B Minutaglio is the author of several acclaimed books, including the
f major biography of President George W. Bush. His book, *City on*
* e*, was named one of the 'greatest tales of survival' ever written by
uire. His work has appeared in the *New York Times, Newsweek,* the
lletin of the Atomic Scientists, the *Daily Beast* and many other publica-
ns. He is a professor of journalism at the University of Texas–Austin.

even L. Davis was born in 1963 and grew up in Dallas, Texas. He is
 author of two books: *Texas Literary Outlaws: Six Writers in the*
ties and Beyond and *J. Frank Dobie: A Liberated Mind*. Davis is a
g-time curator at the Wittliff Collections at Texas State University-
 Marcos. Davis has also edited several books for publication and he
 member of the Texas Institute of Letters.

Praise for *Dallas 1963*

' intriguing exploration . . . Although the authors don't specifi-
c. point the finger at Oswald or anyone else, they contend that it
w Dallas's toxic, extremist environment that made an act of violence
th against the president almost inevitable' *Sunday Times*

'Cas g a clinical eye over the events leading to the death that shook
e orld in November 1963, the acclaimed Texas journalists
pe y put the shocking season at Dealey plaza into context. For
v tics or history buff, this . . . is a must' *Irish Examiner*

'After 'y years, it's a challenge to fashion a new lens with which to
view t ragic events of 22 November 1963 – yet Texans [Minutaglio
 d D ' pull it off brilliantly' *Publishers Weekly*

' bri / written, haunting eulogy to John F. Kennedy. Every
page is an eye opener' Douglas Brinkley, author of *Cronkite*

'All the great personalities of Dallas during the assassination come
alive in this superb rendering of a city on a roller coaster into disaster.
History has been waiting fifty years for this book' Lawrence Wright,
author of *The Looming Tower* and *Going Clear*

Also by Bill Minutaglio and Steven L. Davis

*City on Fire: The Forgotten Disaster That Devastated a Town
and Ignited a Landmark Legal Battle*
by Bill Minutaglio
First Son: George W. Bush and the Bush Family Dynasty
by Bill Minutaglio
The President's Counselor: The Rise to Power of Alberto Gonzales
by Bill Minutaglio
In Search of The Blues: A Journey to the Soul of Black Texas
by Bill Minutaglio
Molly Ivins: A Rebel Life
by Bill Minutaglio and W. Michael Smith
J. Frank Dobie: A Liberated Mind
by Steven L. Davis
Texas Literary Outlaws: Six Writers in the Sixties and Beyond
by Steven L. Davis

Dallas 1963

The Road to the Kennedy Assassination

BILL MINUTAGLIO and STEVEN L. DAVIS

JOHN MURRAY

First published in Great Britain in 2013 by John Murray (Publishers)
An Hachette UK Company

First published in paperback in 2014

1

A CIP catalogue record for this title is available from the British Library

ISBN 978-1-84854-778-0
Ebook ISBN 978-1-84854-777-3

Printed and bound by Clays Ltd, St Ives plc

John Murray policy is to use papers that are natural, renewable and
recyclable products and made from wood grown in sustainable forests.
The logging and manufacturing processes are expected to conform
to the environmental regulations of the country of origin.

John Murray (Publishers)
338 Euston Road
London NW1 3BH

www.johnmurray.co.uk

For Bud Shrake, Shel Hershorn, and Gary Cartwright,
who opened the doors to Dallas 1963,
to Francesco Xavier,
who looked for the American Dream &
to Louie Canelakes, a soulful genius

*America's leadership must be guided by the lights of learning
and reason or else those who confuse rhetoric with reality and the
plausible with the possible will gain the popular ascendancy with
their seemingly swift and simple solutions to every world problem.*
—JOHN F. KENNEDY,
REMARKS PREPARED FOR DELIVERY IN
DALLAS, NOVEMBER 22, 1963

*Dallas, the city that virtually invited the poor insignificant soul who
blotted out the life of President Kennedy to do it in Dallas.*
—A LETTER RECEIVED BY DALLAS MAYOR EARLE CABELL,
DATED NOVEMBER 22, 1963

*President Kennedy has something important to say to each of us
in his death ... He says to all of us that this virus of hate that has
seeped into the veins of our nation, if unchecked, will lead inevitably
to our moral and spiritual doom.*
—MARTIN LUTHER KING JR., NOVEMBER 26, 1963

AUTHORS' NOTE

*D*ALLAS *1963* is not meant to address the many conspiracy theories surrounding the murder of President Kennedy. Our aim is to introduce and then connect the outsize characters and the singular climate in a city that many blamed for killing a president.

Our book begins in early 1960 and ends in late 1963. A product of years of research, the work is informed by access to thousands of pages of archival material, thousands of documents released to the authors by the federal government, along with oral histories, local police reports, eyewitness accounts, interviews, newspaper and magazine accounts, unreleased photographs, dissertations, and film footage. The narrative is constructed with an acute eye toward accountability, toward documenting all the sources in the hundreds of footnotes. The book has been carefully scrutinized by several independent readers to detect and erase any unintended suggestions of political bias.

In the end, *Dallas 1963* is an exploration of how fear and unease can take root, how suspicions can emerge in a seemingly orderly universe. How, as Flannery O'Connor wrote, *Everything That Rises Must Converge*.

How no one—including a doomed president—could have understood the full measure of the swirling forces at work in a place called Dallas.

Bill Minutaglio & Steven L. Davis
Texas, 2013

PRELUDE

On a perfectly languorous Southern California day in September 1959, the bald-headed and bellicose leader of the Soviet Union seems to be bursting out of his skin. Things went so well with Frank Sinatra, but this is no good...no good at all.

Nikita Khrushchev can't get into Disneyland.

Until now, his history-making tour of the United States has been a delicate balance of mirth and diplomacy. He met with President Dwight Eisenhower and he spoke to a group of senators, including John Kennedy of Massachusetts, who has been busy plotting his chances for the presidency. He visited New York City, where over three thousand policemen protected him from the mostly curious, but occasionally angry onlookers.

Then he traveled the country—and it was great fun reaching out to clasp hands with a grinning Sinatra on the movie set for *Can-Can*. He even ogled Marilyn Monroe at a star-studded Hollywood luncheon, although another actor, Ronald Reagan, refused to meet with him, saying, "I believe that to sit socially and break bread with someone denotes friendship, and certainly I feel no friendship for Mr. Khrushchev."[1]

Khrushchev laughed while listening to Shirley MacLaine speaking Russian and then merrily rebuffed her teasing entreaties to dance. Days into his two-week trip, he seemed almost amused with America, with people scrambling to catch a glimpse of him. And perhaps he also sensed what some reporters were suggesting as they filed their stories about the first-ever visit to America by a Soviet head of state. That despite his wide smile, his five-foot-tall fire-hydrant physique, he carried a careening air of impending danger...maybe violence.

Right now Khrushchev is glowering. His aides are huddling,

quietly conferring and then relaying the same bad news to him over and over again: He is not going to be allowed into Disneyland. The police have said they cannot guarantee his safety. Someone already hurled an overripe tomato at him during his Los Angeles motorcade. Worse could happen. Khrushchev, frowning and fuming, is incredulous that he could be killed inside an American theme park.

"I have been told I couldn't go to Disneyland," he sneers. "Why not? What is it? Maybe you have rocket-launching pads there?"[2]

In Dallas, businessmen in their long, fine Neiman Marcus woolen overcoats stop at the Commerce Street newsstand to pick up copies of the morning paper. In the many weeks following the Soviet leader's visit, they have grown accustomed to scanning the headlines for more unnerving news about the snarling Russian bear—and about the thousand other howling uncertainties that once seemed so far removed from the city gates.

With papers folded and tucked under their arms, shivering men troop along the dark, chilly downtown streets toward the humming oil companies, the quietly efficient insurance firms, and the wood-paneled bank towers. Overhead, there is at least one reassuring glow: a fiery red Pegasus—the giant, rotating, neon sculpture that serves as the city's sentinel atop the majestic Magnolia Oil Building.

But for the last several weeks the calm, the soothing confidence often found inside some parts of Dallas, has become as elusive as smoke.

The *Dallas Morning News* reads like a litany of unease. Back in the Soviet Union, Khrushchev is making ominous claims about his nation's power: "I am emphasizing once more that we already possess so many nuclear weapons...should any madman launch an attack on our state or on other socialist states, we would literally be able to wipe the country or countries that attack us off the face of the Earth."

And in the United States, Richard Nixon and John Kennedy are beginning their sharp-edged joust for the presidency. For some, the future of the world might just be at stake. Nixon has already stood up to Khrushchev in Moscow at their "Kitchen Debate." He is even hinting he will be more muscular than President Eisenhower when it comes to confronting communists. But Kennedy seems more deliberative, even cautious, when dealing with the Soviet menace—he says that only peace will breed freedom abroad.

"There are no magic policies of liberation," Kennedy insists. "This is no longer an age when minutemen with muskets can make a revolution. The facts of the matter are that, no matter how bitter some feelings may be, or how confident some are of a victorious war for liberation—freedom behind the Iron Curtain and world peace are inextricably linked."[3]

At almost the exact same time, a lean young ex-soldier named Lee Harvey Oswald is being personally welcomed by the mayor of Minsk and rewarded with both an apartment and a job. Oswald has left everything that he once knew in Texas so he can begin a new life in the Soviet Union. As the first U.S. Marine to ever defect to the Russians, Oswald expects that he will now be regarded as an important person, that he will finally receive the respect he deserves. Maybe, too, things will become more logical and clear in the Soviet Union than in his corner of Texas.

In the cozy shambles of Sol's Turf Bar downtown, more Dallas businessmen swap theories over pastrami sandwiches and cold bottles of Lone Star beer. A nervous electricity is in the air—scrambling chatter about Eisenhower losing Cuba to the communists, atomic weapons and Soviet rockets to the moon, civil rights protesters, Red China, Supreme Court orders for Dallas to integrate its schools, and the presidential jockeying by Kennedy, Nixon, and Lyndon B. Johnson.

But there is something else building in the conversations—and not just the ones held downtown, but also those in the houses of worship, the sprawling mansions, and the universities across Dallas. In key corners of the city, an urgent confederacy of persuasive, often powerful men is forming. Ministers, publishers, congressmen, generals, and oilmen are meeting—at first informally, and then by clear design—and coming to the same conclusions: Dallas and America are in danger. The East Coast liberals, the big-city Catholics, and the government-loving socialists are sapping the faith and eroding the bedrock of the Republic, weakening the country in the face of a very clear communist onslaught. It isn't paranoia. It is *real*—and too many people are turning a blind eye to the threats.

The members of this small, strong-minded set of citizens are hastily reinforcing each other—and insisting that Dallas should be the staging ground for the battles to protect the United States against all this unraveling, all this unholy unthreading of American traditions.

It is unlike anything in the history of the country: A handful of people in a seemingly staid city begin to set the stage for one of the greatest tragedies in American history. And on that stage will appear Dallas's most famous residents: the richest man in the world, the leader of one of the largest religious congregations in the country, a once revered military general, one of the nation's influential publishers, and the most ideologically rigid member of Congress— all joining forces in what seems to them nearly a second Civil War, a righteous crusade to define and defend all that America stands for.

Marooned in an outpost of super-patriotism, their first, cautionary discussions begin to morph into a cacophony of anger. And with it comes the beginning of a feverish march led by this citizen army... a march that will begin in earnest in the first days of 1960 and that will only subside, temporarily, in the bleak, waning days of November 1963.

As 1960 looms, several Southern states and cities—including Dallas—are still brazenly defying the Supreme Court's *Brown v. Board* decision, refusing federal orders to integrate schools.

Everyone knows that just three years earlier, the governor of Arkansas ordered the men in his National Guard to surround a high school in the state capital of Little Rock and block nine Negro students from joining two thousand white ones. The troops were reinforced by a mob waving Confederate flags and lustily singing "Dixie." Residents rushed to stockpile guns and bullets. A car loaded with dynamite was stopped just one block short of the home where the black children and their parents were meeting. The governor had even issued a warning to the nation: "Blood will run in the streets."[4]

Finally, an anxious President Eisenhower unleashed "Operation Little Rock"—sending in an occupying army of battle-hardened federal soldiers led by Major General Edwin Walker, a tall, stiff-backed World War II hero who had grown up on a two-thousand-acre Texas ranch. Walker's men dogtrotted through Little Rock's streets, forcibly dispersing the civilians with bayonets clipped to the ends of their M1 rifles. Four platoons provided cover as the Negro students were escorted up the front steps of the school. The tense standoff came to an immediate end. Walker had broken down segregation in the soul of the South. Instantly, the national press praised him as a shining example of how Americans will fight for what is right.

But what wasn't reported in the dispatches from the domestic front lines was Walker's aching, private anguish in the wake of the history-making moment—and the way the uncompromising Texan saw America spiraling out of control as it lurched toward 1960.

Walker, like General Robert E. Lee before him, forever wanted to be loyal to the Union. But in the weeks and months after Arkansas, building toward the dawn of the new decade, he was increasingly worried that his country was becoming divided in stark, absolute terms. In Lee's time, the abolitionists were the enemy. In Walker's time, it was the integrationists—and the liberals who blindly refused to believe that the United States was in grave danger of being undermined, even attacked, by the Soviet Union.

Walker had made a career following orders, but now, for the first time, he is deeply regretting his devotion to duty. He begins vaulting from ambivalence, to skepticism, to a sense of outrage.

And by 1960 he is becoming gratefully aware that he is not alone.

There are other super-patriots beginning to realize that so many of their countrymen are dulled to the wicked threats from inside and outside the nation. That carefully masked conspiracies are snaking into and through the United States, and accommodating and unsuspecting politicians in Washington seem clueless. Too many good, ordinary Americans have become complacent while a rash of socialist ideas are taking root and metastasizing like a cancer. From Social Security to fluoridated water to membership in the United Nations. And then there's the greatest threat of all: racial equality, spread by "communist" proponents like Martin Luther King Jr.

Walker makes discreet inquiries and soon learns that at least one group, the John Birch Society, also believes there is a bona fide conspiracy—not an ensemble of coincidences, but an organized effort that reaches the highest levels of government.

A dramatic, even frightening, thought blinks in Walker's mind: that even Dwight D. Eisenhower himself, the president of the United States, has lost his way, and is falling prey to the enemy—unknowingly becoming a "conscious, dedicated agent of the Communist Conspiracy."[5]

A burning idea persists with Walker: Eisenhower used federal troops—and used him—to forcibly integrate America. Walker had been used, by his own commanders, to unleash the very kinds of government-ordered social programming that would undermine the nation. In a stunning moment, Walker makes a fateful choice: He will abandon his abject loyalty to his superiors, including the president of the United States.

By 1960, the Texan has enlisted in the John Birch Society— and he feels welcome, at home, part of a spiritual awakening. The highly decorated general writes to the Birch Society founder: "I can foresee your movement...equal only in magnitude to Christ's teaching through the Apostles to heathens."[6]

In time, his devotion to the movement, to protecting America, will lead him directly to Dallas. And he will be far from alone.

By the dawn of the 1960s, more and more super-patriots will come from around the nation to Dallas—as if they have been summoned to join a war.

1960

JANUARY

Over the brisk winter holiday, mailmen in Dallas are bundled against the biting winter chill as they place a series of carefully signed and rather unexpected cards into the mailboxes of the city's most influential residents—men living on the exquisitely manicured, tree-lined streets that filter north of the tall downtown buildings.

The front of the card features a crisp photograph of an attractive young family: A handsome, vigorous-looking man is seated in a comfortable chair, book-lined shelves visible behind him. His face is creased into a charming smile, and his posture projects an easy and sanguine confidence. Perched on his lap is his ebullient daughter, peering down at an open book. Standing behind him is his elegantly attired wife, leaning over her well-dressed husband and child. Her manner seems more reserved, nearly brooding. A strand of pearls frames her long neck. She is very attractive but appears as remote as a silent screen star.

The portrait of this young family radiates a sense of dynastic ease, of a kind of practiced and inherited status. On the inside of the card is the raised, gold-embossed Great Seal of the United States: the fierce eagle clutching an olive branch in one talon and thirteen arrows in the other.

Below the seal appears a message: "Wishing you a Blessed Christmas and a New Year filled with happiness. Senator and Mrs. John F. Kennedy."

Each of the cards has been signed in the same careful handwriting: "Best—Jack."

Many of the people in Dallas are startled at the impressive, personalized card. Most of them have never met Kennedy. Many have never ventured into the Kennedy orbits on the East Coast—nor would they ever want to. In the powerful parts of Dallas, there is a mixture of old Southern families and the nouveau riche. And now, in the last few years, the oil money is flowing furiously into this New South city—sometimes seemingly despite men like Kennedy, despite the Northeastern establishment, despite the long and controlling reach of Washington.

Alongside the older mansions, there are newer thirty-room Taj Mahals where even the toilets are made with gold leaf. The most lavish store in the city, Neiman Marcus, specializes in making millionaires' dreams come true—it is preparing to debut its newest gift idea: His and Hers airplanes. People are flying out of Dallas's Love Field to New Orleans for lunch at Antoine's, or to Lake Tahoe to mingle with Frank Sinatra at the Cal Neva Resort. Or to Las Vegas to play poker with Benny Binion—once the most celebrated purveyor of illicit pleasures to the rich in Dallas, now their host at the famous Horseshoe Casino.

But just a few minutes from the mansions in Dallas, there are also clusters of falling-down shacks, with no running water, settling into the gumbo-soil bottomlands. The city's schools, country clubs, and stores are still perfectly segregated...and bonded, through membership and memory, to ominous things that few speak about by name.

With the grand holiday cards from Kennedy in hand, the recipients place calls to friends. They learn that many others have received the very same greeting from Kennedy, not just in Dallas, but all over the country. Some must wonder if it is giving Kennedy some measure of satisfaction knowing that his cards are being talked about in a city like Dallas...in a place like Texas.

The Lone Star State is often like some rogue nation playing by its own political rules, as if it is about to secede and become its own country again. At the family retreat in Hyannis Port, at the place where the Kennedys feel most unfettered and clear-minded, Dallas probably seems at times like a place worth conceding, a place where there is more than just the usual political resistance to everything a Northern Catholic might embody. Some who have never been to Dallas summon up the easy stereotypes: *It is where Bonnie and Clyde came from. Where big oilmen drive huge cars. A distant city populated by gun-slinging cowboys and snake-handling preachers.*

Even if they don't succumb to those cartoon caricatures, the key advisers in the Kennedy inner circle surely share something: a raw sense of Dallas as an outpost for people particularly disconnected to the Kennedy family's very personality, religion, and principles. And John F. Kennedy himself no doubt knows that it will take far more than a soothing family photograph and a handsome, gilt-tinted holiday card to even begin to erode distrust in a place like Dallas.

One thing is clear this January. Kennedy is watching his major rival for the presidential nomination, Lyndon B. Johnson, the crafty Master of the Senate, the Texas boss who has gone below deck to run the Democratic Party machinery during the Eisenhower presidency. No one in party circles knows more about Texas, about Dallas, than Johnson. No one but Johnson has done more to help empower the men who really run things in Texas. For months now, Jack and his brother Bobby have watched and waited for the tall, clever Texan to make his move.

There are certainly windows of opportunity for Johnson. There are coalescing, angry forces in Dallas and throughout the South. There are governors, senators, and mayors still rallying to resist so many things: the revolutionary integration edicts ordered by the federal government, by the Supreme Court, by political forces in the North...as if a modern version of the Civil War is unfolding. But Johnson is coy, refusing to announce his plans. He is both cunning and wary—and wondering if the nation is really ready for a president from the South, from that alternately celebrated and reviled place called Texas.

While Johnson wavers, Kennedy decides to push forward.

He has been visiting every state in the nation. And he and his team have decided to mail those holiday cards, to have him personally sign thousands of them and send some straight to Dallas, straight to the heart of the American resistance.

On January 2, 1960, people in the city open their ultra-conservative morning newspaper and see the big story: John Fitzgerald Kennedy has announced that he is officially running for the White House.

Inside those three-story mansions with the curving driveways in the exclusive quarters of the city, people now understand exactly what Kennedy's lavish holiday greeting was all about. Later in the day, they are meeting, over coffee and eggs delivered by white-gloved black waiters in the private clubs downtown, and talking about the card—especially in light of the news.

It is both foolish and flattering: *Kennedy wants Texas.*

The Reverend W. A. Criswell, the burly and square-jawed pastor of the sprawling Dallas First Baptist Church, knows that the Lord God Almighty is providing him with a special blessing on this brisk initial Sunday in January 1960.

A brazen bigamist, the craggy and philandering Dallas oil mogul H. L. Hunt, is bowing before him and whispering in his unusually soft and cottony voice that he is ready at last to accept Jesus Christ as his Lord and Savior...and Wallie Amos Criswell as his spiritual leader. Criswell looks down, staring at the large, oval-shaped man with the baby-soft skin and the snowy, thinning hair. It is a holy marriage—between the leader of the largest Baptist church in the world and the richest man in America.

At age fifty, Criswell weighs two hundred pounds and has short, slightly curling hair parted close to the middle of his large head. He has a broad face, thin lips, and narrow but piercing eyes. He prefers a dark tie, a white shirt, and a gray three-piece suit. Like the seventy-year-old Hunt, he emerged in a part of the nation where there was nothing even remotely akin to inherited wealth—where a desperate, hungry man usually only prospered by muscling his way forward without waiting for benevolent figures in Washington to lend a hand.

Criswell was born into wretched poverty near the sluggish Red River and the barren Texas-Oklahoma border, where tornadoes routinely scrape away at people's lives. Baptized in an old galvanized tub, he found his calling under flimsy revival tents, and waving his dog-eared Bible in dusty, hardscrabble villages like Muskogee and Mexia. People say he acquired a holy gift for bridging the Bible to the real world, for linking God's ancient words to today's headlines, for using the Bible as a literal tool to make sense of the news events people hear on the radio or see in the *Dallas Morning News*.

Lately, when he sits inside his expansive, book-lined office in his sprawling brick church, he remains obsessed with liberals and socialists in the Northeast—how the men in Washington want to change traditions, push integration. Too, he has deep, lingering suspicions about Roman Catholics—about whether they would be more devoted to the pope than to the American Constitution.

But when Criswell closes the door to his office and writes his fiery sermons, he knows one thing: He doesn't want to risk the kind of agonizing, national blowback he endured the last time he attacked some big sea changes in America.

Four years ago, the governor of South Carolina had insisted the nationally famous Dallas preacher come give a speech to the state legislature, and Criswell erupted in full-throated roar against integration and those Northern socialists: "The NAACP has got those East Texans on the run so much that they dare not pronounce the word 'chigger' anymore. It has to be Cheegro! Idiocy... Foolishness! Let them integrate! Let them sit up there in their dirty shirts and make all their fine speeches. But they are all a bunch of infidels, dying from the neck up! Let them stay where they are... but leave us alone!"[1]

The lawmakers were mesmerized as Criswell rocked on his feet and raised both of his hands to the heavens:

"They are not our folks. They are not our kind. They don't belong to the same world in which we live... There are people who are trying to force upon us a situation and a thing that is a denial of all that we believe in."

The news about his blistering rebukes reverberated around the country, and some of the fallout was disastrous. Baptist preachers hissed that he had gone too far—even if he was saying what many of them believed. But in Dallas, the mysterious oilman H. L. Hunt listened and heartily approved. Hunt and Criswell both knew that the growing civil rights movement was just a way for soft-willed intellectuals and liberals to supercharge socialism, and open the door to a steadfast campaign by communists to infiltrate America. Hunt admires the way Criswell attacks the enemy. He'd like to entrust his soul and his money to the preacher who says:

"Communism is a denial of God...communism is like a kingdom of darkness presided over by a prince of evil...the greatest challenge the Christian faith has ever faced in 2,000 years of history."[2]

Hunt can feel it. Criswell really understands who is leaving America so vulnerable: "The leftists, the liberals, the pinks and the welfare
statists who are soft on communism and easy toward Russia."[3]

Evening is coming on, the January light is playing off the chilly
waters of the Potomac River, and inside the House of Representatives chamber Congressman Bruce Alger can see his colleagues
pushing out of their chairs and beginning to drift toward drinks
and dinner with lobbyists. Still, this is something that the lawmaker
from Dallas has to do, even if there is not a full audience.

The smoothly handsome and impeccably dressed Alger steps to
the front of the House chamber. Some people say the Princeton-
educated, forty-one-year-old could have been a movie star, that he
bears a striking resemblance to the actor Gary Cooper. His shined
hair is combed to perfection, and he walks with a straight, easy gait.

Confederate General Robert E. Lee's 153rd birthday will pass
entirely without notice in the House of Representatives if not for
Alger, the lone Republican in the Texas delegation and one of the
most passionate conservatives in the nation. Invoking personal
privilege, Alger begins a speech—his mellifluous voice rising and
praising the legend and memory of the Confederate leader.

This should play very well in certain parts of Dallas. The city
was once the national headquarters for the Ku Klux Klan. The
city's famous Magnolia Building, once the tallest in the state and
adorned with that giant sign of a glowing red Pegasus, was opened
by a Grand Dragon of the KKK. A Dallas minister named R. E.
Davis—someone well known to Dallas police—is claiming to be
the new Imperial Wizard of the Original Knights of the KKK. He
is saying ominously that he will combat integration and that "this
Republic was founded by and in violence."[4] The current mayor
of Dallas, R. L. Thornton, was named for Robert E. Lee and had
once been an unabashed KKK member. There are two towering
Confederate monuments to General Lee in Dallas, including one

that is the tallest public structure in the city. There are statues of Confederate legends Stonewall Jackson and Jefferson Davis—and all-white public schools named for rebel heroes. The Confederate cemetery in the heart of the city is always carefully tended.

Now Alger's heartfelt ode to Lee echoes in the lonely chamber. He doesn't care if there is no one to listen. This speech is, really, for the people who put him in Congress—the people who *run* Dallas. Alger's ode to Lee floats across the emptying room:

"A great soldier...a loyal Southerner...a noble American... and a Christian gentleman."[5]

After Alger finishes his speech, he heads to the airport. When his plane finally touches down in Dallas, he is greeted, as always, by a small army of adoring homemakers and young wives who have taken a sudden interest in politics. Alger seems so personally appealing. He seems fully aware of those unseen threats lapping at Dallas.

Immediately, the *Dallas Morning News* issues an editorial thanking Alger:

> *It was fitting, though ironical, that a Republican—Bruce Alger of Dallas—was the only congressman to get on his feet and salute Gen. Robert E. Lee on his birthday.*
>
> *Fitting, because Lee fought for the rights of the states. By resisting big government in Washington. So is Alger.*
>
> *Where were the Democrats—the so-called party of the South? Courting the support of . . . the NAACP?*[6]

At home, Alger is often regarded as a folk hero despite the fact that he has never passed a single piece of legislation. He has introduced doomed bills to withdraw from the United Nations, to break off all diplomatic relations with the Soviet Union, to privatize the federal government. He opposed the civil rights bill of 1957, condemning it as placating "the troublemakers of the NAACP who seek to incite race hatred and discontent which did not exist."[7] And, finally, he cast the lone vote against a federal program to provide surplus milk, free of charge, to needy elementary school children.

The congressman was assailed across the country, but the

leaders of the *Dallas Morning News* rushed to his defense: "Here we are telling ourselves that we must strain every nerve and conserve every penny to meet the assault upon our way of life by the Russians and the spend-it-all folk in Washington come in crying about the milk-hungry children."[8]

Alger has other stalwarts in Dallas. The billionaire Hunt sends out a mass letter racing to the support of the Dallas lawmaker: "His acumen, integrity and courage rate him as one of the 5 or 6 truly great men among the vanishing good men in Washington."[9]

But it is the prosperous stay-at-home wives waiting for him at the Dallas airport that really form the soul of Alger's political vanguard. They constantly spring to his side, excitedly host luncheon forums and fund-raisers in their homes, work for hours on phone banks, and parade door-to-door with his yard signs. Dozens, sometimes hundreds, routinely appear at his public events, applauding wildly. To some skeptics in Dallas it is almost too much—and some are quietly speculating about what inspires so much passion. There are even rumors about his marriage, about why the congressman and his wife have recently separated.

Now, in the city after his Capitol Hill salute to Robert E. Lee, Alger simply goes from one January appearance to another, engulfed by the well-dressed women who have braved the winter weather to welcome him back. As they listen, perched on the edges of their seats and clapping, they hear him hammer home what they know to be true: *There is something poisoning the hallways of power in Washington. There is a cancer. Washington is filled with blind men, liberal men: "the most liberal since the heyday of the New Deal."*[10]

Towering over the women, he lowers his head to tell them he has more work to do in Washington. And often, before he leaves the city to go back to Washington, Alger will do something else: drive downtown and take the elevator to the top floor of an office tower on Commerce Street for a closed-door meeting with his high-ranking backers from the Dallas Citizens Council—the group of fifty or so wealthy white businessmen who meet to chart the city's fate, decide the next mayor, and map out the increasingly twitchy matter of race relations...and how to keep what is happening in Alabama, in New York, anywhere else where protests have occurred, completely out of Dallas.

Alger probably knows that there are people in Dallas who have another name for these men, many descended from the city's founding families, who hold his political fate in their hands: Some call the group the Dallas *White* Citizens Council—leaning in to whisper the word *white*.

As waiters move in and out of the room with tumblers of cool beverages, Alger relays the news from the front lines in Washington: Insiders in the nation's capital are beginning to worry that the Democrats are becoming increasingly soft on civil rights, and that there is something even worse—the Catholic, Jack Kennedy, is beginning to outflank his major rivals for the presidential nomination.

The aging publisher negotiates the old roads leading to the west side of downtown—and to the *Dallas Morning News* building with the Texas and American flags out front, set on an entire block close to the murky Trinity River. The publisher can stare out the car window through the winter weather and consider how much the city has grown since what he calls "the diaper days of Dallas."

Day after day, Ted Dealey, sixty-seven, a short, wiry man with thick glasses, has told himself to be vigilant on behalf of Dallas and all that it stands for. Under his direction, the paper he inherited from his father routinely goes to war with the United Nations, the NAACP, labor, liberals, and—lately—the Supreme Court. In the wake of the *Brown v. Board of Education* decision desegregating America's schools, Dealey's paper charged that the justices had "surrendered to subversion." His editorials mock the high court as the "Judicial Kremlin" and "Courtnik."

As the publisher commutes downtown in January, he is perhaps still marveling at the way that Dallas Congressman Alger invoked splendid references to the Old South and General Robert E. Lee, right in the heart of Washington, DC—a place that Dealey's paper sometimes calls "the Negro Capital of the U.S."[11]

The *Dallas Morning News* was founded by a Confederate officer who served in the North Carolina Fifty-Fifth Regiment before making his way to wide-open Texas. There is a deep Confederate affection in the publisher's family—he has fond memories of his father installing twenty extra beds in their mansion for old rebel soldiers and relatives coming to Dallas for the national Confederate reunion. He grew up with boys named for Robert E. Lee. When the *Dallas Morning News* built its new headquarters a little more than a decade ago, the governor of Texas and the citizens council members who came to the opening were handed a brochure underscoring the fact that the building had separate dining facilities for whites and blacks.

By 1960, Dealey is the most outspoken keeper of the city's history and what some call its Southern traditions. He is, beyond most of the men on the Dallas Citizens Council, the public protector of old Dallas. And he sees his paper serving a vital civic function: reminding readers of "the Dallas way of doing things"—one that he and the handful of those other entrenched leaders in the city's boardrooms single-handedly shaped, nursed, and promoted with uncompromising passion.

Dealey always liked to write. He grew up in the newspaper. As he ages, Dealey also likes to think about one day compiling his increasingly personal reminiscences—ones reflecting on the way things had been in what he felt were the truly innocent days of Dallas. They are nostalgic memories, including how he remembers the black people he had grown up with: Merity would deliver lunch to him wherever Dealey was in the city; jangly Boswell would drive him in the family Cadillac; Viola and Josh lived in a backyard bungalow when they were not cooking and cleaning; Miles polished cuspidors at the newspaper (but locked himself in a small closet to do it, because it reminded him of his close-quarters work as a railroad porter); the miniature, bowlegged, and bald Boykin would fetch things for him; Johnson was your man when you needed someone to check coats at a dinner party in Dallas . . . he had an uncanny ability to remember every fine coat and every owner.

Yet a parallel universe exists in Dallas, a world seldom glimpsed in the pages of Dealey's newspaper: The black janitor from Dallas castrated by a rural Texas mob in 1941. The president of an all-Negro junior college who tried to serve on a Dallas jury in 1938, but who went blind after being shoved hard down the courthouse steps. Thurgood Marshall, the prominent civil rights attorney for the NAACP, chased through city streets by the gun-wielding Dallas police chief, who was shouting: "You black son of a bitch...I have you now."[12]

When Dealey had assumed control of the paper in the 1940s, he began to see the persuasive editorial pages as an important and necessary bully pulpit. He had always felt that when he and the other city leaders gathered downtown at the famous Baker or Adolphus Hotel for power breakfasts, the highest goal was making the city prosperous, making it bustle with quiet, unflappable efficiency... *because it is good for business, good for everyone.* And there really is an order, a way, in Dallas: The citizens council sets the political and economic agenda. Alger then carries their messages in Washington. Criswell becomes the moral compass, the preacher who surrounds things in biblical inviolability. And, finally, Dealey spells them out inside the *Dallas Morning News.*

He is now convinced, like the other men, that Dallas is a singularly remarkable place. You come upon it in the middle of the seemingly endless Texas prairie, hours and hours from other major cities. It emerges from the vast expanse of North Texas for almost no natural reason at all—no impressive waterfronts, no immediate natural resources. But Dallas has been willed into existence by creative, nimble entrepreneurs. They did it by remaining united, by tamping down divisiveness. If it is bad for business, it is not allowed to thrive. It is exactly why the KKK only reluctantly abandoned its national headquarters in Dallas in the 1920s—there were tens of thousands of members in the city, dozens of leading businessmen, but Dealey's father had convinced the most influential men of all that all the brazen KKK displays and parades would doom the city's long-range prospects, that it would chase away profit and all the things that would make the city grow for decades to come.

For the last several years, Dallas has been quietly loping along with little fanfare, little infamy, few distractions. There have been no racial upheavals, no fitful bouts of integration. No outsize calamities making national headlines and tarnishing the city's image. The mayor doesn't talk about his years in the KKK. The district attorney, police chief, and sheriff have quarantined most of the slithering vice in the city—it's still very much there, but instead of it spilling out all over the streets like it used to, you have to know where to find it once the sun goes down. Dallas seems tight, in order.

But now it is a presidential election year, and there are profound choices. It seems like the entire nation is hurtling toward a searing crossroads. There are dangers at home, around the world. And Dealey sees Dallas facing its gravest challenge—just as the nation's attention is turning to a charismatic Democrat named John F. Kennedy.

And the fiercely protective publisher decides to move into action, to guard Dallas. Dealey and his paper want the city to know what dangers are lurking: "On the one side will be those who want to carry the nation farther along the road toward socialism. They will advocate expanded Social Security, federal health insurance and federal aid to the schools, bringing with it federal control.

"1960 may be a crucial year in America's history. It still is uncertain that most voters will have the discernment to choose freedom over candy-covered socialism."[13]

That same month, in Augsburg, West Germany, Major General Edwin A. Walker sweeps into one of the elementary schools on the sprawling military base he commands with unyielding precision.

He is the tough-talking leader of the Twenty-Fourth Infantry Division of the U.S. Army, at the very front lines of the Cold War. At age fifty, Walker is trim, with deep blue eyes and his hair neatly combed into place. He grew up on his family's sprawling ranch northwest of San Antonio. His ancestors fought for the South during the Civil War, and his Confederate sympathies still smolder. At the behest of his devout, conservative mother, he attended West Point. A poor student, he was hell on the polo fields, and ultimately fearless in battle. During World War II he became a daring commando officer, parachuting behind enemy lines to lead bloody night raids. He rose quickly through the ranks. At the end of the war, he boasted a chestful of medals and a reputation as one of the finest, most reliable men in the military.

At formal banquets, he dressed in his crisp uniform, and women gravitated to his side. He was considered a prize catch. But Walker has never married. Instead he is surrounded constantly by young, eager soldiers who serve as his personal aides. Word spread that Walker's chauffeur recently committed suicide, and though there are whispers, no one knows exactly why.

As Walker enters the school, he is quickly escorted to the cafeteria, where two hundred expectant people are gathered for a January Parent Teacher Association meeting. Walker steps onto the stage and approaches the microphone. Before he begins, he looks out at the soldiers, mothers, and children seated before him. They are attentive, eager. Walker is a no-nonsense warrior, and his quick temper is well known inside military circles—but everyone is expecting a version of the usual America-and-apple-pie homilies that go with an address to little children. Some inspiring words to the kids, some cheerful reminders and allusions to the general's old days in the classroom. Maybe a story of self-discipline, courage, or camaraderie. Maybe a gentle joke or two.

The auditorium grows quiet as Walker begins speaking in his loud, flat Texas monotone. He is blistering, withering: Despite the army's best efforts, the enemy is taking over America. Some 60 percent of the U.S. press is already controlled by communists. The leading journalists—Walter Lippmann, Edward Murrow, and Eric Sevareid—are "convinced Communists."

The wary parents in the audience can sense his anger. They begin to turn and murmur to each other: *What is he talking about? Is something like this really happening?*

Walker presses on as the families stare at him: *The communists are relentless, ready to topple America. People at the very top have subversive sympathies. Even former First Lady Eleanor Roosevelt and President Harry S. Truman are "decidedly pink."*[14]

Inside his art-filled, book-cluttered office on the sixth floor of Neiman Marcus, the exquisitely dressed but gnomish-looking Stanley

Marcus shakes his head in disbelief as he considers the latest chess moves by Dallas's self-appointed super-patriots.

Someone has just mailed out six thousand reprints of a January article in a conservative journal, the *American Mercury*. The story is mercilessly attacking Marcus's invention, the Dallas Council on World Affairs: "In Dallas, Leftism's most familiar masquerade is internationalism, in the seemingly innocuous guise of the Council on World Affairs."[15]

The *Dallas Morning News* is also piling on, running stories about the sweeping controversy, and copies of the *Mercury* are even sold out at local newsstands. Marcus is already well known in the city for his cultural inclinations—some that seem to skitter close, in some estimations, to outright socialism. He has used his immense wealth to become a noted art collector and he has also shaped Dallas's symphony orchestra and arts museum.

But sometimes he also can't help but feel that he is in someone's crosshairs, as if he has pushed for too many new things in old Dallas. Marcus co-sponsored, along with TIME, Inc., a *Sports in Art* exhibition at the Dallas Museum of Fine Arts, with works by internationally recognized artists, depicting figure skaters, baseball players, and fishermen. As the museum prepared for the opening, hundreds of prominent, angry people quickly joined forces to protest that the art was done by communists.

Their spokesman Alvin Owsley was the former ambassador to Ireland and national commander of the American Legion, now living in one of the grandest homes in Dallas. "It is one of the basic premises of Communist doctrine that art can and should be used in the constant process of attempting to brainwash and create public attitudes that are soft toward communism," he insisted.[16] "The works of the Red hand and the black heart hating America do not deserve to be exhibited to our citizenship...Let those who would plant a Red picture supplant it with the Red, White and Blue. White for purity, blue for fidelity, as blue as our Texas bluebonnets."[17]

The incident humiliated Marcus when his worldly friends asked him exactly how intolerant Dallas could be. Marcus told them it was just an aberration, an anomaly. For years he had also been bringing in speakers from all over the world as part of his careful plan to elevate Dallas into a consequential city, more sophisticated, more urbane, and less of a down-market, forgettable place in the hot, remote backwaters of Texas.

But now he is holding in his hands this damning screed in the *American Mercury*, and reading that he and his Dallas Council on World Affairs are being blamed for "trying to force their internationalist brand of collectivism on a community which doesn't want it...Dallas is fortunate that it has citizens who are courageous enough to expose this creeping indoctrination and to combat it."[18]

Marcus is fifty-six, a Harvard-educated native of Dallas, and a marketing genius who has turned his family's clothing store into an international symbol of opulence. As the oil boom flooded Texas with petrodollars, Marcus brought mink coats—and Coco Chanel—to Texas. He also brought legendary customer service to his richest clients. He is a soft-spoken man, yet a demanding perfectionist. It is not unusual for Marcus or one of his salespeople to hop into a plane and fly hundreds of miles to close a sale.

Marcus is also a Jew and achingly excluded, along with blacks, from the city's best private clubs. Yet outside the city, he might be the most welcome Dallasite in New York and Europe: He consorts with movie stars and is on a first-name basis with European royalty. He publishes articles in *Fortune* and the *Atlantic*. He helped outfit the wedding party at Grace Kelly's ceremony to Prince Rainier, and he provided First Lady Mamie Eisenhower's inaugural gown. He has stayed overnight at Eisenhower's White House. He is even friendly with Senator John F. Kennedy after they met while serving together on Harvard's board of overseers.

In Dallas, his store is regarded by many as the social center of the city—and even a reassuringly elegant beacon of segregation, since blacks are barred from eating in the Neiman Marcus restaurant. Despite the segregation, city boosters always make a point of bringing Northern executives—ones thinking of relocating to warm-weather, low-tax Dallas—to the emporium. Maybe Marcus's cathedral to the high life will reassure ambivalent magnates from New York and Connecticut that Dallas is on the brink of cosmopolitan splendor.

Marcus always loves the chance to praise Dallas, to tell people the city is marvelously reinventing itself. Marcus can live anywhere he wants—but he loves Dallas.

"It's stimulating to live in a city that's on the make," he tells friends.[19] But he also hears the stinging stereotypes when he travels: Dallas is an uninteresting, uncultured, xenophobic, anti-intellectual city where hoary Old Southerners mingle with the crass New West *nouveau riche*. For years, more than anyone in the city, Marcus has been on a mission to change the image. And with a presidential election year unfolding—one that offers truly defined choices—he is convinced it's time for him to do more to dethrone the hidebound traditions and suspicions that men like Dealey, Criswell, and Hunt are clinging to.

To Marcus, Dallas simply needs to be more worldly and welcoming...and maybe even integrated, even if it means finally opening his store's restaurant to blacks. Something, someone, needs to change in Dallas, in the whole damned South.

In January 1960, Marcus quietly wonders if it could be his old friend and big-spending customer Lyndon Baines Johnson: If LBJ is given power, will he usher Dallas, Texas, and the rest of the South into some sort of fresher, progressive phase?

The two men go way back: Johnson is one of Marcus's best—and most maddening—customers. For years, Marcus has put up with Johnson's braying need for attention. The senator once returned an expensive monogrammed bathrobe to Marcus because the letters *LBJ* weren't large enough to suit his taste.

Marcus decides to call Johnson and have a guarded discussion even before Johnson publicly announces he is a presidential candidate.

LBJ listens as Marcus offers to co-chair his Dallas campaign and raise money for him.

And Marcus wonders if LBJ is really going to try to distance himself from the racist tendencies of the South—and if LBJ has bold plans to drag Dallas away from its past.

FEBRUARY

O
n a bitterly cold Monday afternoon, steam rises from city grates and a light rain falls outside the five-story, limestone-colored Cokesbury Bookstore in downtown Dallas. Cokesbury is just up the street from Neiman Marcus, and some like to suggest it is *the* largest bookstore in America. It regularly brings visiting writers to town—including John Steinbeck and William Faulkner—but neither the store nor the city of Dallas has ever seen an author event like the one unfolding today.

Six hundred people are standing in a line that spills out of the doorway and stretches an entire block. In the damp chill, men have pulled their fedoras tighter over their heads. Women are congregating under umbrellas. Everyone is here for the same reason: a chance to see the reclusive Dallas billionaire reputed to be the wealthiest person on earth. He, as it happens, has just published a novel.

Puffs of mist form as people talk in low, expectant voices, waiting patiently to take another step forward. Many have seen the advertisement for the February book signing in the *Dallas Morning News*, featuring an odd, blurry photo of an old man with glowing eyes and the look of someone trying to duck away from the camera at the exact instant the shutter clicked. The ad for his book *Alpaca* reads:

"ALPACA is as real as today's headlines about Cuba…H. L. Hunt, one of the financial leaders of the world, has taken time from a busy life to write this book. Of permanent importance, it makes a contribution to the welfare of our country and to the world."[1]

Hunt is, really, a phantom Midas that people exchange fantastic rumors about: *How many wives does he really have? Did he really produce more oil during World War II than all the Axis powers combined? Can he really forecast the future?*

★   ★   ★

H. L. Hunt lives in a replica of George Washington's Mount Vernon—though Hunt's home is conspicuously larger—set on a ten-acre estate overlooking White Rock Lake. The acreage surrounding the mansion is not like those of Dallas's other wealthy. There are no palace gardens, statues, or fountains. Instead, a few tame deer patrol the grounds, along with some chickens, a couple of peacocks, and a goat. The property line is marked by a standard-issue chain-link fence. But there is something else. As if to discourage visitors, a very large cannon is stationed at the front of the house, pointing out toward the padlocked gate.

John Paul Getty tells people that Haroldson Lafayette Hunt is the lord among lords in the pantheon of the American rich. He makes more money, more quickly, than anyone else—an electric ability that doesn't jibe with the fact that he looks like a dime-store owner and eats his lunch out of a brown paper bag. And who is surrounded by mystery as much as fact. People routinely pass along the gossip: *He has not one, not two, but three wives and families in different cities. He believes he is from a superior race, someone whose genetic coding is so advanced that his gift to mankind is his offspring. He has a son, a savant, who has been lobotomized and kept hidden in the Dallas mansion—and whom Hunt has tried to cure by arranging for his son to have boundless sexual encounters with beautiful women. Hunt refuses to shake hands with people, fearing he will become contaminated by the contact. He travels in the company of young, blond, full-breasted women; he introduces them as either his "niece" or his "secretary."*

A few things are clear: His various businesses earn him an average of $200,000 a day, but money is no longer the endgame. It is, he believes, best understood as the consequence of his profound genetic makeup. He could own every restaurant in Dallas, buy out Neiman Marcus, but he packs figs and beans in oily lunch bags and drives a bruised Plymouth to his downtown building six days a week, finding the cheapest lot to park in.

His office on the seventh floor of the Mercantile Building is across the street from Neiman Marcus, but he rarely ventures inside. Instead, Hunt prefers saggy suits from off the rack, and drab bow ties that he buys in bulk for eighty-eight cents. He even trims his own hair. He was once a big Cuban cigar smoker, but he gave it up after he did the math in his mind: He had wasted $300,000 in time and money each year, with all the hours spent taking the wrappers off, lighting the cigars, and nursing them.

Hunt has known from an early age that he possesses special powers. He taught himself to read by age three. He can endure great bouts of intercourse, drinking, gambling. He wagers $100,000 on football games. His belief in his own supernatural force is so strong that twice he's tried to lift automobiles off people at the scenes of accidents. He has the genius gene, and it is his civic duty, his moral obligation, to seed planet Earth with his progeny. Hunt also has a vision for utopia, for what America should look like. And now he has published that vision in the form of a novel, *Alpaca*.

"I am the best writer I know," Hunt tells people.[2]

He believes his book to be of "permanent importance." Nevertheless it is printed in the cheapest manner possible. The paper is flimsy, just one grade above the kind used to print the *Dallas Morning News*. The binding is held together with a few dollops of crude wax, rather than glue. He has self-published the volume, listing the publisher as "HLH Press," and his book is very small, only about four inches across.

A novel, a cautionary fable, is the right way to reach ordinary Americans who might otherwise never understand what needs to be done. In *Alpaca*, he has created his own country with the perfect form of government. The men who amass the greatest wealth receive more votes than anyone else—up to seven votes each. The bottom 40 percent of taxpayers get no votes at all. The wealthy can purchase additional votes if they desire. Few government services exist in Alpaca—not even public schools. And, finally, the nation must enshrine the "oil depletion allowance"—a massively lucrative tax break for Texas oilmen—as part of the constitution. It is, in fact, the highest law of the land. "The people of Alpaca...were generally happy with the new Constitution," he writes.[3]

This February afternoon, the people lining up outside the bookstore are extremely eager but patient, as if their politeness will be acknowledged and maybe even rewarded when they buy the billionaire's book. As people step inside and begin inching toward Hunt's signing table, they suddenly hear tiny voices floating in unison. Hunt's ten- and eleven-year-old daughters, Helen and Swanee, are holding hands. They sway together in time as they stand behind their seventy-year-old father and sing to the tune of "Doggie in the Window":

> *How much is that book in the window?*
> *The one that says all the smart things.*
> *How much is that book in the window?*
> *I do hope to learn all it brings.*
> *How much is that book in the window?*
> *The one which my Popsy wrote.*
> *How much is that book in the window?*
> *You can buy it without signing a note.*

As they conclude, the little girls shout: "ALPACA! Fifty Cents!"[4]

Hunt is listening and nodding his head, flecked with silky threads of white hair, in time to the tune. He has written the lyrics himself.

As people near him, they can see he came prepared for the winter weather. His white long johns peek out from beneath his blue suit. He is sporting a blue bow tie, blue suit, and blue socks. The girls are also dressed in blue. Hunt occasionally beams and turns his haunting eyes—the same color as his suit—to the customers approaching with copies of his book.

Hunt believes that Dallas is populated by well-meaning but ill-informed people who are very much like the children standing behind him: innocent, a bit naive, hopeful...and looking for someone or something that will give them a purpose in life.

He watches with quiet satisfaction as people pick up his book.

Alpaca is not Hunt's first foray into educating Americans.

In the 1950s he poured millions of dollars into his nationally syndicated radio program, *Facts Forum*. He hired three of Senator Joseph McCarthy's former aides and an ex-FBI agent living in Dallas to run it. *Facts Forum* reached millions of listeners every day, becoming the first wide-scale pro-conservative radio show in America.

Senator McCarthy was a guest on the show, as was Congressman Bruce Alger. During a *Facts Forum* debate on Social Security, Alger received ten minutes of airtime to attack the federal program. The speaker in favor got thirty seconds. Listeners were then invited to order books personally endorsed by Hunt: *We Must Abolish the United Nations* and *Hitler Was a Liberal*.

There were also persistent attacks on the plans to desegregate, by force if necessary, the schools in America: "Remember that the Negroes, when first brought to America, were not free people reduced to slavery. They were merely transferred from a barbaric enslavement by their own people in Africa to a relatively benign enslavement in the Western Hemisphere."[5]

By 1958, Hunt shuttered *Facts Forum* in favor of a new program: *Life Line*, combining religion and politics. He hired a preacher who adopted Hunt's preferred terms: *Constructive* for devout conservatives and *Mistaken* for those on the road to communism. Hunt's Dallas-based show is aired on hundreds of radio stations across the nation. Now, a favorite target of *Life Line* is the United Nations and those internationalists—like Stanley Marcus—who support it: "We were sold the UN on a promise of peace. What we were not told and what we failed to realize was that this peace was to be on communist terms—in fact, it was to be a total victory for the international Mistaken conspiracy against free men."[6]

Hunt's program, like Dealey's newspaper, is equally condemning of the Supreme Court. The justices in Washington seem part of a thickening conspiracy. "Majority rulings of the Supreme Court of the United States actually have had the effect of giving the green light to subversive and criminal elements in our country."

Life Line issues a sharp warning: "Rulings of the Supreme Court are not, in reality, the supreme law of the land."[7]

Ten million Americans tune in every single day to hear Hunt's program, but no one is more devoted than its creator. Hunt puts LIFE LINE stickers on the bumper of his Plymouth and insists his employees do the same. His wife in Dallas wears *Life Line* earrings. Hunt installs a six-foot-high, twelve-foot-wide pink-and-blue sign in the front yard of his home: LIFE LINE, 6:15 P.M., DIAL 1090.

In his Dallas office he keeps a specially built AM radio that allows him to monitor broadcasts in a dozen different states. He makes his children listen to the program during dinner. Hunt's grip on his radio empire is firm. Occasionally, however, his announcers will stray. Once, Hunt heard the host of *Facts Forum* describe democracy as "a political outgrowth of the teachings of Jesus Christ." Hunt rushed to corner the man, yelling that America is a republic and not everyone should be able to vote:

"The American founding fathers knew, and Jefferson said in specific terms, that a democracy is the most evil kind of government possible . . . the handiwork of the devil himself . . . a phony liberal form of watered down communism."[8]

When he was alone, Hunt sometimes marveled at his transcendent ability to see into the future. He knows which women are destined to bear his children. He can divine where the oil will come blasting up from the ground. Now a new vision is becoming clear, and it is alarming: *Negroes will soon be allowed to vote in large numbers . . . people who have never contributed to America in my genetically superior way will be entitled to the same number of votes as me.*

"H. L. hated niggers," one of his employees says. "It pissed him off that they could cancel out his vote."[9]

As H. Rhett James, a tall, lean thirty-two-year-old preacher with an open face and black-framed glasses, drives to the nighttime meetings at the historic New Hope Baptist Church, he can see the buildings downtown and how they almost seem to cast a shadow over the old freedmen's town zone—where the first freed slaves in the city lived, and where his church has its roots. Where some of the hidden graves of the slaves are being simply paved over as new Dallas highways are built.[10]

Almost since the minute he arrived two years ago to become pastor of New Hope—a house of worship founded by former slaves and where Booker T. Washington, Langston Hughes, W. E. B. Du Bois, and others have come bravely to speak—James has been picking up the phone late at night, while his children are asleep, and hearing strangers hissing death threats. He tries to scare them back: *The FBI is listening in on this conversation.*[11]

He quickly joined and prodded the civil rights movement in the city. He also devoted himself to the John F. Kennedy for president committee in Dallas. And now people are branding him "an Outside Agitator." It is part of the swirl, the dizzying mix: If you support Martin Luther King Jr., if you push for immediate integration, you are preaching social disorder, and socialism, and ultimately communism. The black newspaper—the only outlet in the city that regularly features stories about King—has been running headlines about James and his work: DALLAS BRANCH NAACP WEARY OF WAITING FOR SOCIAL JUSTICE.

James often implores the older black leaders in Dallas to come to meetings at New Hope—perhaps the first black church in Dallas, and one that has a long history of fighting against lynchings and the remaining, hidden elements of the KKK. He has learned a lot from them in his short time in the city: About the black families in South Dallas who tried to move into white neighborhoods but had their houses bombed. About the four hundred white men who invaded the small town outside of Dallas that federal officials had picked as the first place in the state to try to integrate a white school. The mob hung effigies of black figures and they waved signs: DEAD COONS ARE THE BEST COONS and $2 A DOZEN FOR NIGGER EARS. The governor dispatched the Texas Rangers to support the mob and make sure that integration *did not* occur.[12]

As James drives near downtown, he can spot an area most black residents call the Bottoms. It is a zone defined by dirt levees meant to contain the Trinity River, and dotted with clumps of tar-paper shacks that look like they are slouching toward oblivion. There is a Negro Park at the foot of a small hill that finally descends to the river—and at the top of the hill there is a collection of barely tended cemetery plots for the first white settlers in the city. In the graveyard are small six-by-six-inch blocks of limestone or granite; those smaller blocks mark where black servants have been buried at the feet of their white masters.

If James looks closely, there are unpaved dirt paths that drop from the hill, down to the river. At night, the black families in the miserable bungalows might pull their children inside when they see a car, sometimes a police car, bumping deeper into the lowlands. It's an open rumor that almost everyone has heard: There are hidden spots in the Bottoms where brutalizers still regularly mete out unsanctioned punishments to the unfortunate. And sometimes, the bodies of dead black men simply slip off the Trinity River banks as if those poor souls are being pulled by something intrinsic and unyielding. There are whispers about the men who committed "suicide"—by shooting themselves in the back, by beating the backs of their heads. Sometimes black families go to James or other preachers and plead for help: *Please find out about my son. Can you find some justice? Can you talk to the police? Is there something you can do?*

Sometimes they go elsewhere for answers:

There is an old lady who lives in the Bottoms who knows how to find the bodies consumed by the river. She is a seer, some people say, and she will ask a mother or father or wife to fetch a shirt that once belonged to their missing black man. Someone from the Bottoms rows her onto the water, she throws the shirt to the river, and when it stops, she tells people to dive in that spot—that's where the dead black man will be found.

James, a father of four, has accepted the fact that, for many, Dallas is inscrutable. But he tells the black lawyers and preachers who assemble at his church—many of whom have lived in Dallas for decades, far longer than James has been in town—that he is impatient. That he wants to finally force Dallas to integrate its public schools—to finally do what every other major city seems to be doing. He'll start by running for the school board, to challenge an entrenched white incumbent. James has other announcements. He wants to aggressively ramp up the level of civil rights protests in Dallas—and he wants Dallas to be part "of the national movement." He wants to bring Dr. Martin Luther King Jr. to Dallas.

The other black leaders, particularly the preachers, have learned to study James carefully. There have been mild protests in Dallas before. They've almost always been rebuffed—and James is certainly not the first to try, though he is, without question, the boldest newcomer. If Stanley Marcus has an intellectual counterpart in black Dallas—which makes up a third of the city—it is James, one of eight children, and whose father was also a minister who preached courage and independence.

James quoted Aeschylus, Tolstoy, and Emerson. He immersed himself in studying Gandhian civil disobedience. He traveled the nation, pursuing several advanced academic degrees. And perhaps more than any other public figure in the city, he admired Dr. King—the very man Dealey, Alger, Criswell, Hunt, and so many others in Dallas equate with communism. King might be the one man most feared by the Dallas Citizens Council. King is the kind of activist who would be *very bad* for business.

The older men who listen to the firebrand James often exchange knowing glances. Many of them have lived in the city their whole lives. They know there are people, a handful, who really run the city. Not at City Hall, but in the hushed quiet of the boardrooms and private offices.

There are frightening reasons that someone like Martin Luther King Jr. hasn't been invited—or allowed—in Dallas for years.

This winter, by now, James should know how Dallas really works.

MARCH

Juanita Craft, a bespectacled fifty-eight-year-old widow who lives in a small clapboard house not far from Stanley Marcus's old family home, is taking her seat and guiding the young people who seem to follow her everywhere she goes. She has a legacy, and people in black Dallas know it: Her grandfather was a slave. Her mother died after she was refused treatment at an all-white hospital in Dallas. Craft was the first black woman to cast a vote in Dallas County.[1]

People greet the woman with the graying hair and stand to say hello. Craft asks about their children—and whether those children will be joining the NAACP. She has enrolled thousands of people in the NAACP, and she has helped create two hundred chapters by traveling around the state into places where black men and women are immobilized by fear. She has a few hundred young people in her youth brigades in Dallas, and she led them when they first tried to integrate the famous State Fair in Dallas five years ago.

Truth be told, she never thought she'd see this March day: Dallas's Memorial Auditorium filling up with sixteen hundred people, from Floridians to Californians—most of them black. And she knows why NAACP leader Roy Wilkins has accepted the Reverend Rhett James's invitation to come to Dallas—and why the NAACP has *really* selected Dallas for its regional meeting.

Maybe what is happening elsewhere in the South can finally happen in Dallas in 1960: A month earlier, four black college students in Greensboro, North Carolina, staged a sit-in at a whites-only lunch counter inside a Woolworth drugstore. The students were refused service, but they stayed in their seats until the store closed. The next day they returned. By the fourth day, they were joined by three hundred other black supporters.

Craft hopes that maybe that kind of fire, the fire of change, can

come to Dallas. Stanley Marcus's restaurant inside Neiman Marcus is segregated. So are all the public schools. So are the movie
theaters—and the downtown lunch counters. Dallas is remarkably
segregated, perhaps the largest American city with such a widespread sense of apartheid. Maybe this NAACP convention will
jump-start the movement in Dallas.

Ted Dealey, the publisher of the *Dallas Morning News*, is less
than welcoming to the NAACP, which he refers to as the National
Association for the *Agitation* of the Colored People: "Any way you
take it, NAACP means trouble. It means ill will. It means loss in
Dallas of a cordial and friendly relationship between good white
citizens and good colored."[2]

From her seat in the auditorium, Craft watches as Wilkins,
the NAACP's national leader, takes the stage. Reverend James has
wanted him to come to Dallas for a long time. The *News* calls him
"Agitator Wilkins." This is not his first time in Texas. A few years
earlier he helped attorney Thurgood Marshall beat back an attempt
by state officials to outlaw the NAACP.

As he peers at the audience, Wilkins notes several empty chairs.
Plenty of people braved the racist outbacks of East Texas to arrive
in Dallas for the convention. *But where are all the Dallas people?*

Looking down from the lectern, his voice drops an octave as
he departs from his carefully prepared remarks: "I regret the spineless attitude of some Negroes who are afraid to stand up and be
counted on the side of freedom...They ought to know that they
can't be free until they think they are free."[3]

A skeptical *Dallas Morning News* reporter approaches "Agitator
Wilkins" to ask if he really believes that the sit-ins will soon be
coming to Dallas. He quickly replies:

"That depends on the young people of Dallas. And if I know
them, the demonstrations will be here soon."[4]

Downtown, in the boardrooms and pulpits, it is not merely a
forecast...it is a warning.

After the rally, back at her home, Juanita Craft is often by herself.
She misses her husband, Johnny. She likes to cook from the old

family recipes, and she loves to look at her ever-growing collection of rocks. She finds things, buttons or pieces of glass that are thrown away, and tries to make them into little handicrafts that she can give to her "adopted children." Johnny died before they could have their own children and now she has these hundreds of young people all over Texas who call her their aunt, their second mother, their cousin, their grandmother. They call themselves "Craft's kids."

She has a favorite chair, one where she reads and closes her eyes and summons things seared in her mind: When she worked as a maid at the Adolphus Hotel, she was ordered to clean a mess in a high-dollar suite. There was a gang of white men, hollering and laughing and drinking. A live pony was in the room with them. Sitting on the horse was a pretty young woman, completely naked except for a mask and a glittering ring.[5]

There was the time she met First Lady Eleanor Roosevelt at the hotel: When she entered her room, Roosevelt pulled her aside. She saw something in Craft. She told Craft to keep her head up, to not give up, that change was coming as long as people continued to push for it. Craft was quiet, it really wasn't her place to tell the First Lady of the United States all that she knew about Dallas. That a black man had once been attacked by a mob, sexually mutilated, hung from a tree, and set on fire. That there were places along the fetid Trinity River, not far from the hotel, where black men were tied to trees and whipped. That the First Lady could walk out of the front door of the Adolphus and find a store where she could buy a postcard showing a black man lynched in the heart of downtown Dallas.

And most of all, Craft can summon the night she thought she was going to die because of the color of her skin: She was on a train coming back to Dallas, and as it approached the Texas border, the conductor told her to move to the back—to make way for white passengers. She refused. The conductor stared down at her, swaying with the rolling train, and said he would order her removed from the train and Texas justice would be served. She knew what that meant. There were men whipped, and probably worse, in the woods. Somehow, she got to Dallas without harm. She immediately asked the NAACP to launch an investigation into her terrifying Texas train ride. There was a flurry of urgent telegrams to the railroad from the national NAACP offices. Nothing ever came of it.

Now, at her bungalow in South Dallas, Craft can think about the way things are for black people in Dallas in March 1960: There are dozens, maybe hundreds, of families who live in dirt-floor shacks, who have no running water, who are exposed to cholera and other diseases. The forests of hackberry trees just outside the city limits are still tainted by the occasional bloody mystery—a body is found, no one knows what happened, the case is never solved. Some of the Dallas district attorneys have a name for it: *TND—Typical Nigger Deal.*[6]

She reaches into a box filled with letters she will never throw away. There is one in there from one of her kids—one of the young people she inspired to join the NAACP, to take to the streets in Dallas. She tried to get him enrolled in an all-white college outside of Dallas, but he was refused admission. He finally left home and found a school close to New Mexico that allowed blacks. From there, he watched Dallas and listened to Reverend Criswell howl against integration and the dirty, filthy race mixers in America.

Dear Miss Craft . . . It deflated my ego, hearing the statements of Dr. Criswell. But I have news for him. It will be a sad commentary on our life and time if future historians can write that the last bulwark of segregation based on color was God's church.[7]

Craft folds the letter and puts it back in the box.

She knows that Criswell isn't the only one in Dallas who has been using the Bible as a weapon—and equating integration with communism . . . and the end of a certain way of life in Dallas, Texas.

Another Dallas preacher, a cousin to the governor, has written a popular book called *God the Original Segregationist*. He is shipping thousands of copies from his Dallas church office. That preacher says that black people are made black by God, on purpose, to keep them segregated by color. They are descendants of a wayward tribe in the Bible. Too, race mixing will weaken the nation:

"There is absolutely nothing the Communists would love more than a mongrelized America that they could easily enslave ... When those meddlesome white politicians and troublemakers leave them alone, the Negroes are quite happy and satisfied in their segregated condition ... God knows my heart, and He knows I am anything but a 'nigger-hater' ... the land of Dixie has always been a veritable Paradise for the Negro."[8]

Sometimes Craft reads these booklets, these pamphlets, and instead of throwing them away, she will take her scissors from the room where she likes to do her arts and crafts, and she will carefully cut out some pages and put them in other folders or in boxes ... sometimes right next to the treasured mementos from her life.

Spring is coming on. Some things in Dallas, bad and good, are worth remembering.

APRIL

Lady Bird Johnson is arriving at Dallas's soaring, brand-new downtown office complex, the Southland Life Center. Many locals compare it to New York's Rockefeller Center. Two box-shaped skyscrapers rise from a concrete slab, straight grids of blue glass obediently fastened to the sides. Dallasites proudly inform outsiders that the forty-two-story north tower, which houses an insurance company, is the tallest building west of the Mississippi.

Mrs. Johnson's destination is the south tower, the gleaming twenty-eight-story Sheraton Dallas Hotel. She is scheduled for an early April coffee with five hundred women in the grand ballroom.

A pageant of red, white, blue, and yellow greets her. The yellow is for the roses placed around the room in her honor. American and Texas flags are everywhere. Many of the women are debuting the "Ladies for Lyndon" spring ensemble: white skirts, white shoes, white gloves, red-and-white candy-striped jackets, blue scarves, and white "straw boater" hats with white-and-blue bands reading LYNDON B. JOHNSON.

Stanley Marcus has commissioned his designers at Neiman Marcus to create the outfits for the 1960 LBJ campaign—even though Johnson, maddeningly, still won't announce that he is a candidate for president. Marcus has to wonder why LBJ remains hunkered down in the Senate while John F. Kennedy tours the country, charming delegates.

Lady Bird is delighted with the outfits. "I just got a whole costume for my 16-year-old Lynda Bird," she tells everyone. "She's gonna look right sharp in it."[1]

At age forty-seven Lady Bird has jet-black hair and a kindly, intelligent face. Her expressive, sparkling eyes radiate calmness and competence. The daughter of wealthy Texans, she received her first Neiman Marcus charge account at fourteen. Today she manages the Johnson family's business interests, now worth millions of dollars.

She is an exceptionally loyal wife; she has long ago acclimated herself to her husband's sexual dalliances. It is a sacrifice that she sees many wives of public men make. She has certainly heard the wicked gossip about the Massachusetts playboy her husband is battling for the Democratic nomination.

Although she is a petite five feet, five inches, she also knows how to handle a .28-gauge shotgun during dove hunting season, and a rifle during deer season. She dropped an eight-point buck on her very first hunt at the LBJ Ranch. When the similarly slight Robert F. Kennedy paid a visit to the ranch in December 1959, Lyndon took him deer hunting and handed him a high-powered weapon. Bobby fired and the recoil knocked him to the ground. Johnson looked down at him. "Son, you've got to learn to handle a gun like a man."[2] Now, of course, Bobby Kennedy is managing his brother's presidential campaign and is steadily outmaneuvering Lyndon for the Democratic nomination.

At the Sheraton, Lady Bird graciously greets the admiring women, even those she doesn't know, as dear old friends. There are hugs and long periods of hand-holding. She makes some short public remarks. Modestly, she tells the assembled women, "My life is just so easy and pleasant and happy. The big decisions, the hard thinkin', the heavy load are not mine. It makes me feel a little guilty sometimes."[3]

Polite applause fills the room. Then the lights dim and a film projector cranks into gear. On a large screen appears her husband. His voice booms through the loudspeakers. He never mentions the presidency. He tries to appear statesman-like, telling everyone that while others chase the presidency he is remaining in the nation's capital, guiding the U.S. Senate.

He has no other ambitions, no lust for power.

JULY

In those moments when he is truly alone, those meditative times building up to when he will be required to deliver his pre–Fourth of July sermon to an increasingly eager throng, W. A. Criswell can think about the biggest journey he ever took away from Dallas. It was a little like Saul going to Damascus—the journey turned him into a new man once he saw the insidious influence of socialism and communism firsthand:

He had spent four months traveling the globe on a trip funded by generous donations to the church. He stopped in Brazil, Germany, Japan, Nigeria, Greece, Switzerland, North Africa, Israel, Italy, and India. He kept saying to himself: *There are so many lost souls out there. Millions of lost souls.* There were half-naked juju men outside of Lagos, who they decorated their places of prayer with dung. And all the time he was wondering if the six anti-malaria pills he had wolfed down had caused reality to stretch and bend in unnatural ways.

The juju men were especially pretentious animists. They were among the millions lost in a place he calls the Dark Continent. And then in Rome, he studied how the papists created golden altars for themselves, crafted something far beyond a cult of idolatry, and worshipped the bones and relics of saints. It dawned on him: These were just like the conjurers with their juju fetishes in the outback in Nigeria, all designed to control people they assumed to be ignorant.

Back home in Dallas in July, he tells people it is "ridiculous" the way Catholics—so obedient to their regal papal leader—cling to their rituals. *If man allows himself such supremacy over God, how can he do God's work?* There is not really that much distance between the lost souls in Lagos and the Catholics in Rome. And in the end, he decides it is all a problem of gullible people surrendering their independence to some controlling hand: Millions of people around the world are moving toward the creeping control of either Catholics or communists.

One time when he was in Tripoli, he went to the outskirts of the city, where it gives way to the great desert, in order to watch the huge camel caravans. He stared at the long line of animals and their drivers.

A Bedouin stared back at him and asked: "Americano?"

Criswell yelled proudly, enthusiastically, in reply: "Yes, Americano!"

The Bedouin unleashed a gob of phlegm at Criswell and shouted: "Americano no good... Stalin good!"[1]

If guests arrive, Reverend Criswell likes to walk them through a tour of the global artifacts inside his inviting two-story mansion along one of Dallas's finest streets. The houses on his block are stately, set back from the sidewalks by rolling lawns, so someone walking by can gain the true measure of the craftsmanship put into the stone-and-brick structures. Inside, guests can linger with the accumulated treasures, including some china he had bargained for in postwar Germany that had been commissioned by Adolf Hitler.

Now it is Sunday, the day before the Fourth of July, and the congregation at the church will be standing-room-only inside the towering house of worship, as it has been every Sunday for the last few years.

In a few days, the Democrats will begin arriving in Los Angeles for their national convention. John F. Kennedy, fresh from winning several primaries—even in heavily Protestant states—is the odds-on favorite to become the Democratic nominee for president of the United States. It is, for Criswell, more than maddening.

Criswell rereads his sermon for today, "Religious Freedom, the Church, the State and Senator Kennedy." He wants Dallas to know there is something tantamount to a holy war coming: Roman Catholicism "is not only a religion, it is a political tyranny" that "threatens those basic freedoms and those constitutional rights for which our forefathers died." When Americans pay income taxes,

they unknowingly are paying to prop up the Roman Catholic Church. And in South American countries run by Roman
Catholics, dozens of Protestant churches have been destroyed or
confiscated—and dozens of Baptist leaders have been murdered.

Criswell knows it: If John F. Kennedy becomes president, there
is a very real possibility that "one church above all others will rule
America."[2]

As always, Criswell's spellbinding sermon leaves his congregation excited and energized. One of his newest congregants is
especially enthused. H. L. Hunt absorbs his new pastor's broadside
against the Catholic Kennedy—someone who might also want to
destroy the precious oil depletion allowance—and it is like a call to
arms. Criswell's bold oratory, cloaked in biblical inviolability, might
just be the way to destroy John F. Kennedy's presidential ambitions.

On July 8, waving his tan Texas cowboy hat, Lyndon B. Johnson
descends from a plane as a roaring crowd jockeys to see him. A
brass band plays "Everything's Coming Up Roses" while Lady Bird
graciously accepts a dozen yellow roses. Daughters Lynda Bird and
Luci are beaming in their candy-striped "Ladies for Lyndon" jackets.

An even larger crowd, over one thousand boisterous supporters,
fills the block-long lobby of the Biltmore Hotel in Los Angeles as
Johnson arrives for the Democratic Convention. Dozens of "Ladies
for Lyndon" join together to hold hands and form a human chain
to keep the crowd from crushing the Johnsons and their daughters.
A podium has been set up, and LBJ steps before it. Referring to his
opponent, John F. Kennedy, he tells his supporters:

"I'm not against young people. I'm for them."

Significant pause.

"For Vice-President."[3]

The crowd goes wild. Many believe that they have a chance to
nominate the first Southerner in a hundred years for president. The
city is filling up with conventioneers. Campaign signs and buttons
are everywhere. Even the new theme park, Disneyland, is getting
in on the action: The Magic Kingdom is passing out campaign
buttons for Mickey Mouse, Goofy, and Tinker Bell.

The official Democratic platform is finished, and it contains the most bracing civil rights endorsement in party history—hammered into place over the vociferous objections of Southerners:

"The time has come to assure equal access for all Americans to all areas of community life, including voting booths, schoolrooms, jobs, housing, and public facilities."

The platform pointedly endorses the sit-ins at segregated lunch counters, the ones that Dallas has never allowed: "The peaceful demonstrations for first-class citizenship which have recently taken place in many parts of this country are a signal to all of us to make good at long last the guarantees of our Constitution."[4]

When John F. Kennedy arrives in Los Angeles on July 9, he is greeted by even larger crowds. His brass band pumps out "Anchors Aweigh," a nod to the senator's famous wartime service aboard PT-109. The senator's glamorous wife, Jacqueline, has stayed behind in Hyannis Port to rest and avoid stress. She is four months pregnant and has suffered a miscarriage before.

As delegates arrive from all over the country, Johnson can finally see that while he was playing statesman in the Senate, Kennedy had been outflanking him—by rounding up votes. Johnson is pacing, trying to figure out the right moves. And the convention is buzzing with rumors that Kennedy may even win on the first ballot.

As noisy crowds mill around Johnson's campaign reception room at the Biltmore, a spooky-looking older man with wispy white hair lingers near the free soda pop stand. He is wearing a dark blue suit and a white "Johnson for president" tie.

A woman walks up to him, holding her young son by the hand. Assuming he is in charge of handing out the sodas, she politely requests a beverage from him.

"I'm sorry," the man says vacantly, nearly looking through her. "I can't help you."

The woman wheels around.

"Come on, Junior," she says, pulling her son along. "They're just cheap here."[5]

H. L. Hunt watches her leave. He didn't come to the convention to pass out soda pop. He is trying to find a way, any way, to stop Kennedy from winning the nomination—even if it means supporting Lyndon Johnson. Hunt hasn't informed anyone that he's coming, and when he tries to barge in on LBJ's entourage, Johnson simply refuses to see him.

But without LBJ or his team knowing a thing, an increasingly sullen Hunt has a secret, alternative plan. He's already begun putting it into place. When he heard his Dallas minister's sermon last Sunday about Kennedy's insidiously internationalist religion, a thought blinked on in Hunt's mind: *This is a potent weapon.*

As LBJ tells his aides to not let Hunt into the room, Hunt has already arranged to have tens of thousands of copies of Criswell's anti-Kennedy sermon reprinted and quickly mailed to Protestant ministers across the country. *It will unleash a massive backlash against Kennedy. The Democratic Party will have to refuse to nominate a Catholic—and it will have to thank H. L. Hunt from Dallas.*

Lady Bird Johnson and her daughters are stepping out of the long black cars in front of Los Angeles's convention hall.

Tonight, July 13, is the culmination of years of hard work and delicate positioning, all those socials, teas, and luncheons in a thousand different places. Lady Bird has heard the predictions that Kennedy will win, but she still believes in her husband.

Lynda Bird and Luci are still wearing their "Ladies for Lyndon" outfits. Lady Bird is dressed with somewhat more dignity, as befitting a candidate's wife: a gray plaid box-skirted dress from her favorite store, Neiman Marcus.

She and the girls are watching from their private box when Speaker of the House Sam Rayburn, a longtime mentor to Lyndon, rises before the Democratic Convention and places his fellow Texan's name in nomination. Southerners go crazy as a gurgling demonstration erupts in Johnson's favor. Marchers parade across the floor carrying a huge thirty-gallon hat. Signs are waving: BLUE GRASS FOR JOHNSON, OKLAHOMA SOONERS FOR JOHNSON, GEORGIA PEACHES FOR JOHNSON.

Many of the delegates from the Northern states remain silent. As the pro-LBJ parade continues—ten minutes, then fifteen, then twenty—a group of Texans abruptly storms the Massachusetts section and tries to rip the Bay State's banner down. Fistfights break out as the Massachusetts delegates fight back. The Texans are forced to retreat to their seats.

A few minutes later, John F. Kennedy's name is placed in nomination.

As the Kennedy-for-President demonstration springs to life, hundreds of balloons with the senator's name are cascading in the auditorium.

The Texans begin scrambling after them, using the ends of lit cigarettes to pop the balloons. Other Southerners are joining the melee. It's clear that plenty of people are drunk.

The resistance is futile: Kennedy is nominated on the first ballot.

Kennedy surprises nearly everyone when he chooses Johnson as his running mate. But the decision actually comes easily. Kennedy has done the electoral math and knows that he needs the South to win. Johnson is his best hope, and the two men have formed an uneasy political alliance. Kennedy and Johnson both realize that the pro-civil-rights stance by the Democrats will be an uphill battle in the South. And now, a week after his July 13 nomination, Kennedy has just received an opposition research report on Texas. The number one problem, he learns, is Dallas:

1. Is the stronghold of Republicanism in Texas. It has the only Republican Congressman (Bruce Alger) in Texas.

2. the Dallas County Democratic Executive Committee is controlled and run by Alger—Democrats who are and have been anti-Johnson.

3. the world's largest Baptist Church is located in Dallas.

4. the world's largest Methodist Church is located in Dallas.

5. the world's largest Presbyterian Church is located in Dallas.

6. one of the largest Masonic bodies in the U.S. is located in Dallas.

7. *is the weakest labor city of large cities in Texas.*
8. *Dallas is Johnson's weakest county in Texas.*

The dirt-digging memo identifies other enemies in Dallas:

A) Baptist- Dr. Creswell [sic], the pastor of the largest Baptist Church in the world has already denounced Kennedy. This influence will drift out over Texas in all of the Baptist churches. They are well organized and have and will get plenty of money. The small country church members will be extremely vocal in their position, and, of course, will be effective in their communities.

1. Carr P. Collins, Sr.—is one of the outstanding lay leaders of the Baptist Church in Dallas [Criswell's church] and in Texas. He is extremely wealthy. On Friday, July 15, 1960, Nixon called Collins, and the next day (Saturday, July 16, 1960), Carr was in Nixon's office in Washington. This meeting took place before the Republican Convention and immediately after Kennedy and Johnson had been nominated—this is significant. It could be that Nixon discussed campaign contributions with Collins—also, to what extent the Baptist would oppose Kennedy, in Texas, could very well have been discussed. In any event, the meeting was significant, particularly, as to the timing.

And, finally, the report probes Lyndon Johnson:

He, of course, should campaign for the ticket <u>outside of Texas</u>. It is extremely doubtful if he can be effective in Texas. It is impossible for him to justify his adoption of the platform.

In fact, the more he defends it in Texas, the more it will hurt.[6]

SEPTEMBER

Richard M. Nixon's plane touches down in Dallas on the twelfth, a day before Kennedy and Johnson are due to arrive in the city.

All day, Nixon's aides have been whispering and eyeing him. He looks like a man possessed, not healthy at all. He is gaunt, down ten pounds in weight. He is limping from a nasty knee infection. He had a morning campaign event in Baltimore, flew to Indianapolis, and now is racing to Dallas—for just two frenzied hours before flying out to San Francisco. His doctors have been warning him to cut back on his schedule and regain strength in time for the first presidential debate, coming up in less than two weeks.

Nixon ignores them.

Dallas should be welcoming, invigorating. It's impossible to think of a city that is more supportive. There are those powerful old friends from Washington who have decided to make Dallas their headquarters for anti-communist campaigns. And, best of all, waiting for him in Dallas, just as Nixon expected, is Ted Dealey, publisher of the *Dallas Morning News*—who brags that his paper is the first in the nation to endorse Nixon for president.

There is, of course, the mighty Reverend Criswell, who has been blasting Kennedy as an Irish Catholic minion who will remain on bended knee to the pope in Rome. And trusty Congressman Bruce Alger is on hand—and he will have the honor of introducing Nixon at Dallas's Memorial Auditorium. There is also another powerful and wealthy man, someone named in that secret Dallas opposition memo given to Kennedy: Carr P. Collins, the insurance magnate and prominent layman in Criswell's First Baptist Church, who is now the head of "Texans for Nixon." He's buying radio time all over the state to attack Kennedy.

As he greets his allies, even the jaded Nixon is impressed at what Dealey, Alger, and the others have arranged for his two-hour September visit: A grand motorcade will take him through downtown Dallas, led by the famous Texas college drill team, the high-kicking Kilgore Rangerettes, who have traveled 120 miles for the occasion.

Enthusiastic crowds gather to see the vice president, waving American flags, NIXON signs, and occasional Confederate flags. Confetti rains down on Nixon from the upper stories of the Adolphus Hotel. With his knee still not quite right, Nixon emerges from his car and wades into the friendly crowds, shaking hands. Dealey's editors at the *Dallas Morning News* are already writing banner headlines touting Nixon's visit.

Nixon knows where he is, and what people in Dallas want to hear: *The Democrats are drunk on "extremism" . . . and not faithful to states' rights. The oil depletion allowance is in safe hands with me.* "There's nothing like a good crowd to cure a bum knee," he says.

Back at Love Field, as he limps up the stairs to his plane, he turns to offer a final promise to his fanatical supporters in Dallas:

"We'll carry Texas."[1]

As Nixon is embraced in Dallas, John Kennedy makes his way to Houston, where he has scheduled a live September 12 television appearance to explain his Catholic religion before three hundred highly skeptical Texas ministers, including fervent allies of W. A. Criswell.

The speech can't be avoided. Kennedy's religion has become a major issue in the campaign, thanks in large measure to Reverend Criswell's staggering attacks on Catholicism. H. L. Hunt's reprints of the sermon may have come too late to deny Kennedy the nomination, but they are surely having an impact on the general election. By now, through Hunt's efforts, almost two hundred thousand copies of Criswell's sermon are circulating, making it one of the most popular pieces of campaign literature this year.

In Texas, Carr Collins's blaring pro-Nixon radio broadcasts are reaching hundreds of thousands of people, and anonymous flyers attacking Kennedy as the "Papist" are being nailed to telephone poles across the state.

A few days earlier, the Reverend Norman Vincent Peale, one of America's most prominent religious figures, led a group of 150 Protestant clergymen who issued a joint statement: "Faced with the election of a Catholic, our culture is at stake."[2] The Baptist-dominated Solid South seems to be slipping away from the Democrats. Kennedy's poll numbers are dropping fast. He has no choice but to come face the enemy.

As he stands to address the somber ministers in Texas, Kennedy starts slowly.

In truth, he is not nearly as well versed in the nuances of Catholic doctrine as the Baptist preachers staring at him. But he is a quick study, and he's improving each day as a public speaker. His voice begins to ring with a fine, clear timbre as he reminds everyone that there were no religious tests when his brother died fighting for America in World War II.

In a stroke of genius from his speechwriter Ted Sorensen, Kennedy brings up the Alamo, the cradle of Texas liberty—the most revered symbol of Texas independence, the very embodiment of Texas's wish to chart its own course. He suggests Irish Catholics were among those who spilled blood to keep Texas free:

"At the shrine I visited today, side by side with Bowie and Crockett died McCafferty and Bailey and Carey—but no one knows whether they were Catholics or not. For there was no religious test there."[3]

The Texas ministers burst into hard applause as Kennedy finishes his formal remarks. The question-and-answer session goes even better. He is graceful and poised, and his calm, rational explanations seem to assuage the men braced to resist him.

Afterward, some of the preachers speak glowingly about Kennedy. Kennedy's campaign aides are ecstatic. Maybe they have finally put the "Catholic issue" behind them.

But not everyone is swayed. Criswell had wanted to be in Houston; he had been looking forward to throwing scorching questions at Kennedy. But he stayed behind in Dallas to meet with Nixon. And he had made a point of watching Kennedy's appearance on Texas television. Criswell was fuming: *It is all a farce, bordering on a lie.*

"The more I listen to him," he tells Dallas reporters, "the more I [go] 'Ha-ha.'"

Leaning in, he unleashes his thunderous voice:

"One, he is either a sorry Catholic, in which event he ought to get out of the Church. Two, if he's a good Catholic, he shouldn't be President."[4]

No one is quite sure what to expect as the Kennedy-Johnson caravan arrives in Dallas the next day, September 13.

Kennedy and his team have been hearing nothing but praise since the candidate's charm offensive in Houston—except, of course, from Dealey's *Dallas Morning News*, which is arguing that Kennedy's entreaties to the Protestant ministers in Texas will blow up in his face.

House Speaker Sam Rayburn is traveling with the Kennedy campaign in Dallas, and today he has been busy trying to explain who Ted Dealey is to the Kennedy campaign—and where men like Dealey, Hunt, Criswell, and all the others in Dallas who despise Kennedy really come from: "Freedom of the press," Rayburn huffs indignantly. "The people who were the worst broke, and got the richest under Roosevelt and Truman, hate us the worst. And that applies to a lot of people here in Dallas."[5]

The Kennedy motorcade leaves Love Field and pulls out slowly onto the city streets.

Kennedy and Johnson are riding next to each other in the open air, each perched atop the backseat of a convertible for maximum visibility...so people can get close to them, maybe even shake their hands.

LBJ is waving his cowboy hat. Kennedy, bareheaded as usual, raises his hands in the air and grins his wide, polished smile.

The candidates point approvingly at the banners proclaiming BAPTISTS FOR KENNEDY.

Almost instantly, it is apparent that the crowds in Dallas are huge and adoring. The roar can seemingly be heard for miles, echoing through the canyons of downtown skyscrapers as the motorcade progresses. There are thousands of women jumping, waving desperately at JFK, begging him to stop. Some break into the street toward him, only to be restrained by Dallas police. People are surging toward the convertible. Kennedy asks the motorcade to pause and the crowd washes over them, radiating goodwill.

Johnson is amazed. He's never seen anything like it. LBJ certainly hasn't expected this kind of miraculous reception for an Irish Catholic in deeply Protestant Dallas. No one has. Many in the crowd are so fervent, it's nearly terrifying. Several seem frantic to touch Kennedy. Dallas Police Chief Jesse Curry estimates that 175,000 people have turned out to see the Democrat—far more than came to see Nixon.

It is the largest assemblage of people ever convened on the streets of Dallas.

But already, some are saying that surely a large part of the crowd is there to put a face to the enemy's name. Dealey's *Dallas Morning News* downplays Kennedy's electrifying visit. Nixon's motorcade had received a front-page headline: 100,000 WELCOME NIXON TO DALLAS.

But the 175,000 who turn out for Kennedy go nearly unmentioned. A day after trumpeting Richard Nixon's parade, the *Dallas Morning News* headline reads:

KENNEDY AUDITORIUM TALK CHEERED BY 9,500.

OCTOBER

The shoeshine boys and the security guards are wondering where the hell old man Hunt has gone. It is as if he has disappeared. He often has flights of fancy—hiding out for days, playing $1,000-a-hand poker in back rooms on the outskirts of town, driving off with one of his many pneumatic "secretaries." His sexual appetites are often spontaneous, excessive, even after he has allowed himself to be dipped in the baptismal waters by Criswell at the big church downtown.

He is no longer seen at the Mercantile Building across from Neiman Marcus. His old Plymouth with the LIFE LINE stickers no longer frequents the cheapest parking lot downtown. And now it's not just the shoeshine guys and security people wondering what has happened to the billionaire.

Justice Department and Senate investigators are trying to figure out who has been distributing thousands and thousands of copies of Reverend Criswell's bristling sermons attacking Kennedy and Catholics. There's no question that the sermon is Criswell's. His name is listed right on the pamphlet. But the reprints are being circulated anonymously—and in violation of federal election laws.

For days in October, Hunt has been carefully monitoring the investigations. He has former FBI agents on his payroll. He and some of the other oilmen in town have had J. Edgar Hoover as a special guest at their homes. Hunt has resources beyond the ordinary.

As Hunt hides, Criswell tells investigators that the mailings have been paid for "by people who write in and send $5 or $10... Someone in the church will give some money now and then. But it's not any kind of concerted effort."[1]

Investigators don't believe him. There are far too many pamphlets in circulation to be explained away by nickel-and-dime donations. What about Criswell's prized, wealthy parishioner, H. L. Hunt—the world's richest man?

"Mr. Hunt hasn't given anything for the pamphlets," Criswell insists.[2]

Finally, the Senate investigators discover that at least a hundred thousand of the pamphlets with Criswell's anti-Kennedy diatribes have been printed in New York by a company with a mailing list of two hundred thousand Protestant ministers.

And the firm has a very good client: H. L. Hunt of Dallas. The investigators are closing the loop. Hunt, as it turns out, has paid for several anti-JFK pamphlets. The Criswell sermon is merely one of many.

The news about Hunt's involvement quickly leaks out. Reporters are calling all over Dallas—calling Criswell, calling Hunt's office. A national manhunt begins for Hunt, with newsmen and investigators searching from coast to coast. His wife claims not to know where he is. His office will say only that the billionaire is "out of town."

As the drama unfolds and Hunt remains in hiding, a man from Dallas arrives at a Kennedy campaign office carrying two large suitcases. The staffers look gingerly inside the suitcases—which are stuffed with cash. The Kennedy campaign aides are not sure of the total. They are afraid to touch the piles of neatly stacked bills. They huddle, make calls, and await instructions. The obviously big stash of money remains uncounted.

Workers are told to send the suitcases back to Dallas. The Kennedy campaign doesn't want H. L. Hunt's money.

As the days click down to the increasingly contentious November election, Dealey's reporters in Dallas are bringing him polls showing Kennedy within striking distance of Richard Nixon in Texas. Last month there were clearly tens of thousands of ordinary people in Dallas who not only supported Kennedy, but practically seemed to worship him when he came to the city.

Dealey orders the *Morning News* to more aggressively embrace the anti-Catholic crusade and to again hammer home the notion that Kennedy will bend and sway whatever way the pope, cardinals, and bishops tell him:

"In the opinion of the *News*, such a man ought not to be in the White House... The President of the United States should be a man who can be trusted to fear God and honor his oath of office, no matter what all the bishops in the hierarchy may presume to order."[3]

The October 30 editorial is passed around in Kennedy-Johnson circles, and Bobby Kennedy is livid about what is happening in Dallas: During his years investigating organized crime for Congress, he was surprised to learn that there had been a barely known, crooked underground in the city. And now he also believes that a religious zealot and an angry newspaper publisher are aligned against his brother in Dallas. The editorial is being picked up and dissected around the nation—just when he and Jack both thought the anti-Catholic bile had finally been defused.

Dealey is whipping up last-minute resistance to Kennedy—and he will not let it go. The "opposition research" teams working for the Kennedy campaign are coming back with reports clearly showing that Dealey is friends with Nixon. And that Dealey is friends with Criswell. And that there is something deeper, intransigent, circulating in the upper levels in Dallas—something running completely counter to the fact that tens of thousands of exuberant Kennedy supporters had just lined Dallas's streets.

A few men in Dallas are seemingly in league against Kennedy—and they happen to be the most persuasive, most powerful men in the city.

NOVEMBER

His aides are watching him as election day looms. Lyndon Johnson has always been sensitive to the smallest slights from others, but campaigning for Kennedy across the South is spiraling him into a welling paranoia.

He's seen the big picket signs at campaign stops accusing him of being a traitor to the Southern cause. His closest ally and mentor in the Senate, Georgia's Richard Russell, a leading segregationist, has flatly refused to campaign for the JFK–LBJ ticket. Johnson's not sure if JFK will be able to win Georgia. Hell, he's not sure he'll be able to win Texas.

During the campaign swing through the Lone Star State with JFK, Johnson often seemed so defensive, so jumpy, that Kennedy finally turned to him: "Lyndon, I believe you're cracking up."[1]

Johnson possesses an uncanny feel for the politics of his home state. Polls show Nixon and Kennedy close, but he's scared that the actual turnout for Kennedy will be much lower... all of it depressed by the anti-Catholic blitz that Dealey, Hunt, and Criswell are ramrodding with such vehemence.

As election day zooms closer, Johnson suddenly turns to one of his aides. The pain is in his face and in his voice. Johnson rarely has doubts when it comes to political campaigns, and if he does he hardly ever reveals them. This kind of candor is rare.

The aide listens as Johnson admits: "I am deeply disturbed about Texas." *And what if we win the national election ... but lose Texas?* He moans at the very thought: "Imagine how the new administration will look upon us."

For sure, he knows exactly what Bobby Kennedy will say. He has mocked Bobby in front of reporters, run his hands through Bobby's hair like he was a little baby boy. And he once had the balls to curse Bobby out when he came to his suite and tried to talk Johnson out of running against his brother Jack. He knows what Bobby will say if Johnson doesn't deliver Texas—and the goddamned election. Bobby says there was only one reason why Johnson was allowed on the Kennedy ticket in the first place:

"We put that son of a bitch on the ticket to carry Texas."[2]

With only four days left until the election, Johnson makes a manic, last-ditch effort to carry his home state. The entire election hangs in the balance. Carry Texas and Kennedy-Johnson can win the White House.

Johnson tells Lady Bird they are headed to Texas—and to the most difficult city of all.

Dallas.

Congressman Bruce Alger, his face defined by a soothing smile and deeply set and welcoming eyes, is appraising the three hundred women bobbing in front of him on November 4. He is impeccably groomed in a close-fitting business suit, tie, and well-shined shoes. And he seems utterly oblivious to the brisk North Texas winds whipping down the corridors along Commerce Street on this cold Friday morning. He's concentrating on the well-dressed women and the big signs they are carrying.

It is just four days before people vote for either John Kennedy or Richard Nixon in what some are predicting will be the closest presidential election in American history. Everyone knows that Texas will be crucial, and Alger has a wicked surprise in store for Lyndon B. Johnson.

Alger's bare-knuckled positions in Washington, DC, have made him a hero in Dallas—particularly among the crush of women who are here to follow his marching orders. He has beaten Democrats in every election thanks to these faithful women, and he has turned the city into a rugged Republican outpost deep in the heart of the Democratic South. There is, his colleagues grudgingly admit, absolutely no one like Bruce Alger in public office—even with those hothouse whispers about his private life, about the way he has treated his wife.

Lynn Alger long ago gave up on her marriage, calling herself "a political widow." On the evening her husband won his first election, she claims in her divorce petition, he brought a prostitute into their hotel room, forcing her to watch as he made love to the woman.[3]

As he became more popular among Dallas women, phone calls about her began coursing through the city. She perhaps chalks it up to jealousy—and to all those damned women in Dallas who might think she is too tawdry, too cheap, too beneath her husband. *She isn't good enough for him. She is uneducated. A trophy wife. She makes him look bad. Especially if the GOP grooms him to be a vice president.*

Right now, this Friday, her divorce papers are at the courthouse and a messy civil trial could be in the works. The news hasn't hit the papers yet, but plenty of whispers are going around. Alger tells others he doesn't think the trial will hurt his standing as a congressman. "Personal life never hurt a political career," he says. "It's how you do your job."[4]

And today, Alger is focusing on his job. He often says that he consults only two things in making his decisions: the Bible and the Constitution. But he doesn't need either as he faces the Dallas ladies assembled before him:

"The prettiest bunch of women I ever saw in my life," he murmurs with approval,[5] observing the city leaders' wives and daughters, the former debutantes, the members of the Junior League, the graduates of Southern Methodist University, the people with lines of credit at Neiman Marcus—the same ladies who do the volunteer work at the charity galas, the big churches, the local schools and country clubs.

All morning they have been arriving in blue dresses, white blouses, and red vests with NIXON stenciled across the back in large letters. Perched on their heads are demure coif hats—a cross between a pillbox and a beanie. Several are wearing mink coats, purchased from Neiman Marcus just down the street. When they're not wearing them, the women store the mink coats—alongside twenty thousand others—in a special, climate-controlled warehouse that Stanley Marcus provides in the city for his customers.

As Dallas businessmen push past the women, heading to their offices, some are joking that the unlikely gathering looks like a mink coat mob.

Alger is calling it Tag Day in Dallas, and the women are racing up to every stranger to pin NIXON buttons on shirt collars or lapels. Many of the men are delighted, beaming as the young ladies press the election buttons into their jackets. Newspaper photographers are angling for shots. Television news crews are setting up. It is as if Dallas's flannel-suited business district, home to banks, insurance firms, law offices—and Criswell's sprawling First Baptist Church—has become a Republican street festival.

But Alger has much more in mind than simply tagging businessmen with Nixon buttons. Last night, he and his volunteers went downtown to Commerce Street to take over the burnished brownstone Baker Hotel—the luxurious home of the Petroleum Club, and famous for its Peacock Terrace Ballroom. They carefully lettered anti-LBJ placards, stashing them in a spare ballroom. Alger told the women to meet him again at 7 a.m. sharp. They would do some early-morning "tagging"—and reconvene in front of the Baker when they were done.

Now the ladies are back, as instructed. And Lyndon and Lady Bird Johnson are due to arrive at the Baker any second.

Bruce Alger knows that the women excitedly fidgeting in front of him form a bulletproof vanguard. Many are from the city's thoroughbred homes. They and their husbands make Dallas run. *Who is going to stop them?*

As the Johnson motorcade speeds into downtown Dallas, escorted by motorcycle-riding policemen, one of the cops signals to LBJ's driver.

"They're having a little disturbance at the Baker Hotel," the policeman says coolly.[6]

The convoy decides to avoid the Baker's front entrance and instead pulls to a side street.

Out in front of the hotel, Bruce Alger is whipping up the crowd: *If Khrushchev could vote, he'd choose Kennedy-Johnson!*

His women shout their agreement. Suddenly, someone yells that the Johnsons have been spotted, and the group rushes toward the black Lincoln.

As Johnson steps out of the car, a look of utter dismay washes over his hangdog face. Dozens of Alger's Tag Girls are running toward him. They are screaming: "TRAITOR!" "JUDAS!"

The mob lurches to a halt just a few feet short of Johnson, jeering at him.

He turns to his wife, Lady Bird, helping her as she gingerly steps onto the sidewalk. She is fastidiously attired, wearing a lovely red suit from Neiman Marcus. She has a pair of white gloves in one hand. She stares at the protesters and seems to almost freeze.

She knows that her husband isn't popular in Dallas. But she has always imagined the city to be a bastion of Southern gentility, possessed by a kind of Christian civility and even entrepreneurial formality. Now she is facing women of her same social class, and yet they are screaming red-faced insults at her and her husband.

The Johnsons and the protesters regard each other for a moment. Suddenly, one of the Tag Girls darts up and yanks Lady Bird's gloves away, throwing them in the gutter. The women let out a cheer and begin pressing closer to the Johnsons.

Shouts fill the street. Two Dallas police officers and LBJ's bodyguards encircle the couple, pushing the angry women out of the way. The Johnson group bustles its way into the Baker, with some of the Tag Girls in pursuit. They jeer, boo, and push against Johnson's entourage as the senator aims for the hotel elevators.

When the elevator doors open, LBJ whirls to face the mob. He raises his hand and, almost oddly, it goes quiet.

He says: "I recognize that many of you are Republicans, and you have every right to be."

From the crowd, a mocking voice emerges: "Louder!"

Johnson looks at the picket signs, the flushed faces: "I have many friends who are sincere and committed Republicans."

The boos erupt again, echoing across the marble floors of the old hotel: "Socialist! Pinko!"

Finally, Johnson and his wife retreat into the open elevator.

Johnson stares back at the women and summons his most commanding voice: "You ought to be glad you live in a country where you have the legal right to boo and hiss at a man who is running for the vice presidency of the United States."

For a second, the mob seems stilled. Then someone in the back screams out: "Louder and funnier, Lyndon!"

Cheers and laughter bounce around the hotel lobby as the elevator doors close.[7]

In the hotel suite, the frazzled Johnsons try to assess what the hell just happened to them in downtown Dallas. The campaign has been brutally intense, the rhetoric even more polarizing in the last week. Everyone is on edge, but this mob anger from Dallas's leading citizens is surreal.

Johnson and his aides review the logistics: He is scheduled to go across the street to give a speech at the equally famous and plush Hotel Adolphus in fifteen minutes. Everyone knows that he will have to brave a gauntlet to get there. Should he even go? No one has to remind Johnson of the obvious. There is no choice.

There is a knock at the door. Johnson's old friend Stanley Marcus walks in, visibly flustered. The well-dressed Marcus had walked excitedly over from Neiman Marcus to personally greet the Johnsons—but then he witnessed the sudden ambush.

Normally unflappable, Marcus is shaking. He has been very quietly supporting the Kennedy-Johnson ticket—and walking a fine line between his political inclinations and avoiding antagonizing his most prized customers. Yet he's just seen his best customers, women who are personal friends, or daughters of good friends, many wearing mink coats that he has personally sold to them, and they all have come completely unhinged and are screaming at their senator...maybe the next vice president of the United States.

As Marcus tries to calm himself, there is another knock on the hotel suite. A Dallas policeman enters and quickly outlines the situation: The ranks of the protesters are swelling, and Commerce Street is now crammed full of people waiting for the Johnsons. The women have been joined by dozens of businessmen on their lunch hour, drawn by the spectacle they can see from their office windows.

All eyes turn to Lady Bird as she says she is not going to cross that street; she is staying in the room.

The policeman suggests a plan. He and other officers can sneak the Johnsons out a side door of the Baker and into the Adolphus through a back door.

Johnson doesn't like the idea: "We will walk straight through the shouting crowd. We will contrast their boorishness with our civility. And I do *not* want a police escort."

Then Johnson turns to the cop: "If it has come to the point in America where a citizen cannot walk across a public street with his lady without being accosted, then I want to know it."

With Lady Bird on his arm, Johnson steps grandly out of the suite, followed by his campaign aides and Stanley Marcus.

A thunderstorm of boos erupts as the elevator doors open to reveal the Johnsons. Hecklers fall in behind them, jeering as the Johnsons stolidly walk out the front door and onto Commerce Street.

Once the Johnsons appear, it is as if an electric current snakes through the streets. Alger's women are bustling, waving signs, yelling louder. The crowd seems to be getting bigger, angrier. If John F. Kennedy's triumphant motorcade a few weeks earlier summoned Dallas's sunny side, Lyndon Johnson is now running into a full-fledged thunderstorm.

Catcalls cascade over the street. Some hear curses. The placards are being stabbed in the air: TEXAS TRAITOR. JUDAS JOHNSON: TURNCOAT TEXAN. LET'S BEAT JUDAS.

Alger stands a head taller than everyone around him. His sign reads: LBJ SOLD OUT TO YANKEE SOCIALISTS.

The crowd forms a rolling circle around the Johnsons. Someone swings a sign in close to Lady Bird's head, brushing against her hat. The reddened faces are closing in. LBJ clutches his wife.

Another voice shouts: "Judas!"

Alger can be heard yelling: "We're gonna show Johnson he's not wanted in Dallas."

One of Johnson's party pushes desperately through the crowd, aiming for Alger: "It's out of line for a U.S. Congressman to take part in this. Put a stop to this."

Alger responds loud enough for his supporters to hear him: "I don't think it's rude to show a socialist and traitor what you think of him."

Off to the side, Stanley Marcus watches in horror. He is devastated. He feels like every shout of *traitor* or *Judas* is aimed at him as well.

Marcus always had a vision for Dallas—a place of taste, culture, and refinement in the heart of Texas. A place where reason, art, and insight were the outgrowths of so much money pooling in one place on the planet. It would be a sort of beau ideal, a place where people relish and celebrate and share the finest things humankind can create.

In the background are the second-floor dives where $2 would earn you admission to one of nightclub owner Jack Ruby's "exotic dance" joints. Down the block you could see the faint curl of the polluted Trinity River—and beyond it what some say are the worst inner-city slums in America.

Perhaps the gallant veneer Marcus has cultivated so assiduously for Dallas is dissolving right before his eyes, right here on Commerce Street. Right now he knows what is happening: Longtime customers are spotting him and they are already deciding to close their charge accounts at his store.

Inside the Adolphus, the swanky Beaux-Arts hotel built by the founders of Anheuser-Busch, the gleaming wood-and-brass lobby is packed with sign-waving protesters. It is another gauntlet. There is shoving, jockeying, and elbows are flying. Some people are pulling off their Nixon buttons and using the pins to stab at the handful of pro-LBJ supporters. Two women from the Kennedy-Johnson campaign are clutching their faces, pressing their hands to their broken noses. Other people are limping, being helped outside and to hospitals.

Reporters and photographers push in to get a better view. The local NBC-TV affiliate, tipped off to Alger's protest, has already set up a camera to capture the melee.

At six feet, four inches, Johnson towers over most of the throng in the normally hushed lobby. He can see the flashbulbs popping. He can see the eye of the television camera taking everything in. In an instant, just as the storm seems its darkest, his political instincts kick in. Johnson understands political theater. Suddenly, he orders the police to stand aside and waves at his aides and bodyguards to get out of the way.

A woman holding a LET'S GROUND LADY BIRD sign jabs at Mrs. Johnson's face.

Some are spitting. Johnson looks at the contorted faces and Lady Bird flinches. Suddenly, she loses composure and begins shouting back at the crowd, but her husband quickly presses his smothering hand over her face. He leans close to her ear.

"Let's just let them do all the hollering," he says.

With his arm securely around his wife, Lyndon Johnson assumes a pious look of supreme martyrdom as the couple inches forward, toward the elevator that will take them to the second-floor ballroom.

Lady Bird realizes what is happening. Her husband is purposely slowing down, allowing the crowd to press in on them. He's a big man and he could force his way through if he wanted to.

Johnson knows what the television images will show: the helpless vice presidential candidate and his demure wife trapped by an angry horde of hissing and spitting protesters.

As the mob closes in and the cameras click and whir, Johnson thinks of how the images will play on the television screens at the Kennedy compound in Hyannis Port. No one can blame him now for losing Texas—not when they see just how crazed some of the people in his home state really are.

One of LBJ's aides is a young Baptist minister named Bill Moyers. He understands exactly what Johnson is doing: "If he could have thought this up, he would have thought it up. Tried to invent it."[8]

Within hours, television newscasts around the nation are running footage showing Dallas's best-dressed citizens rioting against Lyndon

B. Johnson and his frightened wife. The images of Lady Bird being jeered at by Nixon supporters are particularly disturbing—especially egregious in the South, in places where attacking a candidate's wife is considered truly off limits. The *New York Times* begins reporting that new signs are already appearing at campaign rallies: THE REPUBLICANS DECIDED ME TODAY: I'M FOR KENNEDY AND JOHNSON.

And when reporters ask him to react to the uncontrolled mayhem in the finest hotels in the city of Dallas, Johnson summons some righteous indignation:

"No man is afraid to facing up to such people. But it is outrageous that in a large civilized city a man's wife can be subjected to such treatment. Republicans are attacking the women, and the children will probably be next."[9]

The backlash against Dallas is beginning.

With only two days to the presidential election, Democrats feverishly circulate handbills featuring a photo of Bruce Alger at the protest, and prominent but reluctant Republicans are being forced to condemn the outburst. Momentum bleeds from the Nixon campaign, and Alger suddenly finds himself on the defensive. Perhaps he has unwittingly unleashed something welling, something ugly inside of Dallas that even he didn't realize was there.

Alger decides to announce—in the newspaper, in a paid ad—that he personally witnessed no really unruly behavior. He is a Princeton man, after all, and he offers his "sincere apology" to Lady Bird in case she felt threatened by his supporters.

But he refuses to apologize to LBJ: "The sign I picked up and held aloft expressed my feelings precisely."

In Dallas, the women who had formed his army are equally steadfast. One of them, a Dallas housewife, tells the *Dallas Morning News*:

"LBJ deserves a lot worse than he got."

On November 8, Americans retire for the night not knowing who their next president will be. It is one of the closest presidential elections in the nation's history. The final numbers come down to Illinois and Texas. By morning, the fog has cleared, and John F. Kennedy has carried Illinois by the slimmest of totals, thanks to some suspicious late returns from the Democratic-controlled Chicago region that he visited the same day LBJ went to Dallas.

Richard M. Nixon carries Dallas by nearly a two-to-one margin—his largest victory in any city in the country. But in the rest of Texas, the Kennedy-Johnson ticket stages a dramatic come-from-behind win, beating Nixon by a scant forty-six thousand votes.

The triumph in Texas seals John F. Kennedy's election—and an irony begins to emerge: Kennedy is being sent to the White House because of Dallas, Texas. Because a brawling mob in Dallas led last-minute voters to suddenly throw their support to Kennedy and Johnson.

Nixon watched and knew it: "We lost Texas . . . because of that asshole congressman, you know."[10]

It is, for many in Dallas, almost too much to bear:

The November attempt to crush Kennedy in Dallas has catapulted him to the presidency of the United States.

1961

Secret Service agents are huddling, trying to decide if the seventy-three-year-old man picked up in Florida for plotting to assassinate President-Elect Kennedy needs to be confined in a federal mental health facility. The agents want to continue to assess the stocky man taken into custody two weeks ago—and determine whether he is a lone would-be assassin, or part of some bigger, ongoing plot against Kennedy.

The hatred toward Kennedy is emerging elsewhere. One man in Chicago was arrested at a Kennedy rally in November, after police found him carrying a .38 revolver in a brown paper bag. Another man, also in Chicago, was arrested after he began running toward Kennedy's motorcade; it took over a dozen officers to wrestle him to the ground and rip open his pockets to find a .25-caliber automatic pistol.[1]

Now, with this new case in Florida, the agents are digging deeper. One thing is emerging: This would-be murderer possessed enough explosives to blow up a small mountain. They take turns questioning him. He is a ruddy-faced former postal clerk with a shock of snow-white hair that contrasts with his striking, almost black eyebrows. His arms and hands are wrinkled, and he rarely smiles. He has apparently been meticulous in his planning.

He spent part of December on the highways along the East Coast, and then slowly driving his Buick by and scouting the Kennedy compound in Hyannis Port—and the Kennedy homes in Georgetown and Palm Beach. He was taking photographs, looking for patterns, for any bit of information that could help him pull it all off. He had even been circling the churches and airports used by the Kennedy clan in Florida.

He also went shopping and spent hours putting things together: There were several sticks of dynamite, plenty of blasting caps, enough wiring. He was getting rid of a lot of things as well. All of his furniture, his clothes. He didn't need any of it anymore. He wasn't coming back.

One Sunday, he watched as Kennedy came out of his front door in Palm Beach, on his way to church. He watched from down the street, engine running, his car packed with dynamite. The Secret Service hadn't noticed him. He was going to ram Kennedy's car and blow everyone sky-high. But then he saw Kennedy turn back toward the door. He could see Kennedy telling his wife and daughter good-bye. And the wife was holding a newborn baby in her arms. He decided at that moment that while he was still going to kill the man, he wouldn't do it in front of his family.[2]

Later, driving through Palm Beach, he veered across a white line—something not that unusual with so many retirees in the city. But a nearby cop decided to turn on his lights and pull the man over. He stuck his head inside the car . . . *there is the dynamite . . . the bombing gear.* The word spread quickly at the cop shop, at the newspaper. Reporters managed to shout some questions at him as he was led into custody: *Why'd you do it?*

"Kennedy's money bought the White House and the presidency," he yelled back. "I wanted to stop Kennedy from being president."[3]

Now the indictments against him are being drafted, and arrangements are being made to send him to the intimidating federal psychiatric evaluation center in Springfield, Missouri, a place where the government sometimes confines people viewed as serious threats to the president and the nation. The news about the would-be assassin will appear in papers around the nation, including the ones in Dallas.

It has been weeks, but it is still as if many in the city refuse to believe that Kennedy has actually won. Ted Dealey at the *Dallas Morning News* is among those having the hardest time letting go.

He has remained in regular contact with the defeated Richard Nixon, someone he has grown close to. He reminds the outgoing vice president that Dallas voted overwhelmingly for him. He also speculates that the Kennedy forces stole the election. He refers, mockingly, to Kennedy and Johnson as "friends": "If the count in Illinois and Texas had been honest," Dealey tells Nixon, "I rather think you would have been President today instead of our friend, John Fitzgerald Kennedy."[4]

Dealey wants Nixon to know something else: Just because Dealey is from Dallas it does not mean he has any ties at all to someone like Lyndon Baines Johnson—or by extension John Fitzgerald Kennedy. He wants Nixon to know there is no "Texas loyalty" at work.

"Just between you and me and the gatepost," Dealey tells Nixon, "I doubt whether our friend Lyndon will turn in nearly as creditable a record as you did...and you can more or less read between the lines, as I say this, what I personally think of our South Texas friend."[5]

Day after day, Dealey's paper relentlessly runs stories that are not just skeptical of the president-elect, they are barely contained personal attacks: KENNEDY CONSIDERS KIN FOR JOB, JACK PRESCRIBES BAD MEDICINE, JFK URGED TO GO AFTER DIXIE FOES, DANGEROUS THEORY OF GOVERNMENT, WHITE HOUSE WILL BE ONE OF MANY KENNEDY HOMES.[6]

The *News* is also running a lengthy anti-Kennedy story that is sure to anger people in Dallas who vehemently hate unions, dating to the days when the ballsy, cigar-chomping vice president from Texas, John Nance Garner, battled like holy hell against FDR's support of national labor unions. The Dallas newspaper story is guaranteed to make the anti-union core livid: LABOR VOTE KEY TO KENNEDY WIN.[7]

Another incendiary attack on Kennedy suggests that the president-elect will take away the precious oil depletion allowance that has helped make so many people in Dallas rich, allowing them to buy ridiculously expensive baubles and furs at Stanley Marcus's store, or to print anti-communist diatribes, or to fund billionaire oilman H. L. Hunt's "Constructive" radio shows.

And, perhaps more alarming than anything else: NEGRO VOTES CREDITED FOR JFK WIN.

Race, of course, is the shadow element in the now swirling anti-Kennedy fervor in Dallas. And as the first weeks of 1961 unfurl, the publisher of the *Dallas Morning News* feels liberated to sanction stories and editorials that are thinly veiled barbs at any Kennedy effort to promote diversity in his administration. When Kennedy announces that he will appoint a black man, someone who once served as an adviser to FDR, to be the head of the federal housing agency, Dealey's paper runs an item titled: A NEGRO IS HOUSING BOSS. "No doubt the Negro can do the job. And maybe he can do it excellently. For that matter, a thousand others could do the job and do it excellently. Truth is, the appointment is a gesture to the race which played so vital a part in electing Mr. Kennedy... How do the Southerners feel now?"[8]

Even as John Kennedy is inaugurated as president, the *News* publishes a cutting editorial referring to him as "our most promising young man." The paper does not intend to be complimentary. Kennedy is simply peddling false hope of change: "Mr. Kennedy made 220 promises during his campaign. *The News* neither expects nor hopes that the new President will be able to make good on those promises."[9]

On a frigid Monday afternoon, Reverend Rhett James pushes open the doors to one of the city's leading stores, Titche-Goettinger, and quietly leads five other black residents of Dallas into the segregated, all-white restaurant area. James, dressed in his usual suit and horn-rimmed glasses, tells his people to sit down and place their orders. They are refused service.

James and his group do not budge. They are going to stay in their seats until the store closes that night. As the sit-in begins, James tries to fathom this small victory. At least he is not being thrown out of the store that is just a short stroll from his church. At least he is not being barred from entering the dining area: Just last Tuesday, when James tried walking past all the white customers in the store and heading to the restaurant, there was a line of store employees cordoning the place off. They raced to put up a rope so none of the black people, including James, could even get inside. James could no doubt feel the palpable hatred as people stared at him.

It came the same week a drugstore owner sprayed insecticide over some college students, black and white, trying to integrate a lunch counter near the all-white Southern Methodist University. It is as if some boulder has started rolling and can't be stopped. James has been walking on the downtown streets—a one-man protest, or sometimes he is joined by a few friends. Juanita Craft, the widow who heads the local NAACP's youth council, is also rushing to be involved, organizing high school students to join the protests. Flyers and posters are being printed in black-owned printing shops, urging people to not spend their money at Neiman Marcus, at the drugstores, the candy stores, the Continental Bus Station, anyplace segregated.

Now, all afternoon in the big department store, James and his five friends wait and wait. No one serves them. And when the store finally announces that it is closing, the preacher leads them into the night.[10]

At the minimum, he has plenty to write about in his regular, popular column in the *Dallas Express*, the leading black newspaper. It is called "Dateline Dallas" and with it he hopes to scare the Dallas Citizens Council, or Dealey, or Criswell, or Alger. Maybe they'll realize that sit-ins, even a wholesale economic boycott, are bad for the bottom line—the only thing the men downtown might understand. James begins writing his newspaper column, an open letter to Dallas:

"If the people of Dallas shop at stores that discriminate... they do not want freedom...Freedom is always purchased with a price...Are you willing to pay your share?"[11]

FEBRUARY

It is two weeks after John F. Kennedy's inauguration, and at their offices, Congressman Bruce Alger and publisher Ted Dealey are opening the same letter that is deluging thousands of elected officials and journalists across America—each one written by members of an underground organization just seeping into public view: The John Birch Society, once known to only a small coterie, is unleashing a massive public campaign to impeach Earl Warren, chief justice of the Supreme Court. The group claims that Warren—a Republican appointed by President Eisenhower—has "voted 92 per cent of the time in favor of Communists and subversives."[1]

Envelopes carrying the letters are stamped with the Birch Society's slogan: *This is a REPUBLIC, not a democracy. Let's keep it that way.* Many of the mailings include an incendiary tract depicting the chief justice on a WANTED poster. Among the charges against him:

*"The DESEGREGATION DECISION, which aids and abets the plans of the Communist Conspiracy to (A): create tension between Negroes and Whites; (B): to transform the South into a BLACK SOVIET REPUBLIC; (C): to legalize and encourage intermarriage between Negroes and Whites **and thus mongrelize the American White Race!"***[2]

Newspapers and magazines anxiously scramble to patch together any information they can find about the group. The stories are nearly too fantastic to believe: Birchers are convinced that a secret cadre of communists is taking over America through the guise of seemingly innocent programs: Social Security, the progressive income tax, membership in the United Nations. Even campaigns to add fluoride to city water supplies are regarded as a plot to prepare the populace for communist mind control.

The top levels of the federal government and the news media

are already communist-dominated, according to the Birch Society. Churches are suspect, particularly ones that advocate solidarity with other nations and cultures. The organization's *Blue Book* claims, "Fully one-third of the services in at least the Protestant churches of America are helping that trend... And some actually use their pulpits to preach outright communism."[3] The last three American presidents—Roosevelt, Truman, and Eisenhower—are considered communist dupes at best. The Birch Society's founder, a retired candy maker named Robert Welch, describes Eisenhower as a "conscious, dedicated agent of the Communist Conspiracy."

Politicians from both parties denounce the organization. North Dakota Republican Milton R. Young says that Welch's accusations are outrageous: "Far beyond anything the late Senator Joe McCarthy even thought of. To label some of our most loyal and dedicated people as Communists plays right into the hands of the Communists"[4]—and Welch is renounced as "a little Hitler" and a "right-wing crackpot." President Truman growls that the Birch Society is easy to describe: "Nothing but the Ku Klux Klan without the nightshirts." Even the rising conservative Barry Goldwater, sympathetic to many of the Birchers' political positions, concedes that the Birchers "have hurt the conservative movement."[5] Around the nation, there are calls for a full-scale investigation into the secretive group. The nation's new attorney general, Robert F. Kennedy, even mocks the Birch Society: "It's an organization that's in the area of being humorous."[6]

As one of the most aggressive ultra-conservatives in Congress, Bruce Alger receives a personal appeal from Robert Welch, asking him to join the Birch Society and vote to impeach Justice Warren: "I can assure you that the favor will be appreciated by a lot of people besides me who are now giving their whole lives to supporting patriots like yourself, in an effort to save for our children and their children some semblance of the glorious country which we ourselves inherited."[7]

As the Birch movement begins its edgy, polarizing dance, Alger, Dealey, and other public figures in Dallas now have to weigh their options. Most come to the same conclusion. As much as they agree with the fundamental principles defining the Birchers, it's political suicide to endorse them. In editorials and newsletters, Alger and Dealey try to map out a delicate distance between themselves and the John Birch Society.

And almost instantly, other hard-core extremists in the city begin to castigate the two very men they had assumed would be at the forefront of the public anti-Kennedy armies: Alger and Dealey are deluged with angry letters from local Birch Society members blasting them for their lack of support. The letters are heated, severe, frightening. It is a wake-up call for Dealey and Alger. Maybe they've underestimated how resilient—and aggressive—the anti-Kennedy movement is in Dallas. Maybe there is more going on in the city, maybe there are far more people ready for more muscular action. The Kennedy administration has only been in office for a few weeks—but some people in Dallas are enlisting for a long march of resistance. Already the bumper stickers are appearing on cars: K.O. THE KENNEDYS.

Ted Dealey's *Dallas Morning News* is refusing to linger on the protests in downtown Dallas led by Rhett James and Juanita Craft. It is as if his paper believes that their demands will vanish by refusing to acknowledge them. The paper has even suggested that black Dallas is divided, splintered, that a few activists are presuming to speak for the entire black populace.

James's renegade campaign for the school board ended in defeat. But he'd gained more votes than any previous minority candidate. That symbolism, he knew, meant something to those who ruled Dallas. And now he is positioned as a clear leader of Dallas's black community. James decides to take on Dealey and the *Dallas Morning News*: "When the local morning paper comes out...to infer a division in the Negro community, we see the head of the Southern Divider attempting to spread its influence into the Negro citizenry."[8]

One thing is clear: The first few weeks of 1961 are bringing extraordinary change in Dallas. And it isn't just in the active protests at the downtown restaurants; it is also going to finally come inside the schools. After years of stalling, fighting in the courts, the local school board has just announced that Dallas will cease being the largest American city with completely segregated classrooms.

Integration in the Dallas public schools will finally commence in the fall.

When he hears the news, James sits at his typewriter and begins composing a headline that he knows will startle many already uneasy people in downtown Dallas: DALLAS PREPARES FOR THE INEVITABLE! INTEGRATION![9]

It is Abraham Lincoln's birthday, February 12, and Juanita Craft has organized her eager teenage volunteers for another protest: a "stand-in" outside the segregated Palace and Majestic Theatres in downtown Dallas. The students stand quietly in line, waiting for their turn to purchase a ticket at the box office. They ask for seats inside the theater—not in the segregated balcony. When they are refused, they simply walk back to the end of the line and start the entire process all over again.[10]

Craft monitors the action and approaches every now and then to offer them drinks and snacks she has prepared for the long day. Dallas cops are watching, too. But they make no move to arrest or interfere with the students. Decisions have been made: The Dallas Citizens Council has decided that the city needs, at all costs, to avoid any mayhem, any rioting, any economic backlash.

Many of Craft's NAACP volunteers have brought Bibles. They read passages while waiting in line. As the hours go by, some young women in the group become tired of standing for so long, walking back and forth over the same few feet of pavement. They take off their shoes and walk in their hose or socks.

By 3 p.m., fifty white college students from nearby Southern Methodist University arrive to offer support. The SMU students join the line. As they reach the box office, they ask if they can sit with a Negro friend inside the theater. When they are refused, they go back to the end of the line.

Last year, Craft had begun sending her teenage volunteers into the big H. L. Green drugstore downtown. Blacks were allowed to shop there, but not eat at the lunch counter. She gave her teams enough money to make a modest, yet very visible purchase. They walked inside in pairs and bought a big tablet of drawing paper, or anything else that could be wrapped in a large paper bag. Holding their bags, they went to the lunch counter, took a seat, and ordered soda. When the waitress told them they couldn't be served, they held up their shopping bags: *I just bought this over at the other counter. How come I can buy that there but can't be served here?* Meanwhile, two other young volunteers entered the store and did the same thing. The cycle was repeated, over and over, until the frustrated manager was called.

Back then, and now today on Lincoln's birthday, the police never interfered. There are ugly stares, some hateful shouts, from people passing by. But compared with the dangerous moments endured by activists elsewhere in the South, Dallas is quietly acquiescent. There is no violence, no thudding batons, no unleashed dogs. It is almost as if the powers-that-be are treating the protests like a benign irrelevancy—as if ignoring them will suck the oxygen from them.

Craft has always followed politics with a keen interest. She wonders if Kennedy will really change things. She has seen politicians make promises before, and she has helped shape the NAACP, to give life to it, in the most dangerous moments in Dallas and Texas. She knows that Kennedy is forecasting a new future, even if some people feel he is being too careful.

She has decided that she admires Kennedy. She likes his deliberation. She would like to meet President Kennedy if he ever comes to Dallas.

A number of customers have been sending Stanley Marcus confrontational letters. Each of them is a variation on the same theme:

> *I plan to visit your store soon and am bringing along a friend. However, I've been told that since my friend is a Negro we won't be allowed to dine in your Zodiac restaurant. Could you please clarify your policy for me? I didn't realize that Neiman Marcus is segre-*

gated. Should I take my friend somewhere else to shop so she won't
feel uncomfortable in your store?[11]

Marcus puts the letters down and mulls his decision, and the way Dallas has been changing, and the way he has envisioned its future. For years he's been a lonely voice on the Dallas Citizens Council, quietly lobbying the other men to consider integration. The others have continually put him off, refusing to even discuss the matter.

Marcus has been negotiating a tightrope. He knows that many of his best customers will abandon his store if he is the first to cross the color line. So even as he retains Neiman Marcus's official apartheid, he makes private financial contributions to Negro causes, perhaps hoping to assuage his guilt. And now the walls are crumbling. Everyone can feel it. Organized protests against segregation are spreading across the South, and newspapers are filling with stories of mobs and violence.

The Dallas Citizens Council is coming to a consensus built on enlightened self-interest: *We'll have to bend ... or risk destroying what we built in Dallas.*

The movie *Spartacus*, starring Kirk Douglas, is generating fanfare, and critics are already predicting it will win Academy Awards. President Kennedy has seen the film twice in Washington. And today, the Adamson High School band is assembled in front of the Capri Theatre as local dignitaries join the crowds lining up to see the movie. The dignitaries' names are printed in the papers.

Over the next several days, letters begin arriving at their homes:

I'm shocked that a good American such as you would attend the showing of this Communist-backed movie.

Meanwhile, a grocery chain in Dallas is found to be selling small wicker baskets made in Yugoslavia—and the stores are besieged by letters, phone calls, and visits from angry people demanding that "the communist products" be stripped from the shelves. The store managers anxiously confer and decide to comply.

The Dallas Freedom Forum, tied to a national organization called the Christian Anti-Communist Crusade, is planning its next meeting at the Baker Hotel—the same majestic hotel where LBJ and his wife were cornered last fall by the mink coat mob. The leaders in Dallas are drafting the themes for the meeting—ridding the State Department of socialists, outlawing the Communist Party, imposing a 100 percent trade block on the Soviet Union, and ending foreign aid. The guest list is being drawn up: The lead attorney for H. L. Hunt will be invited. So will the Dallas School Board president—a staunch anti-communist who has already readily agreed to allow national officers of the Christian Anti-Communist Crusade to address high school students.[1]

And the John Birch Society is racing ahead. In dens and living rooms all over the city, more and more groups of up to twenty-five people are gathering for coffee, doughnuts, and recruitment and indoctrination sessions. Prospects are shown a film of Robert Welch reading from his *Blue Book*, and Birch publications are offered for sale. Dozens of new members are joining every week. Welch is prophesying that his organization will soon have one million members.

The negative publicity from the mainstream media toward the Birchers has had the opposite effect among so many in Dallas: "Maybe the Communists didn't like what the society was doing," muses one Dallas member, "and ordered this rash of bad publicity."[2]

All over the city, people watch as Welch appears on NBC's *Meet the Press* and offers his critique of the Eisenhower presidency: "In 1953, internationally, the nearest Communist dominion to us was probably East Germany, 3,500 miles away...but go ahead for eight years to the end of 1960 and see what had happened. The Communists were 90 miles from our shores."[3]

Hearing Welch, several people in Dallas suddenly feel that they have finally found a group, a patriotic organization that understands their frustrations and fears about where America is headed. For some, it anchors men and women in a common belief.

"I was tired of just sitting around and talking about it," says one Dallas member. "I wanted to do something—something concrete—and the society gives me the opportunity and the encouragement."[4]

In Dallas, hundreds of people quickly respond when Welch begins asking for something more from his members—their help compiling a master blacklist:

"The most complete and most accurate files in America on the leading Communists, Socialists, and liberals...who are trying to change the economic and political structure of this country so that it could be comfortably merged with Soviet Russia in a one-world socialist government."[5]

One Dallas homemaker knows her life has changed since this new crusade began taking hold in her city. It has given her purpose and deep meaning:

"I just don't have time for anything," she says. "I'm fighting communism three nights a week."[6]

APRIL

Major General Edwin A. Walker's Twenty-Fourth Infantry Division leads the Seventh Army in combat readiness. The Texan requires daily calisthenics for all thirteen thousand men under his command—even the desk jockeys and once overweight majors are now in top physical shape. A roaring lion, which paces in its cage near headquarters, serves as the Twenty-Fourth's mascot. The animal is said to have the rank and pay of a sergeant.

Walker's division is equipped with nuclear weapons: MGR-1 "Honest John" missiles mounted on the backs of trucks. His well-drilled men can have the rockets ready to fire in five minutes.

There are at least three hundred thousand communist troops massed across the East German border, but the general is increasingly focused on the communist subversion back home. Quietly, some of his soldiers believe that the bachelor general's obsessions are bordering on madness: They've attended his fanatical lectures where he shows a giant map depicting the world's communist penetration—every single country, including the United States, is shaded red. The soldiers have seen Walker lose his temper—shouting that newsman Edward R. Murrow is a communist. They've seen him, eyes glowing with anger, as he rips up a copy of *MAD Magazine*—the children's spoof publication—denouncing it as a subversive influence on American schoolchildren. Walker is speaking constantly about psychological warfare, about brainwashed Americans, about the soldiers he knew who had been tortured by the communists during the Korean War.

By now, it's not just the rank-and-file soldiers who are looking at him. Walker has already been warned twice by the European commander, General Bruce C. Clarke, to stay clear of political proselytizing.

But Walker has reached his critical crossroads, committed to do something that flies completely in the face of all that he has been trained to do during a lifetime as an unswerving soldier: He has decided to disobey his orders, his commanders. He is serving a higher cause. The future of his country—indeed, of all Christianity—is at stake. He begins telling his friends that the hour is late . . . that drastic and immediate action is needed.

He's developed a "Pro-Blue" education program for his division that is identical to the teachings of the John Birch Society. He brings in Birch-affiliated speakers for patriotic lectures, and he recommends his soldiers read *The Life of John Birch* by Robert Welch—the book is stocked in dayrooms throughout the division. The Twenty-Fourth's newspaper, the *Taro Leaf*, reprints articles from the Birch Society's official magazine.[1]

During the buildup to the 1960 election, Walker became even more agitated about the direction of America. Despite pleas from his subordinates, he used his "Commander's Column" in the *Taro Leaf* to urge his men to vote for conservative politicians.

And then, shortly after Kennedy's victory, Walker began experiencing massive headaches. The pain became so severe that he checked himself into the base hospital. Rumors have been circulating that Walker has a brain tumor. Many of his troops believe it's the only way to explain his increasingly erratic behavior. He loses his temper frequently. He is becoming a chain-smoker, nervously lighting one cigarette after another as the puffs swirl around his head.

For some reporters, the rumors about Walker are too good to ignore.

The Overseas Weekly, a sensationalistic tabloid aimed at the enlisted men in Europe and created as a dishy alternative to the more staid *Stars and Stripes*, specializes in true crime stories and photos of half-naked women. The magazine is very popular—fifty thousand servicemen read it religiously. Army officers call it "Oversexed Weekly." Walker is disgusted by the magazine and he's tried, unsuccessfully, to prevent it from being sold at his base.

Walker believes that a *Weekly* reporter has been spreading rumors about his mental state. He has the reporter kicked off his base. In turn, the newspaper's publisher contacts General Clarke, the European commander, and demands that the reporter be reinstated. The publisher warns Clarke that the paper has plenty of information to run a damaging exposé of the general. Clarke feels blackmailed and curtly dismisses the publisher. Now, today, April 15, the newest edition of *The Overseas Weekly* hits newsstands.

A sultry, beautiful blond woman is on the cover. She's lying on a bed and appears to be wearing little more than a blanket. "She's lovely, young, and single," the headline advises.

Above the photo is a larger, more serious headline: WHAT'S GOING ON AT 24TH INF. DIV?

The story begins: "For the past year the 24th Infantry Division has been exposed to a propaganda barrage on the philosophy of the anticommunist John Birch Society."[2]

American newspapers have already been publishing exposés about the John Birch Society for weeks. And now it appears that a high-ranking U.S. Army officer is also involved in the organization. The *Weekly* has scooped the entire stateside press. Each of Walker's political transgressions is detailed, including his contemptuous comments that President Truman and First Lady Eleanor Roosevelt are "definitely pink."

And overnight, General Edwin A. Walker becomes the most controversial man in the American military. He is on the front page of the *New York Times* and he is the focus of headlines around the world, including Dallas.

While President Kennedy grapples with the massive fallout from the CIA's bungled attempt to invade Cuba at the Bay of Pigs, General Walker holds a press conference in Germany to blast the *Overseas Weekly* report. Walker begins calmly enough, reading a written statement denying that his Pro-Blue program is affiliated with the John Birch Society.

But as questions mount about the details in *The Overseas Weekly*, Walker suddenly snaps and begins shouting heatedly at the astonished newsmen:

"We have Communists and we have *The Overseas Weekly*. Nei-

ther is one of God's blessings to the American people or their soldier sons overseas. Immoral, unscrupulous, corrupt and destructive
are terms which could be applied to either. If the costs of the bad
effects of *Overseas Weekly* could be accounted in dollars, it would
be in terms of hundreds of millions of dollars—without including
all the benefits to the enemy."[3]

By now, European commander Clarke is appointing a special
inspector general to investigate the allegations against Walker. The
investigator is a friend of Walker's. General Clarke expects that
the crazy accusations will die down and he will go through the
motions of delivering a mild admonishment to Walker.

Then, Clarke is told by an aide that there is an urgent phone
call from Washington, DC. The secretary of the army is on the
line, and Clarke listens as he tells him that President Kennedy is
demanding that General Walker be relieved of his command—
effective immediately.

Clarke hangs up and decides, simply, to follow the executive
mandates as quickly as possible: He sends news to Walker that he is
being reassigned, summoned to work in Clarke's European Army
headquarters. Walker will be deputy chief of staff while the investigation is conducted. It is a subordinate position, a clear affront to
the proud, feisty Walker.

Clarke admits that he knows Walker feels belittled: "The reas-
signment is very humiliating."[4]

Back in the States, the political establishment backs Kennedy's
action. Wisconsin Congressman Henry S. Reuss essentially calls
Walker crazy: "Generals are entitled to whatever lunatic private views they wish to espouse. They are not entitled to use the
machinery of the U.S. Army to try to corrupt our troops."[5]

Wisconsin Senator William Proxmire is even more scornful:
"The incident shows that the fight against communism should be
taken over by intelligent people and not left to morons."[6]

But the moves against Walker are also galvanizing plenty of people searching for something to cement their distrust of Kennedy.

Thousands of letters and telegrams begin to pour into the White House. One complains: "This is a new low in American history—demoting a General for patriotism and, conversely, it certainly must have given aid and comfort to commies—to realize their insidious infiltration in high places."[7]

Another writer is more direct: "Our traitor president has committed treason against the United States."[8]

Among the messengers bombarding the Kennedy White House is Mrs. George Pinckney Walker of Center Point, Texas. She is General Walker's mother. Her telegram reads: "Another Communist victory if Maj. Gen. Edwin A. Walker is not cleared of subversive accusations."[9]

And in Dallas, Dealey and the *Dallas Morning News* are running several pro-Walker stories and even conducting an investigation into *The Overseas Weekly*. The *News* describes how the magazine that brought down Walker "carries full page, nearly nude girlie pics." Dealey's paper pins down the *Weekly*'s motives:

"Is it to besmear the GI and make him unwelcome and loathsome wherever in the world he may go?"[10]

The *News* issues an editorial: HE SIMPLY TALKED TOO MUCH. It references Walker's denunciations of President Truman and First Lady Eleanor Roosevelt:

"As to Harry Truman, he did the Reds a great service when he ordered MacArthur not to win in Korea and almost as great a service when he fired MacArthur. But Mr. Truman is no pink. He is definite, but not pink."

The piece continues, "As for Dame Roosevelt, it is wrong to say that she is definitely pink. It is kinder to say that her whole thought process is indefinite. She means well in a pastel shade, as it were—rubescent at times, but still it is merely pastel."

And Kennedy has not just erred by exiling Walker from his command, he has cracked the door open to far worse things: "If the Pentagon keeps issuing orders...to soften up instruction on how to counter the Reds, the conclusion is going to be widespread, whether it be accurate or not, that infiltration has been successful at the top."[11]

*   *   *

H. L. Hunt's *Life Line* radio show runs three consecutive programs defending General Walker and his crusades. The program's excitable host, the Reverend Wayne Poucher, reads aloud from the non-controversial portions of Walker's Pro-Blue campaign. These excerpts, he cautions listeners, are presented "with the hope that you have been able to judge for yourself whether these Pro-Blue lectures have been detrimental to our men in the armed forces."[12]

In Texas, John Tower, the state's new Republican senator, the first one since Reconstruction, resorts to religious imagery: "General Walker has been crucified for his patriotism."[13] Congressman Bruce Alger races to help form a Justice-for-Walker Committee. A petition begins circulating in the House of Representatives calling on Kennedy to reinstate Walker—and to even give the general a promotion.

Just as quickly, the spreading backlash against the Kennedy administration moves from Texas to key allies around the nation: Strom Thurmond of South Carolina, the Senate's most ardent segregationist—and someone who once enjoyed listening to Reverend Criswell's denunciations of integration—rises to attack the Kennedy administration for killing Walker's career. Echoing Tower, he also says Walker has been tortured like someone from the Bible: "This brilliant officer and fine commander has been crucified for his patriotism and devotion to his country."[14]

In Europe, General Walker is overwhelmed by his rising celebrity status.

He is busy ordering his young aides to send out thanks to the growing number of supporters—the generals, soldiers, politicians, and people across America writing him notes.

He contemplates his next action.

The general's mother, interviewed at her family's Texas ranch, isn't quite sure what he'll do. But she knows her son:

"He's aggressive and tenacious...and he doesn't back down from a fight. Things will start popping as soon as he comes back."[15]

JUNE

With John F. Kennedy looking on in the White House Rose Garden, General Curtis LeMay is sworn in as the new air force chief of staff.

A pugnacious, cigar-chomping warrior, LeMay directed the bombing campaign against Japan during World War II. He is a big believer in airpower, and why shouldn't he be? His planes ended the Pacific war by obliterating Hiroshima and Nagasaki. LeMay is already suggesting that he can solve America's current troubles in Indochina by bombing Hanoi, the capital of North Vietnam.

Kennedy despises LeMay, but he has no choice other than to appoint the popular general to the Joint Chiefs. "We would have had a major revolt on our hands if we hadn't promoted LeMay," says Kennedy's deputy secretary of defense, Roswell Gilpatric.[1]

The president's relations with his military are at a nadir. His refusal to commit U.S. troops at the Bay of Pigs and his decision to relieve Walker of his command have made the military and its vocal supporters in Congress more than suspicious of him. Kennedy had campaigned as a fierce cold warrior, accusing the Eisenhower administration of letting a "missile gap" develop. Once in office, he realized the truth: A missile gap does exist—but it is overwhelmingly in the United States' favor. The U.S. has 185 intercontinental ballistic missiles and over three thousand deliverable nuclear bombs. The Soviets have only four intercontinental missiles and a few dozen nuclear weapons.

Kennedy also begins to learn that his top military commanders are jockeying to exploit the United States' nuclear advantage, especially as tensions with the Russians mount in Berlin. But Kennedy refuses to issue nuclear threats to the Soviets in order to keep Berlin open. "It's not a very nice solution, but a wall is a hell of a lot better than a war," he says.[2]

His Joint Chiefs don't agree. And Curtis LeMay is only in his post a few days before he causes his first big stir. He attends a fashionable dinner party in Georgetown and is seated next to the wife of a leading senator. He tells her that a nuclear war with the Soviet Union is coming soon—probably before the end of the year. He calmly explains that every major American city—Washington, New York, Chicago, Los Angeles—will be reduced to glowing ash. For his part, LeMay plans to be safely ensconced inside an underground bunker, directing the U.S. strikes on the USSR.

The woman is shocked. She's heard the doomsday scenarios before, but not from the top air force general. LeMay's belief that such an event is imminent is terrifying to her. She mentions her children and grandchildren and asks if there is anything she can do to guarantee their safety. LeMay advises her that the best course of action is to pack a tent and head for the open desert in the West.[3]

When LeMay's comments make the papers, the general denies everything. But Kennedy's generals *are* planning for a nuclear war.

JULY

Kennedy walks into the newly created "Situation Room" located underground beneath the White House's West Wing. It is July 20, and alongside him are his closest aides and Secretary of State Dean Rusk. The Joint Chiefs have prepared a special presentation.

General Lyman Lemnitzer begins by explaining that the military has a plan to launch a surprise nuclear attack against the Russians. Using a series of flip charts on easels, Lemnitzer points out which cities will be blasted off the face of the earth. He concedes that a few retaliatory bombs will strike American cities, killing millions of people in this country. He also admits that the resulting radiation will have untold consequences for the planet as a whole. But this is the price America needs to pay in order to win the war against communism.

Kennedy taps his front teeth with his thumb and runs his hand repeatedly through his hair as Lemnitzer speaks. JFK's aides know that these signals usually indicate his intense irritation.

When the general finishes his presentation, Kennedy gets up and stalks out of the room.

He turns to his secretary of state: "And we call ourselves the human race."[1]

Kennedy really does seem anxious to avoid nuclear war at all costs. He later tells his advisers: "We're not going to plunge into an irresponsible action just because a fanatical fringe in this country puts so-called national pride above national reason."[2]

To counteract the Soviet threat in Europe, he instead calls for a massive buildup of conventional forces. At the same time, he wants to send signals to Khrushchev that he is interested in negotiating a nuclear test ban treaty.

Curtis LeMay and other high-ranking officers are convinced Kennedy is naive. LeMay is certain that America will eventually have a nuclear war with Russia—*so why not start it now, while we have an overwhelming advantage in weaponry?*

And one of LeMay's former bomber pilots during World War II, Congressman Bruce Alger, agrees completely. Alger is one of two congressmen to vote against Kennedy's proposal to strengthen the United States' conventional forces while seeking to tamp down nuclear hostilities.

"We must stop the farce of pretending that we can negotiate with Russian leaders," Alger is saying. The United States, instead, should resume nuclear testing and begin issuing ultimatums to the Soviets.[3]

As other congressmen listen, some are shaking their heads. Alger has often been too extreme, too isolated. This is no different. But even though his views ostracize him in Congress, he finds full support from the unwavering powerbrokers in Dallas:

"Alger is eminently right in thinking that we must look for victory primarily through use of nuclear arms," says Dealey's *Dallas Morning News.*

"Our wisest course should be reliance primarily on strength for nuclear warfare. If, with the first crossing of the West German border by Soviet troops, we can sweep over their heads and strike Moscow with atomic devastation, the Kremlin leaders will have something to think about—if they are still alive to think."[4]

SEPTEMBER

Rhett James fears the worst. It is a scorching day, headed to ninety-six degrees, and the thick mat of warm air is like an advance warning for marauding Hurricane Carla, which is just entering the Gulf Coast and taking dead aim at Texas.

The long summer passed by with almost daily, stunning turns of the wheel: Following the mandates of the Dallas Citizens Council, blacks are now allowed to eat at lunch counters. They are allowed inside any sections of the movie theaters. Those who could afford it can even dine at Stanley Marcus's Zodiac restaurant. The newspapers have barely said a word about the sea changes in Dallas. It is as if an invisible lever was just pulled—and all without any "outside agitators," including the odious Martin Luther King Jr., coming to the city.

But today is the final, perhaps ultimate, test in Dallas: James is trying to integrate the city's schools for the first time in its history. The preacher understands that the handful of wide-eyed children he has helped to handpick are wondering: *Why are there so many white policemen, why are my parents coddling me as if they never want to let me go?*

As James stands outside Travis Elementary, there are at least 750 Dallas police scattered around the city...waiting, watching for how the city will respond. The first-graders stare up at James— they are unaware of the mad swirl of history they are making. They are in their carefully cleaned and pressed clothes, their faces scrubbed and shoes shined. Some of the little girls have bows in their hair. They look, for all the world, as if they are about to go to church—as opposed to marching into the annals of history.

Dallas has fought it, cleverly and then without subtlety. City leaders, from Congressman Alger to former Mayor R. L. Thornton to the new mayor, Earle Cabell, have talked for years about the dilemma:

It is the Supreme Court's law, but it is not what anyone really wants. But the federal orders that General Walker once enforced in Arkansas have finally been too much to ignore in Dallas—the city has been drawing national attention for being more resistant to the laws of the land than even the deepest Southern cities.

Finally, the white men on the Dallas Citizens Council agreed to meet a carefully coordinated group of seven black leaders who came bearing a proposal: *Begin the integration or Dallas loses face. Begin the integration before Dr. King is invited to town. Begin the integration before Freedom Riders, Northern activists, begin occupying the city.*

There were more meetings in the tall buildings, and then Reverend James and the others were told that Dallas would integrate its schools—but only one grade at a time. Starting with the first-graders. Then, the next year, the second grade. And so on, and so on. It was, for people in black Dallas, quintessentially just like white Dallas...slow, hesitant, cautious, and with plenty of time for white residents to move the hell away from any school that had black children in it. It was, in the end, the only way Dallas would ever bend toward integration—it was the only palatable plan for the Dallas Citizens Council.

For the last several weeks, James has carefully helped select these eighteen bright little children, ones who promise to be firm and polite and attentive. There are ten girls and eight boys. He has met with their very wary parents, and he has counseled them about what to expect: At the best it would be a tension-filled but violence-free day. At the worst...well, all he could promise was that he would do his best to protect their babies.

He has studied all the precedents, the perversely insidious ways that school districts across the South have tried to block black students—sometimes by claiming they didn't have the proper health certificates, suggesting that they are like filthy animals carrying communicable diseases. James has made sure that all eighteen Dallas children have been vaccinated, that they have the proper paperwork.

The first integration will take place at William B. Travis Elementary—a name familiar to many of the children in Texas who are required to study Texas history, as if Texas is still its own nation. Travis was, many children can tell you, the commander of the doomed forces at the Alamo, the site of the defining battle in Texas history. He is famous for sending out his letter: "To the People of Texas & all Americans in the world—... The enemy has demanded a surrender at discretion, otherwise, the garrison are to be put to the sword, if the fort is taken. I have answered the demand with a cannon shot, & our flag still waves proudly from the walls. I shall never surrender or retreat. Then, I call on you in the name of Liberty, of patriotism & everything dear to the American character, to come to our aid, with all dispatch... Victory or Death."

At 8:45 a.m., fifteen minutes after school opens, the Dallas school superintendent makes a public announcement: All eighteen Negroes assigned to previously white schools are inside the schools. But four children were not allowed inside classrooms. One didn't submit a birth certificate. One had siblings in a Negro school—and the Dallas School Board will not allow children with siblings in Negro schools to go to white schools. Two were prevented from taking classes because "there was no reason for them to transfer from their school area."[1]

But the majority of the children are in class with white children, and they are safe. Dallas has, in its paternalistic way, done its job. James begins thinking about the next step: *Is it really integration after all? Is it really equal footing and equal education? What will the children hear, what will they be forced to read?*

At that very moment, there are also many people in Dallas who are thinking about the next steps—ways to stem any more integration, any more socialism. Maybe they can pursue a kind of intellectual segregation. Maybe seize control of the classrooms and the books being distributed to children in Dallas.

The hawk-faced sixty-year-old J. Evetts Haley, the prominent Texas historian who once waged a racist campaign for governor, has formed a group called Texans for America. Even as James leads the children into the schools, Haley and his group are insisting that the state ban schoolbooks that are "not American enough" and that are "too soft on communism."[2] His group assails any textbooks favorable to racial integration, the United Nations, the Supreme Court, Social Security, nuclear disarmament, the New Deal—and even the use of the word *democracy* to describe America. That is a charged word, a false word, a word that the billionaire H. L. Hunt in Dallas loathes as well: *America is a republic, not a democracy.* And a republic honors the rights of its states. A republic respects the aims, the ideals, of the states with blood ties to the Confederacy.

A handful of little black children have walked up the steps to Dallas's white schools, almost seven years after the *Brown v. Board of Education* decision.

Now, James knows, there are people trying to make sure that children never read about integration—or even democracy. Instead, they are demanding that the Texas Education Agency assign textbooks that extol Christianity, anti-communism, and carefully selected patriots and their heroic acts: J. Edgar Hoover, Senator Joseph McCarthy, General Douglas MacArthur, even Chiang Kaishek. Virtuous acts—like MacArthur's plan to drop atomic bombs on communist China—should be praised in Texas schoolbooks.

Right now, though, James is relieved for those eighteen children.

Somehow there has been no violence. But still, Dallas is going to stair-step its integration, drag it out for years and years. It is as if the city is still bound by some clutching ambivalence. It is as if there is something holding Dallas back from, once and for all, condemning its worst impulses.[3]

OCTOBER

A thin moon hangs on the horizon as a convoy of three automobiles arrives at Perrin Air Force Base, seventy miles north
of Dallas. The cars are carrying a small contingent of John
Birch Society members. The group is closely followed by reporters
from Dallas who have been alerted to their moves.

Just yesterday, the *Dallas Morning News* broke a major story:
This modest base is training communist pilots from Yugoslavia to
fly F-86 interceptors. The *News* was tipped off by a Dallas insurance man who doubles as a major in the Texas Air National Guard.

"In view of the unprecedented reprimand of a patriot of the
magnitude of General Walker, it is obvious that today the multiple
criminality of communism is honored above God-fearing American patriotism. I remain an unreconstructed, unliberalized, unso-
cialized, uncommunized American!" the Dallas insurance man
tells the paper.[1]

The United States has supported and even armed communist
Yugoslavia for years—ever since 1948, when Marshal Tito broke
away from the Soviet Union. Tito became Yugoslavian president
in 1953, and American policy makers now view Yugoslavian independence as a strategic asset against the Russians. But the Dallas
insurance-man-turned-major is unconvinced: "All Communists,
regardless of nationality, are enemies of America. This is a treasonous situation any way you look at it."[2]

The cars come to a stop at the front gate of Perrin AFB and ten
protesters emerge. They have created three red, white, and blue
picket signs on short notice. One reads: WE PROTEST THE TRAINING
OF RED PILOTS IN THIS COUNTRY. The group begins marching in
front of the gate. After forty-five minutes, press coverage assured,
they climb back into their cars for the drive back to Dallas.

Outrage is mounting as the news spreads that Yugoslavian

communists are being trained on U.S. soil. An irate woman phones the *Dallas Morning News* and demands to know, "Are they making our airmen salute those Red officers up at Perrin?"[3]

Congressman Alger doesn't need to wait and hear from his constituents to know what to say. He summons his secretary and dictates a telegram to President Kennedy:

"The American people are vigorously opposed to exposing our techniques and military weapons to representatives of nations which are part of the world-wide conspiracy dedicated to our destruction."[4]

One of the picketers at Perrin AFB is Frank McGehee, a burly, hard-drinking six-footer who piloted fighter planes in Korea. At age thirty-two, McGehee runs an auto repair garage in Dallas and is trying to put himself through law school. He's a man of strong political convictions and great ambition. He understands that the ultra-conservative movement in Dallas is booming—and it is well funded.

The city is now headquarters to several surging patriotic organizations, many of which have sprung up since Kennedy's election: the Dallas Committee of American Freedom Rallies, the Committee for the Retention of the Poll Tax, the Committee for the Monroe Doctrine, the Dallas Committee to Impeach Earl Warren, the Conservative Independent Voters Information Service, and the Dallas Freedom Forum, which promises: "We'd reduce Russia to a mass of glass for a thousand years."[5]

Women's clubs are also becoming politically active, including Women for Constitutional Government and the Public Affairs Luncheon Club. Even the Dallas Junior League is growing politicized: Its members have just forced the removal of a "communist-inspired" Pablo Picasso painting from a charity art exhibition.

And the John Birch Society remains home to many of Dallas's leading citizens—and there are dozens of individual chapters in the city. McGehee is as outraged about the Yugoslavian pilots situation as anyone else. He also senses a prime opportunity. He quickly arranges to rent the Dallas Memorial Auditorium and begins spreading the word among the Birch chapters: *It's time to come together as a unified force to express our outrage, our indignation.*

On Saturday evening, October 14, the day after the angry picketing at Perrin AFB, three hundred people show up for a meeting that McGehee calls the "National Indignation Convention."

As the self-appointed chairman, McGehee welcomes the crowd: "We want to demonstrate that we are sick and tired of traitors in our government." Dallas, he says, is the beginning of a national crusade: "We must contact every conservative in the United States—that is, every patriotic American."[6]

McGehee appeals for donations because the fight against atheistic communists is too important to quit after just one night. He wants to keep renting the auditorium, and he needs everyone's help to do so. Dollar bills begin filling the buckets McGehee has thoughtfully provided.

The next day the crowd has quadrupled. Some twelve hundred people are now inside the big civic auditorium in Dallas. Clouds of cigarette smoke hang in the air, and many in the crowd are waving small American and Confederate flags. The occasional rebel yell can be heard above the din. The outrage over training communist pilots has struck a deep chord in America, and the National Indignation Convention is rapidly gaining national publicity.

McGehee describes Dallas as the new front line in the war against communism: "The entire United States is looking to see how indignant and how resolute we are."

The chief speaker this evening is Sidney Latham, a senior vice president and chief counsel for H. L. Hunt's oil company. Latham receives a standing ovation as he blisters the Kennedy administration for its treatment of General Walker: "I'm tired of seeing military officers busted out of command for teaching their men that the enemy is bad."

McGehee is awash in donations, and he's now planning to rent the auditorium for a week straight.

On the third night, the rapt audience hears a recorded message from Hollywood actor Ronald Reagan, who tells them, "The progressive income tax was spawned by Karl Marx a hundred years ago." On stage is Dallas's nationally known radio commentator and newsletter writer Dan Smoot, the ex-FBI agent who had once helped run H. L. Hunt's *Facts Forum*. Smoot raises the Cuba issue: "Does it make sense that we are planning to fight Communists in Viet Nam and then not fight them 90 miles away in Cuba?" McGehee collects $3,500 in donations and predicts future crowds of up to twenty thousand people.

On the fourth night, the large crowd is the most boisterous yet, with foot stomping and flag waving. The National Indignation Convention is drawing headlines around the country, and people in Dallas are proud to be at the forefront of the movement. Several politicians have expressed statements of support; even the Kennedy administration now says that it will "review" aid to Yugoslavia. The *Morning News* is also on the bandwagon: "Down in Texas, we may be a little dumb, but it seems to us that to arm an enemy amounts to inviting a rattlesnake to dinner."[7]

McGehee lobbies Congressman Alger to come address his convention. Alger declines to appear in person, but he does agree to speak to the audience by telephone via a loudspeaker hookup. At the appointed moment, McGehee is on stage, announcing that he has spoken personally to Alger this very morning and that he will now call the congressman for his remarks. With great fanfare, McGehee begins dialing a telephone. The speakers broadcast the sound of the phone ringing... and ringing... and ringing some more.

Alger is not answering. McGehee believes that he has been double-crossed.

"We came here to fight—not to be lied to," he shouts as he slams the phone down. He begins stalking around the stage in a fury, pounding his fist into his hand. He looks up at the rafters and shouts: "Bruce Alger has signed his political death warrant!"

The auditorium is erupting with jeers and boos for Alger.

One man—an Alger aide planted in the audience—struggles to make himself heard over the noise. "There might be a misunderstanding," he yells toward the stage. He begins pushing forward, trying to get McGehee's attention.

McGehee hears the man and points fiercely at him: "Anyone who doesn't agree with the National Indignation Convention should get up and walk out." Several people begin leaving the auditorium.

The man persists. "Please, please, I think there's a misunderstanding." He reaches the stage and confers quickly with McGehee.

As it turns out, McGehee has simply dialed the wrong number. When he calls again, Alger answers on the first ring. Now the crowd turns on McGehee.

"Apologize!" people are yelling.

McGehee sheepishly explains to Alger that he thought the congressman had betrayed them.

Alger responds in his exacting Princeton diction: "That was rather precipitous, wasn't it?"

The next night, attendance drops off, even as other cities across the country are beginning to stage their own indignation conventions. Hunt Oil executive Sidney Latham is back. The *Dallas Morning News* files a story saying he called the Kennedy White House "traitors"—and suggested it suffer "death and imprisonment" as outlined by Texas laws. But the *News* is forced to issue a front-page correction after Latham denies that he specifically referred to the Kennedy administration when calling for the death penalty.

On the final night, twenty-five hundred people pack the auditorium to hear Tom Anderson, a conservative publisher and founding member of the John Birch Society's national council.

Anderson suggests that "treason trials" are needed and that they should begin in Franklin Roosevelt's hometown: "Hyde Park, which is handy to Hyannis Port." The crowd laughs and cheers at the reference to Kennedy. Anderson says that he knows what the United States should be doing with its old fighter planes. Instead of giving them to communist Yugoslavia, we should be giving them "to somebody on our side—like Franco."

Anderson ends his talk by calling the John Birch Society "the best plan, the best program I know of to save America." And he issues a stirring call for impeaching Chief Justice Earl Warren.

He is followed on stage by J. Evetts Haley—the segregationist founder of Texans for America, the ex-gubernatorial candidate, and the man who wanted to banish the "communist-influenced" textbooks used in Texas public schools. Haley once condemned vegetarians as socialists, arguing that American freedom depends on beef eaters. And he was once invited to the old Dallas courthouse to join preachers condemning race mixing.

Today, Haley has driven four hundred miles from West Texas to make the National Indignation meeting in Dallas. He strides on stage in pressed jeans and black cowboy boots, holding a ten-gallon cowboy hat. He looks out at the audience with a sly smile and steps forward to the microphone.

"Ol' Tom Anderson here has turned moderate," Haley says, gesturing toward the man who preceded him. "All he wants to do is impeach Earl Warren—I'm for hanging him."[8]

The cheers shake the hall, and dollar bills fill the buckets being passed in the Dallas auditorium.

Ted Dealey considers the telegram that has just arrived at his office. It is addressed personally to him from President John F. Kennedy, but Dealey knows a form letter when he sees one. In fact, several other publishers in Texas are receiving the exact same message:

> It would be useful to me to have an exchange of views with you on state, regional and national problems. Therefore I would be most pleased to have you as my guest at a luncheon on Friday, October 27th at 1:00 p.m. at the White House Washington. (Enter the Northwest Gate on Pennsylvania Avenue.) I hope it will be possible for you to attend. It would be appreciated if you would kindly reply to Press Secretary Pierre Salinger.[9]

Dealey sets the telegram aside. He knows Kennedy has been playing the seduction game, hosting a series of similar meetings with publishers. The president's stated rationale may be a desire to "exchange views," but Dealey knows what he is really up to.

Kennedy is going to try to charm the press into giving him better coverage. He is going to peddle his soft soap, this time to a bunch of Texans.

Dealey has already made his own feelings about Kennedy quite clear in his newspaper. He heard from his sources in Washington that the *Morning News*'s combative editorials are causing Kennedy pain. As Dealey will tell anyone who would listen, "I am not particularly fond of brother Kennedy."[10]

Dealey quickly calculates the cost of a trip to Washington. With airfare, hotel, food, and drink, it will cost several hundred dollars. It's easily worth it. Not many people are given the opportunity to tell the president of the United States to his face exactly how they feel about him.

His father, George B. Dealey, founded the *Dallas Morning News* in 1885, seven years before Ted was born. It was the dominant newspaper in Texas, and it was, really, the world the young Dealey grew up in. He always saw being publisher as a civic calling, as important as any elected office. Even when he left the city and played football for the University of Texas in Austin and then earned a master's in philosophy at Harvard, he knew he was destined to take control of his father's paper.

He made his first mark on the news venue back in the 1920s, when the Ku Klux Klan chose Dallas for its national headquarters. The Klan staged its grand parades down Main Street during the day and it terrorized at night, with cross burnings and whippings and unexplained disappearances of young black men. The city's establishment fell into line and Klansmen were elected to city offices. The managing editor of the competing newspaper, the *Dallas Times Herald*, resigned to become the Klan's public relations director. Dallas, never really known for much, earned a reputation as the KKK bulwark in America.

The young Dealey lobbied his father to stand up to the Klan. Thanks to his efforts, the *Morning News* led a public campaign against the KKK, even withstanding advertising boycotts and angry mobs gathering outside the paper's headquarters. It emerged stronger and more influential than ever. It had no rival as the state's leading newspaper. For the next twenty years, the *News*'s politics was squarely within the traditions of mainstream America. The paper endorsed Franklin D. Roosevelt for president and even supported his New Deal programs, one of which helped cement the Dealey family's legacy in Dallas: One of FDR's Works Progress Administration projects was a small park built in downtown Dallas, just three blocks from the *Morning News* building. It was named in honor of Ted Dealey's father, and it featured a twelve-foot-tall bronze statue of the older man. It became known as Dealey Plaza.

Ted Dealey liked seeing the towering statue. Too, he liked that he had enshrined the family's vision for their newspaper in a quote carved into a panel four stories high above the front entrance to the *Dallas Morning News* building:

> **Build The News upon the rock of truth and righteousness. Conduct it always upon the lines of fairness and integrity. Acknowledge the right of the people to get from the newspaper both sides of every important question.**

Dealey's father had been a moderate man with a finely attuned sense of social decorum. Now, in 1961, the son is striking some people as occasionally caustic or even callous. He is, his friends say, fiercely intelligent and filled with a crackling wit. He is considered the paper's best writer, and he spends time with the editorials. But he is talking openly of his "masturbation period" and he tells one *News* executive, "Some day when you're sitting in that fancy new office of yours, keep in mind that at one time in that exact location stood the finest whorehouse in the entire city of Dallas."[11]

And, in 1961, under his leadership, the *Morning News* has clearly abandoned political moderation—or anything hinting at its old support of the progressive politics of the New Deal. The *News* began to describe Roosevelt's remedies for the Great Depression as the actual *cause* of the economic collapse. The *News* now refers to the New Deal as the "Queer Deal." It lashes out at any hint of government meddling, which it believes will sap Dallas's vitality and the economic miracle the city represents:

"When our forefathers stepped on the west bank of the Mississippi and headed west to carve an empire, did they look back over their shoulders to the National Government for 'welfare' and help? No—with an ax and a Bible and a wife, the pioneer did it himself."[12]

The *News* is ferociously uncompromising. As one of its own reporters observed, the editorial page is "not just dissenting, but insulting."[13]

On the issue of welfare, the *News* asked: "Should we continue to spend tax money on illegitimate babies, when we need it for missiles?"[14]

As his anti-Kennedy campaign marches on, Dealey has begun hearing from a few people in the city. Quietly, some of them are telling him that, in fact, Dealey is doing the very thing he always preaches against: He is ruining Dallas's image around the nation. He is polluting potential business deals.

Stanley Marcus, for one, has been talking to Dealey and saying that he doesn't like the way the paper is leaning ever harder to the right. It is a ginger dance, because Dealey needs Marcus to continue to buy the big display advertisements in his paper. Marcus has been quite clear when it comes to his feelings about the paper: "An ultraconservative journal, opposed to social progress, the United Nations, the Democratic party, federal aid, welfare, and virtually anything except the Dallas Zoo."[15]

But Dealey has a ready answer when Marcus and other people complain that the *News* is imbalanced. Dealey counters that readers might "get confused" if they see a column advocating liberal ideas next to one promoting the conservative line: "We feel a duty along the lines of leading them in thought among the proper channels."

Besides, it isn't that he and his paper have changed.

"The left has just moved farther left," Dealey argues to men like Marcus. "The leftist influence has gotten so much stronger that we have got to holler louder to make ourselves heard."[16]

As Dealey prepares to travel to Washington to have lunch with President Kennedy, he reviews his intelligence on JFK's previous meetings with other publishers. He has asked his Washington reporters to do some background research on what Kennedy does at these meetings, what Dealey can expect when he is in the room with Kennedy. For additional insight, he asks friends in the publishing fraternity who have already seen Kennedy at the White House.

And by now, he knows that the White House generously plies the newspaper guests with alcohol. One publisher, a close friend of Dealey's from Kentucky who is also a staunch segregationist, tells him that Kennedy "has Negroes...all dressed up fancy."[17]

Dealey's sleuthing confirms his suspicions about what the hell the invitation to lunch is really all about: While Kennedy is pretending to solicit the newspapermen's views, the meetings are just social affairs meant to seduce and mollify the media. There is little in the way of focused discussion. Instead, there is plenty of banter, served up with helpings of the famous Kennedy charm. The president is obviously using the occasion to lobby the newspapermen, to cajole them into going easy on him. And now it's time for the collection of Texas publishers, led by Dealey, to submit to Kennedy.

As he mulls over his trip to Washington, Dealey reads a letter he has just received from one of his readers in Dallas—one of the "grassroots" people:

"I want to be one of the many, many people of Dallas who congratulate you and the News for the type of news coverage that is being furnished to us...it is only through making the public aware of our terrible danger from communism that we can preserve the American way of life and our wonderful heritage...I can only hope that when you meet with the president that you will stand up for the rights of the Free Press."[18]

Before catching his flight from Love Field, Dealey decides to write her back:

"Just between you and me and the gatepost, I am not particularly fond of brother Kennedy... You can bet your bottom dollar that I will stand up in the manner that you suggest."[19]

Dealey and eighteen other Texas publishers are gathered in the elegant Red Room, which has recently been redecorated at the behest of Jacqueline Kennedy. Cocktails are served by uniformed waiters. The visitors from Texas chat amiably under exquisite portrait paintings done by American masters. Vice President Lyndon B. Johnson is circulating, slapping people on the back and dominating the conversation, as always. He and Dealey barely acknowledge each other.

The president has not yet arrived. Press Secretary Pierre Salinger steps forward to remind everyone of the ground rules for the luncheon. This is strictly an off-the-record event, in order to allow the president and the publishers to exchange frank views. The president will make some opening remarks, and then he will take questions.

Kennedy enters the room with some aides, and the publishers quickly line up to shake hands with him. Dealey notices that Kennedy looks thin, but that his grip is strong. The group adjourns to lunch around a long, elegantly laid-out wooden dining table that stretches almost from one end of the room to the other. Waiters circle, filling water glasses. The publishers, all dressed in business suits, unfold linen napkins and drape them on their laps. Dealey is seated and picks up the menu: *Gnocchi a la Parisienne, Truites Grenobloise, Haricots Vert au Beurre, Beignets de Salsify, Peche Melba, Petits Fours Secs, Demitasse.* He puts the menu in his pocket.

Kennedy begins by offering some greetings, some welcomes, and then he segues into well-practiced comments, pleading for sympathy from the media because he feels like a "fugitive" in the White House. He offers a quick review of the foreign affairs priorities that the administration is handling—the Bay of Pigs, the Vienna Summit with Khrushchev, the crisis in Berlin.

As he gives his overview, the well-dressed waiters quietly circle the table and refill wineglasses. The publishers eat delicately while listening to Kennedy's talk. Some jot down notes. Some nod in assent as Kennedy speaks, and they chuckle at his splashes of self-deprecating wit.

Dealey stares at the president. Like a reporter, he takes note of the details: *Kennedy is only picking at his food. He is sipping from a glass of tomato juice. He really does look awfully thin. Lyndon Johnson quietly excuses himself because he needs to fly out for a scheduled speech in Florida.*

As Kennedy continues, Dealey glances at his watch impatiently.

Hasn't the president invited us here to get our input? When is he going to quit monopolizing the conversation and listen to someone else for a change?

Dealey swivels and looks around the table. Kennedy is clearly charming the people from Texas, the ones Dealey has known for years.

They seem to be in awe, whether of the man or the office it is hard to say. Either way, it is disgusting. Texans aren't supposed to be so easily brainwashed.

Dealey can't stand it. Leaning forward, half out of his seat, he suddenly interrupts Kennedy and speaks forcefully across the elegant dining table:

"Isn't one of the purposes of this meeting to get an expression of grassroots thinking in Texas?"[20]

Kennedy smiles, perhaps unsure where things are headed, and slowly nods in agreement.

Dealey abruptly growls: "Well...that being the case, I will present the grassroots thinking in Texas as they have been presented to me and as I understand them."[21]

The clinking and scraping of silverware against the china comes to a halt. The room is silent, except for the sound of Texas publishers shifting uneasily in their seats.

The entire room stares at Dealey, whose shoulders are hunched as he cradles a batch of papers he has pulled out of his suit jacket. Kennedy has a slight smile of amusement playing across his face as he regards the old man confronting him. Dealey holds a nine-page, five-hundred-word statement he has written out that very morning on hotel stationery from the Statler Hilton in Washington. He begins reciting in a loud voice:

"The general opinion of the grassroots thinking in this country is that you and your administration are weak sisters. Particularly this is true in Texas right now.

"We need a man on horseback to lead this nation—and many people in Texas and the Southwest think that you are riding Caroline's tricycle."[22]

Dealey pauses and looks around the room.

The other publishers are horrified, the blood draining from their faces. He looks at Kennedy. The president's smile has disappeared, and his face, it appears, is turning red.

Dealey keeps reading:

"The American people are aroused, and rightly so...We should lead from strength, not from weakness...We can annihilate Russia and should make that clear to the Soviet government. This means undoubtedly that they can simultaneously destroy us. But it is better to die than submit to communism and slavery."

Dealey rages on, and the room is as silent as stone.

"We want desperately to follow the administration as long as the administration displays courage, but we will not follow its policies like a bunch of driven sheep if it gives in to Russia one iota. The American people are sick and tired of being bluffed, of negotiations when there is nothing to negotiate.

"These state meetings with the press should not be social meetings. You cannot proselyte the newspapers of America and win them to your side by soft soap...

"We are not morons to be led around the nose by an invested bureaucracy."[23]

Dealey finishes and leans back in deep satisfaction as the luncheon erupts.

Several people begin speaking at once. Some of the publishers rise to their feet and yell: "No, no."

Others begin shouting at, apologizing to, Kennedy: "We don't agree, he's not speaking for us."

One livid publisher lights directly into Dealey: "Ted, you're leading the worst fascist movement in the Southwest and you don't realize that nobody else is with you."

Another publisher is waving his arms, trying desperately to calm everyone down while his admonitions are lost in the din: "This is the dining room of the President of the United States!"[24]

Finally, Dealey's voice rises above the commotion. He is turning back to Kennedy. The room, just as suddenly, is quiet again. Several of the publishers crane their necks, trying to get a good look at Dealey, trying to hear what he will say next.

"My remarks were not meant to be personal in nature," Dealey murmurs. "They are a reflection of public opinion in Texas as I understand it."[25]

The men in the room swivel to look at Kennedy. The president has lost his smile. He is clearly no longer relaxed and friendly. He speaks quietly, forcefully, as he rebuts Dealey. When the stories about the luncheon appear, the two men will have vastly different memories of Kennedy's rejoinder.

As the luncheon breaks up, Kennedy turns to his press secretary. He is speaking half in jest, but the humor is cold.

"Don't subscribe to that newspaper," he tells Salinger, pointing toward Dealey. "I'm tired of reading its editorials."

Salinger shrugs: "But I have to read them."[26]

News of Dealey's face-off with Kennedy sweeps the nation.

Dealey tells reporters: "I may have stuck my neck out, but the President wanted the grass-roots opinion, so I gave it to him."[27]

Privately, Dealey is happy with the notoriety. He'd used "weak sisters" and "Caroline's tricycle" in "a deliberate attempt to swipe some headlines." He tells a friend: "And apparently in that I was eminently successful."[28]

The *Morning News* publishes the complete text of Dealey's statement along with a photo of Dealey offering a rare smile as he descends from his plane after returning to Dallas. Dealey prints his own version of events in the paper—there will be other versions, far different, in the upcoming days and weeks. Dealey leaves out any mention of a response by Kennedy. His account reinforces Dallasites' worst impressions of Kennedy: The boyish president, so flummoxed by Dealey's courageous attack, was apparently unable to muster a single word in his own defense.

Dealey eagerly follows the way other publications cover the incident, ordering his staff to send him updates of how the story is being reported around the country. But aside from a few sympathetic editorials in right-leaning papers, Dealey finds a wave of denunciation, even among other papers in Texas. He is derided as a boorish crank, a man so lacking in basic civility that he can't even be trusted to have lunch with the president of the United States.

Dealey fires off telegrams to the other Texas publishers, asking for their opinion of his behavior. The telegrams come roaring back, one after another, almost every single one of them critical.

"I think you were rude to President Kennedy," responds Jim Chambers, publisher of Dealey's major competitor, the *Dallas Times Herald*. "We were his guests in his home. You could have had your say in your paper, in a letter, or at a regular press conference without embarrassment to anyone." From Waco, Pat Taggart writes: "Your truculence and phrasing were inappropriate."

El Paso Times publisher Dorrance D. Roderick tells Dealey: "I did not vote for Mr. Kennedy but was encouraged that he did not blow his top at your remarks . . . I think this restraint will stand the president in good stead in future prolonged negotiations with Khrushchev. Probably Harry Truman would have taken your [lunch] plate away from you."

Houston H. Harte, who owns a chain of newspapers across the state, writes, simply: "Please let the matter die. Texas has been embarrassed enough."[29]

There is only one conclusion for Dealey to make: These other publishers in Texas are also weak sisters.

NOVEMBER

The army is asking him to transfer to a command post in Hawaii. But there is something else happening, and fast, something tantamount to a movement, maybe a revolution welling up in the heartland. He is almost caught off guard. His phone has been ringing non-stop. Millionaires are offering jobs in the private sector. Some offer sinecures. Congressmen are asking him to come to their districts to speak. Dozens of organizations are calling for him to attend rallies. Thousands of letters are pouring in, many stuffed with dollar bills. The letters often say the same thing: *Run against John F. Kennedy in the 1964 election*. Some just say that Walker, radiating confidence and rugged handsomeness, is the "man on horseback" who can protect and lead the United States of America.

He calls a press conference and announces that he is resigning.

"My career has been destroyed," he says, reading from a prepared statement. "I must find other means of serving my country in the time of her great need... To do this, I must be free from the power of little men who, in the name of my country, punish loyal service to it."

And Walker promises to continue his anti-communist crusade: "It will be my purpose now, as a civilian, to attempt to do what I have found it no longer possible to do in uniform."[1]

The far right movement, divided and even marginalized toward the end of the Eisenhower administration, is suddenly bursting wide open in reaction to Kennedy's presidency. Membership in the John Birch Society skyrockets, and hundreds of other new organizations are springing up. The Minutemen preach armed resistance to the domestic communist takeover. The National States Rights Party and the American Nazi Party fight against court-mandated integration.

And, without his ever pursuing it, General Edwin Walker from Texas has seemingly, suddenly, been propelled to the head of the movement. His coronation occurs when *Newsweek* places him on its cover under the headline: THUNDER ON THE RIGHT: THE CONSERVATIVES, THE RADICALS, THE FANATIC FRINGE.

In Washington, Kennedy and his brother have been blindsided by the zealotry. They are not alone. Many political insiders had considered the extreme right reduced to a hodgepodge of often disconnected, amateurish activists in the wake of Joseph McCarthy's censure in the mid-1950s. The far left had become a much bigger security concern, as evidenced by J. Edgar Hoover's aggressive FBI investigations of political leftists. For many political watchers and journalists, the "rise" of a new far right "movement" just seemed, at first, like a benign irrelevancy: *People believe that the government is attempting mind control by fluoridating their water? That Eisenhower was a communist dupe?*

But now the initial head-shaking and skepticism have given way to the startling reconnaissance arriving at the White House on a regular basis: Kennedy's team is learning that there is something overtaking parts of America, boiling over into a rage, and a desire to not only defeat, but utterly destroy opponents.

For Kennedy and his brother, Dallas was a pivot point in the presidential election. And it was, especially for Bobby, a place he saw through the prism of crime—perhaps he was convinced that the city had a hidden criminal machine led by Mafia men. The kind that could only exist if some in the city simply didn't pursue them hard enough. Either way, the Kennedys were becoming convinced that Dallas might be a threat for hard-edged political reasons.

Whatever delay President Kennedy has experienced in recognizing the new political landscape, he catches up in a hurry after Ted Dealey's stampede through his White House luncheon, and the wave of popular support for General Walker, the rogue general who is already approaching hero status in Dallas.

Immediately following his resignation, Walker gives his first-ever interview—an exclusive to the *Dallas Morning News*. In the conversation, Walker hints strongly that he would like to make Dallas his permanent home.

An office has already been set up for him on the seventeenth floor of a downtown skyscraper. Enthusiastic volunteers are sending out fund-raising appeals on his behalf. One missive reads: "Remember that if our grandfathers had fought the Indians and Red-Coats like we are fighting the Communists, we wouldn't be alive today."[2] Letters of support are already pouring into Walker's office in Dallas.

Many of his followers, not knowing Walker's address but understanding the link between him and Dealey's *Dallas Morning News*, address their letters simply:

GENERAL EDWIN WALKER, C/O DALLAS MORNING NEWS.

U.S. Attorney General Bobby Kennedy steps to the podium at the Sheraton Dallas, waits for the applause to die down, and looks up at the dozens of editors and publishers at the national Associated Press Managing Editors meeting. Outside, six cars are repeatedly circling the hotel, filled with angry protesters from the Dallas-headquartered National Indignation Convention.

By now, the Kennedy White House is redefining its relationship with Dallas. The city has become the home for a concentrated pocket of political extremists. Bobby Kennedy has been continually frustrated by spending the last several years trying to solve the mystery of the Dallas underworld. The president's brother has been traveling the country, making speeches, pushing his brother's domestic policies, and talking about two things: organized crime and communism. They are twin themes to talk about in Dallas. The APME meeting is also always a captive audience, a way to reach top editors, editorial writers who are gathering from around the nation.

He decides to start with a joke. He knows everyone here will get it—everyone in the room knows how much *Dallas Morning News* publisher Ted Dealey loathes his brother. And how Dealey insulted President Kennedy to his face, right inside the White House.

"I would have liked to have had lunch with Mr. Dealey. Some of the gang and I had got together in Washington and written a memo that I wanted to read him," Bobby says, his face breaking into a toothy smile.[3]

The room rocks with laughter. After everyone quiets down, Attorney General Kennedy turns serious. "The situation now is that the major figures of organized crime have become so rich and so powerful that they and their operations are in large part beyond the reach of local officials," he says, measuring his words.

"We would rather work two or three years to bring a major underworld figure to justice than to bring a number of cases against less important hoodlums just to make the record look good."

It has to be a nod to the way he really feels about Dallas—"beyond the reach of local officials." Kennedy has already tried to get anyone—crime bosses from New York to New Orleans—to talk about that underworld in Dallas. They have all invoked the Fifth Amendment. Kennedy moves on to something else—those six cars that have been circling the hotel, protesting the presence of a member of the soft-on-communism Kennedy family. He blasts the Dallas men protesting outside, their National Indignation Convention, and the John Birch Society.

"I have no sympathy with those who are defeatists...Nor do I have sympathy with those who, in the name of fighting communism, sow seeds of suspicion and distrust by making false or irresponsible charges, not only against courageous teachers and public officials and against the foundations of our government—Congress, the Supreme Court and even the presidency itself.

"The John Birch Society has been looking for Communists, and found only one—President Eisenhower."[4]

He lets his words settle on the editors and publishers. Anyone who has been following Bobby Kennedy's arc, the way he is waging scorched-earth war on organized crime—and waging a running battle against people saying his brother is soft on communism—has to know that Kennedy has come to engage the battle here in Dallas.

He makes one final appeal to Ted Dealey, urging him not to fall into league with men like General Edwin Walker:

"As newspaper editors you have a special responsibility not to be hoodwinked or stampeded by the fearful Americans of our time."[5]

★   ★   ★

Joe Civello reads the story in Thursday's *Dallas Morning News*: The attorney general of the United States is in town. Bobby Kennedy has come railing against the mob, talking about the unfinished investigations he started a few years ago. Civello, fifty-nine, is a short, slender man who likes to wear straw fedoras with wide cloth bands. He has black-framed glasses that make his eyes seem especially wide—and he often has a slightly bemused look on his face, as if he is looking at something only he can see.

When he was thirty-five, he had been busted in Dallas for his role in the largest heroin, morphine, and opium operation in the South—and he was given a decade and a half in the federal prison at Leavenworth. He had also once fired a sawed-off shotgun into a man's stomach as they stood inside a Dallas drugstore. The murder charges were somehow dropped. Now he tells people he helps run an imported food store and dabbles in construction. Bobby Kennedy, for one, is convinced Civello represents something rotten at the core of Dallas.

He first heard about Civello four years ago, after the Dallas man had driven with friends onto the twisting country lanes a few hours north of New York City. The gang arrived at an imposing stone country mansion owned by a man named Joe "the Barber" Barbara, passed under the grand entryway, went inside, and began shaking hands and offering hellos to the dozens of men who were already there. The smell of expensive cuts of meat being grilled wafted through the air.

Without warning, someone shouted that the New York State Police were nearby. The troopers were staggered: They had caught dozens of the most infamous Mafia chiefs in America: Vito Genovese, Carlo Gambino, Joe Bonanno, and others, from cities like New York City, San Francisco, Boston, Denver, Cleveland, Tampa, Chicago, Los Angeles, and Pittsburgh—and Dallas. The meeting gave the lie to FBI director J. Edgar Hoover's assertion that there really was no big organized crime syndicate in the United States, that the communists posed a far bigger threat. This was proof that there was something crooked in Dallas: probably a city where some of the "local officials"—the ones Bobby Kennedy talked about yesterday at the Sheraton Dallas—had looked the other way.

Bobby Kennedy was the lead investigator for the Senate Rackets Committee—and his brother, Senator John F. Kennedy, was a committee member. Bobby grilled Mafia figures, over and over again, about Civello. He told a reporter from the *Dallas Morning News* that he was watching Dallas, that Civello was someone he clearly wanted to investigate.[6] He called people like Civello "the enemy within."

Civello was finally found guilty of "conspiring to obstruct justice by lying" about the national Mafia meeting. The judge said that he needed to be "segregated from society...he is a high-ranking criminal who cloaked himself with the facade of legitimate business."[7] Civello hired Percy Foreman, the most flamboyant attorney in Texas, to handle his appeal. Foreman was famous for representing a breathy Dallas stripper nicknamed Candy Barr, who was said to have made the first pornographic movie in America, filmed in a Dallas hotel when she was sixteen years old. Foreman got Civello's conviction magically reversed.

Bobby Kennedy could not have been pleased.

Criminals were already leaving Dallas, one way or another. Benny Binion went to Las Vegas to open up casinos. Lewis McWillie, who used to help run the dice games at the Deuces and Top O' Hill Terrace, went to Cuba to manage the Tropicana for Meyer Lansky. H. L. Hunt had especially liked coming to Top O' Hill—he would arrive like a hurricane, ready to drop tens of thousands of dollars. He brought in groups of twelve buddies, headed to a private room, and made a beeline for the food spread. When Hunt finally went home, he never, ever left a tip.[8]

In downtown Dallas, the only truly open nods to the slinky side of life are the girlie clubs by the Adolphus and the Baker Hotels. They are mostly a dirty little circus within walking distance of Reverend Criswell's First Baptist Church. And Civello, the local district attorneys, and several reporters and admen from the Dallas newspapers know all about the bustling, back-slapping Jewish guy who runs one of the soft-core stripper clubs: Jack Ruby is like some sort of giggling, manic gatekeeper—a grinning barker calling you inside, wrapping his arm around your shoulder, and leading you upstairs to a good table with a view of his "classy" girls. Ruby is always trolling brazenly for new talent to work at his clubs; he wants Candy Barr to dance for him.

Civello might use an Italian word for someone like Ruby. He is *pazzo*. He is crazy, a buffoon. He hires a colored man named Andy to work the bar—and to take Polaroid pictures of drunk customers. He sells $2 bottles of champagne for $17. He sells pizza to beer-soaked out-of-towners, and he grins when another "Bus Station Girl" walks into his office—it's another teenager off the ranch, off the farm, from someplace like Big Spring, Texas—and she wants a job, she needs money, and she came through Fort Worth and then into the bus station that's a short walk from the Carousel Club in downtown Dallas.

On the surface, perhaps, Ruby is no different from many of the people who have come to Dallas over the decades: He arrived on the new frontier and invented a life, a business. He almost willed his way into the nightclub arena, carving out his slice of the downtown action. As time went by, just like Civello, he attained a sense of comfort and ease in the city. Police routinely patronize his place. So do prosecutors. So do some members of the Dallas Citizens Council. Ruby makes sure to know their names, treat them to drinks and quiet introductions to the women.

As long as things are kept relatively clean, Ruby is allowed to prosper. For a while, it seems good for him: He even dreams of bigger things, bigger clubs, more legitimate ambitions—anything that will allow him to *really* be taken seriously by the powers-that-be in Dallas.

On November 18, just days after Dealey's White House showdown, after General Walker's resignation and Bobby Kennedy's blast at the crooks and right-wingers in Dallas, President Kennedy flies to California for a speech at the Hollywood Palladium. There are twenty-five hundred Democrats assembled inside. Outside some three thousand anti-Kennedy protesters are picketing. Kennedy is finally ready to publicly rebuke Ted Dealey, Edwin Walker, power-hungry generals, and the entire far right movement. Though he is in Los Angeles, it is almost as if he is talking directly to Dallas, to the things welling up in that city:

"There have always been those fringes of our society who have sought to escape their own responsibility by finding a simple solution, an appealing slogan or a convenient scapegoat...convinced that the real danger comes from within. They look suspiciously at their neighbors and their leaders. They call for a 'man on horseback' because they do not trust the people. They find treason in our finest churches, in our highest court, and even in the treatment of our water.⁹

"They equate the Democratic Party with the welfare state, the welfare state with socialism, and socialism with communism. They object, quite rightly, to politics intruding on the military, but they are very anxious for the military to engage in politics."

Kennedy asks that America refuse to succumb to hysteria: Let "our patriotism be reflected in the creation of confidence rather than crusades of suspicion."

Kennedy even reaches across the political aisle for support. Former President Eisenhower agrees to make a public show of solidarity by joining Kennedy when the president returns to Washington.

Eisenhower also goes on television to make his case against political extremism:

"I don't think the United States needs super-patriots. We need patriotism, honestly practiced by all of us, and we don't need these people that are more patriotic than you or anybody else."

Eisenhower lashes out at General Walker and Kennedy's restless military command. It is "bad practice—very bad," Eisenhower says, for any military officer to express opinions on "political matters or economic matters that are contrary to the president's."¹⁰

Stanley Marcus is reading the Sunday magazine section of the *New York Times*—there is a lengthy story about the extremists, about "the Rampageous Right." It includes a photo of John Birch Society founder Robert Welch—and Welch is pictured speaking to adoring admirers in Dallas.

For weeks, Marcus has been paying increasingly close attention to the way people, including Ted Dealey and General Walker, are joining forces against Kennedy. Marcus strongly supported JFK's and Johnson's campaign and even grew friendly with the president. After taking office, Kennedy appointed Marcus as a trustee of the new National Cultural Center/Kennedy Center. Kennedy also appoints Marcus to two other presidential committees dealing with the arts.

Marcus grins and tells people he knows what's behind the appointments: "I guess this is what you would call a political payoff."[11]

Still, from his position near the front lines of Kennedy opposition in Dallas, Marcus can see things moving beyond the usual partisan political games. It is as if he is witnessing the very wellspring of the most aggressive resistance to the president.

And as he sees the spiked anger at Kennedy, Marcus is deciding to move further from his ambivalence than ever before. He has defended the "communist" artwork in the museums. He has pushed for peaceful integration in Dallas—and admitted his own restaurant needed to be in the vanguard. He has obviously thrown his shoulder behind LBJ and then Kennedy. And he has even told Dealey to make his newspaper more moderate.

Now he wants the full support of the other citizen kings in the city—he wants them to step forward, boldly, and renounce whatever the hell is percolating in the city. Marcus quickly makes several copies of the *New York Times* article showing the Birch Society founder in Dallas and sends it to various Dallas Citizens Council leaders, including the mayor. Marcus's message should reverberate loud and clear: *People in other parts of the country are beginning to equate Dallas with intolerance. It's not good for business.*

After his secretaries have mailed out the copies of the article along with his cover letter, Marcus waits to hear back—surely, some leaders in the city will realize how the extremism is blackening Dallas's image.

Marcus hears from no one.

Fresh out of the army, with the entire country to choose from as he starts his bold new life, Edwin Walker chooses the place that seems most hospitable to him. He is shopping for a home in Dallas—and looking at houses just down the road from one of the grandest monuments ever to General Robert E. Lee.

He is arriving in the city at a time when the local news reports are seemingly filled with one sensational story after another, and some people are worrying that Dallas is in mortal danger of unraveling:

A mother of three young children beats her husband to death with a baseball bat.[1] A woman shoots her boyfriend at point-blank range—and he is dying because no white ambulances will come for him and he has to wait for the Friendly Ambulance for Negroes. A seventy-eight-year-old white grocer reaches into a candy box behind his counter, pulls out a .32 pistol, and pumps three shots into what the *Dallas Morning News* calls a "Negro bandit."[2] The police say there are thousands of sodomites organizing homosexual rings in Dallas. A Dallas radio reporter is insisting he has a tape recording of Russian cosmonauts dying in outer space—and that he wants the State Department to use his "death rattle" tapes as anti-Russian propaganda, to prove that the Russians are killing their own people.[3]

Walker is not deterred. And the mayor of Dallas and other city leaders have arranged for him to give his first public speech in America—in the grand Dallas Memorial Auditorium. Workers have been busy arranging the enormous letters on the marquee outside: TEXAS WELCOMES GENERAL EDWIN WALKER.

He decides to hold a press conference before the event. Before he speaks, he issues ground rules: Only Texas reporters are allowed to attend—no national media. Walker has a list of approved questions—they are the only questions he will agree to answer. He has already written out, in longhand, his answers to each of his own questions. One reporter asks Walker a pre-approved question about censorship. Walker is pleased that the conference is going the way he wants, the way it should—otherwise the media will distort everything. He responds:

"I feel that censorship is very important...Censorship can be a line through words or a line through a country. Both have affected preparedness and the national security. Censorship can also be accomplished by little or no funds, and has been for 16 years in fourth-dimensional warfare training."

The reporters look up from their notepads, quizzical looks on their faces. Walker takes a long drag on a cigarette—and blows a cumulus of smoke at them.

One of the newsmen asks: "Does this mean you're advocating censorship, or did I miss the boat some place?"[4]

Walker ignores him and ends the conference.

Inside the auditorium, there are almost six thousand fervid supporters. Former Texas Governor Coke Stevenson, who serves as the chair of the "Texas Welcomes Home General Walker Committee," warmly introduces the general.

Dressed in a suit, the lanky general strides onto the stage and is engulfed in a standing ovation.

Standing completely straight, Walker adjusts his black glasses, pulls out a sheaf of papers, and begins reading his speech. In the audience, people wave American flags and hiss when he mentions the State Department. Those close enough to the stage can see that Walker's hands are shaking:

"Tonight I stand alone before you as Edwin A. Walker. I have been charged with nothing. I have been found guilty of nothing. I have been punished for nothing.

"I welcome the opportunity to stand before you as the symbol of the capability to coordinate the inspired and unchallengeable power of the people with the strength of our military forces. Such unity of purpose and spirit would cause an immediate capitulation of Reds and Pinks from Dallas to Moscow to Peking."

Walker's voice quavers and cracks. He mispronounces words and fumbles passages. He leans over his papers, his eyes darting up occasionally for a glimpse of the crowd. It is the biggest audience he has ever addressed as a civilian. But his followers don't mind his halting delivery. He seems real, and they are cherishing every word.

But Dealey and some of the other men on the citizens council are also watching and wondering if this really is the man on horse-back, the man who can overthrow the little boy Kennedy on his tricycle. The content in the speech is good, quite good, but Walker will have to work on his delivery. *Kennedy's cronies in Washington will eat him alive.*

When Walker describes how he has resigned from the military because he "could no longer be a collaborator," the crowd rises to its feet.[5]

He rails against the media. He warns that the international communist conspiracy will include the takeover of American churches and schools. And he insists that U.S. generals such as himself could have easily eradicated the Soviet threat a long time ago...if they hadn't been throttled by meddlesome politicians in Washington.

"To this day," he says, his voice rising in indignation, "the military are censored in their control of the nuclear weapons they need in combat. Every senior officer in your military establishment for the past ten years has been concerned or involved directly in the struggle to release atomic weapons from bureaucratic civilian control."[6]

The crowd in Dallas goes wild.

"Russia...would be no threat to anyone."[7]

As Walker drives his speech home, everyone is standing, applauding, shouting his name. It is overwhelming. After ninety minutes, he finally walks off stage having been interrupted with applause more than one hundred times.

Now it is time for an encore.

Dallas's mayor, Earle Cabell, steps forward. Cabell, like Walker, has deep ties to the John Birch Society. Cabell was present when the first local branch of the society had been formed two years earlier. Cabell knows, from his own family experience, about how generals running afoul of John F. Kennedy are treated—and he shares Walker's loathing of Kennedy: His brother, General Charles P. Cabell, was recently fired by Kennedy as deputy director of the CIA after the Bay of Pigs fiasco.

The Dallas mayor, whose father and grandfather were mayors of the city, also has ancestral ties to the Confederacy. His grandfather was a Confederate general, and his likeness is enshrined in the grand Confederate Memorial just a short walk from the auditorium.

Cabell knows Walker is already receiving substantial financial support from people in Dallas, and that Walker has established his temporary headquarters in the city. The mayor is anxious to seal the deal—and he wants to do it in front of six thousand witnesses.

He steps to the microphone. As Walker stands proudly by his side, Mayor Cabell presents Walker with a fancy Western hat, along with a certificate honoring him with a "Dallas Citizen's Award":

"It is my pleasure and privilege, General Walker, to present to you at this time, this certificate endowing you with all the... privileges of honorary citizenship in this great city of Dallas."

Walker clutches his cowboy hat and beams while listening to the mayor.

He is, truly, at home.

1962

JANUARY

Ted Dealey has arrived downtown and is placing a call to a new friend in the city: Robert Morris is one of the most dedicated communist hunters in America, and the former chief counsel to the Senate Judiciary Subcommittee on Internal Security, where he formed a close alliance with Senator Joseph McCarthy.

One of Morris's targets, a Canadian diplomat, committed suicide in the heat of Morris's investigations. Some blamed him for a smear campaign, but to Morris, the man's death was a vindication of the evidence he had amassed. After a failed bid to win a Senate seat from New Jersey, Morris was offered the presidency of the University of Dallas, and he moved to the city in 1960. Almost upon arrival, he was embraced by Dealey and others as someone worth knowing.

Morris still has superior connections in national security circles in Washington and New York—and Dealey hopes that Morris will jump-start some sleuthing into rumors that he has been hearing about Kennedy.

As Morris pulls up to the newspaper building, he should be able to see the grand railroad passenger terminal and the viaduct that leads over the Trinity River into a part of Dallas called Oak Cliff—a leafy place with a few rolling hills. It is the part of town where strip club owner Jack Ruby is thinking of moving. Morris can also see, just a one-minute walk away, the steam heat rising by Dealey Plaza and the Texas School Book Depository.

Morris walks through the low-slung lobby and across the gleaming floors, takes an elevator up, and is ushered past the framed images of the newspaper's founder, the bearded Confederate colonel from North Carolina whose wealthy family had owned several slaves, a foundry, grocery stores, and pieces of a railroad company.

Morris knows he is in his comfort zone whenever he visits Dealey. The publisher likes learning about the John Birch Society, where Morris is a high-ranking member. Dealey's paper has been writing glowing stories about Morris, and about any ardent anti-communist in America. Dealey has also invited Morris to begin contributing editorial columns to the paper, and Morris has happily complied.

The *News* is still running commentary, news stories, and even cartoons supporting General Walker—including one showing Walker on his hands and knees, a gaping and bloody wound in his back, while a huge and mysterious hand clutches a knife adorned with the hammer and sickle. The unsubtle message is that a hero like Walker has been stabbed in the back by the powers-that-be... by the Kennedy White House. Only a few months ago, President Kennedy had urged Americans to consider building bomb shelters—and more than a few people in Dallas believed only Walker, not Kennedy, possessed the combative will to stand up to the Soviet nuclear threat.[1]

As Morris settles into a chair, Dealey tells him he is convinced that the president of the United States has been leading a secret life. He doesn't have to tell Morris that he is also convinced that the Kennedys are out for retribution... against Dealey... and against Dallas.

The chance of exposing Kennedy as a fraud is almost too perfect not to pursue: A conservative columnist in New York named Victor Lasky has written to Dealey, congratulating him for his upbraiding of the president, and suggesting he has been doing spadework investigating the possibility that Kennedy has been married before. Dealey is instantly intrigued, he writes back, and the men begin an ongoing correspondence.

It is eating away at Dealey, to the point that he has ordered his most trusted journalists to investigate the rumors. He tells other staffers to make copies of all the Kennedy-related editorials and journalism that the *Dallas Morning News* has done over the last few years—and ship it free of charge to Lasky, who is working on his second attack-Kennedy book, one that will include suggestions that Kennedy has been deliberately exaggerating his military record.

The marital dirt about Kennedy has been bouncing around big-city newsrooms for a while. But it only gained a beachhead among the conspiracy-minded, anti-communist, anti-Kennedy stalwarts. The innuendo is tied to an alleged genealogy of "the Blauvelt family" that purports to show that a woman from Illinois named Durie Malcolm quietly married Kennedy in 1947—and that Kennedy's unforgiving and calculating father wanted the marriage quietly dissolved and all public records of it expunged and destroyed.

Dealey orders his assistant managing editor Tom Simmons to make inquiries, to pull together some leads. He continues to stay in touch with Lasky. And now he has summoned Robert Morris.

In his office, Dealey explains what he is after. Morris has also heard the rumors about Kennedy's secret marriage, and he personally knows those who are investigating the president. While Dealey looks on, Morris picks up the publisher's telephone and makes a long-distance call to a trusted friend in New York, a publisher named Lyle Munson who specializes in printing and distributing anti-communist literature.

The man tells Morris that, yes, he has heard the Kennedy marriage rumor: He has already done his own digging and has actually gotten the woman in question on the phone. He asked her point-blank: *Have you ever been married to John Fitzgerald Kennedy?* Without hesitation, the woman uttered four straight curse words before slamming the phone down.[2]

Morris thanks his friend and turns back to Dealey—and relays the news that the investigation has reached a dead end. The publisher is perhaps disappointed, but certainly not ready to give up.

Dealey keeps folders that are by now bulging with excoriating telegrams from the men he once considered part of his warm publishing fraternity—the men he would meet, every year, at the newspaper and publisher conventions around the nation, the men he'd sent Christmas cards to, the men who were part of his family's

whole inherited world of journalism. It is like a family shunning—
and he is perhaps thinking, late into the night, that this is what
it must be like to be the lone warrior. Even in Texas, where his
family has been considered one of the enduring newspaper dynas-
ties, there are people telling him that he has been an utter asshole.
A moron. A boor. That he might be speaking for a few people in
Dallas, but not for the rest of Texas.

Maybe worst of all, there are even people sending him copies
of a nationally syndicated column written by the hugely popular
journalist Drew Pearson. The column says that, eight years earlier,
Dallas police had arrested Dealey for drunk and disorderly conduct
and cursing like holy hell at the police.

His wife was driving their Cadillac when it slammed into
another car. Dealey threatened to attack the policeman who arrived
at the scene, and told the officer he would "whip" his ass if the officer took off his uniform. As the policeman tried to restore order,
someone inside the Dealey car began screaming: *"You can't arrest
him! He's Ted Dealey and owns half of Dallas!"*[3] Dealey reportedly
yelled at the officer over and over again—even at the police station.
Fines were paid, some friends came to take the Cadillac, and the
matter eventually went away.

Now Dealey wonders how anyone found out about the incident and whether a liberal drone like Drew Pearson was in fact
working on behalf of the Kennedys. The story is being seen in
hundreds and hundreds of papers, from coast to coast.

He has carefully built an image of himself as the newspaper
publisher who is also the sturdy social and political conscience of
the city. Looking out the newspaper window into a wintry Dallas,
anyone could see a city wrestling with itself.

When his secretary peeks her head in the door and then brings him
the morning mail, there is often another story tucked inside the
handwritten letters to him—this one a syndicated column that is
appearing in various newspapers or magazines, clipped out and put
in those envelopes simply addressed: TED DEALEY, DALLAS MORNING
NEWS.

This article is a long piece suggesting it has the "real story" of the showdown between Dealey and Kennedy in the White House. In Dealey's version, published in his paper, he left the impression that the young president had been so wounded by Dealey's attack that he had been unable to muster any intelligible defense.

This new story, however, indicates that Kennedy had actually eloquently rebutted Dealey: "The difference between you and me, Mr. Dealey, is that I was elected president of this country and you were not. I have the responsibility for the lives of 180 million Americans, which you have not.

"Mr. Dealey, I may not be in the White House more than four years but I do not want it ever said that a Kennedy brought war to the United States. I have been in a war myself. I lost a brother in the war and a brother-in-law, and I know what war is. Wars are easier to talk about than they are to fight. I'm just as tough as you are— and I didn't get elected president by arriving at soft judgments."[4]

This spreading story stings Dealey. And it is one he is convinced is being peddled by Kennedy's willing media servants. Dealey decides to do some digging, ordering his own reporters, again, to find out what the hell the Kennedys are up to. His staff sends him confidential memos: The columnist who reported Kennedy's alleged remarks to Dealey is a well-known friend of the Kennedy clan named Charles Bartlett. Dealey's sources tell him—incorrectly— that Bartlett was JFK's best man at his wedding to Jacqueline.

Dealey writes a note to Bill Steven, an old friend and the editor of the *Houston Chronicle*, and tells him that he has been doing some digging into the Kennedy media machine. That he has found things out about the minion who was no doubt summoned by Kennedy to savage Dealey in a story about how Kennedy had rebuked the Dallas newspaper publisher: "It is my understanding that this (reporter) was the best man at President Kennedy's wedding and that he is at the present time engaged in forming an all nigger club in Washington..."[5]

Dealey then dictates a note to his champion Washington correspondent, Bob Baskin, thanking him for keeping him posted on all the Kennedy machinations in Washington. He tells Baskin to alert him if Kennedy is planning group meetings with any other American publishers. Dealey says he wants to "encourage them to speak up like I did instead of sitting around the President like a bunch of graven images."

Dealey signs off on his note to his bureau chief: "Regards to you and all the other folks in nigger town."[6]

To the women watching him inside Dallas's grand old Baker Hotel, the ex-general Edwin Walker seems to be losing control, fighting some sort of battle within himself. Hundreds of well-dressed members of the Dallas Public Affairs Luncheon Club and the local chapter of the Daughters of the American Revolution are fixed on him:

"I am convinced that a soldier, to live a full life, must know how to live—and how to die," says Walker.

His voice has broken and he is trembling, quavering, clearly on the verge of tears. Through misty eyes, he looks down at his prepared speech and then at the audience. The words refuse to come. He blinks, trying to regain his focus.

The women have heard speeches from decorated veterans before, and some of them are married to men who served in the military. This doesn't seem to be the stiff-backed man from Dallas who is becoming the face of the anti-communist movement in America—the man who stormed the Nazis during the war, the one who wants to bomb communist Russia into submission, the one who has the spine to stand up to the prancing Kennedy.

Trying to gather his composure, to stop from bawling like a baby, Walker looks out over the friendly faces—these women had just passed a resolution, earlier, to condemn the "military censorship" of Walker. He is, of course, inside the same hotel where the Judas, Lyndon Baines Johnson, was attacked by the mink coat mob in November 1960 when one of Walker's staunchest political allies, Bruce Alger, tried to blow up the Kennedy-Johnson presidential election bid.

Maybe if Alger had actually succeeded, maybe if some of these very same women had succeeded back then, Walker wouldn't be here right now. He'd still be in the military, on the road to bigger things—and a greater hand in controlling U.S. foreign policy. He wouldn't be feeling his own voice grow faint and weak, fighting back tears—because Kennedy would never have won. And Kennedy wouldn't have forced him out of the military, out of the mission he had given his entire life to.

Sometimes, when Walker tries to articulate his deepest fears, he gets lost. He drifts, loses concentration, stumbles and stares at the notes in front of him as if they are suddenly blank. Finally, haltingly, he begins to speak again—about his soldiers, the ones who served with him in Europe, or who are still facing down the communist menace and guarding the borders and checkpoints in Berlin and Eastern Europe. They are not bending toward socialism:

"The man standing near the barbed wire is not too liberal," Walker tells the women.

Then Walker goes after LBJ—who has been traveling to Asia, monitoring the United States' relationships with China and Vietnam: "When Lyndon Johnson comes back to this country from Asia and says that changing the standard of living is the answer to communism, then he is badly misinformed."

Walker reaches for a handkerchief. Choking with emotion, he suddenly begins talking again about the men from his old army unit in Germany. The Dallas women are rising to their feet and applauding him—and the troops.

He shouts out: "If the men of the 24th could hear you today— they would raise the roof!"[7]

General Walker's towering home along bucolic Turtle Creek Boulevard is already becoming a tourist destination in Dallas. The house is impossible to miss. Three American flags are stationed on the outside perimeter of his front lawn, and his name is prominently labeled on the mailbox: GENERAL EDWIN A. WALKER. Two more flags—a Texas and a Confederate banner—are positioned near his front entrance.

Walker has also installed a large sign in his yard—a billboard, some people call it—so that he can display a patriotic message. Today's appeal reads: GET THE U.S. OUT OF THE U.N.

Walker often patrols the grounds, allowing himself to be seen by those driving or walking past. Sometimes people stop and ask to take photographs with him. The two-story gabled house has about five thousand square feet, and its living room is dominated by a very large, gold-framed painting of his mother, Charlotte, looking strong and regal in a fine pink dress. Mrs. Walker personally delivered the painting when she came to help her son get settled into his new home.

If people in Dallas think the mansion is too much for one person, the truth is that Walker has plenty of company. In addition to being his private residence, it also functions as his new command center. Inside, volunteers who have enlisted in Walker's cause are busy opening letters with cash donations inside—or are sending out patriotic pamphlets and fund-raising appeals.

Desks, filing cabinets, and stacks of booklets with Walker's speeches are everywhere. Walker decides to set up what he calls a "Patriotic Telephone Service." Callers receive a three-minute recorded message from the general, which ends with his plea for donations to his mission. Three hundred to four hundred calls are coming in every week.

Visitors who ring the doorbell at the home, people who want to get him to sign one of his pamphlets, can't help but notice that there is always a bustle of earnest, well-groomed young men inside the stately home. Walker has plenty of overnight company, many of them muscled, clean-cut former soldiers. As they march through his home, carry boxes, or move file cabinets, Walker affectionately introduces them to others as his "adjutants."

A patrolman in Fort Worth, the segregated twin city just thirty miles west of Dallas, is gunning his car toward the Ahavath Sholom Synagogue. It is close to 1:30 a.m. on a jet-black, chilly Saturday. The police department has just gotten a tip that someone is going to plant a bomb at the temple.

Through the blanketing darkness, as he carefully pulls closer to the building, he can make out two figures moving furtively in the dark. They are carrying something.

John F. Kennedy campaigning in Dallas, September 1960. *Photograph by Shel Hershorn. Briscoe Center for American History, University of Texas at Austin.*

LBJ and JFK are delighted by the unexpectedly warm welcome they receive in Dallas during the 1960 presidential campaign. *Photograph by Shel Hershorn. Briscoe Center for American History, University of Texas at Austin.*

John F. Kennedy addresses a capacity crowd in the Dallas Memorial Auditorium while campaigning for president in 1960. *Photograph by Shel Hershorn. Briscoe Center for American History, University of Texas at Austin.*

Ultra-conservative billionaire H. L. Hunt of Dallas signs copies of his self-published utopian novel, *Alpaca*, as his two daughters sing in the background. Hunt's novel called for apportioning votes based on income. The bottom 40 percent of wage earners – those who pay no federal income taxes – would receive no votes. Billionaires such as Hunt would receive up to seven votes each, and could purchase more. *Photograph by Shel Hershorn. Briscoe Center for American History, University of Texas at Austin.*

Stanley Marcus gives Coco Chanel a tour of his family's store, Neiman Marcus, in downtown Dallas. Marcus tried to broker a peace between Dallas ultra-conservatives and President Kennedy. *Photograph by Shel Hershorn. Briscoe Center for American History, University of Texas at Austin.*

The Reverend W. A. Criswell of Dallas's First Baptist Church – the largest all-white Baptist church in the country. His sermon lambasting Kennedy's Catholicism became one of the most widely distributed pieces of campaign literature in 1960. Criswell had earlier denounced those in favor of civil rights as "a bunch of infidels, dying from the neck up." *Dallas Morning News*.

Juanita Craft boards a train and bids farewell to an unidentified friend. Craft was the longtime NAACP youth coordinator in Dallas, and her "kids" were often on the front lines of the battles against segregation. *Texas/Dallas History and Archives Division, Dallas Public Library.*

The Reverend Rhett James hands out literature in front of the H. L. Green drugstore in downtown Dallas while the Reverend E. W. Thomas carries a picket sign. James pushed for a more forceful approach to integration than most black Dallas leaders were comfortable with. *Photograph by Marion Butts. Texas/Dallas History and Archives Division, Dallas Public Library.*

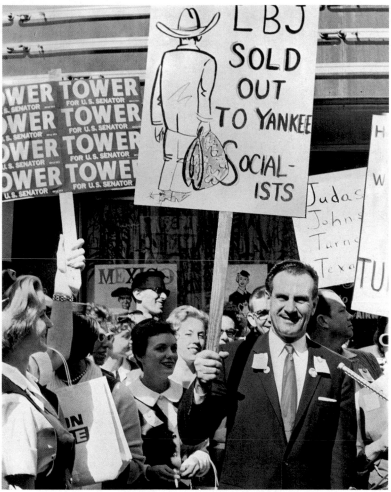

Congressman Bruce Alger protesting LBJ in Dallas with the mink coat mob shortly before the 1960 presidential election. Richard Nixon would later refer to Alger as "that asshole congressman." *Photograph by John Mazziotta. Lyndon Baines Johnson Presidential Library.*

Lyndon and Lady Bird Johnson move slowly through Dallas's infamous mink coat mob. *Photograph by John Mazziotta. Lyndon Baines Johnson Presidential Library.*

He yells for them to halt and the figures freeze as he carefully approaches. The officer is stunned: It is two young boys—and they are armed with charcoal, sulfur, saltpeter, and gunpowder from fireworks. They are twelve and fourteen, a seventh- and a ninth-grader.

They tell the police that they want to blow the synagogue up. But that they have "no ill feelings toward Jewish people" and that they "intended no harm." One of the boys also has a knife and when the policeman examines it, he notices it has been etched with a Nazi emblem. He orders the children into his car.

It is creeping toward 2 a.m. As the arresting officer drives them for booking downtown, one of the boys suddenly stabs his arm out the open window of the patrol car—and seems to let something flutter into the wind. The officer slams the car to a halt and runs back to where the object has landed. There is something dark at the side of the road. It looks like a piece of cloth. He reaches down, picks it up. It is an armband with a black swastika symbol.

He climbs back in the car, with the Nazi armband, and continues to the police station. The building is infamous for having what some black residents in North Texas call "the Showdown Room"—a place where elderly black men are taken, told to drop their pants, and then whipped with belts by various cops... while being asked which of the policemen is whipping harder.[8]

A booking officer picks up a phone, calls the children's parents, and tells them their sons have just been arrested.[9]

Walker is speeding from Dallas to West Texas, to the remote patch of desert where the Bush dynasty has sent George H. W. Bush with hundreds of thousands of dollars in seed money for the family's forays into the oil patch. Walker has been asked to give a speech in this remote northwestern corner of the state—there are loyal oilmen out there, people who hate the Kennedy family, who know Kennedy wants to take away the oil depletion allowances. This part of Texas, especially, is ready to go to war over socialistic regulation, Big Government, and attempts to tax the oilmen to death. They are convinced that they are producing the nation's lifeblood—and they are doing it on their own dime, on their own goddamned faith and sweat.

Going to West Texas is like visiting another country. You spend endless hours driving across flat expanses of nothing—until a West Texas oil town wells up like some sort of metallic Oz on the prairie. As he travels, Dallas is still very much on his mind. He has never broken down in public like that. It isn't like him. The women in Dallas were so forgiving, accepting. They cheered him, comforted him.

When he arrives in the rugged, industrial city of Odessa, there is a message that the National Indignation Convention in Dallas needs him to speak to the faithful—and *now*. He quickly agrees to be patched back by telephone.

The NIC is anxious to expand into a national organization, and it is naturally turning to General Walker; it stands to gain more followers by enlisting him in the cause. At convention rallies, Walker is praised as a modern-day George Washington and his speeches are handed out along with the same John Birch materials that Walker once ordered his own troops to study.

In Dallas, in the cavernous Memorial Auditorium, the audience cheers as a telephone is held before a microphone and Walker's voice comes crackling out of the loudspeakers:

"The press in the United States were the willing servants and propagandists of the Soviet Union. If anyone needed to know that the press was filled with leftists, all they had to do was look at how magazines had named Nikita Khrushchev 'Man Of The Year.' "

He clamors on, name checking the media, confirming everyone's worst fears that reporters and editors and publishers are entranced by the kind of liberalism that leads to socialism...and total government control:

"The Soviet propagandists. The left wing press...The New York Times, NBC and CBS."

As Walker's voice echoes in the Dallas auditorium, it is cold and icy out on the streets of the city. The neon lights on Commerce, near the slinky nightclubs with the showgirls, are beginning to

blink on. There are Greyhound buses pulling into the nearby terminal. There is an old millinery shop that stays open late and when
you walk by you can often see women leaning over, sewing into
the evening. At the Dallas Farmer's Market, just a few blocks from
the auditorium, the wind will sometimes rattle the big metal sheds
and the sound will echo in the night.

Frank McGehee, leader of the National Indignation Convention, is disappointed that the audience isn't larger—he blames it on
bad weather. But the crowd is fiery, raucous—and people are yelling as Walker lights into the media. And it isn't just Dallas that's
hearing Walker. His voice is also being transmitted to other meetings across the country—on the "National Indignation Committee Freedom Network."[10]

It is still hard for him to fathom that he can speak so freely—and
even be paid for it. The requests for interviews and speeches are
ceaseless. Walker is especially bold during one stop in Jackson,
Mississippi: "Three decades of Potomac pretenders—New Dealers, Fair Dealers, red herrings, co-existence artists and U.N. One
World New Frontiersman—have conspired in the liquidation of
our constitutional government."[11]

Every time he returns to his home in Dallas, there are stacks of
inquiries, more open invitations: *Can he come to the Crown Theater
in Chicago to speak to five thousand people attending a meeting of a new group
called the Pro Blue Organization? Will he address the segregationists with
the Capital Citizens' Council in Little Rock, Arkansas?*

It is building, for sure, to another decision. He wants to file his
name in the governor's race in Texas. That should be a good pre-
lude to running, from Dallas, his presidential candidacy.

He suddenly decides to take a quick, begrudging trip to San
Antonio to speak to two hundred members of the Texas Press
Association. He dislikes most people in the media, except for Ted
Dealey in Dallas. But he also presumes that there are far more
conservative publishers in Texas than liberal ones—though maybe
none ballsy enough to confront Kennedy the way Dealey once had.

"I must compliment Texas. Texas has been very responsive to the difficulties and dire perils of our world crisis. Texas is a state much farther advanced than most. This the press deserves a great deal of credit for," he tells the crowd.

Walker still hates speaking to a civilian public, but he knows enough to understand that he has to plant some seeds. If there is to be a takeover of the corrupt powers in Washington, a takeover that he is framing as an overthrow of a totalitarian regime led by John F. Kennedy, then he has to simply go all the way:

"One half to two-thirds of the thousands of letters I have received since I left the Army refer to some sort of elective leadership."[12]

The media people in the audience look at each other and know it can only mean one thing: Walker is going to run for office—and it is all aimed at ultimately removing Kennedy and his passel of liberal socialists from the White House.

FEBRUARY

It is going on hour four as Walker presses the phone to his ear at his headquarters in Dallas. It has been a grueling conversation, and it is going around and around in circles. Walker is quiet and attentive, but he is unbending. Two allied senators, one Democrat and one Republican, are still working hard to convince him to drop out of the gubernatorial race even before he starts.

Strom Thurmond from South Carolina and John Tower from Texas are two of Walker's greatest supporters and perhaps the two most powerfully strident conservatives in the Senate. They have been rattling sabers, demanding congressional inquiries into the way Walker's military career ended—they're calling it the "muzzling of the military," as if Walker has been silenced by taking away his freedom of speech. They desperately want to turn the congressional inquiries into an anti-Kennedy witch hunt, a way to show how the Kennedy brothers bullied a good soldier like Walker straight out of the military after a lifetime of fighting for America.

Walker listens patiently as Thurmond and Tower employ every trick they know. They both tell him he is a super-patriot: Entering the governor's race in Texas is going to steal conservative votes. It is going to make it easier for Johnson's "boy" John Connally to win the governor's office. *That is not what the solid conservatives, in either party, want. Save your ammunition for bigger battles.*

If the nation really is beginning to see an avalanche of wholesale resistance toward Kennedy—and people are more willing to hear from a war hero who isn't a career politician—then there is always a chance that Walker can join Tower in the Senate...or go all the way to the White House. He is in every major newspaper, on every major TV outlet, and he is the most valuable political chip in Dallas—and one that needs to be played at just the right moment.

By the end, Thurmond and Tower are in unison: Now is not the time to run for governor.

Walker finally thanks them and hangs up. Within minutes he receives another call, this one from an agitated Congressman Bruce Alger.

Alger tries the same tactics, tries being reasonable, but just as clear and as insistent: Everyone knows that LBJ's protégé John Connally is going to win. Why doesn't Walker wait and take on liberal Texas Senator Ralph Yarborough in 1964? The right is already salivating at the prospect of Barry Goldwater running against Kennedy in 1964, and with Goldwater's coattails lifting Walker there is a real chance to give Texas two Republican senators.

Walker tells him that people from Dallas are calling him and forming "Win with Walker" committees around the state. He has women in Dallas rising to their feet and soaking in his unbridled emotion. If he can reach them, if they are still cheering an old soldier overcome with tears, then he can win votes in Texas. He is speaking the truth about Kennedy, and people in Dallas are responding to it.

By the time they are through talking, Alger is teetering on anger. But he knows that blowing up at Walker won't do any good. He is beginning to realize that Walker will chart his own path, that he is immune to advice.

Walker packs a bag for his trip to Austin, walks outside and bows his head as he ducks into a car. An aide drives him a few minutes north to Dallas's Love Field, where a supporter has a private plane fueled and waiting on the runway.

After a forty-five-minute flight, the plane touches down in Austin, where another supporter, a wealthy Texas stockbroker, is waiting to whisk Walker straight to the Democratic Party offices not far from the towering Texas Capitol on Congress Avenue. As they drive, Walker can see the massive granite statehouse and the Confederate memorial out front.

At party headquarters, Walker posts the $1,000 filing fee to enter the gubernatorial race. When asked for his occupation, he writes, simply: "Soldier."

*   *   *

Looking out at the five thousand people waiting for him to speak in Chicago two weeks later, it almost feels more like a national religious crusade than any kind of political event.

He has accepted an invitation to speak to a nascent Pro-Blue group. It is his first speech since he announced he would run for governor of Texas. He doesn't care if it seems odd that a gubernatorial candidate in Texas would kick off his campaign in Illinois.

From Dallas, Bruce Alger is watching Walker's tour around the nation. He is dumbstruck: Not only has Walker rejected his advice, he's entered the race as a Democrat. If he'd filed as a Republican, Walker could have at least won the nomination and been the party's standard-bearer against Connally in the fall election.

Alger shakes his head in disbelief as he tells a *Dallas Morning News* reporter: "I am very disappointed—more than I can tell you—that General Walker is running as a Democrat."[1]

In Chicago, Walker is not thinking about Alger. Or even Texas. He is drilling harder and harder into Kennedy. *He is worse than a traitor. Kennedy has essentially exiled Americans to doom.* The crowd shouts its approval. It is, says Walker in his speech, as if the Russians have taken control of Kennedy's mind and essentially put every American at risk of being annihilated in a nuclear attack:

"If we are not to survive, it will be because our national administration does not plan for us to survive. We are not only in dire peril, but the course of national leadership has involved deception and misrepresentation.

"It is impossible to tell what strange drug has bewitched this nation in recent years—especially at the top."[2]

Later the same day, Lyndon Johnson holds a secret meeting in his office with NAACP Executive Director Roy Wilkins. They are agreeing on the things that Johnson and his staffers have been conveying to Dallas—and to the preacher Rhett James, who has embarked on an aggressive campaign to convince Johnson that the only way to crush segregation is by providing jobs and appointments to black people. By demanding that the white businessmen who run the city offer better pay, equal pay, to black people. By demanding that they do a hell of a lot more than allow a few little children into white schools—or black people into movie theaters downtown.

Johnson promises the NAACP leaders that his next major initiative in Washington is going to be the final desegregation of the American workforce. And the news is instantly shared with James, who is still thinking of how far he can push the NAACP into confronting Dallas.

Johnson wants to like James, in large part because he delivered votes to him and Kennedy—even when the powerful black leaders in Dallas still wondered if Johnson had some deep-rooted Southern bigotries. James had been one of the first people to sign up for a JFK-LBJ steering committee in Dallas. And James had been dutifully pushing to help LBJ get John Connally elected governor of Texas—and Connally was another figure held in great suspicion by black leaders and white liberals in Texas. James clearly had his own mind, his own fortitude when it came to the climate in Dallas.

Johnson decides to send a private message to James: He will fly him to Washington so the Dallas minister can deliver the invocation for the U.S. Senate and become the first Negro in America to serve as the acting chaplain.

It is a dance, of course. Johnson's people know that James is someone who can still handily serve Kennedy and Johnson—and maybe pivot some black votes when the reelection wars commence. They know damned well how close, how tightly tied to Dallas, the presidential election was last time—and how tight it will be the next time. Texas still won't come easy.

The Kennedy-Johnson machine can use every bit of help in the city, whether it is from an influential figure like Stanley Marcus, or an indefatigable widow named Juanita Craft, or a studious-looking but unafraid preacher like Rhett James.

As James prepares his Sunday sermons at New Hope, he understands the stakes in Dallas have gotten more dangerous and outsize than ever before. Running for the local school board was one thing. But, now, presuming to vault over the Dallas Citizens Council—which still has no blacks, Hispanics, or women as members—and right to the White House is another thing entirely.

James writes to the vice president of the United States: "I was the first Baptist minister to issue a national news release defending the right of a Catholic to run for president. This was done during the time when several Baptist ministers in the Dallas area were issuing statements, in my opinion, contrary to our Democratic ideals."[3]

In Washington, Johnson appears before Kennedy's committee on equal employment and delivers a stern speech about how integrating business in America is the key to ending racism:

"If at all possible, we are going to try to find some long range recommendations to make up for many years of neglect. The real problem is to break down old habits of thinking and old ways of doing things so we can end the injustice and the discrimination."[4]

In Dallas, as he learns what Johnson has to say, Reverend James is no doubt pleased. It is as if LBJ is on the top floor of the Magnolia Building, the First RepublicBank, the *Dallas Morning News*, or the Mercantile Building in downtown Dallas, speaking to the few dozen white businessmen who effectively run the entire city.

By now, it has to almost be too much to bear for Dealey, Criswell, Alger, Walker, and Hunt: Integrating schools is one thing, but Kennedy must be ordering LBJ to broker new rules that will force changes in industry and employment. There may be room for a handful of black children in the first-grade classrooms. But now, there is this smothering sense of uncertainty about what Kennedy has planned in terms of federal regulations, bills, and appointments—things that are all about business, about the bottom line. *And what will happen next?*

MARCH

Frank McGehee has been basking in the heady, cash-swept days of the National Indignation Convention. He's now ready to expand, to franchise his idea. He has traveled to Washington, DC, and called a press conference to announce his plans: He is forming the "National National Indignation Convention."

Reporters are confused: "Don't you have too many 'nationals' in that name?"

McGehee responds: "No, it will be the National National Indignation Convention. It speaks for itself, logically and clearly."[1]

The chairman is anxious to distinguish his organization from all competitors: "We're far to the right of the John Birch Society. We think the John Birchers are far to the left. The National Indignation Convention denounces the liberal taint of the John Birch Society."[2]

McGehee is planning to stage a huge rally in Washington, DC, and he brashly decides to invite some very special guests. He sends a letter to President Kennedy: "The National Indignation Convention hereby extends an invitation to you, the Vice President, all members of the Cabinet and National Security Council to listen to our Convention Program."

McGehee suggests that he is sympathetic to the fact that the nation's leadership may have pressing time demands—and so he suggests a solution in case President Kennedy cannot attend his rally: "For your convenience and comfort, we will make all necessary arrangements to have this program broadcast within the confines of the White House. Please let us know if you desire to accept."[3]

Kennedy's aides in the White House receive his invitation and ignore it. The proposed rally in Washington fizzles out due to a lack of interest. But McGehee does win enough financing from donors to tape a one-hour radio broadcast of his thoughts on the communist menace.

He quickly makes his remarks available to radio stations nation-wide. Several of them accept. The broadcast begins: "The ultimate aim of the militant communist is to prove that there is no God."

After a pause, McGehee commands: "Never forget that statement."

He is in rhythm now, pointing out the differences between communism and Americanism:

"One is the envoy of Satan . . . the other the disciple of Christ."

He closes the program by reading a patriotic poem, calling for men on horseback to join his cause:

"Tall men, sun-crowned, who live above the fog in public duty."[4]

General Walker's campaign for governor of Texas—and hopefully higher office—is off to a rousing start. H. L. Hunt has heartily endorsed him and has written out a personal check that he grandly presented to Walker along with his blessing. Hunt has also sent one of his former employees, a Yale PhD named Medford Evans, to help the general plot his election strategy. Evans, an arch-conservative writer and intellectual, was once associated with William F. Buckley Jr., and now has close ties to extremist pro-segregation groups across the South. He tells others that Walker is not just an old war hero, he is a savior: "The most important individual in the United States is General Edwin A. Walker."[5]

Another Walker supporter has gifted the general with a catchy campaign song, "Win with Walker," sung to the tune of "Put on Your Old Gray Bonnet":

> *Put on your Pro-Blue Bonnet*
> *With the Lone Star upon it*
> *And we'll put Ted Walker on the way*
> *For when he's in Austin*
> *From LA to Boston*
> *Texas leads the USA*[6]

Walker's opponents for governor are barnstorming the state, giving speeches on the lawns of rural county courthouses and passing the hat at barbecue fund-raisers.

The general, however, is continuing his national speaking tour, enthralled by the thousands of people lining up to hear him, many waving WALKER FOR PRESIDENT signs. He gives them what they've come for, roaring about Kennedy submitting to the Russian bear.

In Dallas, his efforts are increasingly aided by an unflaggingly passionate pair of new volunteers: a thirty-six-year-old printing salesman named Robert Surrey and his twenty-three-year-old wife, Mary.

The Surreys were among the group of ten John Birch Society members who picketed at Perrin Air Force Base last October, helping to launch the National Indignation Convention. Born in Oak Park, Illinois, Surrey graduated from Northwestern University and moved to Dallas in the 1950s. He works for Johnson Printing Company, one of the city's major printing firms. Surrey also owns some stock in the company, and he and his wife reside in fashionable Highland Park, not far from General Walker.

Surrey has become very active in political groups, including the Committee for the Retention of the Poll Tax. The Surreys are so conservative that they even regard the *Dallas Morning News* with suspicion. A few months earlier, Mary Surrey sent the paper an angry letter for printing what she termed a "blasphemous" article about General Walker:

"It appears that the *News* has been taken over by the left-wingers. It is so disappointing to find that a paper you have always considered on the side of America has suddenly capitulated to the enemy...Shall we run up the white flag now?"[7]

As Walker launches his campaign, Mary Surrey quickly becomes his personal secretary. Meanwhile, her husband offers Walker his considerable experience in printing and publishing. The men form American Eagle Publishing Company, which operates out of Walker's home, selling and distributing "patriotic" material across the nation: from General Walker's speeches to booklets denouncing JFK, Earl Warren, and the United Nations.

Some people who unexpectedly receive American Eagle litera-ture are shocked by what they deem to be violently anti-Jewish and anti-Negro content—and when they call the local police or FBI to complain, they're told that the publishers are protected under the First Amendment.

The police are perhaps unaware that Robert Surrey—Walker's business partner—is also becoming secretly active within the upper reaches of the American Nazi Party.

There is a frisson of celebrity by now, a proximity to power, just by being at General Walker's home. He is shoulder-to-shoulder in terms of name recognition with Dallas's most famous residents—Hunt, Criswell, and Marcus. Being here with Walker, being at his home, is a window into something bigger than anything most of them had ever experienced in Dallas.

Yet at the end of the day, when Walker's supporters finally leave his home headquarters and walk down the pathway from his tow-ering front door, one young man will often linger and wait for him in the upstairs bedroom. No one knows—or admits it if they do. No one in the media asks why Walker has never married.

Walker has secret lovers, and if word ever emerges, it will rip his credibility—certainly in Dallas where Reverend Criswell preaches that homosexuality is a perversion of God's will.

Somehow Walker's lovers remain discreet.

Walker's crusade is carrying him to Washington, and the general has made arrangements to stay with one of his relatives, an elderly widow who lives near the Capitol. Walker and several members of his campaign team take over the woman's home, staying for several days, smoking cigars and drinking bourbon and beer, plotting how to get Kennedy out of office.

Walker's relative secretly listens to the fiery conversations. It's beyond the pale, beyond the normal political complaints. The men seem powerful, scary, spurred on by something that is alarming her. She places a call to a close friend and asks her to please come for a visit—and to stay with her for protection.

On the morning that Walker leaves, she wishes him and his comrades good luck, and closes the door behind them. Once they are out of sight, she immediately goes to a local FBI office to tell them that she has been terrified, that she has heard Walker and his men plotting and planning. She tells them that Walker poses a real danger to the president.[8]

The FBI agent dutifully takes down her report, which is added to the growing file the FBI began building on Walker from the minute he resigned from the military and his associations with the John Birch Society became known.

At the Justice Department, Walker's case is being reviewed. One FBI agent who is doing reconnaissance at Walker's speeches tells his superiors that Walker has to be a paper tiger. He is a plodding public speaker. He seems loony. The agent shares his field reports: "Walker was decidedly unimpressive in this appearance . . . He appeared to be sincere but completely out of his element."[9]

If the man knows that Walker is homosexual, it is not in his report. Any good agent knows that J. Edgar Hoover is homosexual . . . and hates communists. It might not be wise to write a report noting that Walker has gay lovers.

Even if the FBI agent wasn't riveted by Walker's speaking style or his sexual proclivities, there is now a very long line of radio stations—ones inspired by the anti-communist programming invented and paid for by H. L. Hunt—that are jumping to carry Walker's speeches. All thirty-five radio stations in Mississippi are suspending regular programming to carry Walker's remarks: "There will be no rock and roll heard over Mississippi radio stations for at least an hour Saturday night."[10]

In radio broadcasts and speeches, Walker is identified as a citizen of the intensely patriotic city of Dallas, Texas. During the previous decade, if some outsiders thought about Dallas at all, it was as some distant metropolis crammed with benign, tumbleweed hicks who punched holes in the ground and became oil millionaires and billionaires. Or in kinder moments, as the place where the sophisticated and urbane Stanley Marcus has tried to import culture—

and cleverly gotten fabulously wealthy by catering to those yahoos from the oil patch.

In a short time, really in a year or two, the national image of the often overlooked, even forgettable city has radically changed: Alger, Hunt, Criswell, and Dealey are making coast-to-coast news for either anti-Kennedy, anti-Catholic, or anti-communist attacks. Too, the welling national fascination with the specter of organized crime occasionally turns toward Dallas and men like Joe Civello.

But now Walker's flamboyant presence in the city, and his constant, direct identification with Dallas, is hurtling the reputation to yet another level. And more than a few people in Dallas feel that a handful of strident men have almost commandeered the city. Men who don't speak for everyone—not even the majority. There is a sense that Dallas is being hijacked—and being branded a city of hate.

As Walker travels from Dallas to spread his call to arms, his mother is never far from his mind. Back in Texas, the seventy-six-year-old Charlotte Walker is still vigorous, and still combatively protective of her bachelor son. Walker's associates quietly confide that she is his best political asset.

The mother and son speak on the telephone almost every day. She also sends him notes, pointers, campaign advice. She gives him tips on how to improve his public speaking: "1. Going to the podium with your speech clearly written and with NO changes inserted and 2. Reading aloud, over and over, until you are thoroughly familiar with every word, for twenty-four hours, more or less, before delivery."[11]

Even as he is addressing crowds numbering in the thousands, she is hunched over her desk, sending out hundreds of letters, drumming up support. She writes to generals, senators, congressmen, and ordinary citizens. In her impassioned notes, she echoes her son and indicts President Kennedy. She knows what Kennedy is doing: "Bordering on treason."[12]

Mrs. Walker sends out pleas for donations, as if it is still World

War II and money needs to be raised to defeat the enemy: the communists and Kennedy. Across the country, people open up hand-addressed letters from her. She says her son needs their faith, their support, and their money. Supporting him will save the nation: "If he folds up for lack of funds, the commies will have won another victory."[13]

She also aggressively monitors coverage by the socialist media. She is quick to personally challenge journalists who disappoint her. She lights into one Associated Press reporter: "Your ... reports carry news of all gubernatorial candidates EXCEPT Gen. Walker. Why is this?"[14]

She knows that Dealey's *Dallas Morning News* is usually supportive. Her son granted one exclusive interview during his entire campaign—to the *Dallas Morning News*. And his mother followed suit, granting her only campaign interview to the paper. One day, she writes Dealey a note: "It's gratifying to see people concerned over the subversive elements in this country."[15]

And she also decides to write a note to the paper's chief editorial writer, Dick West: "If we had more editors like you with the courage of their convictions, TRUTH would be established instead of propaganda spread by liberals."[16]

Walker doesn't really want her campaigning, especially at her age, but she insists on making at least one formal appearance. In the embracing city of Dallas, she has been invited to speak before five hundred women at the sprawling, manicured Dallas Country Club. As the uniformed waiters offer refreshments, she is given a rousing welcome. And she can feel it, too. Here, it seems, people know how endangered America is. How anemic and unsuspecting men rule Washington. How they have conspired to crucify her son—a war hero, a super-patriot, a man who loves his country and its Constitution more than the spineless Kennedy and his cronies in the White House.

Charlotte Walker's appearance cannot, however, mask the fact that her son is rarely in Texas. Now, more than a few voters—and newspapers—are questioning how Walker's ongoing national crusade really relates to what he might do to help Texas. People are beginning to wonder: *What do his constant anti-Kennedy rants have to do with governing Texas?*

Walker decides to return to Dallas just long enough to issue an official platform: "All state business will be conducted with a prayer for divine guidance...my platform is the Constitution of the State of Texas."[17]

He assures voters that there is a reason they should care about his battle against communism: Texas is "a prime target of Soviet attention," according to the ex-general.

Back in his home state, he also makes his segregationist stands clear, announcing that he is for "state's rights." He is, as one newspaper reports, the only gubernatorial candidate who is not even making a nod toward wanting the black vote.[18]

Walker's fervent segregationist rhetoric flies in the face of the elders in his adopted city, the ones who have finally, reluctantly, recognized that legalized desegregation is becoming a reality. But Juanita Craft, Rhett James, and Stanley Marcus know that not everyone is ready to just flick that lever and surrender the "Southern traditions." Walker knows it, too. And now it's almost as if he is speaking directly to those disempowered in the city, the ones who felt betrayed by the begrudging but united front presented by the mighty Dallas Citizens Council.

While Dallas may have temporarily retreated in the face of the "socialist pro-integration" enemy, Walker is raising the banner of segregation high, waving it fearlessly for everyone to see. He is doing more than trying to slow integration; he is trying to win back lost territory.

He tells reporters that Jim Crow is not only proper, it is: "Actually a source of unique cultural benefits."

APRIL

An overflow audience pushes into the marble-walled Caucus Room of the Old Senate Office Building. General Edwin Walker is in Washington for the long-awaited "Walker Hearings"—his appearance before a controversial Senate committee investigating charges that the Kennedy administration is "muzzling" high-ranking military officers like Walker.

He is dressed in his best suit, his hair combed to perfection. He has been waiting for this. He is excited, and he knows there will be people watching around the nation. This widely anticipated event, a dramatic showdown in the nation's capital, should provide the ultimate stage to launch his attacks against Kennedy. This will be a perfect chance to make his case to the American people, to offer them a contrast between himself and John F. Kennedy.

All eyes turn toward him as he enters the room flanked by his attorneys. There is a bustle as reporters jockey for positions and senators study Walker while they sip from glasses of water. Among the spectators is a haunting-looking man that some recognize as George Lincoln Rockwell, the stormy leader of the American Nazi Party. Rockwell has turned out to show his support for Walker. The neo-Nazi is telling everyone who will listen that General Walker is the man the country needs in the White House: "A good leader for a national coalition of patriots."

Rockwell is prominently displaying a swastika lapel pin on his jacket. Just as the hearings are about to begin, House security officers approach Rockwell and ask him to remove the swastika. He refuses. The officers grab him by the arms and attempt to forcibly escort him from the building. There is jostling, shoving, as a small melee breaks out. As the leader of America's Nazi movement is dragged outside, he shouts out his support for the man from Dallas.[1]

Walker looks nonplussed as he settles in front of a microphone.

The official proceedings finally begin, and Walker is invited to offer some opening remarks. He arranges sheets of paper in front of him and begins reading, in a slow and deliberate monotone, from a nine-thousand-word statement. He has worked hard on it, and it is a manifesto. It is a distillation of things he feels about America and about Kennedy.

I am a Christian martyr, personally victimized by the international Communist conspiracy. Being assigned to command the 24th Infantry Division in Germany had amounted to entrapment. There are enemies within. People with 'powerful backing' are against me. The Kennedy Administration is filled with communists.[2]

As he marches through his speech, some Democratic senators are visibly sighing, shrugging. Others are leaning forward, trying to pick up any specifics, any details, in Walker's charges. As he speaks, some senators are already deciding that Walker is worse than Joseph McCarthy—who at least occasionally offered some actual evidence of a treasonous communist conspiracy. As Walker drones on, even conservative senators begin shaking their heads as they hear Walker say he has been "framed in a den of iniquity."[3]

When he is finally done, some of the senators seem almost relieved. They begin to pepper him with questions.

General Walker is not used to being questioned. And unlike at his lone press conference in Dallas, Walker doesn't know the questions ahead of time. Even the friendly queries seem to take him by surprise. He is openmouthed and speechless as he looks at the senators, trying to summon thoughts or words that refuse to come. After several excruciatingly long pauses, his attorneys whisper suggestions in his ear.

Walker begins speaking in a halting manner, his voice cracking. Walker's two attorneys begin trying to answer for him, but the senators cut them off.

Democratic Senator Stuart Symington from Missouri is eager to grill Walker. He starts by saying that Walker has denounced many books as communist-inspired, including *What We Must Know About Communism*—a favorite target of the John Birch Society. He adds that President Eisenhower had once recommended the book as a good and useful study of communism, and that he thoroughly agreed.

Symington demands an answer from Walker:

"What then did you find objectionable about the book?"

Walker looks at Symington. There is an infinite pause. Finally, stammering, Walker says that he has not actually read the book.

The Caucus Room is quiet, almost in sympathy with the awkward moment. Under further questioning, Walker is forced to admit that he has not, in fact, read *any* of the books he has been ferociously denouncing as communist-inspired. Some senators are staring aghast at Walker, clearly disturbed that they have let this man take up so much of their time.

Reporters are scribbling in their notebooks, ready to race outside to bang out stories or aim for telephones so they can call their editors.

Suddenly, without prompting, Walker begins describing how a "real control apparatus" is out to get him.

The senators press him to explain. *Who . . . or what . . . is out to get you?*

Walker stares back at them and gulps:

"I cannot identify those that are completely in control of the apparatus."[4]

His testimony is called to a halt. Walker and his attorneys begin to pack their briefcases.

As Walker finally exits the suffocating atmosphere of the Caucus Room, he is confronted by a swarm of reporters, including Tom Kelly, a correspondent for the *Washington Daily News*. The five-foot, five-inch 155-pound reporter steps up to Walker and asks whether the general will disavow the support of American Nazi Party leader George Lincoln Rockwell.

Walker glares at the reporter. And suddenly, violently, he raises his right arm, rears back, and punches Kelly in the right eye, snapping the reporter's head back into a camera.

Walker doesn't speak. He marches on, refusing to look back or answer any questions.[5]

★   ★   ★

Bruce Alger has been crafting a speech, one that will take a full two days to deliver on the floor of the House. He wants it to explain how Kennedy is dooming America and everything it stands for. He decides to call his speech "Requiem for a Free People."

He steps to the floor and begins reading his carefully composed words. As the other congressmen listen, it must seem like the man from Dallas is comparing the Kennedy administration's "dictatorial" tactics to those used in Nazi Germany or the Soviet Union:

"I wonder how long we will be able to speak freely in this House. I intend to speak out as long as I can... We have read news stories of private citizens and newspapers being aroused in the dark hours of the night by agents of the federal government to answer questions... Are we, the citizens of the land of the free, now to expect the thunder of boots in the night, the knock at the door, the summons to appear to justify our actions whenever we say anything or do anything that does not meet with the approval of the President and the planners who surround him?"[6]

Alger wouldn't be faulted for wondering about the wood-lined, top floors of the downtown buildings, where the city's future is daily mapped out by men from the Dallas Citizens Council—and where the million-dollar oil and real estate contracts are signed, where the fate of the entire Dallas school system is being shaped, where the very look of entire neighborhoods is really decided. Of course, none of it has its true genesis in City Hall—he knows that by now. It begins in the hushed dining rooms at the RepublicBank, inside the private clubs atop the Baker Hotel, in the *Dallas Morning News* executive offices, even in the pastor's office at First Baptist. Dallas is still tight that way, coordinated that way, and that is the real reason it has never exploded.

Alger knows it, anyone who spends time at the Dallas Country Club knows it. The city's history is firmly guided by its citizen kings, always has been, always will be. He perhaps wonders if there is dissatisfaction, now, with his own role. If he has begun to strike some of the men who brought him to office as ineffective. Truth be told, he was never part of the legacy structure in the city: He wasn't wealthy enough to gain a seat at the head table alongside the Dallas Citizens Council leaders. He didn't have the roots in the city to be one of the primogenitor kingmakers. Do they see him as flailing, pushing for political trophies he can't win? Perhaps Dealey and so many others in Dallas are asking each other: *Is Alger really good for business?*

Maybe he is no longer protecting and promoting Dallas's image as a place that desperately wants to be taken seriously. He had been rebuked by former Speaker of the House Sam Rayburn, and by one Kennedy minion after another. No one has told him, but perhaps he can sense it, the way the powers-that-be in the city are beginning to think of options. Maybe someone with deeper roots, links to the viziers that have run the city for decades. It could be that Alger never recovered his bearings after he was attacked for the unhinged protest in Dallas against Lyndon and Lady Bird Johnson two years ago—the one that helped catapult Kennedy to the White House.

Whatever it is, Alger is on uncertain, shifting turf. In Dallas, decisions are being made beyond his ken or even his understanding. The wives of the downtown men are even whispering at the Dallas Country Club: *Alger is getting divorced, it is becoming "racy"* . . . [7]

And Dealey is serving, as he usually does, as the public voice for any dissatisfaction inside the upper reaches of the hierarchy. The editorials in his paper are like press releases from the pantheon, the civic curriculum delivered straight from the Dallas Citizens Council. Lately, Dealey's paper has been slapping Alger for not knowing that he needs to befriend, and abide by, the hidebound ultra-conservative Southern Democrats . . . the ones with a long, loyal history of fighting integration, fighting FDR, fighting for states' rights.[8] They are nominally Democrats, of course, but in many ways they are more conservative than the most conservative Republicans. Dealey perhaps is staggered that Alger cannot understand it: *It would take an army to overthrow Kennedy and Johnson.*

Too, there is something else. Something that reveals how

Kennedy might feel about Dallas. Alger has been trying, unsuccessfully, to convince the Kennedy administration to greenlight a federal project that could become one of the biggest money-making deals in the history of the city—a grand plan to build a federal center on the crappy western edge of downtown. It would be a massive complex that would make several Dallas millionaires even richer because they had scooped up, at bargain prices, nearby land that should skyrocket in value. It could irrevocably change the face of the city. It might mean huge construction dollars, acres seized by eminent domain, rail lines diverted, tunnels built under the city, convention centers, hotels, and even a new home for City Hall.

The Dallas Citizens Council decides that for once it would be appropriate to bring a huge federal project to Dallas—but without it appearing that Dallas is on bended knee to Washington, or slavishly addicted to federal handouts. It would begin with a towering government building just minutes from Dealey's newspaper, from Criswell's Baptist church, from Hunt's oil company headquarters.

The pieces are all in place but the Kennedy administration has clearly put a lid on it. Federal approval is delayed. Something, someone, is stalling it. The *Dallas Morning News* isn't letting its reporters note the specifics of the deal or the principals involved. And at least one skeptical reporter is so frustrated at not being able to write a story connecting the dots between the business cabal and the federal project that he tells the chaplain at his church—and the chaplain advises him to go get drunk. Some brave reporters in other parts of Texas are calling the handful of Dallas investors "the Syndicate."[9]

In Washington, Alger knows what he has to do.

He goes back to the floor of the House, this time blaming the delays on the Kennedy machine: The Kennedy White House is out to punish Dallas, is out to crush the entire damned city, because it voted against Kennedy...because the city insisted on reelecting anti-Kennedy warriors like Alger.[10]

On top of it all, Alger has another reelection campaign on his hands. He is running for Congress for the fifth time. The Dallas

Citizens Council is impatient. They can always find another conservative to represent the city in Washington. Maybe someone like Mayor Earle Cabell, the man who welcomed Walker to Dallas, who attended the founding meeting of the John Birch Society in Dallas.

Alger decides to ramp up his anti-Kennedy attacks. On the floor of the House, Alger is more unfiltered than ever: The Kennedy administration is assuming "almost unlimited power" and hell-bent on denying some things for Dallas because it is a city that clearly dislikes the Kennedy insiders.[11]

Alger says he will make the Kennedys pay—and make them suffer a "number of rebuffs."[12]

MAY

With the election for governor only days away, Walker is back at home on Turtle Creek Boulevard after his disastrous appearance in Washington. He is greeted by a small legion of housewives and former soldiers.

They try to cheer him up. Even his mother is there, his fiercest supporter. As he settles in his study, Walker has time to dwell on how the Kennedys are probably smugly enjoying the accounts in the left-wing media. How their friends inside the news ranks will make a mockery of him.

Yet even ardent conservatives are now turning against him. William F. Buckley Jr., editor of the *National Review*, says Walker should be "consigned to history's ashcan."[1] Dealey is also chagrined at Walker's performance. It doesn't help things—and it certainly hasn't made Dallas look very good. Walker had been lauded in stories, editorials, and even editorial cartoons in Dealey's paper. And now the paper is being forced reluctantly to report, with studied understatement, that Walker "tended to roam in his answers and many of the questions had to be repeated by senators to elicit responses."[2]

Walker is unfazed. He begins mapping out his battle plan for the final week of campaigning. There is a special, last-minute maneuver. As the days wind down to election day, thousands of Texans are suddenly riveted to urgent messages blaring from their radios:

A speech, written and delivered by one of Walker's wealthy faithful, is thundering over the airwaves, pleading with Texans to vote for Walker—because it is the only way to stop Kennedy, to save America before it is too late:

His "gang of Fabian socialists" are committing "wholesale treason"—"You had better be working too for the election of General Walker...before Red Chinese troops start pouring across the Rio Grande to occupy Texas."[3]

At his final campaign event—an address to the National Indignation Convention in Dallas—the untold story is that the right-wing organization is falling on hard times. Frank McGehee's donations are drying up; he has to book a banquet room at a local Holiday Inn instead of renting the Dallas Memorial Auditorium.

Speaking to five hundred people at the motel, Walker unleashes another furious attack on the president. Kennedy "is leading the country toward a totalitarian state," he tells them. He predicts a ruinous future for Dallas, and all of America unless he becomes governor:

"Your vote for Walker may be your last chance to vote for a free candidate—unless I am elected."[4]

On May 5, Texans go to the polls.

At his home, his mother nearby, Walker tries to follow the tallies. He doesn't appear upset by the early reports that he is losing—and the final reports showing he will place last among the six Democrats on the ballot. Still, he garners 138,000 votes, far more than political veterans had ever expected, and well ahead of the leading Republican vote getter in the GOP primary.

There is gnashing in the extremist circles in Dallas: If Walker had only listened to Alger's advice and run as a Republican, he would have been the party's standard-bearer in the fall.

Walker's Dallas supporters had hoped that the general's campaign would be the lightning rod for a sweeping movement against Kennedy—and maybe even a chance to turn back the tide on forced integration.

In defeat Walker remains unbowed. Speaking to a still-energized assembly of faithful supporters in Dallas, he calls the people who voted for him "an army." They are soldiers joined together to defeat a common enemy:

"There is hope for our salvation as shown by the 150,000 free votes I received. An army of 150,000 patriots is a great force which must be extended."

As his "soldiers" listen and cheer, Walker's argument is clear to them: He hasn't earned enough votes to win an election, but he has enlisted enough warriors to start a revolution.

Shortly after waking up on July 17, John Kennedy is informed by aides that a Soviet MiG jet fighter has buzzed a U.S. government plane flying into West Berlin. He hopes this hostility is not a harbinger of the day ahead.

It is a Tuesday morning, the day of a much-anticipated vote in the Senate on the president's controversial plan to establish a "Medicare" program to ensure health care for older Americans who can't afford health insurance. Resistance from conservatives has been fierce, and Washington is tense with anticipation—all one hundred senators are in town for the vote. Both sides are predicting victory.

But before the Senate acts, Kennedy has a meeting with a delegation of business leaders from Dallas, led by Stanley Marcus, a man close to LBJ. The timing of Marcus's visit is beyond inauspicious—his city is at the forefront of the public resistance to Kennedy's Medicare plan.

Just a few weeks earlier, Bruce Alger made national news by aggressively challenging Abe Ribicoff, Kennedy's secretary of health, education, and welfare, accusing him of carrying a bill on behalf of a liberal lobbying group, Americans for Democratic Action.

"This is an ADA bill as presently drafted," Alger said. "As an ADA member, do you want to change it?"

Ribicoff replied: "I am not a member of the Americans for Democratic Action."

"No?" said Alger, with mock incredulity. "I'll have to check my sources."

"Go ahead," said Ribicoff.

"Since this is another socialized scheme, I assumed that the ADA would be for it," countered Alger.[1]

The *Dallas Morning News* quickly praised Alger as Ribicoff's "chief tormentor."[2]

An editorial claims that JFK's support of Medicare sounds suspiciously similar to a pro-Medicare editorial that appeared in the *Worker*—the official publication of the U.S. Communist Party.[3]

And on the radio, H. L. Hunt's *Life Line* fills the airwaves with dozens of assaults on Medicare, claiming that it would create government death panels:

"This plan provides a neat little package of sweeping dictatorial power over medicine and the healing arts—a package which would literally make the President of the United States a medical czar with potential life-or-death power over every man, woman and child in the country."[4]

Given the vitriolic attacks by Alger and the *Morning News* on the health care proposals, Marcus and the other men from Dallas are lucky to even receive an audience with the president.

It took Marcus's skillful maneuvering, working through Lyndon Johnson, to finally get Kennedy to agree to a meeting. Marcus has been desperate for some kind of dialogue with the White House ever since Dealey's eruption at JFK last October. He wants Kennedy to know that not everyone in Dallas subscribes to ultra-right orthodoxies, that the city is not run by extremists like General Walker or gangsters like Joe Civello—that Dallas is, at its core, an efficient, business-like American city that the president would come to love if he only spent more time there.

Marcus is joined on his trip by the publisher of the rival newspaper in Dallas, the more moderate *Times Herald*, along with Erik Jonsson, the co-founder of Texas Instruments who has been tapped to become the next president of the Dallas Citizens Council.

The three men have been watching with unconcealed dismay as rival cities in Texas scoop up millions and even billions in federal spending: Austin and Fort Worth are getting new federal centers and Houston has landed a plum prize with the Space Center, which is currently under construction.

Vice President Lyndon Johnson leads Marcus, his old friend, into the Oval Office, where the president receives him and the other men from Dallas with reserved politeness. Marcus and the others explain that Dallas has eight thousand federal workers—more than any other city in the Southwest—and without a new federal center the government is forced to lease office space at high prices. Investing in a permanent facility could save the federal government millions in rental fees.

Kennedy listens carefully. Then he explains coolly that the concerns about the federal budget have forced everyone to cut back on large expenditures. But his real point is obvious to everyone present: It is those in Dallas who have been the most vocal in demanding that Kennedy slash federal spending.

Kennedy offers a face-saving gesture. He picks up the phone and arranges for the men to visit officials at the General Services Administration, which oversees federal office spaces. He assures them that convincing the GSA of Dallas's merits is really the first important step toward getting the millions of dollars that Congressman Bruce Alger has so far failed to secure.

By now, the president is ready to brush the men out of the Oval Office. But before he can do it, Marcus abruptly invites Kennedy to visit Dallas.

Perhaps Kennedy can come for the opening of the grand State Fair in October, or maybe to see a football game? He can see firsthand what a fine city it really is.

Kennedy studies the men, shakes hands, and promises to consider coming to Dallas one day soon.

After Marcus leaves, Kennedy and Johnson return their attention to the dramatic Medicare fight unfolding in the U.S. Senate.

The final vote is exceedingly close. And yet, in a stinging rebuke to the president, several Southern Democrats join Republicans to oppose Kennedy, and Medicare fails by two votes.

Kennedy is devastated by the loss. He holds an impromptu press conference, and is as angry as the public has ever seen him. This is his worst day on Capitol Hill as president.

Back in Dallas, the *Morning News* cheers the Senate vote, declaring Kennedy's initiative "a legislative corpse."[5]

The timing for Marcus couldn't be worse. It almost seems

like he is doomed in his hope of building a bridge from Dallas to Kennedy.

Something is clearly changing for Edwin Walker in the wake of his ruinous, rambling discourse before the Senate and his hopelessly quixotic race for governor. Rock-ribbed conservative allies like Senator Strom Thurmond now refuse to return his phone calls. Bruce Alger, who had once pushed his way to the front of the line to praise Walker, now pretends not to notice the general when Walker shows up at Alger's campaign events in Dallas. Even the uncompromising billionaire H. L. Hunt is distancing himself. He tells others that Walker had lost the governor's race because "he was too unresponsive to my suggestions."[6]

Walker is learning that in a city like Dallas, winning is everything. Losers, especially ones who embarrass the city, are ostracized. And that, perhaps, explains why a city inspector named Bob Stapleton showed up at the general's door.

Walker listens as the inspector politely informs him that neighbors are complaining about the general conducting business in a residential zone. The inspector mentions people coming in and out, and the numerous boxes of publications for Walker's publishing company, American Eagle, being shipped from the house. He writes up a citation and presents it to Walker for his signature.

Glaring at the man and his papers, Walker steps menacingly from his house. He crunches the piece of paper in his fist, hurls it at the city official, and finally chases the man past the high-flying American flags on his front lawn.

As the man retreats, Walker returns inside. Before too long, he is contacted by the *Dallas Morning News*. Walker is still livid:

"If every woman wearing a dress is a secretary, the world is overloaded with secretaries. If every typewriter in a house makes it an office, we are overloaded with offices."

And now the petty bureaucrats from Dallas City Hall are knocking on the door of his home, his national headquarters?

Walker adds: "If they are as liberal as Khrushchev or Kennedy with their ideas of property rights, then I don't want to see them."[7]

Walker is outraged that the *Morning News* would report such a trivial incident but refuse to print the "important message" he had just cabled to a national meeting of state governors.

Even though he hadn't been elected governor of Texas, he was anxious to let the public know that he still stood for the rights of the individual states, and that he had warned every governor in the Republic that President Kennedy was planning to surrender control of the U.S. military to the United Nations.

The more he mulls things, the angrier he becomes, and he decides that maybe the time has come to create his own patriotic news service. He invites a pair of sympathetic journalists to his home and explains to them that his new organization will be like the Associated Press, except that it will only report news that is friendly to conservative positions.

One man is incredulous at Walker's proposal, telling him that it could cost as much as "a hundred million dollars."

Walker uses his finger to draw a line down his desk. He asks the man what side he stands on:

"It is not possible to straddle the fence."[8]

SEPTEMBER

James Meredith, a twenty-nine-year-old Korean War veteran who has applied to the University of Mississippi, meets all requirements for admittance, save one. He is black. The case has gone all the way to Chief Justice Earl Warren's Supreme Court, which ruled that Meredith cannot be denied entrance on the basis of his race.

The *Dallas Morning News* has reacted with outrage, accusing the Supreme Court and the Kennedy administration of "an effort to force Reconstruction II on a region which resents that force."[1] The *News* is increasingly adopting the rhetoric of the grassroots ultra-conservative movement: "To inflict civil wrongs in the name of civil rights is not the path of the patriot or the peaceful."[2]

In Mississippi, Governor Ross Barnett is refusing to back down. He has traveled to the campus to physically block Meredith from registering. Surrounded by state police and flashing news cameras, Barnett shouted: "We will not surrender to the evil and illegal forces of tyranny!" A crowd of white protesters yelled: "Go home, nigger!"[3]

Now the standoff is in its second week. President Kennedy and his brother, the attorney general, are negotiating directly with Barnett on the telephone. Kennedy, like Eisenhower before him, is not anxious to use federal troops to enforce integration in the South.

Barnett refuses to budge and Attorney General Robert Kennedy jabs back at the governor, telling reporters, "Mr. Meredith will be registered."

Inspired by Barnett's resistance, a large crowd of pro-segregationists gathers at the edge of campus on September 27. Crosses are burned and students at a pep rally shout, "Hotty, toddy, we want a body."[4] The white resistance has learned its lessons since Little Rock. This time the mob is much bigger. And it is heavily armed.

The standoff represents the most serious challenge to federal authority since the Civil War. Governor Barnett, belatedly recognizing the seriousness of the situation, begins desperately negotiating in secret with the Kennedy brothers to reach a face-saving settlement. And General Edwin A. Walker of Dallas decides that this is a moment he should and will seize—it is the perfect cause to use to personally confront John Kennedy, and to rescue Dallas and the rest of the South from enforced integration.

From his base of operations in Dallas, Walker makes a nationally broadcast radio speech. His audience is estimated in the millions: "It is time to move. We have talked, listened, and been pushed around far too much by the anti-Christ Supreme Court. Rise...now is the time to be heard. Ten thousand strong, from every state in the union. Rally to the cause of freedom, the battle cry of the Republic...bring your flag, your tent, and your skillet. It's now or never."

Walker apologizes for his earlier role in integrating Central High School in Little Rock: "The last time, in such a situation, I was on the wrong side. That was in Little Rock, Arkansas...this time I am out of uniform and I am on the right side. And I will be there."[5]

Walker's followers begin to gather ammunition and weapons. The FBI issues urgent memos to its field staff, warning that armed men under Walker's control are going to Mississippi to resist federal troops.

Senator Wayne Morse of Oregon stands on the floor of the Senate and denounces Walker as a "fascist-minded ex-general" who is trying to lead an armed rebellion against the U.S. government.[6]

In Dallas, the regional secretary of the NAACP, Clarence Laws, calls Walker "irresponsible and dangerous."[7]

When reporters phone Walker's home, his staff tells them: "We are just telling them what patriots should do at a time like this. Someone stood at Concord."[8]

★　　　★　　　★

President Kennedy and Governor Barnett speak three times by telephone over the next two days. The mob surrounding the University of Mississippi grows larger and more menacing, and the governor is concerned that his state police cannot guarantee Meredith's safety. Kennedy knows that the time has come to act. With great reluctance, he issues an executive order to federalize Mississippi's National Guard. He also orders five hundred U.S. Marshals to Oxford to ensure that Meredith can be enrolled.

Meanwhile, Walker is flying in a private plane to Mississippi. Groups of armed men are driving to Oxford to join him: Two hundred from Mobile, Alabama. Busloads from California. Caravans from Florida, Oklahoma, and other states. Another forty-five college students from the University of Texas at Austin.

Among those heeding Walker's call to arms is one of his adjutants, Ashland F. Burchwell, a handsome twenty-two-year-old who had been one of Walker's soldiers in Germany. Burchwell, who often volunteers for duty at the general's Dallas mansion, has loaded his car with necessary supplies for the trip to Mississippi: a fully loaded .357 Magnum pistol, a fully loaded .303 army-style rifle, three .22-caliber pistols, one switchblade, and three thousand rounds of ammunition. He also has blankets and changes of clothing.

Dallas police spot Burchwell speeding on his way out of town. As they look over the car, they realize that he is transporting a small arsenal to join the general in Mississippi. Burchwell is arrested and detained in Dallas.

Once Walker arrives in Mississippi, he holds a press conference at the airport. Facing the television cameras, the general announces: "I call for a national protest against the conspiracy from within. Rally to the cause of freedom in righteous indignation, violent vocal protest and bitter silence under the flag of Mississippi and the use of Federal troops."[9]

Walker promises reporters that "thousands and possibly tens of thousands of people from Florida to California" are on their way to support him.[10]

★   ★   ★

On September 30, heavily armed U.S. Marshals arrive on campus with James Meredith. Dressed mostly in civilian coats and ties, the marshals are wearing white helmets and orange armbands identifying them. They carry loaded .38s, although they are under strict orders from President Kennedy not to fire their weapons unless Meredith's life is at stake.

The marshals mistakenly believe that their show of force will quell the crowd, just as Walker's own troops had experienced at Little Rock five years earlier. They manage to get Meredith onto campus, but soon find themselves pinned down by the ever-swelling ranks of protesters.

By evening, twenty-five hundred people are surrounding the campus, chanting "Go to hell, JFK," and "Yankee Go Home." Some are waving Confederate flags. Others are dressed in Confederate uniforms. Many are carrying weapons. The crowd believes that Meredith is inside the Lyceum, the administration building, and they are trying to storm the building, shouting "Give us the nigger!"

The marshals form a defensive line, standing shoulder-to-shoulder facing the crowd. By now, many of the marshals have donned orange vests stocked with tear gas canisters.

General Walker is now arriving on campus, ready to lead his volunteers. But Barnett's state police turn him away. The governor, already in plenty of trouble with the feds, wants nothing to do with Walker. The general retreats to the courthouse square. There he chats with deputies and offers his assistance to Sheriff J. W. Ford, who politely declines.[11]

At 8 p.m., President John F. Kennedy takes to television to deliver a live statement from the Oval Office. He has decided he needs to explain to the nation why he is sending federal marshals to Mississippi: "Had the police powers of Mississippi been used to support the orders of the court…instead of deliberately and unlawfully blocking them, a peaceable and sensible solution would have been possible without any Federal intervention."[12]

While Kennedy is speaking, Walker is eating a steak at Oxford's Mansion Restaurant, along with his close supporters.

Watching the president on television, Walker mutters: "Nauseating, nauseating."[13]

Abruptly finishing his dinner, he walks up to the counter and asks for an entire carton of cigarettes. He knows it is going to be a long night.[14]

While Kennedy appeals for order and calm, all hell is breaking loose on the university campus. The mob, steadily growing as Walker's reinforcements arrive from all over the country, is surging forward toward the school's Lyceum—and the federal marshals are hell-bent on protecting it.

Rocks and eggs, bricks and bottles are thudding down on the marshals. Rifle shots begin ringing out in the night. The marshals are firing tear gas back at the crowd.

The mob retreats and gathers under the twenty-nine-foot-tall statue of a Confederate soldier. The group is joined by a tall, dark-suited Texan wearing a big white Stetson. The protesters immediately recognize the man, and a joyous cry goes up: "General Walker is here! We've got a leader!"[15] Another protester, seeing Walker, yells out, "Sic 'em, John Birch!"[16]

Walker appears very calm as he greets the protesters. He looks over at the U.S. Marshals.

Someone calls out, "General, will you lead us to the steps?"

Walker, smoking steadily, confers with the group for a few moments, then announces: "Well, we are ready."[17]

Under Walker's command, members of the mob move toward the marshals, but are driven back once more by the tear gas.

As Walker's volunteers reconvene under the statue, an Episcopalian minister from Oxford named Duncan Gray recognizes Walker. Gray has come to campus to try to stop the rioting. He approaches Walker and pleads for his help in calming the mob.

Walker snorts at him: "You are the kind of minister that makes me ashamed to be an Episcopalian."

Walker calls on the mob, and a group of his followers jump on the minister and begin beating him. Walker is pointing back toward the line of marshals and shouting "Go get 'em boys... charge!"[18]

Soon parts of the campus are in flames. Shots are ringing out as marshals fall to the ground, gravely wounded. Walker's men steal a fire engine, and it races toward the Lyceum. Protesters hook a high-pressure hose to a fire hydrant and begin blasting the marshals with water.

The marshals are running out of tear gas, but they are able to drive the protesters back enough so that they can cut the fire truck's ignition wires and shoot holes into the hose. More shots are zinging back at the marshals, and, incredibly, Molotov cocktails are now being hurled. Suddenly a bulldozer appears, and it is aimed at full speed into the line of federal agents. Desperate shots are ringing out in response as the bulldozer comes under a hailstorm of fire. It comes crashing to a stop just thirty feet from the Lyceum.

Walker is striding purposefully through the smoke and chaos. He is in his element: In contrast with his milquetoast appearance before the Senate committee, Walker is exuding calm, even serenity, as the fighting roars around him. It is like leading the charges in Europe during World War II.

He tells the protesters: "You're doing all right—riot, riot. You are getting news all over the country. Now you've got casualties."[19]

After midnight he leaves the campus for a time. He is seen with a group of men who approach a gas station. They fill a five-gallon container full of gasoline and grab an empty case of soft drink bottles. Restocked with the ingredients for more Molotov cocktails, they speed back to campus.

The long night becomes a series of pitched battles as the beleaguered marshals continue to desperately fight off the mob, waiting for reinforcements that never come. Cars are overturned and set on fire. The journalists not holed up in the Lyceum are singled out by mob members. Many are chased and beaten, including a television reporter from Dallas whose newsreel camera is smashed.

Another reporter is found murdered, shot in the back at close range.

★   ★   ★

Bobby Kennedy has been on the phone, fielding the frantic reports
from aides in Mississippi who are trying to monitor every move by
Walker. Now he's huddling with his brother to see what presidential orders can be dispatched.

"General Walker's been downtown getting people stirred up...
Can we get it arranged to get him arrested?" he asks.

President Kennedy says: "By the FBI."

His brother thinks about it for a second. "Well, let's see if we
can arrest him," he says. "Will you tell the FBI that we need an
arrest warrant?"

President Kennedy needs to know something first. "What's his
crime?" he asks his brother.

"He's been stirring people up," says Bobby Kennedy.

"Inciting," adds the president.

Bobby Kennedy suggests that there is one more thing that they
can probably charge Walker with: "Obstruction of justice."

It is like a war room, really, as White House aides run in and
out with scraps of paper, huddle in corners, check their watches.
The two brothers continue quickly trading solutions to the Walker
dilemma.

"Would the FBI have trouble arresting him...How many
agents do you have down there? I think you ought to get those
MPs [military police] into there and over by the airport. I don't see
what you've got to lose," observes President Kennedy.

His brother mulls it over. "Yeah, OK. All right. I'll do that,"
he replies.

The brothers hunker down some more. Aides sprint in with
news about gas masks, riot gear, how it could turn into a "war."

"General Walker," says the president. "Imagine that son of a
bitch having been the commander of a division up till last year?
And the Army promoting him?"

One of his aides mentions the bestselling novel *Seven Days in
May*—a book many people believe is based on Walker. It centers
on a treasonous conspiracy by right-wing military commanders to stage a coup d'état and overthrow a president they believe

has endangered the United States by bending to the Soviet Union. Kennedy has read the book.

Suddenly, Bobby speaks up: "He's getting them all stirred up. If he has them march down there with guns, we could have a hell of a battle . . . Walker's baiting them. They need to keep an eye on him."

The president listens to the back-and-forth, the bits of information being phoned in from the Kennedy aides who are on the ground in Mississippi—they are trying to stay on some phone lines in the basement of a campus building.

"I haven't had such an interesting time since the Bay of Pigs," says President Kennedy.[20]

The president and the attorney general are beginning to realize that five hundred federal marshals aren't enough. One of Bobby Kennedy's men manages to get through on the telephone and tells his boss: "It's getting like the Alamo." Bobby grimaces and responds, "Well, you know what happened to those guys, don't you?"[21]

The president orders two battalions of army military police to go to Oxford immediately to reinforce the marshals. Yet as the hours pass the help fails to arrive. Kennedy finally tells his aides that Khrushchev would have gotten "those troops in fast enough. That's what worries *me* about the whole thing."[22]

OCTOBER

As the new day dawns, two people are dead. Of the 350 marshals who had been guarding the university's Lyceum Building, 180 are injured—27 wounded by gunfire. Fires are still burning as broken glass and burned-out automobiles litter the campus. America is awakening to the shocking scenes of devastation.

As the extent of the rioting becomes clear, Kennedy orders fifteen thousand federal troops into Oxford. It is the biggest military force used to quell a civilian insurrection since 1865. And as the U.S. soldiers stream into Oxford in military convoys, they are greeted by the sight of Confederate flags flown at half-mast. Hundreds of jeering civilians are lining the streets, many of them hurling bottles and insults at the army trucks as they rumble down the littered streets. A contingent of U.S. Marshals briskly escorts James Meredith to the Lyceum. He had been hidden away in a guarded dormitory room overnight. Inside the administration building, Meredith pays his tuition with $230 in cash and is officially enrolled.

Walker, unaware that Meredith has been registered, enjoys a victory breakfast and is now walking to Oxford's courthouse square. Supporters shout his name, race to his side, and he smilingly poses for photographs. A radio reporter thrusts a microphone toward him and he speaks elatedly about true patriotism, about Americans rising up.

The mood is still edgy. Little brawls and skirmishes are erupting and the federal troops are chasing people away. Suddenly, a military officer recognizes Walker and strides toward him, ordering him to leave the area. Walker glares at the man and refuses. Several soldiers march over, pointing their bayonets at Walker, and finally force him away.

★   ★   ★

Just after 9 a.m., President Kennedy orders an aide to quickly find Solicitor General Archibald Cox. Kennedy has had time to sleep on it. He knows what he wants to do.

"Good morning," Kennedy says when his call goes through. "We want to arrest General Walker, and I don't know whether we just arrest him for disturbing the peace or whether we arrest him for more than that."[1]

Walker piles into a car driven by his chief aide, Robert Surrey. With them is J. Evetts Haley, the Texas segregationist who was a hero to the National Indignation Convention in Dallas.

The car hurtles down the road, trying to flee the university scene, but heads unknowingly right toward a roadblock set up by two armed soldiers. One of them, Walker notes, is a Negro. After some brief questioning, the soldiers remove Walker from the car and take him into federal custody.

Under orders from Attorney General Robert F. Kennedy, Walker is arrested on four federal counts, including rebellion, insurrection, and seditious conspiracy against the U.S. government.

Back in Washington, Bobby Kennedy begins making urgent, insistent calls. Something has to be done with Walker. The attorney general orders federal officials to begin a drilled-down examination of everything they can find on Edwin A. Walker: his strange behavior in front of the Senate committee, his confrontational public statements in the media—even his internal files from the army report, including the one that mentions his "psychosomatic disorders."

Bobby Kennedy also turns finally to Dr. Charles E. Smith, medical director and chief psychiatrist of the Federal Bureau of Prisons. Smith provides a report on Walker to a sympathetic federal judge in Mississippi—the report says that Walker's recent behavior indicates "essentially unpredictable and seemingly bizarre outbursts of the type often observed in individuals suffering with paranoid mental disorder."

Even though Walker has not been examined by an independent psychiatrist, nor by Dr. Smith himself, the judge quickly agrees and orders Walker committed to a federal psychiatric prison for evaluation.

As Walker is spirited away by the federal agents, his supporters back in Dallas quickly spring into action. His attorney is Robert Morris, whose rabid anti-communism proved too much even for the University of Dallas—Morris left a few months ago to form a group called the Defenders of American Liberties.[2] He still writes editorial columns for the *Dallas Morning News*, and he is still willing to help Ted Dealey with any reconnaissance on Kennedy.

Morris calls a press conference to decry the treatment of Walker. He describes Walker as "the United States' first political prisoner. One would think we're in Havana or Budapest, the way General Walker has been treated." Thousands of angry telegrams and letters begin arriving at the White House, demanding Walker's release. Hundreds of protesters arrive at the U.S. Medical Center in Springfield, Missouri, where Walker is incarcerated. Some of them wave Confederate flags and hold signs that read: INTER-RACE MARRIAGES WILL RUIN THE WHITE RACE.

Morris knows the visuals will not win Walker sympathy across the country. He asks the picketers to please go home.

In Dallas, the *Morning News* rushes to embrace the general. It claims that Walker's actions in Mississippi had been peaceful. It is the Kennedy administration, the *News* argues, that has been the violent aggressor by sending marshals to the South.

Bruce Alger, who has received a flood of pro-Walker phone calls and telegrams from his constituents, calls Attorney General Robert Kennedy personally. Alger releases public statements defending Walker and takes to the floor of the House of Representatives, charging that the Kennedys' actions mean that "the freedom of every citizen of this land is in jeopardy."[3]

Reporters are dispatched to Walker's house on Turtle Creek to see if they can get some reaction from his headquarters. The first reporter to arrive, from the *Dallas Times Herald*, is ordered off the premises. Then a freelance photographer named Duane Robinson shows up. A former photojournalist for United Press International, he's just received a magazine assignment to photograph General Walker's home. Robinson sets up his camera and is preparing to take his picture when a man emerges from Walker's house and demands the film. Robinson refuses, noting that there is no law against taking a photograph of a house. Walker's aide lunges at him, and Robinson runs for it. Another Walker aide comes charging out of the house, and the two men chase Robinson through the streets of Dallas, finally catching him. They begin beating Robinson, then grab his camera and run away with it.

Later, Walker's house has an armed guard standing watch by the front door. Dallas police officers show up at the house to ask about the photographer's missing camera, but they are turned away.

The guard tells them: "The badge is not good enough. You've got to have legal papers to get in here."[4]

In custody, Walker remains silent, refusing to provide anything but his name, rank, and serial number.

Another psychiatric prisoner in the facility, however, is attempting to get messages through to Walker.

The prisoner writes to the general: "My case started... when I made charges of organized homosexuals in government and of their influence and power. I am still making the same charges. And I still have evidence and proof of it. I also now charge there is a homosexual–communist alliance to undermine moral codes of decency."

The man closes his letter: "I am still on record in the Justice Department as being 'insane' and so are you..."

Walker decides not to reply.[5]

Finally, Walker's attorneys and the Justice Department agree that Walker will submit to an independent psychological examination in Dallas. Walker's supporters raise the general's $100,000 bond, and he is freed after spending six days as a prisoner of the federal government. He exits the medical center at Springfield into the waiting arms of his mother, who has come from Dallas to meet him.

Walker flies home, arriving to find a joyous crowd of some 250 Confederate-flag-waving supporters. The throng also holds signs reading HAIL THE HERO! and WALKER FOR PRESIDENT IN 1964.

Walker briefly addresses the crowd, telling them he doesn't understand why the Kennedys imprisoned him, since he had only gone to Mississippi to see a football game.

Everyone laughs and cheers. As the general exits the terminal at Love Field, people burst into song: "For he's a jolly good fellow!"

Walker is nearly tearing up.

"I appreciate this very much. It is wonderful to be back in Texas," he tells them.

People in the crowd murmur in turn:

"God bless you ... we're with you."[6]

As Walker settles back into Dallas and plots his next move, a lean former marine marksman named Lee Harvey Oswald is settling into his new city. He has found a job making photographic reproductions at a graphic arts company. He is looking for a home for his Russian bride and his young daughter. He is also renting a PO box downtown, where he can receive his copies of the *Worker*, the weekly paper published by the U.S. Communist Party. News about Dallas's General Walker is everywhere, and the *Worker* is no exception. The radical left is as paranoid as the radical right, and for some of the open communists in America, Walker's forays into Mississippi are drumming up fears that the right really is planning some sort of violent, fascist takeover of the nation.

Walker is bidding for the "Fuehrer Role" says the *Worker*: "The first open candidate for leadership of the mass movement which the military-monopolist-pro-fascist plotters are now hoping to organize throughout the nation."

The newspaper is convinced that Walker would never be able to live so well in Dallas and travel the nation at ease if he was not supported in the city by "financial backers of the extreme right wing groups."

It calls for "action against him and his allies."[7]

As he reads the *Worker*, Oswald understands more clearly than before that America's violent right wing is headquartered in the city where he has brought his family.

He was born in New Orleans, moved around the country with his mother, and then joined the marines when he was seventeen. He spent three years in active duty, developed a fascination with communism and Russia—and abruptly decided to abandon the United States and make his way to Moscow in 1959. He was ready to start a new life, to stay, perhaps, forever. He met and married a quiet woman, Marina; they quickly had a child named June.

But by the spring of 1962 he was frustrated and wanted to move back to the United States. It took months of paperwork, cajoling, letter writing, until he and his family finally made it back to Fort Worth, just west of Dallas, where they would live briefly with his relatives.

Despite the way his dreams in the Soviet Union dissolved, he is still fascinated by communism—and alert to threats of fascism.

As he finds his way in Dallas, he can see that some in the city have consistently embraced General Edwin A. Walker and his allies—and no one is doing anything to stop them.

The race riot in Mississippi is eclipsed by startling news. Two weeks after the confrontations in Oxford, a U-2 flight over Cuba provides evidence of everyone's worst fears: The Soviets are stocking the island with nuclear missiles aimed at the United States.

Kennedy's top military commanders brief the president. Led by air force chief Curtis LeMay, the generals call for a direct strike on Cuba. LeMay argues that the best solution for Cuba is to "fry it."[8] Kennedy asks the general how the Russians will respond if the United States bombs Cuba.

"They'll do nothing," LeMay shrugs.

"Are you trying to tell me," Kennedy asks, eyes widening in disbelief, "that they'll let us bomb their missiles, and kill a lot of Russians and then do nothing? If they don't do anything in Cuba, then they'll certainly do something in Berlin."[9]

LeMay is insolent. He informs his commander in chief that his failure to order a military strike "would be almost as bad as

[Neville Chamberlain's] appeasement at Munich." Other chiefs jump into the exchange, endorsing LeMay's call to bomb Cuba.

Kennedy raises more objections. LeMay warns the president that he risks being viewed as "spineless" by "a lot of our own citizens."[10]

JFK instead calls for a naval blockade, an incremental step designed to put off the Soviets without immediately starting a war. For days the world stands poised on the brink of nuclear holocaust. Finally, the Soviets blink and turn their ships back.

Many Americans, including plenty who had been either ambivalent or opposed to Kennedy, erupt in cheers. The young president has stood toe-to-toe with the Kremlin and forced Khrushchev to back down. But the generals are convinced that Kennedy has yet again squandered a golden opportunity to destroy the enemy.

General LeMay fumes: "We had a chance to throw the Communists out of Cuba. But the administration was scared to death [the Soviet Union] might shoot a missile at us."[11]

NOVEMBER

Oswald has grown increasingly cold and remote. He has been screaming at Marina, and she is afraid of him—afraid for herself, and for the baby. Tonight, she decides to take the child and move away from the small duplex he found for them in the Oak Cliff section of Dallas, just a few short blocks from where the girlie club owner Jack Ruby shares an apartment with a friend.

He has to wonder if he will ever be reunited with Marina and the baby. She was, perhaps, stronger than he had imagined she would be. Ready to challenge him, in her native Russian, and then to simply pack her bags and move out.

At home, by himself again, he studies the latest news about Kennedy, about Cuba, about Castro. He is just as angered by Kennedy's actions as the American generals: Kennedy is really just furthering U.S. imperialism in Latin America—and the Cubans obviously always face a massive military threat from the United States...so why shouldn't they be able to arm themselves?

Truth be told, he was once complimentary of President Kennedy. He'd even pointed to a photo of Kennedy on the cover of *Time* and remarked how he looked different from "the other ratty politicos."[1] But now Kennedy seems so ready to crush Cuba and Castro.[2]

Oswald's interest in extremist politics is taking a knife-edged turn. He has petitioned to join the Trotskyist Socialist Workers Party, but his application is rejected since no chapter exists in Dallas, and there are few prospects of starting one. He does, however, obtain a subscription to the party's weekly paper, the *Militant*, which attacks General Walker and President Kennedy's Cuban policies with equal fervor.

The *Worker* preaches non-violence, but the *Militant* is much more forceful, calling for "revolutionary violence when necessary."[3] The *Militant* is quickly supplanting the *Worker* as Oswald's favorite paper.

As per the conditions for his release from the federal psychiatric facility, Edwin Walker presents himself to Parkland Hospital in Dallas for his sanity exam.

The tests are going to be administered by Dr. R. L. Stubblefield, who has been overwhelmed with telegrams and phone calls from Dallasites condemning him for questioning the mental health of a patriot like General Walker.

Stubblefield studies Walker and notes that the ex-general is very cooperative throughout the testing.

"Mr. Walker appears to be able to deal freely and accurately with his recollections of the incidents leading up to his arrest and present charges...It is our impression that the court in this case at this time is NOT concerned about Mr. Walker's ability to understand fully the more complex and subtle aspects of his motivation in regard to the acts for which he is charged. If it were, and if we were asked to evaluate these kinds of questions, it would be necessary to conduct a much more penetrating exploration of Mr. Walker's psychological operations."[4]

Walker is released from Parkland on November 10. It is his fifty-third birthday.

His attorney Robert Morris, the legendary communist hunter and anti-Kennedy ally to Dealey, announces to the *Dallas Morning News* that Walker has passed his examinations with flying colors.

The tests reveal that Walker is more than sane, according to Morris:

"Functioning currently at the superior level of intelligence."[5]

DECEMBER

Forty thousand people gather in Miami's Orange Bowl on December 29 to hear President Kennedy speak. He decided to come to South Florida to greet the surviving Bay of Pigs veterans released from prison by Castro after some quiet negotiations—in exchange for their release, Kennedy has agreed to deliver $53 million in food and medicine to Cuba.

Emotions are running high as Kennedy accepts the Cuban brigade's battle flag. Departing from his prepared text, the president suddenly says:

"I can assure you that this flag will be returned to this brigade in a free Havana."[1]

The roars in the stadium echo through the tropical air, even as Kennedy's civilian staffers grimace. The last thing the country needs, after the delicate negotiations with Castro, is more saber rattling over Cuba.

The *Militant*, Lee Harvey Oswald's favorite publication, has determined that Kennedy has reached a new level of evil:

"The most barefaced and disgusting display of immorality, ignorance and bad taste ever put on by a U.S. President."[2]

1963

JANUARY

This is the night Rhett James has been dreaming of for Dallas. He has finally succeeded in luring Dr. Martin Luther King Jr. It is King's first visit in seven years—the previous time had been a below-the-radar address to a church youth group—but now he will make a wide-open public speech at the big Music Hall at Fair Park. As the clock ticks past 7 p.m., James goes through his checklist and makes sure his church's gospel choir is ready to provide the music.

There is an electricity, an almost palpable buzz—some people won't be convinced until they actually see King set foot on a Dallas stage. Not everyone is happy, of course: Two hundred protesters huff and stomp outside, yelling that King is a communist.

James knows they are there, but maybe today can be a day of healing, a time for the hate to be put aside. Word is coming in that there are well over twenty-five hundred people in the hall. Looking out, James can see some white people squeezing into the rows up front. James had made a point of inviting staunch conservatives, including the GOP chairman in Dallas—but they declined.

Suddenly, the panicky rumor blurts out: *The police think there is a bomb in the building.*

Fair Park is home to the largest assemblage of art deco public buildings in America. Built in 1936 to celebrate the centennial of the Republic of Texas, the park has been the scene of long-running battles to integrate the State Fair—it was there that Juanita Craft and her teenagers from the NAACP once stood outside, politely handing out literature, dutifully holding signs.

Now there is a bomb scare, and Craft is probably not surprised. She has been openly critical of Dr. King,[1] though she certainly understands his motivations, and those of Rosa Parks, someone she considers a friend. Craft was a front-line warrior in the first unsuccessful attempts to get the State Fair and the Music Hall integrated—but lately she is worried about Dallas, and thinking that violence is in the air, and that blood may be spilled. Maybe it's lunatic to invite King into a place like Dallas—where so many see King as the man unraveling the social order, as the very face of the liberal-socialist-communist insurgency in America.

The first story announcing King's arrival hit the front page of the black newspapers a few weeks ago, while King goes virtually without any mention in the *Dallas Morning News*. He is the one black American the big daily newspaper is most wary of. Dallas has worked too hard, too long, to tamp down any hint of aggressive unrest in the city. The threat King poses is evident in the twenty-minute movie the Dallas Citizens Council had paid for and screened a thousand times all across the city. Narrated by a forceful Walter Cronkite, *Dallas at the Crossroads* featured newspaper editors, ministers, prosecutors, police, and businessmen—all white, all cautioning that Dallas will implode if civic disturbances catch fire. One stern Dallas elder after another stares directly into the camera and speaks in grave tones about the consequences of Dallas acting irrationally:

"Nothing is gained by lawlessness," one of Dealey's editorial writers somberly says.

"Violence, civil disorder, riots are crimes equally punishable under the law... The police will devote their energies to controlling those few who do not have the judgment and character to obey the law: We know who those few are," threatens Police Chief Jesse Curry.

"Dallas is a good city—and we want to keep it that way. Together, we shall show America 'The Dallas Way,'" insists Mayor Earle Cabell.

Right now parents who had wanted their children to see the famous Dr. King are pulling their kids closer. James has to be afraid that this crowning moment, this civil rights flare shot straight from the heart of inflexible Dallas, will be utterly ruined. People can hear the chants from the protesters outside.

One of them, Jimmy Robinson, a twenty-four-year-old from a Dallas suburb, is eagerly telling reporters: "We don't want to start a commotion. We just want to let the people know that we do not believe in what the NAACP and Martin Luther King stand for."[2] He is representing the National States Rights Party, he says, a pro-segregationist group from Georgia whose founder describes Hitler as "too moderate."

Inside the auditorium, James has to consider King's safety, and what all this means for Dallas, and even for himself. He has been working for five straight years to bridge Dallas to the national civil rights movement, and this could be the culmination. He led some of the first wide-scale and organized civil rights protests downtown; he helped spur the integration of Dallas schools. He writes the most hard-charging column in the city, in the leading black newspaper; he leads a church founded by slaves; he serves as head of the NAACP; he is in regular communication with Lyndon Baines Johnson; and now, almost as a capstone, he has finally gotten King to come to Dallas.

He has told people King will address the poll tax.[3] King and James are fighting it on all fronts, while still urging people to figure out how best to pay it so they can continue to vote. But many people are hoping for more. They want to hear King's version of "Dallas at the Crossroads"—not the version from the people downtown. They want to hear how Dallas will change, and how fast it will change.

Maybe that's why someone in the city might want to kill Martin Luther King Jr.—and everyone who has turned out to see him.

In that morning's edition of the black newspaper, James wrote his regular column. He could have written about King's upcoming visit that night. He could have written another one of his scorching indictments of corrupt politics, wretched poverty, or racism. But instead, he wrote about love. About how he hoped that Dallas, in 1963, would have the most peaceful, blessed year in its history:

"Live up to the best that is within you...live each day as if it were your last day on Earth...rise above the trite experiences of life and elevate your life into a sphere of radiant and peaceful union with your inner self and your personal relationships...may this year be your best year yet."[4]

There really are, James prayed, some signs that Dallas is changing. Maybe if people rise to their feet to cheer Dr. King it will be a sign that Dallas is not a city of hate. That Kennedy has a vision for America. That Johnson is squarely at a distance from the haunted traditions in Texas. That he and Kennedy symbolize a union—a joining of the old frontier with Kennedy's New Frontier, a way to move the nation forward beyond its fractured past.

Maybe, in 1963, Dallas can finally move away from the anger, the bile, and the violence.

By 8 p.m. the police have finally determined that the bomb threat is probably, hopefully, just a hoax to drive King's audience away.

The police teams still circulate inside and outside, keeping a wary eye on the roaming picketers. The police push them at least twenty-five feet away from the building, so the attendees can continue to enter in an orderly fashion.

From the front of the hall, James can see the leading rabbi in the city, someone who has been trying to lure Stanley Marcus to join his temple. He can also see the leading black attorneys in the city, the ones who are working directly with Thurgood Marshall to push for desegregation around the nation. There are other preachers and members of different congregations—he can see men from Carter Temple, Lone Star Baptist, Good Street Baptist, the Magnolia CME Church, and many, many more.

James finishes his prayers, the invocation, and the salutations and introduces the Reverend Martin Luther King Jr.

The last time King was in Dallas he was just beginning his crusade, and he had come to speak to that group of young people at a local church. The Dallas teenagers probably had no idea what dangers he was facing, how things were racing toward confrontation and change around America. That was seven years ago. King would no doubt have come back to Dallas if he had been invited—but even many black leaders in the city were afraid of what his visit would unleash.

Staring at the filling auditorium, King is no doubt still thinking about the appropriate message to convey to a city like Dallas. Dallas is complex, with history layered upon history: There is that minister, R. E. Davis, who claims he leads the national wing of the KKK from his home, close to where Jack Ruby and Lee Harvey Oswald have lived; the Confederate cemetery is just a long walk away from the very podium where King is standing; the "stair-step" integration plan is a laughingstock in black activist circles around the nation.

King decides to focus his Dallas speech on "America's Dream."

"Segregation is the strange paradox of the principle that all men are created equal," he begins, his voice ringing over the hushed audience.

Many people in the room have never heard King speak in person.

"We must get rid of the notion, once and for all, that there is a superior and an inferior race."[5]

Suddenly, some people are on their feet, interrupting him with rising applause. King pauses and then seems to echo what James has been searching for, pushing for, hoping for in Dallas since the moment he arrived in the city:

"We must develop a powerful action program to break down the barriers of segregation," and we must be honest "with ourselves and our white brothers: Segregation is wrong. It is a new formula of slavery covered up with nice complexities."

King nods toward politics, toward Kennedy: He has "done some impressive things in civil rights, especially when compared to the previous administration." He talks about Kennedy wanting to open up the business portals, the bedrock things that are the special ken of the Dallas Citizens Council, to black people. To poor people. And says that Kennedy should not stop with any order he has handed down to advance equality in the workplace—in the boardrooms. The Kennedy mandate has to push harder, deeper, into the entrenched realms. The Kennedy blueprint is a start, and even if it scares some people in Dallas, the blueprint is not the end:

"It does not do the full job," shouts King...and President Kennedy "must give the order teeth if it is to work."

In the audience, people are clapping, raising their hands to the roof. Some shout out: "That's right!"

King soaks in the applause and decides, now that he has set the table, he can issue an advance warning—to Dallas, and to America. The movement is prepared to move things to another level, to push for a sweeping boycott of businesses. What has happened in Dallas and other cities, the de facto desegregation, is just a beginning. Any businessman in Dallas can be singled out by black citizens. White businessmen can become "targets of a nationwide 'selective buying' program."

James has been shouting it, writing about it, and now King— the one so many people in Dallas thought was fomenting revolution around the nation—is at a podium inside the once perfectly segregated civic jewel of the city and telling black Dallasites to have the courage to storm the gates.

The crowd bursts into applause at least twenty-five times during King's forty-five-minute plea for justice in America, in Dallas.

"If a man has not found something worth dying for, he isn't fit to live," King shouts, his words echoing to the back of the room.

For a second, he seems almost too harsh, too combative.

King decides to add one more thing: "One can struggle to end the reign of segregation...but yet love the segregationist."

And again, the couple of thousand faithful in Dallas roar their approval. King is waving his hands in the air:

"The Declaration of Independence does not say some men... it does not say all white men...it does not say all Gentiles...it does not say all Protestants...it says *all* men are created equal! If the American dream is to be a reality, the idea of white supremacy must come to an end now and ever more."

Sometimes, the nightmares come back in crystalline detail. A short, solid-looking man named Jack Oran, who now runs a small bicycle and motorcycle shop in Dallas, always remembers what happened to him in the concentration camps:

He is pushing out of a bunk bed filled with six people. There is a dead man in the camp, someone whose pockets can be picked for scraps of moldy food. A piece of old bread, covered with lice, is on the floor and people are fighting for it.

And then he is being summoned, one painfully gaunt man among hundreds, to see Dr. Josef Mengele—the Nazi monster at the Auschwitz death camp. Oran is castrated. No anesthetics are used. He is sewn up, blood is running down his legs, and he is ordered back to work. He is certain his parents, his four sisters, and his brother have all been killed.

Now it is eighteen years later and he is thirty-nine years old.

After the Russians opened the gates to Auschwitz, he found his way to the United States. He got a job as a dishwasher in the Jewish ghetto in New York City—and then followed the promise of jobs, and an American Dream, to Dallas. He met a woman and they adopted three children. He opened up his bike store—he was good at fixing things, working patiently on broken parts and putting them back together.

He has been reading the papers, following what General Walker has been saying, what Reverend Criswell has been preaching, what H. L. Hunt's *Life Line* program has been airing, and what the *Dallas Morning News* has been printing. In the paper, just a few days ago, there was a man from a Dallas suburb named Jimmy Robinson, someone swearing allegiance to an organization founded by an American who thinks Hitler was too lenient. Robinson had come out to protest against a preacher, Dr. King, who is professing equality—and love—as an alternative.

Jack Oran has seen political extremism develop before. Although reticent to discuss his past, he decides that he should no longer be silent: That was the great failing in Europe—too many people were silent. He begins scheduling talks before local groups, to churches, to synagogues, to civic organizations, to veterans' groups, to the Kiwanis and Rotary Clubs. He tells people how he came to have the death camp number 80629 scratched into his body . . . and about how evil really does exist . . . how hatred exists . . .

how it is allowed to fester and then it is fed by indulgence, by some sort of swelling fervor and hysteria. That is how it all begins—until all sense of humanity is ended.

He has been speaking in public for several months now, telling his story. Each time he talks he is flooded with the same emotions and nearly breaks down. Some people hug him, others are racked with tears. Some just bow their heads and pray.

Be aware. There is hatred, extremism, and it is feeding itself like a fire. It is the way it began with the Nazis. Please don't let it come to Dallas.

It is January 25, and it is near freezing, brutally cold. Oran is through with work, finally returning to his modest home. His neighbors like him; he is a dignified but friendly man. A few of them know his history, have seen his death camp tattoo. And a few realize that something is troubling him about Dallas, and making him feel obligated to do something he avoided for years. To talk in public, to address strangers, to warn people.

As Oran pulls onto this street, there is a strange, unnatural glow coming from the direction of his house. There are wisps of smoke and dancing embers blowing over the grass and sidewalk.

He stops and stares. Someone has jammed a giant wooden cross into his lawn and set it on fire. It is roaring, blazing, and people are coming out of their homes to see it, to gape at it. Oran is almost dizzy as he goes inside and calls the police.

It takes days, but Oran finally learns that the police have picked up a suspect. His name is Jimmy Robinson, the same man who was leading the angry protest against King's visit to Dallas.

Oran learns that the man grew up in deep rural Texas and was only drawn to Dallas a few months earlier. Robinson defiantly, almost proudly admits to the police that he set the large cross on fire at the Holocaust survivor's house. He did it, he said, because he didn't like what Oran was saying in his speeches. He pays a $10 fine and is released.

FEBRUARY

A group of leading conservatives in Dallas is meeting on a cold Friday night at the elegantly appointed, comfortable home of Robert Morris—Walker's attorney, the John Birch Society member, and the man who worked with Dealey to investigate whether President Kennedy had once had a secret marriage.

There are several guests at Morris's house, including one of Dealey's top-ranking editorial writers from the *Dallas Morning News*. Also present is a man who has handled public relations for H. L. Hunt and a detective from the Dallas Police Department. And there is a stranger whom Morris has introduced as a former army soldier with an interest in political causes. The compact, intense man, new to Dallas, was serving in Germany when General Walker was being rebuked by Kennedy for speaking truth to power.

For three hours, the men gossip and talk politics over drinks and snacks. At midnight, Morris approaches the ex-soldier, Larrie Schmidt, and asks: "Enjoying yourself, Larrie?"

Schmidt answers briskly: "No, sir, I am not, to be honest with you. I thought we were getting together for business, not to socialize. I am terribly disappointed."

Morris calls for quiet in the room. "It is time to get down to business," Morris tells the others.

He tells the group that the real reason he has invited everyone to his home this evening is because of Larrie Schmidt and his mission. The men turn curiously to the twenty-seven-year-old with closely cropped black hair and dark, flashing eyes.

Schmidt has been preparing for this moment ever since he arrived in Dallas. He tells them that, in his opinion, the conservatives in Dallas have been too passive, too timid. He has come to Dallas to unleash an aggressive action plan to build up conservative forces.

The men stare at him, and Schmidt is basking in their attention. He has been telling people: "Whether I go down in history books as a great and noble man, or a tyrant, I am determined to at least be recorded in the history of our times."[1]

Schmidt was born in the heartland, in Nebraska. He studied journalism in college and dreamed of being able to reach millions of people. He signed up for two tours in the army and, while he was based in Germany, devoted himself to reading about the communist menace that was just out of sight but never, ever out of mind. The more he read the newspapers and magazines from the United States, the more it seemed as if people were in denial—particularly in Washington.

As a specialist fourth class stationed in Munich, Schmidt sometimes envisioned his life after the army—concerned about the kind of country he would return to. He read books by Ayn Rand and Barry Goldwater, and also read the same John Birch Society material that General Walker had given to his soldiers. The more Schmidt studied, the more he became disgruntled with Kennedy, with the way he was constantly appeasing instead of standing up to the communists.

Sometimes, Schmidt wondered what he would do if *he* was president:

If I were president, I would attack the Commies on every front, fighting them abroad and forcing those at home into concentration camps.[2]

One night when he was still in the army, he was holding court in a crowded beer hall in Munich, confident in his outspoken anti-Kennedy condemnations—and one soldier after another gathered to hear him. The soldiers swapped cheerful news about what they were hearing. There was a conservative resurgence in America. But just as quickly, they were sobered by someone saying anti-communist patriots were actually only gaining news headlines... but not gaining any real traction.

How could they with someone like Kennedy in the White House?

Schmidt listened to the soldiers yelling and debating. A thought bubbled up: *Conservatives are too fragmented, and as long as they remain split among hundreds of individual groups they have no chance of becoming an effective political force.*

Somebody had to travel the nation and do the long, hard, slogging work of uniting the conservative organizations. He liked what Ayn Rand had written about unbowed men, super men who were seeking and living their destiny. Walker has been trying to live his destiny, but he was getting whipped, over and over, by Kennedy. Maybe Schmidt can try to pick up the pieces of the splintered movement, and maybe he can at last try to unite the anti-Kennedy forces.

When he first told some fellow soldiers in Germany about his master plan, they thought it was just an amusing addition to chasing local women and steins of beer. Schmidt tried to organize them, tried to demand blood oaths to prove their loyalty. Most of the soldiers laughed and refused.

As he was getting ready to be discharged, he thought long and hard about where to ignite his plan in America. He knew where Walker had gone to make his final stand—and where the bristling, action-oriented wings of the patriotic movement seemed so solid. Dallas seemed to be the most promising right-wing citadel in America, a place where the men in charge—the university president, the publisher, the preachers, the mayor and congressman—were more united than almost anywhere else.

If they gave Walker the keys to the city, they may just do it for him, too.

When Schmidt arrived in Dallas the previous fall, soon after the uneasy conclusion of the Cuban Missile Crisis and Walker's arrest in the violent rioting in Mississippi, he instantly began trying to meet the real conservative heavyweights in the city—Dealey, Hunt, and Walker.

He had saved a little money, enough to live on until he found a job, and he began by contacting the conservative action groups. Few in the city were hiding their allegiances: Walker flew several flags outside his home, the radio stations were filled with right-wing shows, and one of Hunt's former employees was distributing, from Dallas, one of the most aggressive anti-Kennedy newsletters in America.

From a bar stool in Munich, Dallas had seemed a veritable conservative paradise, a utopia overflowing with easy money and right-thinking people who were the only ones in America to so openly embrace Walker. It seemed like a place so gurgling with conservative principles that Schmidt could go right to the top floors, straight to where the Dallas Citizens Council manned the city.

The garrulous Schmidt searched for clubs, grassroots organizations, and even watering holes where he could strike up conversations, make inroads. At first blush, on the street level, Dallas seemed surprisingly like "a hick town," Schmidt wrote to his friends still in the military in Germany. "There are three kind of bars: straight beer joints; bars with beer and liquor (but no mixed drinks, you have to buy a whole bottle and buy mix); private clubs. No great night life."

It didn't matter, really.

He was in Dallas for other reasons—to try to see Walker, to persuade H. L. Hunt to open his war chest: "Am drinking very little. All business. This is no time for games."[3]

Schmidt's first goal was to infiltrate Frank McGehee's National Indignation Convention. It turned out to be far easier than Schmidt could have imagined. McGehee quickly agreed to meet with him. After a short conversation, McGehee suddenly offered to make Schmidt his vice president.

Schmidt wrote to his allies in the military: "It got us everything we had intended to get, 18 months ahead of schedule!"

Schmidt rhapsodized about what he could do with a membership fee of just one dollar for each of the three hundred thousand NIC members: "Think in terms of 300,000 members, $300,000."[4]

The more he learned about the NIC and Dallas, the more he was staggered by the ferocity exhibited by men like Frank McGehee, its founder: "Frank gives me the impression of being rather anti-Semitic," he told others.

This worried Schmidt. One of his allies from Germany, an army soldier named Bernard Weissman, was Jewish. Schmidt suggested that he should convert to Christianity. Religious fervor was one key to success inside the Dallas right wing: "We *must* all return to church. These people here are religious bugs."[5]

Some of them, too, were abject racists. Schmidt had grown up in Nebraska, far from the entrenched apartheid in the South. The enforced segregation in Dallas was something he had never witnessed before. "Down here a negro is nigger. No one—and I mean no one—is ever to say one kind word about niggers. Only liberals do that… On the other hand, the KKK is passé. Don't praise it. Don't preach race hatred. Don't say anything good about niggers—but don't talk about harming them either. The conservative isn't 'agin the nigras,' he just wants to keep him in his place for his own good."[6]

But after a few heady days of enjoying his status as the new vice president for the National Indignation Convention, the truth began to dawn on Schmidt: McGehee's organization did not have three hundred thousand members. It did not even have three hundred members. Those stories were all lies—generated by McGehee to attract media coverage.

Just a few weeks before Schmidt came to town, the NIC rented Dallas Memorial Auditorium for a rally. Less than a hundred people showed up—"There's too much hall here for the few of us," McGehee remarked sadly.[7]

Schmidt could see that the NIC was boiling down to a few hard-core stalwarts in Dallas. Maybe the whole damned movement was collapsing. Maybe someone needed to deal directly with the powers-that-be in Dallas—the real powers. Someone needed to connect the foot soldiers in Dallas with the moneymen.

Schmidt found work selling life insurance, mingled at more conservative events, and buttonholed anyone who would give him time, until he finally gained a meeting with some of the editors at Dealey's *Dallas Morning News*—and it was a breakthrough, as if he was getting closer, moving to that sacrosanct world of the Dallas Citizens Council. Schmidt listened as he heard promises that if he was patient, he would also be eventually introduced to both General Walker and H. L. Hunt.

First, though, he'd be invited to Robert Morris's house to meet a select group of like-minded men, including someone from the *Dallas Morning News.*

On this chilly Friday night, the men assembled in Morris's living room lean in to listen to Schmidt's specific plan. It is well past midnight and it must feel both grave and conspiratorial.

Schmidt studies the faces of the hushed men in Morris's home. He knows that this could finally be his entrée into the upper reaches of the Dallas firmament. Maybe the gateway to his being taken more seriously, maybe the chance to get the support of the men downtown.

He shifts into high energy and tells the men that he has people, strong-willed soldiers, who are willing to relocate to Dallas to join them. He says it is, in a way, a team of loyal, action-oriented conservative fighters who will push Dallas to another level—and make it a pivot point for a changing America.

The Dallas conservatives are sometimes too damned passive and disorganized. If we can marshal our united forces, we can bring real change to America.

As he winds down, the skeptical men in the room seem a bit persuaded by his breathless, almost Bible-thumping speech. They instantly agree to help Schmidt launch a Dallas chapter of Young Americans for Freedom (YAF), a national conservative organization. But they have their doubts about Schmidt, too—and he is not given the president's position. That honor goes to Ken Thompson, the editorial writer from the *Dallas Morning News.*

Schmidt, feeling very proud, shakes hands all around and basks in a final toast from Morris. He heads into the chilly North Texas night. Once he is settled back into his apartment, he begins typing a letter to his soldier friends in Munich:

"We have succeeded, the mission with which I was charged in Dallas has been achieved. Friday night, I attended a gathering of the top conservatives in Dallas…I accomplished my task in Dallas. I need you here soon. I sold these people on each of you, and they are expecting you to come to Dallas and play an important role.

"The days of leisure are over…"[8]

★   ★   ★

On Abraham Lincoln's birthday, February 12, over eight hundred leading black figures from across the nation arrive at the White House for a special gala luncheon to honor the hundredth anniversary of the Emancipation Proclamation.

The famous entertainer Sammy Davis Jr. is there, along with his very blond wife. There are leading officials arriving from many of the national civil rights organizations. Though Dr. King has been invited, he has sent his regrets; he is still somewhat impatient with Kennedy's progress on civil rights.[9]

And there are also two people from Dallas being shown inside: Rhett James and Juanita Craft. Like the other guests, in the preceding weeks they received a gold-hued, engraved invitation from President Kennedy and the First Lady summoning them to the special celebration in Washington.[10] It is, really, as if they have been invited into an orbit that few people from Dallas ever experience— and that a handful would still have aggressively resisted.

But surely this invitation, this trip to see the dazzling president and First Lady, are signs of a new beginning—just as much as Dr. King's triumphant visit to Dallas last month.

Finally, President Kennedy and Jacqueline Kennedy arrive. She is resplendent in a ruby-red velvet-and-silk Oleg Cassini skirt and jacket. The president is smartly turned out in an impeccable suit.[11] As they greet their guests, they are charming, radiant. It is a formal affair, among the most elaborate ever offered by the White House to so many black leaders at one time.

James, for one, feels like he is in the moment but hovering above it. Amid the hubbub of well-wishers, clinking glasses, and camera flashes, the Dallas preacher's mind is wandering. He admires Kennedy, he has been happy with the way the president and his brother moved quickly to address the situation in Mississippi. Even though some criticize Kennedy for being too hesitant on civil rights, he has already done more than many previous presidents. James says that Kennedy has an inner courage—and that he occupies "the loneliest chair in the world."[12]

As President Kennedy mingles and the First Lady poses for

group photographs, the visitors from Dallas must wonder if their city will ever really live up to what Lincoln wanted, what the Emancipation Proclamation spells out. It seems so promising, so close at hand. Dallas really has been changing—for the good. Surely it won't take much longer for true equality in the city?

A thought pops into James's mind: "How long will it take to make this proclamation a reality? Already it has been 100 years."[13]

It is like crossing from one country to another—Lee Harvey Oswald and Marina have left their humble duplex and are now arriving at an upscale residence in Dallas for a party given by a swashbuckling Russian émigré who seems to have connections to everyone, including various intelligence agencies and Dallas oil millionaires.

George De Mohrenschildt and his wife have been providing the struggling young couple with gifts of food, clothing, and household items, often over the proud Lee's objections.

De Mohrenschildt is not the only one inside the tightly knit Russian expatriate community to coo over the polite, quiet Marina. Many of the others seem to loathe Oswald, suspicious that he has been controlling her in some darker ways. But De Mohrenschildt almost seems to have a clinical fascination with Oswald—maybe as a quiet man he can work to draw out.

Oswald knows that De Mohrenschildt is one of the handful of people in Dallas who seem to listen seriously to his theories on the fascists and the right wing. Oswald considers De Mohrenschildt his only friend in the city—and maybe some sort of gateway to respectability.

De Mohrenschildt is from a wealthy Russian family that lost its holdings during the Bolshevik revolution. He speaks several languages, and his range of contacts among America's elite is extensive—he is friendly with everyone from George Herbert Walker Bush to the parents of Jacqueline Bouvier Kennedy. As a young girl, Jackie had sat on his knee during social gatherings, calling him "Uncle George."

He can seem non-specific in his allegiances, willing to mingle and listen to any side: De Mohrenschildt has joined several organizations, from Stanley Marcus's liberal Dallas Council on World Affairs to Ted Dealey's conservative Texas Crusade for Freedom.

But when he is with Oswald, he assures him he is an avowed leftist.

And as they huddle tonight inside his grand house, apart from the swirl of the other guests laughing and drinking, De Mohrenschildt makes no secret of his dislike for General Edwin Walker:

"Anyone who 'knocked off Walker' would be doing society a favor."[14]

On February 27, Walker boards a specially equipped tour bus owned by his close friend, the anti-communist televangelist Billy James Hargis. The two men are departing on a speaking tour to twenty-nine cities, mostly in the South: "To alert the public to the enemy within and without." Taking their inspiration from Paul Revere, they are calling their tour Operation Midnight Ride.

Hargis is a thirty-seven-year-old, three-hundred-pound Texas-born leader of the Christian Crusade, a fervent group of a hundred thousand paid followers based in Tulsa, Oklahoma. He has an unusually boyish and doughy face, prefers tailored suits, and decorates his office with pictures of Jesus and a large flagpole with the Stars and Stripes. He distributes autographed pictures of himself, often signed: *Go With God!*

He possesses an honorary doctorate in divinity from Bob Jones University, a conservative bulwark in South Carolina, and he is armed with an abundant gift for self-promotion. Early in his career, Hargis wrote speeches for Senator Joseph McCarthy. Then he hit upon the idea of getting Bibles into communist countries by attaching them to one million hydrogen-filled balloons that would float over the Iron Curtain. Hargis enjoys traveling in luxurious style, and he personally toured great portions of Europe in order to supervise his Bible balloon launchings into the airspace of the godless nations.

He publishes a weekly newsletter and a monthly magazine along with numerous tape recordings and albums. His daily broadcasts are carried by 250 television stations and can be heard on over five hundred radio stations across the country. And during his religious revival appearances, he will often call out for a $10,000 donation in the name of God. One of his aides planted in the audience will shout out that he has heard the Lord's call and will volunteer the money. The idea is to stampede others into pledging their money, too. Anyone who donates $25 or more receives a free copy of his record album: *The United Nations Hoax*.[15]

Hargis and Walker are at ease with each other. Their politics are apparent. Their loathing of Kennedy, of Washington liberals, of Martin Luther King Jr., makes for a perfect match. What only a few might suspect is that Hargis—like Walker—has a secret sexual life.

Hargis began courting Walker even before the general resigned from the army. Now he's invited him to join the board of the Christian Crusade, and he shamelessly flatters Walker at every opportunity, telling him: "God knows, we need you for President!"[16]

Among Hargis's most devoted followers is Walker's mother. In letters to her son, she likes to sign off by writing: "Go with God, as Billy James Hargis always says."[17]

As they board the bus and begin their tour of America, Walker confesses something to Hargis: *After the failed gubernatorial race and the snuffing out of my American rebellion in Mississippi, I know that I will never be president. The best I can hope for is to be a lightning rod for patriots until the communist establishment locks me up again.*

As the Operation Midnight Ride tour bus, complete with sleeping bunks, begins to curl down the interstate highways leading out of Texas, Hargis tells aides that he and General Walker are on a mission to "expose the communist clergymen" who support civil rights—clergymen like Rhett James in Dallas and Martin Luther King Jr.

MARCH

Staring out the window of the tour bus, as Operation Midnight Ride moves across America, Walker sees crowds of protesters—including whites and blacks from the local NAACP. He stares down at them, his face impassive, as they wave signs: THIS ISN'T OLE MISS, WALKER, and WE DON'T NEED RACISTS HERE, WALKER.[1]

Escorted by police guards inside one venue after another, Walker and Hargis wait patiently until an entire row of American flags is carefully arranged on the stage behind them.

As the caravan rolls on, Walker seems to grow even more fanatical in his opposition to Kennedy, perhaps spurred on by the religious inviolability he thinks that Hargis affords him. Walker condemns the "Kennedy dynasty and dictatorship...There is no law left...We have got to start all over."[2]

He refers to Robert Kennedy as "little stupid brother Bobby, as they call him in Mississippi." The Kennedy brothers are just like the Castro brothers in Cuba: "Jack has Bobby and Castro has Raul."

He describes his arrest in Mississippi as the result of a preconceived Kennedy plot against him.

"I wouldn't conform to the 'National Policy,'" he rails to half-puzzled audiences. "They had to get rid of me because I knew too much about Mississippi."[3]

As the barnstorming tour moves across America, Walker also seems to become increasingly fixated on Cuba. He begins calling on President Kennedy to use military might to remove Castro. And really, not to oust him—but to simply kill him. To assassinate him.

Walker shouts: "I challenge the Commander-in-Chief of the United States of America to...liquidate that scourge that has descended upon the island of Cuba."[4]

*   *   *

Oswald's beatings of Marina are now more frequent—and even more violent. He's gone from slapping her around to actually punching her square in the face, leaving her with purple-and-black eyes. She lowers her head in shame, so the neighbors can't see it—but they do, and they are shocked. His political rhetoric is also growing increasingly strident. She hears him say that she will soon need to take the baby and return to the Soviet Union.

From the beginning of their relationship, not long after they met at a dance in the Soviet Union, she knew he had a remote side to him. But now he locks himself in his room for hours at a time, reading books on communism and writing political tracts. At the typesetting and graphic arts firm where he works, he has created a phony ID card for himself, using the name A. J. Hidell. He orders a Smith & Wesson .38 snub-nosed revolver through the mail, using the same alias. She spots him poring over a city map and the Dallas bus schedule, and he is focusing his attention on a particular stretch of Turtle Creek Boulevard.

Then, three days after Walker's blistering, unfiltered speech about killing Castro, Oswald leaves their duplex and begins doing reconnaissance at the general's home. His mission is entering the action-oriented phase. He takes photographs of the back of Walker's house from the narrow, bush-lined alley.

Back at his home, he must have realized that a pistol will not be sufficient, because he also orders a Mannlicher-Carcano rifle with a telescopic sight from a sporting goods store in Chicago. He pays $19.95 plus $1.50 for shipping and handling. Although inexpensive, the Carcano is a reliable, accurate weapon, similar to the U.S. Army's M14. He achieved "marksman" status in the marine corps, and a few rounds of target practice in Dallas are enough to acquaint himself with his new weapon.

Marina has gotten used to him closing the door as he steps inside a back room. He is preparing his operations manual for the anti-Walker mission, filling a folder with photographs and a map with various routes. It would be easy to hide a rifle along some railroad tracks near the general's house.

He sends a long letter to the *Militant*, which appears in a March 1963 issue under the headline NEWS AND VIEWS FROM DALLAS. In the letter, he describes Dallas as a city where poor renters live at the mercy of exploitative landlords, and he congratulates the paper as "the most informative radical publication in America."

Marina wonders where he goes when he leaves the house for hours at a time. When he returns home he tells her that he was doing target practice, or attending a typing class. There have been so many beatings at his hands that she knows enough not to argue with him.

On the last Sunday in March, Marina is hanging diapers on a flimsy clothesline stuck in the grass in the small backyard. Oswald steps outside, gives her his camera, and shows her how to operate it. He stands facing her, squinting in the sunlight as a trace of a smile plays across his face. He is outfitted entirely in black. He holds the Carcano rifle proudly, even jauntily, pointing its barrel toward the sky. In his other hand he displays two papers—the *Worker* and an issue of the *Militant* that contains his published letter.

The *Militant*'s front page also carries a story about a black civil rights worker who has been shot by three white racists in Mississippi. The message must be clear: The extreme right is engaged in violence, even assassinations. Now is the time for the other side to be heard.

For a second, Marina isn't sure what to make of her husband's odd request to be photographed with his two newspapers and new rifle. She laughs nervously, but takes the picture anyway. He tells her he will send the photo to the *Militant*.[5]

Afterward, Oswald develops the photographs at his job, furtively. He knows by now that he has been steadily alienating his boss and co-workers, just as he has in virtually all the jobs he's ever held. Even back in Russia, one of his supervisors wrote a report on him: "Citizen Lee Harvey Oswald reacts in an over-sensitive manner to remarks from the foremen, and is careless in his work. Citizen L. H. Oswald takes no part in the social life of the shop and keeps very much to himself."[6]

Despite his professed love for the working class, Oswald usually refuses to associate with the other workers in Dallas. He makes a show of reading Russian-language magazines during his lunch breaks. His contempt for his work and his colleagues seems on display at every moment.

The day after Marina photographs him in the backyard, his boss at the typesetting and graphic arts firm summons Oswald and tells him he is being fired.[7]

APRIL

O n the clean-swept streets of Dallas's downtown, a demonstration involving a lone member of the "lunatic left" is
drawing some curious stares. Oswald is there, darting down
sidewalks, staging a one-man picket. He has a placard around his
chest: HANDS OFF CUBA! VIVA FIDEL!

As people walk by, he jabs a hand out and offers "Fair Play for
Cuba" literature.

Two patrolmen spot him and have to wonder what there is to
picket—the stores are integrated, the protesters are dormant.

Oswald is alarmed: "Oh hell, here come the cops."

He drops the leaflets and makes a quick getaway.

Later, safe at his duplex, he sends a report to the Fair Play for
Cuba Committee in New York: "Since I am unemployed I stood
yesterday for the first time in my life, with a placard around my
neck." Oswald notes that he had been "cursed as well as praised."

He requests forty to fifty additional pamphlets for future
actions.[1]

Robert Surrey, Walker's day-to-day aide, arrives at the general's
grand house on April 8 to welcome him home after Operation
Midnight Ride.

The national revolution, this mixture of Christianity and anti-
communism, didn't seem to soar like Walker and his army thought
it would. In Dallas, at least, the Walker team knows the campaign
has been well received and that the *Dallas Morning News* has been
faithful.

As Surrey turns his car into the alley behind the home, he spots
a late-model Ford and two strangers, who appear to be looking
over the fence at Walker's house. Surrey waits until the men get in
their car and drive away. Then he follows them. The car manages

to escape, but Surrey is sure of one detail—it does not have a license plate. He returns to Walker's home to greet the general.

As they slip into the quiet of the home, they both wonder if the place has been bugged. Walker and his aides talk, make jokes, about the possibility that the FBI went into his home—maybe while he was away on Operation Midnight Ride—and put listening devices in the walls. Walker is well aware that his high-profile political activities are making him a target. He knows that the FBI is monitoring him. Possibly the CIA and KGB, too. Who knows who his volunteers really are?

Walker is certain that some of them are undercover officers or double agents. He is convinced that someone is out to get him.

Two days later, Oswald finally confesses to Marina that he has been fired from his job. He blames it on the FBI, claiming that they made his employer nervous by asking questions about him. Near twilight, he finishes dinner and then leaves without telling her where he is going. Marina hopes he is off to his typing class.

It's been unseasonably hot in Dallas. The temperature reached ninety-nine degrees earlier in the day as a wall of hot southwesterly winds stalled over the city. Now it is still warm, close to eighty degrees, as Oswald walks quickly away from the duplex. He moves past the thick-trunked oak and pecan trees, headed for the city bus stop two blocks away. With darkness coming on, he wants to get to that comfortable neighborhood of larger, carefully manicured homes north of downtown.

He did not tell his wife that he left a note behind for her: a very detailed message, written in his careful, flowing cursive. The note is on the dresser in his small private room where he likes to read and think. If he doesn't return home this evening, Marina will be sure to find it:

> *1. This is the key to the mailbox which is located in the main post office in the city on Ervay Street. This is the same street where the drugstore, in which you always waited is located. You will find the mailbox in the post office which is located 4 blocks from the*

drugstore on that street. I paid for the box last month so don't worry about it.

2. Send the information as to what has happened to me to the Embassy and include newspaper clippings (should there be anything about me in the newspapers). I believe that the Embassy will come quickly to your assistance on learning everything.

3. I paid the house rent on the 2d so don't worry about it.

4. Recently I also paid for water and gas.

5. The money from work will possibly be coming. The money will be sent to our post office box. Go to the bank and cash the check.

6. You can either throw out or give my clothing, etc. away. Do not keep these. However, I prefer that you hold on to my personal papers (military, civil, etc.).

7. Certain of my documents are in the small blue valise.

8. The address book can be found on my table in the study should need same.

9. We have friends here. The Red Cross also will help you.

10. I left you as much money as I could, $60 on the second of the month. You and the baby can live for another 2 months using $10 per week.

11. If I am alive and taken prisoner, the city jail is located at the end of the bridge through which we always passed on going to the city (right in the beginning of the city after crossing the bridge).[2]

It is 8:30 p.m. on April 10 and General Walker is settling into the study on the first floor of his sprawling home. His handful of devoted aides have headed for their cars, and he is by himself on this uncomfortably warm Wednesday night. Though he likes to retire early, he decides to stay up a little later. He needs to finish his income tax forms, which are due in five days.

Fastidious and orderly, he rolls up his shirtsleeves, finds a sharp pencil, and arranges his financial statements on a wooden writing desk at the rear of the house. The wood-framed window in his study faces a very narrow, hidden alley lined with a lattice fence and some thin, tall bushes just beginning to bud. Tonight, he has left the window shades open. Most of the lights in the house are on. He sits at his desk, facing the center of the room.

Oswald knows the dark, quiet path behind Walker's home. He arrives close to 9 p.m. He is carrying his rifle, which he has retrieved after hiding it earlier in the week near the railroad tracks. From his vantage point, he can see that the worship service at the chapel on the other side of the general's house is ending. Car doors are slamming and engines start up as people begin driving away. His timing is perfect.

He has a clear view into Walker's home. The general is easily visible, sitting at his desk. A few feet from the window, a squat-bodied gas meter is sticking out of the ground like a little silver-gray figure with spindly arms. There are narrow, ten-foot-high bushes just beyond the gas meter. Oswald quickly surveys the area around him. Now is the time.

He steps up to Walker's pale-colored, wood-lattice fence, formed with pickets that are four to six inches wide and five feet high. The fence, with the open squares in the lattice serving as solid notches, is perfect for resting and aiming a rifle. It is 120 feet from the fence to Walker's desk.

There are escape routes from this vantage point:

Deeper down the dark alley.

A sprint from the alley to the east into the greenbelt and the engulfing woods.

Racing southeast for the hidden trails, those tiny paths, to the railroad tracks. Then a long, quick walk to catch a bus home from a different part of the city.

Oswald lifts his rifle and stares into the window. Surrounding Walker are folders, books, and stacks of packages wrapped in brown shipping paper. The walls are decorated with panels of foil wallpaper embossed with an Asian-style flower motif. Walker's head is in profile. He has a pencil in hand, and he is perfectly still, focused on something at his desk. From outside looking in, it must look a bit like a painting—as if Walker is caught in thought with the right side of his face clearly visible.

Oswald squints into his telescopic sight, and Walker's head fills the view. He looks so close now, and he's sitting so still, that there's no possible way to miss. Drawing a tight bead on Walker's head, he pulls the trigger. An explosion hurtles through the night, a thunder that echoes to the alley, to the creek, to the church and the surrounding houses.

Walker flinches instinctively at the loud blast and the sound of a wicked crack over his scalp—right inside his hair. For a second, he is frozen. His right arm is still resting on the desk alongside his 1962 income tax forms. He doesn't know it, but blood is beginning to appear. A thought instantly blinks in his mind:

A firecracker. Somebody just threw a firecracker at me. How the hell did some damned kid throw a firecracker through the screen?[3]

He realizes now that there was another noise. A brutish punching, thudding sound. He instantly pushes away from the desk so that he is no longer visible through the window. Looking back at where he had been sitting, he sees a large hole in the wall, very near where his head had been. He carefully, quickly, moves upstairs, looking for his pistol. He grabs it and comes down the staircase, and as he does he glances out a south-facing second-floor window.

There is a car beyond the trees, some kind of car, just making the turn out of the alley by the church. Heading to Turtle Creek Boulevard.

Walker makes it to his back door and gingerly steps into the inky night. Gun in hand, he stares hard into the darkness. The taillights he spotted from his upstairs window have vanished.

He returns to the house. By now he realizes that his right arm is bleeding in four or five places. Walker calls the police and asks them to come as soon as possible. Then he calls Robert Surrey.

The first Dallas cops arrive within five minutes. Surrey pulls up to Walker's house a few minutes later, joined by a second police car with detectives from the burglary and theft squad.

Inside the house, one of the detectives tells Walker to sit down.

Patrolmen are in the backyard, trying to see if they can line up the shot, follow its path. There is a chip, a notch, on the fence—maybe a spot that could be used to rest a rifle.

"He couldn't have missed you," one of the officers says to Walker.

"He must have been a lousy shot," Walker replies.

"It was an attempted assassination," adds a detective named Don McElroy.

"What makes you call it that?" asks Walker.

"Because he was definitely out to get you," replies McElroy.[4]

Examining the point where the bullet entered through the window, the cops can see that it slammed into the upper portion of the wooden window frame. That collision was just enough to alter the bullet's trajectory a fraction so that it passed through Walker's hair—instead of boring into his right temple.

When Surrey is allowed inside, he sees Walker seated at his desk as the cops try to reconstruct the affair. Surrey can also see that there is something strange, white and gray, in Walker's hair.

"What happened? What's going on?" asks Surrey.

Walker points to the gaping, exploded hole in the nine-inch-thick wall.

"Oh, you found a bug," laughs Surrey, laying on the sarcasm.

Walker shakes his head. "No," he says, "I have been shot at." He raises an arm and points to the shattered window.

Surrey sees the blood oozing out of Walker's right arm. He reaches down. Walker holds up his wounded arm for inspection and says, calmly, "The jacket of the bullet must have come apart when it went through the window."[5]

Now Surrey can see several pieces of metal sticking out of Walker's skin. He bounds upstairs and finds a first-aid kit. He brings down tweezers, bends over Walker's arm, and begins patiently extracting the bullet fragments as the police continue to ask questions.

As he works and listens, Surrey grows convinced this is not a case for the damned burglary squad.

Surrey hears a patrolman named Billy Norvell say: "I found it."

The cop has gone into another room, on the other side of the hole blown through the wall. There, among the stacks of Walker's patriotic literature, Norvell has discovered the spent bullet. It is resting atop a pile of Walker's most popular pamphlet, *Walker Speaks . . . Unmuzzled!*

Norvell scratches his initials on the base of the bullet and hands it to McElroy from the burglary squad. Later, McElroy will take the squashed, mushroomed bullet for processing at the Crime Scene Search Section at police headquarters downtown.[6]

By now, reporters who have heard the news on police scanners are racing to Walker's home. They mingle easily with the cops and push toward Walker, asking for his reaction.

"Somebody took a shot at me," says the general. "That is the closest I have ever been missed in 30 years of military service."

The burglary detective, McElroy, tells the reporters: "Whoever shot at the general was playing for keeps. The sniper wasn't trying to scare him. He was shooting to kill."[7]

It is close to midnight by the time Oswald finally returns home. If he had a car, he could have easily driven from Walker's house in fifteen minutes. If he took a bus near the general's house and made the easiest connections, he could have been home within an hour. But he played it safe, catching a bus as far away from Walker's neighborhood as possible.

When he enters the duplex, Marina is waiting. She became worried during the evening by his long absence, and she began rooting around the home, hoping to find some clue about what he was up to. She discovered the note he left for her with its painstakingly detailed set of instructions.

When he steps inside, she's relieved to see that he doesn't appear to have any weapons with him. She shows him the note and speaks in her native Russian:

"What happened? What is the meaning of this?"

He looks pale and he brushes her off, telling her not to ask him any questions. He goes to the radio and snaps it on, turning the dial and trying to find a news station. She stays beside him, pleading for him to tell her what is going on.

Frustrated that there is no news on the shooting, he finally tells her: He traveled across town to shoot someone—a man, a former general, who needed to die. She stares at her husband. He is edgy, nervous. She is stunned.

"Where is the rifle? What did you do with it?" she demands.

He says that he buried it. That dogs could find things by a sense of smell. That he didn't want to be caught carrying the rifle.

She listens and begins crying. She is worried about his mind, his mental state. She is worried that the police are on their way to arrest them all. *What happens to our daughter?*

"This was a very bad man," he explains to her. "He was a fascist . . . he was the leader of a fascist organization."

"You have no right to take his life," she replies.

He is very serious. "If someone had killed Hitler in time it would have saved many lives."[8]

She decides not to call the police.

There is their child, June. The child and her husband have been her world. She knows she is almost completely dependent on him in this new country where she barely speaks the language. He has a brutal vein. He has punched her. And now he has tried to kill a man. Yet somehow, she feels that she still harbors some attachment to him.

As night wears on, he takes her into his confidence and explains more. He tells her he has been planning to shoot Walker for the last two months. He tells her about his photographs of Walker's house, his maps, consulting the bus schedules, writing his plans in English in his private notebooks . . . and writing his good-bye notes to her in Russian. He strikes her as being proud of what he did.

Now it is after midnight and he continues to search the radio for news. Nothing yet is being reported. Finally, after another hour, he gives up and goes to bed. She tries but can't sleep at all. Her mind is racing with more questions, but she decides not to ask them.

The next morning Marina finds her husband listening to the radio again and studying the newspapers.

"I missed," he tells her, angry with himself.

She has decided to keep the good-bye note, with his explicit instructions, hidden away in a cookbook. And now she threatens to use the note against him, to give it to the police, if he tries another assassination attempt on Walker. She says that Walker was kept alive for some reason—and that was reason enough for him not to be shot at again.

He promises her he won't try to kill Walker again.

She listens as he shakes his head and repeats that he took aim. *Very good aim.*[9]

Three days later, on the Saturday before Easter, Oswald is still monitoring the news reports. A story announces that one witness reported seeing two men in the church parking lot right after the shooting, and that one of them drove away. The police seem intent on following this lead.

He laughs, scoffing at the way the police are fixated on mysterious getaway cars:

"Americans are so spoiled," he tells his wife. "It never occurs to them that you might use your own two legs."[10]

Later that day he goes out again. When he returns he has his rifle. Carefully, he places it inside a closet and drapes a coat over it. Then he shows her parts of his private notebook. It is written in English, on legal-size paper. She doesn't understand some of it. There are descriptions of Walker's house, notes about distances, notes about the distribution of the windows in a house. There are also photographs inside the book. She asks him what they are.

"Well, this one is the picture of the house of General Walker's— his residence," he replies.

She stares at the notebook. "It would be awfully bad to keep a thing like that in the house," she says.

He goes into their bathroom, carrying the notebook and some matches. He bends over the sink, strikes the matches, and sets fire to the notebook and some, but not all, of the images of Walker's house.[11]

Later that night, unexpected visitors begin banging on their duplex door. Marina is terrified, certain it's the police. She calms down when she hears the familiar voices belonging to two of the very few people she and her husband have grown close to in Dallas. It is the De Mohrenschildts, and they have come to deliver an Easter basket to her child. Like many people in Dallas, the visitors have been reading the stunning news about Walker. As they step inside the duplex, George calls out in his loud voice:

"Lee, how is it possible that you missed?"[12]

It is a joke, of course, but she can see how her husband freezes. Lee seems to shrivel, sink in on himself. He is speechless. The pained silence in the room makes everyone uncomfortable.

At home, as his wounds heal and his security guards stay on high alert, Walker feels validated.

The fact that someone has tried to kill him in the heart of Dallas proves how right he has been—and how successful his national crusade has been. He has been stirring up the snakes around America, and now they are being revealed. He knows that some people in the media consider him a crackpot, that they don't believe his predictions about the thinly veiled menace being uncorked by the socialists and the communists.

He might have officially resigned his military command, but right now he is still a warrior—and still subject to enemy fire. He decides to issue a public warning. Maybe this time people will hear him:

"The Kennedys say there's no internal threat to our freedom. (But) there are plenty of people on the other side. You don't have to go overseas to earn a Purple Heart.

"I've been saying the front was right here at home...in Dallas."[13]

It is a glorious Easter Sunday morning, four days after the mysterious, unsolved assassination attempt on Walker. The temperatures are in the low sixties, and the carefully cultivated azaleas all over North Dallas are just beginning to bloom. It is the time of year, many residents say, when the city looks and feels its finest—the pleasant, slightly cooler month before the onslaught of the brutal, grinding heat that often begins to grip the city in May. At the downtown police station there is, all morning, a flurry of frantic incoming calls. Neo-Nazis have swept through the city during the night, vandalizing the homes of several prominent Jews with a custom-printed decal. The marauders have even located Stanley Marcus's postmodern house on Nonesuch Road. The sticker is blood red with a bold black swastika. Under the swastika are the words: WE ARE BACK.

That same night the vandals strike again. This time they sweep through downtown Dallas, targeting Jewish-owned businesses. Office workers arriving on Monday morning discover the ominous swastikas plastered on at least a dozen stores. Stanley Marcus can see it all over the glittering window displays that families in Dallas normally flock to see: The windows, filled with Easter finery and exclusive haute couture from the Parisian runways, are now covered in swastikas. Many people in the city know Marcus is a Jew. There is a precise reason people singled out the Neiman Marcus windows for swastikas.

At the police station, the cops say they have theories but no suspects. The only thing certain is that the decals are not the work of amateurs. It is clear that they have been professionally printed.

The campaign against Dallas's Jews intensifies. The next week, a desk officer at the police station receives a telephone call from a man about Temple Emanu-El—the graceful home of the city's oldest Jewish congregation, established nearly a hundred years earlier.

"Can you hear me?" the caller says. "There is a bomb in Temple Emanu-El. If you don't want a bunch of dead people, you'd better send someone out there."

Six police cars rush to the scene, where they find bright red swastikas painted on the temple. After a thorough search, no bomb is found.

While the swastikas are appearing around Dallas, the police continue to investigate the assassination attempt on Walker. Even Walker is confused by what is going on in Dallas. He is a professed super-Christian, someone who has just traveled the nation with an ultra-Christian-conservative. Is it possible that some of Walker's supporters are moving into some more aggressive stage that even he would never endorse?

Walker denies any knowledge of the actions, but tells police he "thinks there may be a tie-in" between the recent attempt on his life and the swastikas targeting the city's most prominent Jews.[14]

MAY

Publicly, Walker is blaming "the other side" for having tried to kill him. But privately, the general and his closest advisers believe that it could have been an inside job. The police check into a former Walker aide, someone Surrey has suspicions about, but the investigation goes nowhere.

For weeks, police still are telling reporters that there are no suspects in the assassination attempt. The Friends of Walker organization in Dallas offers a reward for the capture of the shooter. Walker's inner circle seems to grow tighter around him. One of the members of the group, a woman much devoted to the general, believes that the motive is jealousy. Romance, not politics:

"Many women flocked around the general [but] he did not seem to notice them," she tells the police. It was an act of unrequited love. "One of them took a shot at him."[1]

Elsewhere in the city, people are beginning to wonder if there is a bigger price being paid for Walker's presence. Things seem spiraling: An assassination attempt in one of the lavish, most secure parts of town.

And there is Walker refusing to back down—seeming emboldened, validated, by having someone in Dallas fire a gun at him.

As the city surrenders to the unforgiving heat of the summer, another force in Dallas is hammering away at Kennedy. The ex-FBI agent Dan Smoot, who had earlier helped H. L. Hunt spread his radio messages across America, is now the star of his own radio program, *The Dan Smoot Report*, heard by millions of listeners across the country. Smoot's tone is increasingly alarmist as he centers, over and over again, on the communist-Negro-Kennedy conspiracies:

"Kennedy, by Executive Orders which bypass Congress, has already created a body of 'laws' to transform our Republic into a dictatorship," argues Smoot on his broadcast and in his weekly newsletter with a Dallas dateline. His followers learn that it is a "dangerous delusion" to trust Kennedy—who "wants a socialist dictatorship" in the United States.[1]

Smoot, who is friendly with General Walker's inner circle, has also just published a book called *The Invisible Government*—which is rapidly gaining favor inside super-patriot circles and has already gone through five printings. It argues that the Council on Foreign Relations—which includes key members of John F. Kennedy's administration—is in actuality part of an elaborate plot to prepare America for socialism. On his Dallas-headquartered radio show and in his weekly newsletter, it can easily occur to many that Smoot is speaking for most of the city—or a significant portion of the people who run it.

As the summer steams ahead, President Kennedy goes on television to make an impassioned appeal for civil rights legislation. A few hours later, on June 12, in Mississippi, civil rights leader Medgar Evers is returning home from an NAACP meeting carrying T-shirts stamped JIM CROW MUST GO. As Evers walks up to his house, a sniper guns him down, murdering him right in front of his two young children.

Evers had been at the forefront of many integration actions in the South, including James Meredith's efforts to enroll in the University of Mississippi in 1962. His death sparks national outrage against violent segregationists. Even Ted Dealey's *Dallas Morning News* expresses sadness and regret for the murder, while noting: "But the blame for any hotheadedness in the South can be put, in part, on those who are trying to change a way of life too quickly."[2]

Yet in Dallas, Dan Smoot seems unmoved, even seeming to wonder why Evers had been turned into a "national hero." He argues that John F. Kennedy is plotting with the racial activists, ones no doubt like Juanita Craft and Reverend Rhett James in Dallas, to establish a socialist dictatorship ruled by Negroes. Smoot even approvingly quotes Dallas congressman Bruce Alger in his newsletter, printing Alger's claim that, under the Kennedy administration, blacks are receiving far more federal jobs than their population warrants.

As the summer heat expands and fears of violence surge, Smoot finally makes wide-open forecasts that Dallas, and the nation, will soon be drenched in blood because of the president and his insistent embrace of those "negro racial agitation groups":

"John F. Kennedy, catering to this crowd, is sowing the seeds of hate and violence: the nation will reap a bloody harvest."[3]

AUGUST

It's been a hopeful summer for Jacqueline Kennedy. America's First Lady is expecting the couple's third child in September, and she looks radiant. In recent weeks she has been taking her two young children, Caroline and John-John, to Washington-area parks, enjoying picnic lunches while the children scramble over playgrounds. Now she is comfortably settled in a waterfront home on Cape Cod, near the Kennedy family compound at Hyannis Port.

The prospect of a presidential baby is delighting many Americans. Some are hoping that she will choose to have the baby inside the White House. But other arrangements are being made: The *Dallas Morning News* runs a story pointing out that Mrs. Kennedy will go to Walter Reed Army Hospital to give birth, where she will occupy an "elegantly furnished" suite on the fourth floor. The *News* wants its readers to understand one salient fact about Mrs. Kennedy's accommodation: FIRST LADY'S HOSPITAL STAY TO BE FREE EXCEPT FOR FOOD.[1]

While his wife and the children are on Cape Cod, President Kennedy is negotiating a nuclear test ban treaty with the Soviet Union. As the agreement is reached, Kennedy goes on television to address the nation: "The achievement of this goal is not a victory for one side—it is a victory for mankind."[2] The treaty is signed in Moscow on August 5. Now the president must convince a skeptical public and Senate to embrace the treaty.

The *News* runs a bitter editorial, lambasting Kennedy as 50 TIMES A FOOL.[3] The *News*'s lead editorial writer, Dick West, asks, "Is the fear of death now the main foundation of our foreign policy? Are we to be asked, in future negotiations, to surrender some of our cherished institutions to avoid the possibility of 5 million fatalities a second?"[4]

On H. L. Hunt's *Life Line*, the very idea of coexistence with the communists has been under attack for years: "We are told by mistaken spokesmen that if we coexist peacefully for a while, communism will mellow and change...The Marxist-Leninists have dedicated themselves to the task of obliterating from the face of the earth every trace of God...So in the Cold War it is God Himself who is ultimately at stake."[5]

The *Dallas Morning News* wants everyone to understand that it's not just high-level editors opposed to the president's policy: The grassroots is angry as well. The *News* prints a "man-in-the-street" opinion poll that indicates massive resistance: "President Kennedy was censured on several occasions in the poll."[6]

Just two days after the Moscow signing, as her husband is working to build support for the test ban treaty, Jacqueline Kennedy begins feeling sharp pains in her abdomen. She is raced to Otis Air Force Base Hospital in Bourne, Massachusetts. An emergency cesarean section is performed. The premature baby boy weighs just under five pounds, and he is struggling to breathe. He is immediately transferred to Boston Children's Hospital in critical condition.

The anguished president rushes to be with his child and remains by the baby's side for two days. Finally, the boy dies from respiratory distress syndrome. The president and the First Lady had picked out a name well in advance—Patrick Bouvier Kennedy. The baby is laid to rest after a private funeral mass.

SEPTEMBER

Larrie Schmidt is inside his favorite dark watering hole, a sad run-down little place called the DuCharme Club. It's been a year since he moved to Dallas. He's on a break from pushing life insurance policies to people in the city. As he nurses his drink, he has been thinking that the bar might be a good business opportunity, maybe a place to buy, maybe a place to use as a meeting headquarters. The mission, being embedded in Dallas, trying to infiltrate and command the conservative activist groups, is proving harder than he imagined. It's certainly not helping his marriage having to juggle a job and trying to make Dallas his base of operations for his master plan. He is hearing less and less from the soldiers in Munich who were once so gung-ho to join him, to enlist in the cause, to fight for the same thing that General Walker believed in. He had expected at least one soldier, one ally, to join him each month that he was in Dallas. But by now, Schmidt knows that not many—if any—are coming. Even if Dallas is the right place, perhaps the only place in America, to start the revolution.

As Schmidt drinks another beer, he takes solace in the fact that his brother Bob has moved to Dallas and is joining the right-wing army.

Sometimes, Schmidt must wonder if he has been inadvertently outflanked by the conservative elite in Dallas. There is still a chain of command inside the inner circles. There are layers and then layers. Cracking through the layers is easier said than done. It is almost as if he is being tested.

After his exhilarating meeting at Robert Morris's home, he perhaps felt that he had seduced the leading newspaper, the police, and even Morris—the liaison to the most powerful and wealthy conservatives in the city. At his apartment, after the meeting, Schmidt had quickly told his friends in Germany that he had agreed with Morris's plan to form a Young Americans for Freedom chapter in

Dallas—and by agreeing to join it, Schmidt and his friends would have the perfect organization to begin their master plan to seize control of the conservative revolution in America.

But later, Schmidt was in touch with the men from the *Dallas Morning News* who were the nominal heads of the chapter—and they told Schmidt that he and his followers would be required to pay $60 "founders" dues to the Dallas YAF.

It was a steep entry fee for military men making less than $100 per month in the army. Schmidt sent letters to his friends still stationed in Germany telling them that they should still come to Dallas. That once they set up a base of operations, they would soon be making far more income as members of the YAF executive board.

Only one soldier in Germany, Larry Jones, wrote back to express his complete faith in Schmidt. After his discharge over the summer, Jones made the journey to Dallas, lured by Schmidt's promises of big money and major influence.

What he found instead was Schmidt living in a cheap apartment and spending most of his spare time drinking beer at the DuCharme. Among the DuCharme's main charms, perhaps its only charm, was that it sold beer on credit—a practice that Schmidt took frequent advantage of.

As he settled into Dallas, Jones learned that there were no salaries for being board members of the YAF, so he took a job selling used cars. For a time, he listened patiently as Schmidt sat on a bar stool at the DuCharme, suggesting they pool their money, buy the place, and hire some Arthur Murray dance instructors to be hostesses. The ladies could hustle drinks and bring in new customers. They approached a few women about the idea, but each was supremely uninterested. After a few weeks, Jones simply slipped out of the city.

Schmidt is down to one remaining soldier: Bernie Weissman, a Jew from the Bronx. After he was discharged in August, Weissman returned to New York City and found work selling encyclopedias. Schmidt has been pleading with Weissman, regaling him with tales of all the money he is making in Dallas. Schmidt claims to be averaging $342 a week on commissions, a salary nearly four times the national average.

He writes Weissman: "We shall be able to find employment for you with excellent economic opportunities. We have powerful contacts and allies down here."[1]

One day, he clips some help wanted ads from the *Dallas Morning News* and sends them with his next letter to Weissman:

"I have a lot of contacts, both professionally and in business and politics. I know bankers, insurance men, realtors."[2]

As the one-year anniversary of his arrival in Dallas approaches, Schmidt finally dreams that he is coming closer to the top ranks—to meeting with Dealey, with Criswell, and especially with H. L. Hunt. The reclusive oilman is the one man in America who can instantly bankroll the new patriotic revolution.

Schmidt has met with a former CIA operative in Dallas who writes scripts for H. L. Hunt's *Life Line* radio program. Schmidt knows that the ex-CIA officer, Warren Carroll, is being paid the princely sum of $700 per week by Hunt. It is what Schmidt dreams of—earning excellent money for being a patriot.

And, perhaps just as good as this entrée to Hunt, his brother has worked hard to infiltrate the ranks of the young men who are at the heart of General Walker's circle in Dallas. Bob has been volunteering, showing up at Walker's home. One day he boldly asks Walker for a job.

Schmidt receives the excellent news: His brother has been hired to work full-time for Walker as his chauffeur.

Suddenly, low-level insurance man Schmidt thinks he has solid connections to both Hunt and Walker, that he is beginning to seriously infiltrate the Dallas far right. Now that he has connections, he needs more men, and he needs an action plan.

Each time his plane touches down at Dallas's Love Field, Stanley Marcus feels like he is an ambassador returning home—and that he is, in fact, bringing the United Nations straight to a city in the Texas heartland.

As his driver leaves the airport, Marcus can see the tall downtown buildings jutting up like spires on the pancake-flat prairie. His store is in the dead center of it all. He knows his famous emporium is the most visible symbol of globalism in the city.

He has funded major art exhibitions and cultivated his customers' tastes for the finest things from Europe and Asia. And through his Dallas Council on World Affairs, Marcus has arranged the visits of hundreds of foreign dignitaries over the last ten years. Inarguably, he is the city's most prominent internationalist—and the one high-profile figure in the city who fears his home is too often consumed by xenophobia.

Marcus is a world traveler, and he serves on a prominent national committee in support of the United Nations. He is the state chair for the United Nations Day Committee in Texas. One of his highest-ranking employees is president of the Dallas United Nations Association. Marcus is a fierce admirer of Adlai Stevenson, the cerebral U.S. ambassador to the United Nations.

At Neiman Marcus, he has also created an extravagant October festival devoted to the world's cultures. Known as the "Fortnight," the two-week exposition highlights a particular country or region chosen specifically by Marcus. He carefully orchestrates the festival so that museums feature artists from the chosen countries, theaters stage just the right plays, and civic organizations host timely lectures. Marcus convinces foreign governments and his suppliers to underwrite the costs—by pointing out how new markets are being created for their products.

During the Fortnight festival the store remakes itself, immersing customers in a nod to a featured country. National magazines, like *Time*, gush when Marcus turns his attention to France: "From top to bottom the six-story building was like a Gallic birthday cake. The exterior became a reproduction of chic Paris shops. Inside, the first floor was transformed into a three-dimensional scene of the Place de la Concorde." Even the store's restaurant, the Zodiac, is converted into a facsimile of Paris's famous Maxim's restaurant.[3]

Ambassadors and royalty will descend on Dallas for the grand opening of the Fortnight. The ribbon-cutting ceremonies take place at the front door of Neiman Marcus, with a beaming Stanley Marcus shaking hands, posing for pictures, and welcoming high-profile visitors and a parade of eager customers.

He is a showman, really, someone who has learned to appeal to Dallas's vanities—but he is convinced this mercantile angling is also nourishing Dallas's soul, making the city realize that the things from the outside, from the other worlds, are not so threatening. It is enlightened self-interest—it is good for Marcus and it is good for Dallas. He is gifted with enormous profits and the city, in turn, is made more hospitable, more open, more tolerant. In the end, if it helps to tamp down the wicked extremism—the swastikas, the cross burnings, the almost knee-jerk hatred of Dr. King and President Kennedy and the United Nations—it is all good for the city.

He has to be cheered by this fact: The store always posts record sales during these salutes to "foreign culture." People are spending money, to be sure, but perhaps they are also immunizing themselves and the city against the bilious xenophobia.

It is no coincidence that he plans this year's extravaganza to overlap with the annual commemoration of United Nations Day. October 24 recognizes the founding of the international body in 1948. Despite the anti–United Nations resistance emanating from the *Dallas Morning News*, Alger, Walker, Criswell, and Hunt, many people in Dallas have been early and enthusiastic adopters of UN Day—and for years several civic organizations have tried to highlight UN contributions to world peace. Marcus tells people to remember World War II. To think of the United Nations as a bulwark for peace: "The best tool that I know of to prevent an outbreak of World War III."[4]

It has been, thinks Marcus, a pivotal year for Dallas. Dr. King, the man who dreamed of a peaceful and united America, finally came to the city, and he survived his visit without any violence, with the protesters drowned out by the warm embrace of thousands of black and white residents joining together.

The lunatics who tried to kill Walker, who planted swastikas on Neiman Marcus window fronts, had to be just a tiny, seething, foaming minority. Marcus is an optimist, someone who hopes for the best, who assumes that the collective goodwill in the city will rule the day—and that most of the people in Dallas will never let it be hijacked by the bursting anger of men like Walker.

And he is also pleased at the way his ambitious international marketing campaign for Dallas is going. It is a place that he wants people to come to—not just from New York, Washington, Los Angeles, and Chicago, but from London, Madrid, Rome, and Paris. He wants people to think of Dallas as a top-tier city that has artfully blended its history with its promising future:

"A jet-age city with old-fashioned Southwestern hospitality and charm."[5]

Bruce Alger has decided to write a confrontational two-page letter to John F. Kennedy—and then share it with the world. Maybe this last-ditch effort to publicize his extreme hostility toward Kennedy will help him survive in Dallas:

"Kennedy is operating as chief executive without regard to the rule of law and is, indeed, substituting his own judgment and will for the exercise of the constitutional powers by the Congress and the people. He does not trust the people to handle their own affairs, but rather believes in his own infallibility to do all things for them, using, of course, their money."[6]

After three black men are promoted to supervisory positions in city post offices—in the wake of a Kennedy decree pushing for equal employment and promotion opportunities—Alger demands a congressional probe.[7] When an NAACP leader from Dallas comes to visit him in Washington, pleading for Alger to support President Kennedy's civil rights bill, Alger bluntly refuses. He tells the man that the NAACP is helping clergymen incite Negroes into rioting and lawlessness—and it is cleverly staging demonstrations that will surely lead to chaos and violence.[8] Alger knows full well that his powerful rebuke of the NAACP will play well in Dallas—especially for those who have been afraid of Dr. King, Rhett James, and Juanita Craft.

Finally, Alger has decided to launch his public letter at Kennedy. He wants Kennedy to read, and read closely, along with everyone else in Dallas:

The audience reacts to denunciations of the Kennedy administration during a meeting of Dallas's National Indignation Convention. *Photograph by Shel Hershorn. Briscoe Center for American History, University of Texas at Austin.*

Dallas Mayor Earle Cabell, left, welcomes General Edwin Walker to Dallas with an official proclamation and a cowboy hat. Many ultra-conservatives viewed Walker as America's "man on horseback" who could defeat Kennedy. *Photograph by Shel Hershorn. Briscoe Center for American History, University of Texas at Austin.*

Kennedy and *Dallas Morning News* publisher Ted Dealey (seated two places to JFK's left) regard each other during this luncheon hosted by the president for Texas publishers. Dealey's raucous confrontation with JFK in the White House drew national attention – and reprisals from Kennedy's team. *Photograph by Abbie Rowe. White House Photographs. John F. Kennedy Presidential Library and Museum.*

Supporters greet General Edwin Walker at Dallas's Love Field after his release from a federal psychiatric prison, where he'd been confined by the Kennedy administration after leading the pro-segregationist riot at Ole Miss when James Meredith tried to register for classes. *Photograph by Joe Laird, Dallas Morning News.*

Rhett James brings Martin Luther King to Dallas in 1963 for a rally against the poll tax. Left to right: the Reverend Rhett James, Rabbi Levi Olan, J. A. Stanfield, and Dr. King. *Photograph by Marion Butts. Texas/Dallas History and Archives Division, Dallas Public Library.*

Lee Harvey Oswald in Dallas. *Photograph by Shel Hershorn. Briscoe Center for American History, University of Texas at Austin.*

Adlai Stevenson, ambassador to the United Nations, being assailed by angry protesters in the weeks before President Kennedy's arrival in Dallas. *Courtesy of Wes Wise.*

WANTED

FOR

TREASON

THIS MAN is wanted for treasonous activities against the United States:

1. Betraying the Constitution (which he swore to uphold):
He is turning the sovereignty of the U.S. over to the communist controlled United Nations.
He is betraying our friends (Cuba, Katanga, Portugal) and befriending our enemies (Russia, Yugoslavia, Poland).
2. He has been WRONG on innumerable issues affecting the security of the U.S. (United Nations-Berlin wall-Missle removal-Cuba-Wheat deals-Test Ban Treaty, etc.)
3. He has been lax in enforcing Communist Registration laws.
4. He has given support and encouragement to the Communist inspired racial riots.
5. He has illegally invaded a sovereign State with federal troops.
6. He has consistently appointed Anti-Christians to Federal office: Upholds the Supreme Court in its Anti-Christian rulings.
Aliens and known Communists abound in Federal offices.
7. He has been caught in fantastic LIES to the American people (including personal ones like his previous marraige and divorce).

WANTED FOR TREASON flyer. *(public domain) Sixth Floor Museum at Dealey Plaza, Dallas.*

John F. Kennedy and Jacqueline Kennedy arrive at Love Field, November 22, 1963. *Photograph by Clint Grant. Texas/Dallas History and Archives Division, Dallas Public Library.*

"Is Dallas being punished because the people have elected me their representative? Do you deny me the right to criticize your policies, when, in my best judgment they are wrong?"

After his demands for answers, Alger says that he would like to meet Kennedy—soon, and man-to-man.[9]

It is hard to ignore John Birch Society billboards peppering the city: U.S. OUT OF THE U.N. And now the Texas legislature has even taken up a bill to outlaw the display of the United Nations flag or seal on any building funded with tax dollars. The proposal would effectively negate UN Day in Texas—and violators could be sent to a Texas prison for two years.

The *Dallas Morning News* gave a brassy endorsement to the bill, and all nine Dallas-area state representatives voted to support the ban on United Nations Day. The anti-UN bill sailed through the state Senate and seemed destined for certain passage in the House until one lawmaker rose to his feet and condemned it as: "Another attempt to appease the lunatic fringe which contaminates our public life and which holds that patriotism is not the quiet dedication of a lifetime but is frequent outbursts of emotionalism."[10]

City officials are still bitter at the defeat. Congressman Alger describes the UN in his newsletter as "The Soviet's greatest hoax," and warns that the United States would be committing "suicide" by remaining in the organization.[11]

Alger even flirts with the idea of introducing a congressional resolution demanding that the U.S. flag be flown at half-mast on UN Day.

The United Nations is a favorite target of H. L. Hunt's tax-exempt *Life Line* program: "Most Americans who think about the matter must surely by now have reached the reasoned conclusion that the United Nations has turned into a monstrous threat to the interests of the United States."[12]

Dan Smoot, the former FBI agent and Hunt employee in Dallas who writes and broadcasts some of the most virulent anti-Kennedy attacks in the nation, warns that the UN and communism have the exact same objective: "Creation of a world socialist system."[13]

He is unafraid to pin it all on one person—President Kennedy. "If Kennedy stays in power...the drive toward world government will quicken disastrously," Smoot tells his faithful followers. "The nation may not last long enough...unless something is done in 1964 to halt the Kennedy program."[14]

General Walker is also ratcheting up his rhetoric to a new level. The time has come, he announces, to choose between the United Nations and the United States. He prophesies that the issue will be the most important in the 1964 elections.

As Stanley Marcus contemplates matters in his office, sifting through all the reports about that same powerful minority—the barely concealed allegiances connecting the leading newspaper, the leading preacher, the congressman, the former general, and the oilmen—he begins forming a plan: *Why not try to inject Dallas with a wonderful dose of logic—why not bring the very face of American internationalism straight to the heart of Dallas and show how forward-looking the city can be?*

Marcus decides to use his Washington connections to reach out to U.S. Ambassador to the United Nations Adlai E. Stevenson and personally invite him to offer a major speech in Dallas—and to prove, once and for all, that the Kennedy administration is not selling out the nation to communists, not surrendering America to some socialist conspiracy.

Stevenson will offer his erudite logic and calm. And Dallas will hopefully extend its hand.

The morning is dawning warm and humid as Walker lights his first cigarette of the day and reaches for the *Dallas Morning News*. There hasn't been much to cheer him lately as he nears the one-year anniversary of his arrest in Mississippi.

His pro-white states' rights crusade was dealt a major blow nine days earlier with the bombing of a Negro church in Birmingham, Alabama, that killed four young girls. As outrage spreads across the country, segregationists are on the defensive. President Kennedy is now meeting openly with Negro leaders and talking about sending federal troops to Birmingham.

Earlier in the week, Kennedy even went before the United

Nations Assembly and, incredibly to Walker, *apologized* for the United States' race relations: "We share your regret and resentment," the president told the foreign hordes. "We intend to end such practices for all time to come."[15]

Walker is livid that a U.S. president would demonstrate weakness before the entire world. *Soviet Russia is systematically destroying the liberty of millions of people, and Kennedy is apologizing for a few blemishes on the United States' record?*

The front page of the *Morning News* confirms his worst fears about the president. The top headline announces that the U.S. Senate has passed JFK's Nuclear Test Ban Treaty with the Soviet Union. It is a major victory for Kennedy—and the Russians. But the local newspaper, at least, is resisting Kennedy's "Moscow Treaty"—pointing out that the American public is being hoodwinked by pro-communist propaganda, including "the much exaggerated fear of atomic fallout."[16]

Walker glances at the letters to the editor. He is often mentioned, praised, by letter writers. Today, September 25, he is pleased to see a letter complimenting the *News*'s editorial staff and another criticizing the leftist-liberal Kennedy administration for appeasing the Reds.

When he reaches the local news section, there is a large advertisement. The bottom half of the page is dominated by a drawing of a dark night sky, full of stars. White lines between the stars trace out the constellations, but these are not the traditional images of the Big Dipper and Orion. Instead, the lines converge to form images of shoes, glamorous, high-heeled women's shoes. The ad reads:

"It is written in the stars, most beautiful is she who lithely glides in a Neiman-Marcus evening shoe."

There is also a smaller news item tucked in between accounts of a freeway crash and a garbage collectors' strike. The headline reads: U.N. WEEK: ADLAI PLANS DALLAS TALK ON OCT. 24.

The story announces that the U.S. ambassador to the United Nations, Adlai Stevenson, is officially coming to Dallas—and he has been invited by Stanley Marcus and the other Jewish leaders at his store.

Walker knows why Stevenson is coming to Dallas. He is not

just the former governor of Illinois and a two-time candidate for the presidency. He is the country's leading proponent of the UN. General Walker is the top-ranking patriot opposed to the United Nations. Stevenson's visit to Dallas represents nothing less than a direct challenge to him.

Walker convenes a strategy meeting with Robert Surrey and his other closest aides at his headquarters on Turtle Creek Boulevard.

Someone mentions that October 23, the day prior to Stevenson's visit, is officially designated "United States Day."

This annual tribute to the United States had been established by conservatives ten years earlier as a rebuke to UN Day, but the holiday hadn't really taken off. With Stevenson confronting Walker in Dallas on UN Day, however, the juxtaposition couldn't be any clearer. Walker tells his team that they will commandeer U.S. Day.

Alger tried to upstage a Johnson campaign visit to Dallas in November 1960—and the damned plan had horribly backfired. Maybe Walker and his allies can waylay Stevenson's pro-Kennedy, pro–United Nations foray into Dallas. Maybe they can generate, the day before, a big-time patriotic event that will steal the thunder from the Kennedy administration. The pieces begin falling into place quickly.

Stevenson's speech will be inside the Dallas Memorial Auditorium, and Surrey quickly makes his own call to the auditorium and arranges to rent the building for the exact evening before Stevenson's event.

Calls are also made down to Austin and to Texas Governor John Connally—maybe he can issue a proclamation declaring October 23 as "United States Day" in Texas.

In Dallas, bumper stickers are being crafted to read: U.S. DAY OR UN DAY—THERE MUST BE A CHOICE. YOU CANNOT RIDE BOTH HORSES.[17]

Kennedy aides have summoned Bob Baskin, the Washington bureau chief of the *Dallas Morning News*. They are in Jackson Hole, Wyoming, where Baskin has been following President Kennedy on an eleven-state tour around the nation—and this Wednesday night, some White House aides are giving him exclusive confirmation that the president is finally scheduling a trip in the near future to Texas.

Kennedy will visit several Texas cities, and his itinerary will include Dallas on November 22. Baskin knows he has a nice newspaper coup, and as he pounds the keys on his typewriter he makes sure that he notes, in his first sentence, that he is the only one to break the news.

Despite the still-icy relationship in the wake of publisher Ted Dealey's verbal confrontation with Kennedy at the White House, Kennedy's team knows that the *Morning News* remains the bellwether publication in the state. Giving the Dallas newspaper the exclusive news represents a mild overture, a chance to perhaps try to sway the tone of coverage inside Dealey's pages.

Baskin suspects that Kennedy is visiting Texas to shore up the Democratic Party's machinery, which is becoming increasingly fractured between liberals and conservatives. His instincts tell him that Kennedy will try to make sure that his coming reelection campaign will not be derailed by intra-party squabbles.

Dallas is a place, perhaps, where some stalwarts of the Democratic Party can be pressured into giving ground under the threats from the right-wing extremists. Kennedy is coming to Dallas, Baskin speculates, to try to stem the tide. First Stevenson will come—to confront the right wing in the heart of Dallas. Then Kennedy will come—and do the same damned thing. It is clearly a coordinated campaign.

As he finishes typing up his story, Baskin decides to weave in some carefully culled snippets from a speech the president has just given in Montana about how he wants to reason—and negotiate— with the enemies of the United States—specifically communism and the Soviet Union.

"What we hope to do is lessen the chance of a military collision between these two great powers, which together have the power to kill 300 million people in a day."[18]

This part of Kennedy's speech is sure to draw ire from the right.

OCTOBER

In many ways, Bruce Alger's political career remains defined by the searing moment out on the streets of Dallas in November 1960—when the world saw startling images of petite Lady Bird Johnson, her face twisted in fear and then anger, as the mink coat mob swirled around her, some spitting and pushing and screaming. Alger might have believed that the circumspect elders always resented him for it—that, even as much as they wanted LBJ, Lady Bird, and Kennedy assailed, it was never going to help the city's image.

And now reporters are asking questions: *What is waiting for John F. Kennedy, this time, in Dallas? What will Alger do when President Kennedy's motorcade passes through the downtown streets?*

Alger agrees to an interview with Dealey's *Dallas Morning News*. He is careful with his answers. It is a choice opportunity to salvage his conservative mettle. The interview is with Bob Baskin. Alger says he is speaking for his people in Dallas: "We should welcome him if he's prepared to answer questions and get away from pious platitudes. He owes us that courtesy."

Baskin decides that he will round out his story by interviewing Joe Pool, a conservative Democrat and congressman-at-large from the Dallas area. Pool is a savvy politician, someone who knows, perhaps better than Alger, how the men atop the Dallas Citizens Council treasure a somber, subdued discretion—and are repulsed by anything that erodes an iota of fiscal confidence in Dallas. Pool grew up in the areas of Dallas that are now undergoing white flight. And he went to the all-white Southern Methodist University law school. When he speaks to the *Dallas Morning News* about what will happen to the president of the United States in Dallas, it is as if he is actually talking directly to Bruce Alger—and, by extension, to all the men in Dallas who have openly opposed Kennedy.

"While I disagree with the Kennedy Administration on much

legislation, I feel that he is president of the United States and believe that the people of Texas will extend to him a courteous reception.

"I am sure that he will not have any discourteous demonstrations, such as occurred in Dallas in 1960 during a visit of our vice president, Lyndon B. Johnson, and his wife.

"Everyone, both Democrats and Republicans, regrets the 1960 incident, and I for one am hopeful that his visit will receive a typical Texas welcome."[1]

Larrie Schmidt is busy making plans for the upcoming visits. He writes to his friend Bernard Weissman in New York:

"There are to be protests. All the big things are happening now—if we don't get in right now we may as well forget it...The opening is here—all we need to do is pick up the ball and run like hell."[2]

Schmidt contacts Dealey's editorial writer for the *Dallas Morning News*—who is president of the local Young Americans for Freedom chapter. Schmidt's idea is simple: *Let's organize the Young Americans for Freedom to picket Stevenson's appearance.*

He is told no. The YAF, given its direct affiliation with the *Morning News*, wants to steer clear of any street protests. Disgusted, Schmidt abruptly resigns from the organization. It's a dicey game, turning his back on Dealey and his powerful newspaper. But Schmidt knows this chance will never come again—to take direct action against Stevenson and maybe Kennedy. He talks to his brother, the chauffeur for Walker. He contacts the John Birch Society. Surely he can drum up some ideas, money, support for some anti-Stevenson, anti-Kennedy operations.

He also writes to Weissman:

"Watch your newspaper for news of huge demonstrations here in Dallas on Oct 23 and 24 in connection with UN Day and Adlai Stevenson's speech here. Plans already made, strategy being carried out."[3]

General Edwin Walker is scanning the front-page stories touting Adlai Stevenson's upcoming visit. He is irritated. The communists are receiving free publicity, but his own U.S. Day rally is all but ignored.

The local CBS television affiliate announces that Stevenson's speech will be broadcast live. No such provision is made for Walker. The general's aides have been whispering that they might not fill the auditorium. An extensive word-of-mouth campaign is launched. Walker's aide Robert Surrey has designed and printed hundreds of flyers and yard signs: U.S. OR U.N. IN 1964. Advertisements appear in the *Dallas Morning News*: U.S. DAY RALLY! the black-bordered ads read. US OR UN? YOU CAN'T STRADDLE THIS!

Rumors are spreading across Dallas that hundreds of picket signs are stashed at Walker's headquarters. Neiman Marcus executives are worried, and they call Dallas Police Chief Jesse Curry to inquire about protection for Stevenson. The chief assures them there will be no danger.

The *Dallas Times Herald* runs an editorial cartoon crystallizing the anxiety: In it, Stevenson is carrying a suitcase marked DALLAS. Standing with him is Lyndon B. Johnson, survivor of Dallas's mink coat mob in 1960. LBJ has a reassuring hand on Adlai's shoulder, telling him: "Be brave."

A welcoming committee steps into position as the 990 Astrojet arrives from Chicago on October 23. A diminutive woman in a sweeping, Vietnamese-style dress emerges from the plane, and cheers ring out.

Dallas is not on the official itinerary of Mrs. Ngo Dinh Nhu, the vainglorious "First Lady" of South Vietnam. She is scheduled to simply change planes at Love Field and continue on her American tour. But Madame Nhu has heard about the great American patriots in Dallas, and she is intrigued. She has also heard about something even more exciting: Neiman Marcus. She orders a brief layover in Dallas.

General Walker and dozens of his followers are waiting to greet her. At the head of the large Dallas delegation is fifteen-year-old Karen Surrey, the daughter of General Walker's closest aide.

Surrey steps forward and announces that she is representing General Walker's U.S. Day Committee in Dallas. She presents Madame Nhu with a dozen red roses and two small American flags, telling her they are for "a very brave and courageous lady."[4]

Madame Nhu is on a worldwide tour insisting that Vietnam is winning the war against the communists. Her troops, however, have ignited international outrage for their attacks on Buddhist temples. Monks have committed ritual suicide by immolating themselves on city streets. She dismisses the suicides as "Buddhist barbecues."

"If the Buddhists wish to have another barbecue, I will be glad to supply the gasoline and a match," she announces.[5]

President Kennedy has refused to meet her; he is planning to cut aid to her government, and rumors are swirling the CIA is plotting a coup to topple her husband's regime.

Madame Nhu calls Kennedy an appeaser and says that his plans to cut aid to her government are "treason." She wonders why "all the people around President Kennedy are pink?"[6]

Her edgy comments have ostracized her in Washington. But Walker and his comrades are eager to embrace her—especially on a day when Walker is scheduled to blast Kennedy during his U.S. Day speech.

As Madame Nhu greets her admirers, more cheers ring out. Her security chief beams at the crowd and tells a *Dallas Morning News* reporter that the reception in Dallas is the warmest they have received in America.

Fifteen minutes later Madame Nhu arrives at Neiman Marcus, attended by a large entourage, including the Surrey family. It is not quite what she expected. Stanley Marcus has tricked the store out to look like some idealized postcard from Switzerland. The group walks under the display of Swiss flags and approaches the grand replica of Bern's clock, towering over the main entrance. They stare at Father Time, who is attended by a crowing rooster, a group of bears marching in a circle, and a surreal jester clanging a bell. Inside, the elevator doors resemble entranceways to Swiss chalets. There are mountains of fake snow, big Swiss clocks, and even a faux ski lift.

Madame Nhu ignores the reporters and the spreading crowd gawking at her. She focuses on shopping. She picks up a man's shirt and turns to a saleswoman:

"Is this American?" she asks pointedly. "I do not want any-thing foreign."[7]

As Madame Nhu flies away and twilight descends over Dallas, the main event for U.S. Day begins.

Hundreds of people file into the Memorial Auditorium for Walker's rally. Even though it is late October, the heat hasn't bro-ken. Dallas is still waiting for its first cool front of the fall.

Inside, the auditorium is filling up with John Birchers, Minute-men, Young Americans for Freedom, the National States Rights Party. Also in attendance is the former chairman of the now defunct National Indignation Convention, Frank McGehee, as well as Larrie Schmidt, along with his brother, who is still working as Walker's chauffeur.

And still another man is present—he has come by himself.

After being fired from his job, after failing to murder General Walker at his home, Lee Harvey Oswald decided to move to New Orleans, hoping that city would be more receptive to his pro-Cuba, pro-Castro politics. Marina joined him for a while but even-tually returned to Dallas without him. Things in New Orleans spiraled quickly downward for Oswald. There were run-ins with the police—and he found virtually no support for his cause. New Orleans was, in many ways, a miserable experience punctuated with moments of paranoia, loneliness, and a simmering anger at the lack of support for his pro-Cuba agenda.

Now he is back in Dallas.

Walker is still alive. He wouldn't be holding this rally, giving this speech, if Oswald had altered his shot by just a fraction of an inch—if his bullet hadn't hit the wood on the windowpane.

Oswald, dressed in jeans and a white T-shirt, wants to look casual. He blends in perfectly. He finds a seat and watches as people tote huge American and Dixie flags into the auditorium.

General Walker is fidgeting nervously, chain-smoking as he waits for the program to begin. He looks out into the auditorium and sees that many of the seats are filling up—some twelve hundred people in all. It is not a capacity crowd, but respectable nonetheless.

Once everyone assembles, the event begins with the reading of supportive telegrams from patriots in Dallas—Bruce Alger, Hunt's former employee, the ex–FBI agent Dan Smoot, and former University of Dallas President Robert Morris, a close friend of Ted Dealey.

Walker steps to the microphone. Oswald listens to the man he tried to kill five months ago:

"The main battleground in the world today is right here in America, and it involves the United States versus the United Nations."[8]

Pausing to look out at the crowd, his voice acid with contempt, he adds:

"Adlai's going to sell his hogwash, and here's who is sponsoring him in Dallas."[9]

Walker reads a long blacklist, stopping after each name to allow the audience to scream condemnations: the Boy Scouts of America, the YMCA, the League of Women Voters, the Kiwanis Clubs, the Optimists Clubs, and the Rotary Clubs...groups like the ones in Dallas where the castrated Holocaust survivor Jack Oran had gone to speak against hatred.

Walker marches on, name checking churches, temples, even the generally conservative and virtually segregated Southern Methodist University. On and on Walker reads, until at last he finishes indicting what he says are sixty-one anti–U.S. organizations in Dallas.

Then he turns his attention to national figures—Kennedy, Eisenhower, Roosevelt, Truman, the CIA, Nixon, the State Department—and efforts by men like Rhett James, the black Dallas preacher, to repeal the poll tax.

But most of his ire is saved for the United Nations:

"I'll tell you who started the UN," he shouts into his microphone. "It was the communists..."[10]

Walker is interrupted, time and again, by cheers. The huge flags undulate over the crowd. Adlai Stevenson will be appearing on the very same stage in twenty-four hours. Speaking into the very same microphone and gazing out over the same auditorium. It is like the parallel universes of Dallas are bumping up against each other.

"Tonight we stand on a battleground...the symbol of our sovereignty," Walker roars.

"Tomorrow night there will stand here a symbol to the communist conspiracy."[11]

Before he steps away from the microphone, Walker asks the crowd: *Which side will Dallas choose?*

Stanley Marcus's executive vice president is standing on the tarmac at Love Field, where President Kennedy will land in a few weeks. The morning sun is bright and warm as the flight from New York arrives. The Neiman Marcus executive is relieved to see no protesters or picket signs, just a small welcoming group and a handful of reporters. Marcus sent observers to monitor General Walker's U.S. Day rally the evening before, and they came back spooked.

After Adlai Stevenson's plane lands, he walks down the ramp a bit stiffly. He seems older and more frail than in photos. Reporters begin shouting questions:

"Are you expecting a friendly crowd at your speech tonight?"

Stevenson smiles. He knows that the night before, the rogue General Walker had held an anti–United Nations, anti–Kennedy administration rally in Dallas.

"I don't know why not," he replies to the reporter.

Marcus has arranged a limousine for Stevenson, and it takes him to the Sheraton. After checking into the Presidential Suite, Stevenson meets with Marcus—who has sponsored a formal luncheon in the ambassador's honor. Dozens of Marcus's friends in the business sector or local government are in attendance. The group has been carefully screened.

Stevenson receives polite applause and an honorary Texas cowboy hat. Stevenson turns to Marcus: "Having been through Texas several times in my campaigns, I have about sixty-five Texas hats."

Stevenson makes a show of inspecting the hat closely. "But of all of them, this is the best one." He puts the hat on and the room breaks out in cheers.[12]

Stevenson takes friendly questions from the audience as lunch is served. Outside, a small plane is flying over Dallas, methodically zigzagging its way across the city. A large banner tails behind the plane, proclaiming, GET US OUT OF UN.

After the luncheon, Stevenson tours Neiman Marcus, visits the Dallas Press Club to talk to newsmen, and then makes his way to an elevator crowded with a dozen people.

Stevenson is beginning to think that all the stories he's been hearing about Dallas's hostility are gross exaggerations.

As he steps out of the elevator, he hears a derisive voice calling after him: "What the hell's the United Nations for, anyway?"[13]

Marcus's people send a security man back to the police chief to ask for even more protection tonight. Again, the chief assures them that everything will be fine. The police will have everything under control.

Larrie Schmidt is among the very first to arrive at the Dallas Memorial Auditorium, and he has brought company. He used his contacts to roust a small platoon of sign-wielding college students—and now they are striding into the auditorium and setting up a picket line in the lobby.

Marching together, they wave signs: ADLAI, WHO ELECTED YOU? They chant, "GET THE U.S. OUT OF THE UN."

The students are smartly attired in sport coats and ties. Schmidt had insisted on the dress code: "I wanted to show people the difference between conservative pickets and leftist beatniks."[14]

Anxious contingents of UN supporters mix uneasily with Schmidt and pro-Walker supporters. More protest signs are bobbing overhead, and some people are carrying Confederate flags, rattling Halloween noisemakers and shouting as they pour inside.

A man in an Uncle Sam suit is waving an American flag and shouting that the UN is for communist race mixers—he is Bobby Joiner, an infamous Dallas-area segregationist who is running for the state legislature under the banner of the "Indignant White Citizens Council."

As people jostle through the lobby and toward the auditorium, a man suddenly confronts Schmidt's line of well-dressed college-aged protesters. He begins screaming, calling them "Nazis." The man tries to grab a picket sign. Several people push in and for a moment it looks like a fight, or even a riot, might break out.

It is precisely what Larrie Schmidt is hoping for. The shouting man is one of his own people. Schmidt had planned the political theater to make his groomed group look like martyrs. He wants news to emerge that pro–United Nations goons are bullying his peaceful, reasonable picketers in Dallas.

Seats are filling quickly. Walker's supporters are waving their placards and blocking the views of those sitting behind them. More insults are shouted back and forth. Fistfights are even breaking out as emotions boil over. Dallas police are still nowhere to be seen.

Finally, about fifteen minutes before the program is scheduled to begin, cops begin arriving. They break up a couple of fights and take up stations around the arena, looking on grimly. There are now almost two thousand people inside the auditorium.

In North Dallas, Walker is finishing a fine meal at a friend's house. The men retreat to the living room. Walker is leaning in close to the television for the live broadcast of the Stevenson speech. Walker knows enough, after being arrested by Kennedy's people in Mississippi, to stay away from the affair. *Who knows what Kennedy's people would do to him if he showed up in person to challenge their damned United Nations ambassador?*

Above the stage hangs a large banner: WELCOME ADLAI.

The sign had been a curiosity. It was there when the auditorium crew arrived earlier that afternoon. They weren't sure how that had happened, but they left it in place.

From his chair on the stage, looking out at the restive crowd, Stanley Marcus is beginning to realize that the confrontation Stevenson has been avoiding all day is finally arriving…and Marcus is stunned by its scope. It isn't supposed to be this way. He had thought that the arrival of a reasonable, well-spoken man would placate the extremists in Dallas—possibly even win them over. It was, really, the same thing that Rhett James had thought when he invited Dr. Martin Luther King Jr. to Dallas. That having these men in the city, that hearing them, the hard-edged people would be forced to retreat, to surrender to the collective goodwill of the city.

Marcus's role is to introduce Stevenson, but as he walks to the podium a cacophony of boos and catcalls rains down on him. Positioned directly behind him is the official flag of the United Nations. Marcus, who has set the style for Dallas for so long, feels waves of hatred washing over him.

He has not prepared any formal remarks. As he stands under the hot spotlight, sweating and facing an angry crowd, words suddenly flee. He is usually able to spin a gossamer speech at any given moment, but now he is adrift. Visibly rattled, he limps through an abbreviated, halting introduction—punctuated by jeers. He takes a seat on stage, pulls out a handkerchief, and wipes sweat from his brow.

Stevenson acknowledges the cheers and ignores the snaking hisses that echo in the cavernous hall.

Suddenly a large, bulky man near the front row rises from his seat.

"Mr. Ambassador, I have a question for you!" shouts Frank McGehee, the Dallas founder of the National Indignation Convention.

Stevenson ignores him and begins his speech, but McGehee keeps shouting, raising his voice in defiance. Now he is asking why Stevenson insists on negotiating with communist dictators.

Stevenson finally stares down at him and says in a dry voice: "I'll be delighted to give you equal time after I have finished."

As cops move toward him, McGehee keeps shouting.

A small, elderly Dallas schoolteacher is sitting near McGehee—and he stands up and tries to push the larger man back into his seat.

McGehee wrestles the man. The cops finally arrive and grab him by the arms as he tries to twist away.

"Surely my dear friend," Stevenson says loudly, "I don't have to come here from Illinois to teach Texas manners, do I?"

A roar of approval erupts as police march McGehee toward the exit.

Stevenson issues a parting shot: "For my part, I believe in the forgiveness of sin and the redemption of ignorance."

Schmidt and the remaining protesters keep trying to interrupt

Stevenson's rhythm. Hundreds of Halloween noisemakers clack in unison the instant he starts a sentence. People are fake coughing, laughing in exaggerated fashion.

"How about *Cuber*?" some people are yelling, trying to imitate JFK's accent.[15]

One man stands up and chants: "Kennedy will get his reward in hell. Stevenson is going to die. His heart will stop, stop, stop. And he will burn, burn, burn."[16]

People begin streaming into the aisles, holding American flags upside down, a tactic they have learned from General Walker to signal a nation in distress or under attack. Halfway through Stevenson's speech, a group of Walker's commandos dart behind the stage and pull on a rope. The large banner that reads WELCOME ADLAI flips down to reveal another message in huge letters: UN RED FRONT.

One Stevenson supporter turns to another in disbelief:

"This must be what it was like in Munich during the Beer Hall Putsch."[17]

More scuffles are breaking out, but Stevenson is insisting on staying on stage—and directly addressing the extremists in Dallas:

"I understand that some of these fearful groups are trying to establish a United States Day in competition with United Nations Day. This is the first time I have heard that the United States and the United Nations are rivals."

Stevenson continues speaking, and when he finishes his supporters erupt with prolonged cheers. The ovation lasts for three full minutes as Stevenson waves back to the crowd and is finally hustled off stage. In the wings, Marcus leads the ambassador to a small, private reception with members of the Dallas United Nations Association.

Stevenson listens to numerous apologies and receives assurances that most people in Dallas don't agree with the protesters.

Then, a policeman passes the word that not all of the protesters have left the premises. Nearly a hundred people are marching in front of the auditorium. The group is surrounding Stevenson's limousine and chanting anti-UN slogans. Larrie Schmidt's people are among them. They sing "Dixie" and "Onward Christian Soldiers" while a half dozen police officers nervously monitor the situation.

One of the protesters is Cora Lacy Frederickson, the wife of a Dallas insurance executive and a staunch supporter of General Walker. She attended Walker's U.S. Day rally last night. She is carrying a large sign nailed to a piece of wood. It is one of those used by Schmidt's group, and it reads: ADLAI, WHO ELECTED YOU?

Inside the auditorium, police officers confer with Marcus and Stevenson. They decide that it is best for the ambassador to leave from the south stage door, away from the knot of protesters. A police escort helps Stevenson's driver move the limousine. As the car drives away, the crowd rushes after it.

The cops quickly set up a rope line for Stevenson and Marcus to help them reach the waiting limousine. As Stevenson emerges, a buzz goes up and people race toward him, waving their signs and yelling: "COMMUNIST!" and "TRAITOR!"

Police struggle to hold back the crowd. TV and news photographers zoom in to capture the scene as the angry picketers descend on Stevenson. Seemingly oblivious to any danger, Stevenson chats and shakes hands with supporters as he moves toward his car.

Frederickson suddenly flies toward Stevenson, her sign raised high. Flashbulbs are popping as her placard slams down on Stevenson's forehead, just missing his eye. The ambassador steps back under the blow.

A clean-cut college student pushes toward the reeling Stevenson, flailing his fists. The cops and Stevenson's aides push back.

Frederickson is seized by the police.

Stevenson gathers his composure and yells to make himself heard over the crowd. He tells the police not to arrest the woman. He attempts to talk to her, even as the crowd pushes and heaves.[18]

"What's the matter with you?" he asks her. "What's the trouble?"

Frederickson yells at him: "Don't you know?"

Stevenson asks: "Know what?"

She shouts: "I know, everybody knows. Why don't you know?"

Stevenson gives up: "It's all right to have your own views... but don't hit anyone."[19]

The police are flanking him and Marcus, pushing them toward the limousine. Some of Stevenson's supporters have dug into their pockets and are throwing coins at the protesters to get them to disperse.

Stevenson and Marcus have nearly reached the car when two more young men leap from the crowd.

"TRAITOR!" they yell in unison, unleashing gobs of spit at Stevenson's face.

Two cops wrestle one of them, a twenty-two-year-old General Walker loyalist, to the ground. The man spits again, this time into the face of one of the cops struggling with him.

The other man darts into the line of protesters, making a clean getaway. The cops can't chase him because it will leave Stevenson unprotected.

They try to put handcuffs on the twenty-two-year-old. He begins screaming: "THEY ARE BURNING ME WITH CIGA-RETTES!"[20]

One of the policemen wrenches open a door to the limousine and Marcus pushes Stevenson inside, crawling in desperately after him as the cop slams the door shut.

The protesters begin rocking the automobile. The chauffeur appears immobilized by fear.

Marcus barks: "Get the hell out of here!"[21]

The chauffeur guns the engine and the car pulls forward as protesters fall away. The limo hurtles through the parking lot, screeching as it turns a corner. Inside the car, Stevenson takes out his handkerchief and wipes the saliva from his face.

Addressing no one in particular he asks:

"Are these human beings or animals?"

Cora Frederickson, the normally staid wife of the Dallas insurance executive, is explaining to reporters why her picket sign struck the U.S. ambassador to the United Nations on his head.

"It was never my intention to hit him," she tells the newsmen. "Someone must have pushed the sign down on him."

She gestures with her hands: "I felt someone take hold of the sign and push down on it."

Frederickson has a good idea who is responsible:

"There were a bunch of colored people standing around in back of me," she shrugs.

Noticing quizzical looks, she adds:

"I was pushed from behind by a Negro."[22]

In New York, Bernard Weissman's telephone is ringing late in the evening. It is Larrie Schmidt, calling long-distance from Dallas.

"I have made it," Schmidt shouts excitedly. "I have done it for us."

He describes the "hullabaloo" inside the auditorium and how Stevenson had been mobbed and struck while trying to leave.

Schmidt says he helped organize the demonstration.

"It went off beautifully. There is going to be national publicity... newspapers were all over the place." He tells Weissman he has been interviewed for TV and radio. At long last, the breakthrough moment has arrived.[23]

Photographers are racing to darkrooms and frantic newsmen are phoning their offices, telling them to save space on the front page.

A Dallas television reporter was right behind Stevenson, filming the scene as Cora Frederickson's sign hit the ambassador.

"I've got something really hot in my camera!" the TV man shouts as he rushes to air his film on the evening news. Audible gasps are heard in the studio as the film, just minutes old, appears on the monitor for the first time. The entire scene is captured in startling clarity. The dignified Stevenson is surrounded by screaming faces. Then Frederickson enters the frame, her narrowly spaced eyes squinting in fury, her mouth twisted and her tongue sticking out as she raises her sign and crashes it down on Stevenson's head. There are no black citizens anywhere in the frame.

Millions of Americans are opening their morning newspapers to find shocking photos from Dallas. Breathless reports describe a city that seems to have gone insane: Anti–United Nations demonstrators shoved, booed, beat, and spat in the face of Adlai E. Stevenson.

Reporters summon references to 1960, when "a clawing, hissing, mink-coat mob held vice-presidential candidate Lyndon Johnson and his wife at bay in a hotel lobby for almost an hour."[24]

On the evening news, Walter Cronkite seems to frown in disapproval as the footage from Dallas airs. The images are played over and over, with slow motion and freeze frames. The *Washington Post* describes the crowd in Dallas as "creatures from a jungle swamp."[25] *Time* calls them "Dallas' adult delinquents." The lone liberal publication in the state, the *Texas Observer*, says: "If the Birchers had not been in the minority, the Stevenson Riot would have had blood as well as spit."[26]

Having been in Dallas less than twenty-four hours, Stevenson departs early Friday morning. A dozen uniformed police officers and at least six plainclothesmen stand guard as he makes the short walk from the airport terminal to his plane.

Later in the day, after he lands in Los Angeles, Stevenson speaks about the Dallas incident: "I'm glad to be here at all, especially alive, indeed not even wounded."[27]

He decides that Dallas is being objectified—perhaps too much. There are people, like Stanley Marcus, who invited him, who supported him. The crowd of supporters was far bigger than the crowd that assaulted him. He remains gracious and complimentary toward his hosts in Dallas: "I've never had a more enthusiastic reception than in Dallas," he says. The problem was "the violent behavior of a few."

A reporter asks him why he didn't want the woman in Dallas arrested—or even the man who spat on him:

"I don't want to send them to jail. I want to send them to school."[28]

Privately, Stevenson is very concerned about Kennedy's safety in the city.

He takes a phone call from Arthur Schlesinger, a senior White House aide. Schlesinger tells him that Kennedy admires how he had remained calm under fire in Dallas. The two men joke light-heartedly about the incident.

Then, suddenly, Stevenson becomes serious:

"There was something very ugly and frightening about the atmosphere," he says.

He mentions that he had talked to Stanley Marcus and other leading people in Dallas. There was uncertainty, some dread, in Dallas.

"They wondered whether the President should go to Dallas," Stevenson says. "And so do I."[29]

Back in Dallas, a group of one hundred civic and business leaders, led by Mayor Earle Cabell, quickly wires an official apology to Stevenson:

"The city of Dallas is outraged and abjectly ashamed of the disgraceful discourtesies you suffered at the hands of a small group of extremists here last night," the telegram reads. The attackers do "not represent the heart or the mind of this great city."[30]

Mindful of President Kennedy's upcoming visit and the negative consequences for Dallas if the president decides to cancel, the city leaders forward a copy of the telegram to the White House.

The more moderate afternoon newspaper, the *Dallas Times Herald*, publishes a front-page apology:

"Dallas has been disgraced. There is no other way to view the storm trooper actions of last night's frightening attack on Adlai Stevenson...this misconstrued, misguided brand of 'patriotism' is dragging the name of Dallas through the slime of national dishonor."[31]

At his home on Turtle Creek, General Walker is feeling magnanimous. He admits a group of reporters and allows them to ask his opinion about the Stevenson event. He reminds them that he had not been at the auditorium, though he did happen to catch the television broadcast.

"Mr. Stevenson's speech was typically naïve, innocent, and

false... I don't know who they're learning from, or what they are learning, unless it's how to be communists."[32]

When asked if he'd organized the picketing against Stevenson, the general suddenly points to the door:

"I think you have all the information you need right now."[33]

Around the nation, and despite a begrudging apology for the incident from the *Dallas Morning News*, some observers are racing to link the attack on Stevenson with publisher Ted Dealey's running war with President Kennedy.

An ABC News commentator lays the incident directly at Dealey's doorstep, reminding national viewers that spitting and railing at national leaders is nothing new when it comes to some people from Dallas: Dealey "figuratively spat in the eye of the President of the United States himself in the White House itself."[34]

From his executive office on the fifth floor of Neiman Marcus, Stanley Marcus, pen in hand, begins drafting one of the most difficult and important letters he's ever written. The Stevenson incident has left him with "a heavy heart... ashamed for the city."[35]

All day long he's been hearing from angry customers canceling their Neiman Marcus charge cards because of his obvious public support for the United Nations, and by extension for John F. Kennedy.

He patiently answers each complaint in diplomatic tones. But Marcus has also decided to let Ted Dealey know what he thinks— and to do it as directly as possible.

The divisions in the city have been building for years. Marcus is from the old guard, too. His family dates back decades, just like Dealey's. But there are lines of demarcation now, things that Marcus can't abide. He spends hundreds of thousands each year in newspaper advertising. He sees Dealey at all the important galas and Dallas Citizens Council gatherings. They have almost always been diametrically opposed on political things—and only united in their common interest belief: They both want what is good for business in Dallas. Dealey, of all people, should know that the extremism in Dallas has given the city a black eye. That it is exactly what people once told his father about the Ku Klux Klan in Dallas.

Marcus knows Dealey well enough to feel that he might simply toss his letter in the trash. He decides to address the letter to the heir to the Dealey dynasty—Ted's son, Joe, who has recently become the president of the *Dallas Morning News*. Joe has a reputation for being more reasonable than his father. Maybe Marcus can reason with him, and maybe Joe in turn can influence his father:

"I have a criticism to make...and I send it to you, not as an advertiser, but as a citizen of our community...we need to ask ourselves how and why incidents of this type occur in Dallas, for it is only possible to prevent their repetition if we can get the answers to the 'how and why?'

"In the opinion of many people, your paper has been one of the contributing factors to the development of a hard core of unreasonable people intolerant of any views opposed to their own. For many years...your paper has been preaching a doctrine of criticism of the Government and of the United Nations while at the same time giving solace to the extreme rightists like General Walker and his ilk.

"I think that the constant sowing of seeds of intolerance has made it possible for the extreme rightist groups to grow in the city of Dallas with some aura of respectability."

Marcus pointedly reminds Dealey of his own success as a businessman: "I am for free enterprise as much as the *Dallas News* is. I am against communism as much as the *Dallas News* is.

"We need to have a community that can live together and disagree amiably without the deep-seated bigotry and hatred that I sense is burning in the hearts and minds of too large a portion of our citizenship today.

"*The Dallas Morning News* has a great responsibility...to lead as it did in the days of the Ku Klux Klan in bringing the state of reasonableness back into the bloodstream of Dallas."[36]

Once he finishes, Marcus signs his name and places the letter in an envelope, sealing it carefully. The letter goes out immediately. No one ever responds.

In the wake of the attack on Stevenson, Rhett James must feel there is something deeply embedded among a handful of hard-edged people in Dallas, something that nurtures a barely contained toxicity. The newspapers seem to echo it every morning. Day after day, people all over the city are picking up newspapers and reading one unsettling tale after another from the mean streets:

The police fire a volley of shots into the back of a black man as he frantically scales a fence; they think he has stolen a car and now he is dead. White teenagers spit and curse at black students after a high school football game; a tossed beer bottle lacerates a cheerleader's face. For no obvious reason, someone steps up to a woman sitting in a North Dallas café and shoots her in the mouth. A black laborer takes a bus to the home of his late white employer, a cotton merchant—and hammers the man's widow to death. A seventeen-month-old baby is suddenly killed by a stray bullet. A fourteen-year-old black boy is in a coma after being hit and dragged by a speeding car driven by a middle-aged white man. In Oak Cliff, near where Lee Harvey Oswald and Jack Ruby both now live, a black man comes stumbling out of a one-story frame house. Eighty percent of his body is engulfed in flames and he is screaming: "Put me out, put me out." Someone, a stranger, has doused him with a five-gallon can of gasoline and tossed a match at him.

James returns to his pulpit at New Hope Baptist to preach unity and peace. The fact that despite the Stevenson attack, Kennedy is still coming to Dallas, with Johnson, is almost a sign, a miracle.

Through LBJ's urging, James has just been asked to be the Dallas representative at a meeting of President Kennedy's Committee on Equal Employment in Los Angeles. With the appointment, James must feel as if there really are stronger bridges spanning straight from the Kennedy White House to ordinary people in Dallas like Juanita Craft, like himself. And that somehow, magically, those bridges are bypassing the normal hurdles, those hoary "traditions," the Dallas Citizens Council, and even moments like the horrible attack on Adlai Stevenson.

In their way, President Kennedy and his brother both seem unafraid of Dallas. They have to know that inviting black activists from Dallas to the White House—and then signing off on Adlai Stevenson's visit to the city—is bringing the fight to certain intractable elders in the city.

Mayor Earle Cabell has weighed the storm of negative publicity in the wake of the Stevenson debacle, the way people around the nation are now viewing Dallas, and he has made a decision: He is ready to publicly condemn the extremists.

"Let us look these so-called patriots in the face, see who they are, what they have done and where they are leading us...These are not conservatives. These are radicals. Dallas cannot ignore the existence of this element any more than we can allow it to continue as our spokesman...This cancer on the body politic must be removed."

And maybe, despite the embarrassment and humiliation the city has suffered, Dallas will get another chance on November 22, when President Kennedy comes to town. "We have an opportunity to redeem ourselves when the President pays us a visit next month."[37]

The other longtime stewards of the Dallas Citizens Council—in the city, some refer to the twenty-five top leaders as "the Giants"—are taking no chances with Kennedy's upcoming visit. In addition to Mayor Cabell's speech, city officials are promising extra-vigilant protection for the president.

"Any Dallas elements planning to give President Kennedy a reception similar to that accorded Adlai Stevenson may be in for a rude awakening," the *Dallas Morning News* reports. The president's security team "will compile a full report on who might be demonstrating, where and why...By the time the President arrives in Dallas, the men assigned to that segment of his Texas tour will be very knowledgeable about his zealous critics."[38]

The federal agents "are sharp-eyed, alert and cat-like in their quickness. They know what they are watching out for and, usually, whom."[39]

The *News* promises a veritable blanket of ironclad security: "Every inch of the President's route from the time his plane arrives at Love Field to the time it leaves will be thoroughly explored."[40]

General Edwin A. Walker walks out into his front yard and looks up at the three American flags flapping in the breeze. Reverently, carefully, he brings each one down.

Later, commuters traveling along Turtle Creek Boulevard notice a strange sight.

Out in front of Walker's gray mansion are three American flags, as always. Only now they are flying upside down.

Photos of Walker's protest flash across the country. Reporters predictably arrive at his grand home, and he tells them that there is an unseen hand at work in America. That "the invisible government" brought Stevenson to Dallas in order to spread communism.

"Adlai got what was coming to him. He represents the U.N. and since the people can't get to the U.N., they got to him."[41]

Larrie Schmidt is gurgling with energy, anxious to write to his old army ally Bernard Weissman.

Schmidt is inspired by Walker's steadfast resistance, still cresting in the wake of the Stevenson protests and all the national coverage.

Maybe it will finally convince Weissman and others to relocate to Dallas and join the insurgency. It is the only city in America that would have the courage to confront Stevenson head-on—and imagine what it could do when Kennedy arrives next month.

Schmidt writes: "What appeared at first to have been a great blunder of ours has rapidly turned into a great victory."

He has been in Dallas long enough to know who the specific enemies in the city are. He saw them with his own eyes, trying to protect Stevenson from the hard truths in Dallas: "The ultra liberals of Dallas, led by STANLEY MARCUS of Neiman Marcus went too far in pressuring for denunciation of 'extremists' and 'Fascists' in Dallas. As a result, a bomb has exploded everywhere here against them. This town is a battleground and that is no joke. Never before have the Dallas conservatives from the GOP to the John Birch Society ever been so strongly united."[42]

His letter arrives in New York, and Weissman has already seen what everyone else in America has seen—the images from Dallas, the way people were so determined, so unafraid. He packs his trunk with some clothes and points his car south, toward Dallas.

Bruce Alger knows that Mayor Cabell has been essentially denouncing the very man—General Walker—that Cabell, Dealey, and most of the powerful men in Dallas once openly embraced as a heroic savior on horseback.

But Alger decides to stick to his guns, and for a minute it seems as if Dealey's *Dallas Morning News* is back in his corner, allowing him to vent about the weak-willed liberals and socialists who are painting Dallas as a dark-hearted fortress in Texas. The paper allows him space to defend the city: "Why should there be any discrediting of Dallas? Why are good people, with good intentions, taken in and assume a feeling of guilt where no guilt exists, and apologize for a community that has done no wrong?"[43]

Alger also decides to send a special newsletter to his constituents titled "Dallas—proud, courageous—truly the home of the free and the brave."

And finally, he says the twenty-two-year-old man—a member of Walker's organization, and the one who spat on the policeman at the Stevenson melee and had to be wrestled into submission—was really a patriot. He was driven mad by the truth. He "lost his head because of his resentment against the U.N., that threatens his freedom and his country's freedom . . . If you disapprove vocally of such things, are you to be called intemperate?

"The real issue is that the U.N. today is engaging in many actions harmful to peace, to the communist-captive peoples, to the sovereignty of the United States."

Alger denounces any need to apologize for Dallas: "The enemies of the United States are encouraged . . . this all fits with the Communist objective."[44]

Too, he adds that he is encouraged to hear similar stirrings from his voters in his Dallas district. An executive with H. L. Hunt's oil company told him: "Obviously, Adlai was intent on starting something."[45] And another Alger supporter told him the Stevenson attack was just a big political charade, planned in advance to make Dallas look insane, just the way LBJ had "planned" the mink coat melee in 1960: "You will note that the circumstances were so similar with the fiasco set up by Lyndon Johnson . . . that it could have been planned by the same people in advance . . . to try and goad those whom he knew to be his political enemies, to create an issue to use in the coming campaign."[46]

NOVEMBER

It is 3 a.m. and President Kennedy is being told there is a phone call with some desperately urgent news: A coup has been launched against South Vietnamese President Ngo Dinh Diem and his brother, security chief Ngo Dinh Nhu.

The well-coordinated revolt is being carried out by South Vietnam's senior military command, with tacit support from the Kennedy administration. Tanks are rumbling through Saigon's streets as key government ministries fall to the rebels. Diem and Nhu are trapped in the presidential palace, guarded by fifteen hundred loyalist troops. Fighter jets are strafing the building as the opposition forces advance.

The intense fighting continues throughout the day. By 5 p.m. Washington time on November 1, coup leaders announce that Diem and Nhu have surrendered.

As the crisis unfolds, Madame Nhu holds a brief press conference at the Beverly Wilshire in Los Angeles, where she has been staying ever since her visit to Dallas:

"No coup can erupt without at least Americans inciting it or backing it," she tells the jostling newsmen. "I believe all the devils of hell are against us, but I believe that we shall triumph eventually."

When asked if she might seek political asylum in the United States, Madame Nhu loses her temper.

"Never!" she shouts. "Not in any country that would stab my country in the back!"[1]

Later in the day, the news from Vietnam takes a grim turn. Saigon radio is reporting that Diem and Nhu have both committed suicide.

While events in Southeast Asia spiral out of control, Kennedy's aides huddle to map out plans for his Texas trip—and, in particular, for Dallas. They, too, want to avoid any headaches in the city. And they want to ensure that Kennedy leaves Dallas with a political plum, that he is sent off with hosannas in a city that, by now, so many people think of as the epicenter of the right-wing, anti-Kennedy resistance. If Kennedy is embraced by Dallas, if triumphant images of him being engulfed in cheers are broadcast around America, it will be proof that Kennedy can overcome any kind of resistance. His aides devote time to studying the city, reading Dealey's newspaper, looking for clues about what to expect and how to prepare. For one thing, there has been an explosion of money in the city—the rich there seem to keep getting richer. They have only to look at the outrageous pages of the latest, famous Neiman Marcus Christmas catalog, which has just appeared and is making its usual splash from coast to coast—just the way Stanley Marcus wants it.

The store is selling cowboy chaps in white mink. A Shahtoosh muffler, made from the chin hairs of the ibex goat that lives in the Himalayas. Ten-gallon hats for dogs. A wastebasket made from an elephant's foot. And a personal submarine for around $20,000. It's fourteen feet long, weighs 975 pounds, fits two people, and cruises at three to seven miles per hour. "The ultimate in togetherness."

But today Stanley Marcus looks unusually preoccupied.

He is in a meeting with his top executives where the talk is of the publicity the Neiman Marcus catalog is getting and about forecasts for holiday sales season.

Marcus seems ruminative, detached, and he suddenly blurts out:

"I think we ought to see whether or not we can persuade President Kennedy to change his mind about visiting Dallas."

The women and men grouped around the conference table stare at him.

Marcus adds, "Frankly, I don't think this city is safe for it."[2]

President Kennedy is expected to arrive at Chicago's O'Hare Field at 11 a.m. He will be greeted by Mayor Richard Daley and then enjoy a grand motorcade through the city. It is November 2, and Kennedy says he's coming to town to watch the Army–Air Force football game, but the trip has obvious political overtones. Illinois, along with Texas, is one of the two states the president barely carried in the 1960 election. It will be crucial to keep it in his column in 1964.

Before leaving for Chicago, Kennedy closely monitors the situation in South Vietnam with his top national security advisers. In Saigon, people are taking to the streets in jubilation after learning of Diem's and Nhu's deaths.

Then disturbing news arrives: Diem and Nhu did not commit suicide, after all. They were murdered. After surrendering, the two men were placed inside an armored vehicle with their hands tied behind their backs. When they were next seen, both had been beaten and shot several times. Nhu had also been stabbed repeatedly.

Defense Secretary Robert McNamara notices Kennedy blanch when he hears the report.

Kennedy has been assuming that Diem and Nhu would go into exile, not be assassinated.

Kennedy gets up immediately and walks out of the room, obviously distressed.

As he leaves, General Maxwell Taylor, chairman of the Joint Chiefs of Staff, mutters under his breath: "What did he expect?"[3]

Within minutes, a brisk announcement is made. The president's trip to Chicago will be canceled because of the crisis in Vietnam.

Texas's Democratic national committeeman has a problem with President Kennedy's upcoming visit to Texas. The issue is Dallas. Byron Skelton can't shake the feeling that something bad will happen to the president there. It's more than a sense of foreboding. It feels like a premonition. He suggests to friends that the climate in Dallas could easily inspire an unstable person to take action against Kennedy.

Skelton has been reading news of a recent speech by General Walker that seems to practically invite violence against the president.

Skelton carefully clips out a newspaper story about Walker and includes it with a letter he has decided to send to his best contact in the Kennedy administration, Attorney General Robert Kennedy:

"Frankly, I am worried about President Kennedy's proposed trip to Dallas. You will note that General Walker says that 'Kennedy is a liability to the free world.' A man who would make this kind of statement is capable of doing harm to the President... I would feel better if the President's itinerary did not include Dallas. Please give this your earnest consideration."[4]

Bobby Kennedy knows Skelton, and he knows that Skelton is not a man given to histrionics. He also understands that showing the letter from Texas to his brother will be a waste of time.

The Kennedy brothers have been hearing all kinds of warnings about Dallas ever since the trip to Texas was first announced. Senator J. William Fulbright of Arkansas has already told the president: "Dallas is a very dangerous place. *I* wouldn't go there. Don't *you* go."[5]

Several letters have arrived at the White House pleading for Kennedy to avoid the city.

One Dallas woman has written: "Don't let the President come down here. I'm worried about him. I think something terrible will happen to him."[6]

Bobby knows that his brother won't call off the trip, especially after having to cancel in Chicago. Still, he can't let Skelton's letter rest. He decides to pass it along to his brother's close aide Kenny O'Donnell, the man responsible for the president's schedule.

O'Donnell reviews the letter. He understands the issue as well as Robert Kennedy does, but there is no stopping Jack Kennedy from going to Dallas. The idea of him shrinking from a confrontation with General Walker is laughable.

In fact, Kennedy has already decided to deliver a hard-hitting speech criticizing political extremists when he visits Dallas.

Bernard Weissman's 1957 Ford Fairlane convertible pulls up to the Eden Roe Apartments, home of his friend Larrie Schmidt. It is about 5 p.m. He has driven for two days, stopping only for a brief rest in South Carolina.

Although it is six weeks into autumn, summer seems to be lingering in Dallas. Temperatures are still in the eighties as Weissman emerges from his car. The native New Yorker is a tall, slender, neatly dressed man who has just turned twenty-six. He wears black horn-rimmed glasses and keeps his thinning hair combed straight back.

He has someone with him, a twenty-eight-year-old former soldier named William Burley, another friend from the old days serving in Germany.

It wasn't hard to convince Burley, who has been eking out a living selling hearing aids in Baltimore, to come along. Going to Texas, following Schmidt's promises of chasing the money trail on the new frontier for ultra-conservatism, seemed like a far better future. Schmidt has been writing to them, begging them to come to Dallas and join him. He told them the time is right, that he has become quite famous in Dallas ever since the Adlai Stevenson incident: "I am a hero to the right . . . a storm trooper to the left."[7]

Schmidt is glad to see them, he welcomes them inside, and Weissman and Burley, weary from the long drive, spend their first night with Schmidt.

The next day, Weissman finds a cheap apartment about a mile away. He explains to the landlady that he and Burley have just been discharged from the army and that they don't have money for a deposit. He puts on his salesman's charm and sweet-talks her. He asks if they can pay for just two weeks' rent, and then pay the rest after they find work. The landlady agrees to accommodate the two former soldiers. She has second thoughts later when she sees them moving a keg of beer into the apartment.

Weissman and Burley quickly find jobs as carpet salesmen, a thriving occupation in the rapidly expanding city. Weissman has always thought of himself as an idealist, and Schmidt as a politician, a mover and shaker. But they both believe that it takes money, big money, to build a powerhouse conservative machine—and Dallas is the perfect place for that.

H. L. Hunt's chief of security is a former FBI agent, and he enjoys *excellent* contacts within the Dallas Police Department. He knows that the Dallas police have been monitoring some of the city's "extremist" groups. Before it's even filed he knows what's going into an internal police report on security for Kennedy's visit.

The police have been doing their street-level reconnaissance, trying to figure out if any Dallas local extremists are preparing for violence. The bomb threat against Martin Luther King Jr., the swastikas on Neiman Marcus windows, the cross burning on the Holocaust survivor's lawn, the Adlai Stevenson riot—they have all added up to a growing folder of information at police headquarters on extremist activists in the city.

The police report is nearly ready, but before it is issued Hunt's security head sends a memo to Hunt with the details: There are "unconfirmed reports of possible violence during the parade."[8]

He believes that Hunt will be anxious to avoid any incidents in Dallas—if only because people in Dallas, and around the nation, will likely try to blame Hunt for inciting it. He's been blamed for plenty already: funding Senator Joseph McCarthy, spending millions on his right-wing radio programs, spending more money on distributing the anti-Kennedy screeds that featured the sermons of W. A. Criswell, and even donating cash to General Walker.

Hunt's security chief has thought it through. He proposes a solution to his reclusive employer: "I have thought about the problem, and I am wondering if a few letters to the editor might not be a good way of pre-exposing this if, in fact, there is a planned incident."[9]

Hunt is never shy about writing letters to Ted Dealey and the editors at the *Dallas Morning News*. He's sent several over the years. And he knows that when a letter from him arrives at Dealey's newspaper, it carries some freight—the city's richest man should be allowed space in his local newspaper.

When he receives the private memo from his security chief, Hunt mulls it over. He has extraordinary means at his disposal, a preference for dealing in cash, and a tendency to employ former FBI agents. They are very good, loyal employees, and he pays them very well to keep his predilections private. Hunt finally decides against taking action.

Maybe, just maybe, it would be useful for the president to see how little he is liked in Dallas.

Lee Harvey Oswald's name has been showing up again in some of the reports that a longtime FBI agent in Dallas is pulling together on extremists in the area. The local FBI first began tracking him and

Marina in the summer of 1962, when they arrived from the Soviet Union. The FBI in New Orleans kept tabs on him until there was a sense that he and his wife were both headed back to Texas.

When he returned to Dallas from New Orleans a month ago, he checked into a YMCA. He tried to land a job at a printing company but had no luck. Then he moved from one boardinghouse to another in the Oak Cliff section of the city—not far from the duplex where he had mapped out his assassination attempt on Walker.

Two weeks ago he applied for a laborer's job at the Texas School Book Depository, and began work the next day. Two days later he turned twenty-four. Two days after that Marina gave birth to Audrey Marina Rachel Oswald.

Things are still not right between him and Marina. Wary as always, she and the babies are living with friends, and he is alone in his boardinghouse in Oak Cliff. A short bus ride takes him right past the *Dallas Morning News* and Dealey Plaza, not far from Reverend Criswell's First Baptist Church, and straight to the School Book Depository. On weekends he visits Marina and the girls.

Oswald is anxious to immerse himself back into the political climate in Dallas. He has attended a meeting of the American Civil Liberties Union. He monitored Walker's U.S. Day rally. And then, just a few days ago, he learned that a local, veteran FBI agent named James Hosty has started making inquiries in the neighborhood where Marina has gone to live with her friend. Hosty sat down with Marina and her friend and talked briefly to them. Marina seemed nervous and he told her she had nothing to fear, that he was not the Gestapo. He asked where Lee lived and Marina's friend said that she only knew he was somewhere in the Oak Cliff neighborhood.

Later, when Lee talked to Marina, he told her that if the FBI man ever returned, she should get his license plate.

Plenty of people in Dallas say they are one thing when they are really another.

A seasoned Dallas police lieutenant named Jack Revill has uncovered a plot to disrupt President Kennedy's visit to Dallas.

And now Revill has a growing pile of papers on his desk. He has been drowning in work ever since the Adlai Stevenson incident rocked the city. Word has come down from the chief's office—and probably higher—that Revill, head of the Criminal Intelligence Section, has to find out what the city's political fringe groups might be plotting to unleash on Kennedy.

Revill's officers quickly infiltrate several organizations. His detectives conduct surveillance, monitor conversations, and snap photographs of suspicious people and groups: The preacher who says he is the rightful leader of the modern Ku Klux Klan. The Indignant White Citizens Council. The National States Rights Party. The John Birch Society—hell, that could even include the mayor. The White Citizens Council. The General Edwin A. Walker Group. Revill's men are also monitoring the few groups on the left, including the Dallas Civil Liberties Union.

But now Revill is fixed on the one thing that seems tangible. Several college students from nearby North Texas State University have been visiting General Walker's home.

Many of them joined the heated demonstrations against Stevenson on UN Day. The cops ran checks on several of them, and their photographs are sitting on Revill's desk.

His squad has also developed a confidential informant inside the student group. And the informant has news: The group intends to have "well planned demonstrations during the President's visit to Dallas."

The informant has no specifics, but the group's association with Walker is ominous enough. And one of the students, apparently someone the others looked to as a leader, has already issued a verbal threat against President Kennedy: "We will drag his dick in the dirt."[10]

Revill confers with his commanders at the police station, returns to his desk, summons his squad, and tells them they are going to go hard after the students. The Secret Service is also being notified. And then, over the next few days, each student receives a visit from Revill and another officer. On some of the visits, a Secret Service agent joins the officers.

The students abandon their plans.

* * *

On November 7, Kennedy Press Secretary Pierre Salinger announces that Jacqueline Kennedy will accompany her husband on the upcoming trip to Texas.

This is big news—this is the First Lady's very first political trip with her husband since his election. She, in fact, has never even been to Texas before. People in the state are delighted, and the state's newspapers eagerly report the news.

Lady Bird Johnson writes to Jackie from the LBJ Ranch:

"The President's on page five, Lyndon's on the back page, but you're on the *front* page."[11]

When FBI Agent Hosty returns to his office on November 8, the receptionist hands him a business envelope that is blank on the outside. Inside is a folded, handwritten note on bond paper. It is a short note, no longer than two paragraphs.

Hosty studies the letter. He has gotten these kinds of messages, these complaints, before. This one pretty much reads like many of the others: *You've been interviewing people I know, my wife, without my permission. You should stop. If you don't stop talking to my wife, I'll take action against the FBI.*

He notes that the letter is unsigned. Maybe it's that Jew-hating Jimmy Robinson, the man who had protested Dr. King's visit to Dallas—and then burned a cross on a Holocaust survivor's lawn. Hosty was out interviewing Robinson's wife over the summer.

He puts the letter down and does not share it with anyone else.[12]

General Walker assumes that the enemy is everywhere: They're listening every time he picks up his telephone, they're "volunteering" to be his bodyguard, they're eagerly distributing his literature.

As the days count down to the arrival in Dallas of Kennedy, his worst political enemy, Walker is increasingly cautious. He never knows when someone will come for him again, in the middle of the night, just when he is comfortable or settled into his home. He never even considered moving out of his house after the assassination attempt. It would be a sign of fear. He'd have to live like H. L. Hunt, surrounded by ex-FBI agents, sneaking in and out of the city—and maybe, like Hunt, refusing to even shake a stranger's hand. Walker has enough secrets in his personal life; he doesn't need any more.

His inner circle has grown tighter. Among his closest associates, there is just one man who has repeatedly proved himself—by going into battle with Walker in Mississippi, and by pulling bullet fragments out of Walker's arm the night he was almost killed in Dallas: Robert Surrey.

Surrey has never let the general down. And Surrey knows that Walker hates Nazis because of his experience in World War II. But Surrey is a patient man, and he is hoping for the right time to tell Walker that he has cultivated his own secret, other life.

Surrey is fascinated by the racial purity doctrines of the American Nazi Party. He has finally, quietly, joined the group and started studying the beliefs of American Nazi Party founder George Lincoln Rockwell, the man who showed up at General Walker's Senate hearing and refused to remove his swastika. Surrey has a secret name inside the Nazi Party—Max Amman, in honor of one of Hitler's favorite publishers and allies. Surrey is a publisher, too, just like Hitler's comrade. He and Walker are the co-owners of American Eagle Publishing, the company that releases Walker's books and pamphlets.

Surrey sees the other super-patriots in Dallas as driven, committed "storm troopers" who are out to squelch communism and protect racial purity. As far as Surrey can see, there's only one significant ideological difference between the American Nazis and Walker. He has never betrayed Walker's secret. But the Nazi Party is officially anti-homosexual, and Rockwell has said: "If there's one thing I'd rather gas than Communists, it's queers."[13]

Right now Surrey has other things to talk to Walker about. He can keep his growing obsession with the Nazi Party in check until there is a time when Walker might be even remotely receptive to the news. Today, Walker and Surrey are discussing Kennedy's upcoming visit to Dallas.

They regained the national headlines by preempting Stevenson's speech. But Stevenson basically came unprotected and alone, relying only on Stanley Marcus and the Dallas police to keep him safe. Kennedy can count on a much larger force: the Secret Service, the FBI, and maybe even federal troops if necessary. The roiling, planned demonstrations against Adlai Stevenson in a relatively unguarded auditorium came off brilliantly. But attempting to picket or disrupt a high-security presidential event is something else entirely. And now, after the Stevenson event, even the often friendly Dallas police are on high alert.

Walker briefly considered staging something with the help of those students from North Texas State, but obviously the police were tipped off. There are infiltrators afoot. And Kennedy would like nothing more than to catch Walker off guard—or to blame him for any disruptions in Dallas. Walker will be the most likely suspect for any anti-Kennedy action in the city.

The general has made up his mind: He will make a strategic retreat from Dallas while Kennedy is allowed his parade in downtown Dallas.

But still, *something* needs to be done to confront the president.

Robert Surrey places a phone call to a friend from a printing shop where he once worked. Surrey asks if he is willing to do a quick printing order on the side. He knows his friend only makes $35 a week, and he offers him $40 in cash. The man agrees, and later that evening Surrey leaves his home in Highland Park and meets his friend after hours at a small frame building along a commercial strip not far from Walker's house. Surrey explains that he has a customer who wants to print several thousand copies of a handbill as inexpensively as possible.

The two men consider the various options and eventually select an assortment of "dodger stock," cheap newsprint of various colors: green, orange, blue, yellow. Surrey agrees to pay an additional $20 for five thousand sheets.

Surrey has brought along the material for the handbill: two photographs of John F. Kennedy clipped from magazines. One photograph shows the president, unsmiling, staring straight ahead. The other photo is a profile shot, taken from the side. Surrey provides the text, already formatted and pasted onto a board. His friend barely notices the headline accompanying the text and photos of President Kennedy:

WANTED FOR TREASON.

November 11, Veterans Day, dawns bright and sunny with above-normal temperatures in the nation's capital. John F. Kennedy is on his way to Arlington National Cemetery to commemorate the occasion. He decides to bring along his young son, John Jr., who will turn three years old in exactly two weeks.

Members of his inner circle have noticed that the president has seemed unusually gloomy over the last several days. Maybe he is still affected by the murders of the Vietnamese leaders Diem and Nhu. And those closest to JFK know, too, that he is still haunted by the death of his two-day-old son Patrick back in August.

A strange sense of deep contentment always seems to overtake Kennedy whenever he visits Arlington National Cemetery. He's already told others that he would like to be buried here.

John-John bounds out ahead of him, in a playful mood as they walk through the cemetery with their entourage. The president is wearing a dark blue pin-striped suit. John-John is outfitted in blue shorts and a white sweater trimmed with red and blue. Kennedy carefully places a red, white, and blue wreath at the Tomb of the Unknown Soldier.

John-John remains ebullient, even during the somber public ceremony with an audience of several thousand. At one point, he breaks away from his Secret Service minder and makes a mad dash for the stage to join his father. Later, he successfully darts between some of the presidential aides to reach for Kennedy. He hugs his father's legs and lets out a series of happy yelps. Then he begins to walk backward, facing his father, hunching his shoulders in mock seriousness. Though the occasion is grave, the audience is charmed by the display.

As the group leaves the cemetery, Kennedy tells Congressman Hale Boggs:

"This is one of the really beautiful places on earth. I could stay here forever."[14]

The presidential limousine departs and the back window rolls down so John-John can wave good-bye to the spectators.

Bernard Weissman and Bill Burley have only been in Dallas eleven days but already they're beginning to regret moving here.

Larrie Schmidt, despite his big talk, has had very little influence in Dallas. The *Dallas Morning News* refuses to quote him, ever. Schmidt talked up his connection to General Walker, describing how his brother "infiltrated" Walker's group by becoming the general's driver and handyman, but his brother seems far away from Walker's inner circle, content to drink away the little bit of money Walker pays him. And meanwhile, Schmidt seems increasingly obsessed with his scheme to fund the conservative revolution by buying the DuCharme, the ramshackle beer joint where they spend their off hours. At least Schmidt is making a living selling life insurance—Weissman and Burley are failing at selling carpeting.

Instead of the big plans Schmidt promised, the men often wind up after work just hanging out and drinking beer. Sometimes they are joined by the college students Schmidt has recruited—the ones who helped lead the attack on the Stevenson speech.

To Weissman, the scene isn't much different from their days as GIs in Munich—a lot of big talk and beer drinking, but very little action. And when Schmidt does take them out to a conservative political gathering, it is even worse: Weissman can feel the anti-Semitism throbbing when people hear his name.

There is one thing that keeps them going: Kennedy's upcoming visit. At one time they discussed how to unleash major disruptions. But they can see that the city is on alert, that people are being watched: Walker and other leading conservatives are making strategic exits from Dallas. Bruce Alger announced that he is canceling a banquet in his honor on November 22. And the U.S. Senate's most staunch defender of General Walker during his battles with Kennedy, Texas Senator John Tower, has turned down an invitation to appear in the city when the president arrives.

Schmidt talks to his contacts in the local John Birch Society—including an independent oilman named Joseph Grinnan, who is close to Walker, the Hunt family, and other powerful conservatives in the city. The oilman's personal attorney is Robert Morris. There are whispers in Dallas that Grinnan keeps a full supply of arms and ammunition in his car at all times.

The oilman has important news to share. He can get Schmidt financial backing for a major anti-Kennedy propaganda effort: a full-page advertisement in the *Dallas Morning News* attacking Kennedy that the paper will surely print.

The strippers at his club are driving Jack Ruby crazy, and just when he is expecting a flood of customers to come during Kennedy's visit next week.

Jada—her real name is Janet Adams Conforto—has been working at the Carousel Club since the summer but now she is really breaking his back. They have been arguing over money, over her contract, which expires in January. She calls in sick one night and when she comes back the next night Ruby cuts the lights in the middle of her act. Ruby has grown erratic, threatening her, to the point where she is scared.

People can see it; he is chattering and hustling maybe more than ever. He's been juggling things—trolling the streets for new girls, making sure his headliner Tammi True is happy, scouting out locations for a new club, remembering to get his ads in to the *Dallas Morning News*, wondering if the drag queen who makes the costumes for the strippers is going to remain reliable.

The old, wily gangster Joe Civello has met Ruby a few times and learned to avoid him. Ruby is clearly never as discreet as he should be. Civello is trying to stay in the shadows, as far from Ruby as possible. With Kennedy and his people coming, it's simply not a good time. Ruby puts people on edge—and the city is already edgy:

A week before the president is to arrive, a man pulls out a fishing knife and plunges it two times into a friend's stomach until he dies. And a woman shoots her husband dead in the heart. Another man punches a woman in the eye in a tavern—she pulls out a knife and stabs him twice until he dies. Another man turns a garbage can upside down, jumps on it, crawls through an apartment window, and viciously rapes a woman while her six-month-old baby sleeps nearby. She can't tell if he is black or white—but she tells police that she has been active in "civic affairs" and the cops are left wondering if the rape is really also a warning for her to step away from things, to stand down from the big things threatening to overtake the normal order in Dallas.

The Secret Service arrives in Dallas on November 16 to coordinate security for the president's visit. Agents are meeting with Dallas police and the local FBI to review the situation. The Secret Service has only five permanent employees in the city, so it will need to rely on local law enforcement to protect the president.

Kennedy wants a motorcade through Dallas. The plan calls for Air Force One to land at Love Field at 11:30 a.m. on the twenty-second. From there, the presidential motorcade will travel through downtown. Immediately after, Kennedy will attend a luncheon and deliver a speech before twenty-five hundred people.

Civic leaders are insisting to the White House that they have the luncheon at the city's showplace facility—the Trade Mart. The building, however, is a security nightmare. Four stories high with a million square feet, the Trade Mart is arranged around a giant indoor courtyard—and this large open area is the proposed site for the luncheon. Numerous balconies overlook the courtyard, and the building contains a maze of corridors and rooms where an assassin can lurk. Even worse, there are fourteen separate entrances to the courtyard, each of which must be heavily guarded.

The bland, boxy building is on a highway heading north of downtown. The less-than-glamorous place gives the lie to the grand vision that Marcus has always wanted for Dallas—his view of a Paris on the prairie. In reality, the Trade Mart strikes closer to the heart of what Dallas is all about—it is a warehouse, a centralized place in the center of the United States where national, mainstream retailers can inspect and select massive quantities of off-the-rack merchandise to stock their stores around the country.

It is, some say, a perfect metaphor for Dallas. It is big and efficient, but hardly pleasing to look at.

The Secret Service grudgingly agrees to accept the site, but everyone realizes it will require intense planning and numerous officers. Inside the White House, Kennedy's aides know that Dallas poses a unique security challenge—and not just because of the location for the president's luncheon.

Kenny O'Donnell has already received a confidential report on Dallas from the Department of Justice. Special agents have been requesting information from Dallas police and the FBI about "persons of interest." The Dallas police offer several names: There's General Walker, of course, along with Ashland Burchwell, the Walker aide who was arrested with a carload of ammunition on his way to the University of Mississippi. There's also Robert Hatfield, the young man from Walker's group who spat on Adlai Stevenson. There is Jimmy Robinson, who picketed Dr. King and then burned a cross on the Holocaust survivor's lawn.

Pushing deadlines, the various agencies try to create a working portfolio of political extremists in the city. FBI Agent James Hosty does not mention that a communist and former defector, Lee Harvey Oswald, is also in Dallas—and that he has just obtained a job along Kennedy's prospective motorcade route. There is nothing, after all, in Oswald's past, as far as the FBI is aware, to suggest a propensity for violence. He seems merely quirky, a self-absorbed ideologue. The guy can barely keep a job, let alone a marriage.

Security preparations focus on the places where Kennedy will spend the most time: Love Field and the Trade Mart. At those sites, protection will be exceptionally tight. The Secret Service and Dallas police have reviewed film footage of the Adlai Stevenson protests, and they have made still photos of key Dallas demonstrators to distribute among police officers in charge of access at the airport and the luncheon.

The security for the motorcade is a different matter. During these events, the presidential motorcades generally proceed at twenty miles per hour, though they are often forced to slow down considerably in thick crowds. The president will pass in front of hundreds of buildings and below thousands and thousands of windows. There simply is no way to inspect every single building along the motorcade route, despite what the *Dallas Morning News* reported.

The security team drives along the prospective course. As the car makes its way through downtown, a Secret Service agent looks up at the skyscrapers surrounding them. He turns to one of the other members of the security detail and says:

"Hell, we'd be sitting ducks."[15]

Stanley Marcus is in New York on business, and he's pleased to get away from Dallas for a while. He loves his hometown, but he's always energized by his visits to New York, where he enjoys taking in the shows on Broadway. There's plenty to choose from: Neil Simon's comedy *Barefoot in the Park*, which is being hailed for its breakout performance by a young actor named Robert Redford. There's also Zero Mostel in *A Funny Thing Happened on the Way to the Forum* and Edward Albee's smash hit, *Who's Afraid of Virginia Woolf?*

But even in New York, Marcus hears a lot about Kennedy's upcoming visit to Dallas. Several friends have contacted him to complain that local Democrats are being frozen out of the Kennedy luncheon. Dallas's conservative leadership—in the form of the Citizens Council—is allocating the seats at the event, and the invitations are going to their friends and colleagues, rather than the loyal Democrats who have supported Kennedy.

Marcus sighs deeply. It's just another example of small-mindedness in Dallas.

The phone in his hotel suite rings. An operator tells him to hold the line for the vice president of the United States. After a few moments, Lyndon B. Johnson's booming voice comes over the wire.

Johnson explains yet another problem with Kennedy's Dallas visit. The president is supposed to be fund-raising in Texas, but not enough people in Dallas are stepping forward to help foot the bill for the luncheon. Johnson tells him, "Stanley, we need more money to make proper arrangements, and that crowd in Dallas isn't doing enough to get it. We need $25,000 and we need it right away."

Marcus sees his golden opportunity. Maybe the stinginess of the local welcoming committee will be enough to convince the president to change his plans.

"I sure wish to hell you'd persuade Kennedy not to come," Marcus says to Johnson. "It is a grave mistake to come to Dallas."

The vice president is impatient. He's already heard too much of this second-guessing about the president's schedule.

"I don't care what you think," he tells Marcus, "nor does it make any difference what I think about the President coming down to Dallas. He is coming to Dallas, so go out and raise the money."[16]

Reverend W. A. Criswell often works on his homilies well in advance—and he has been carefully preparing a special one to deliver next Sunday, in the wake of President Kennedy's visit to Dallas.

He is going to call the post-Kennedy sermon: "For God and Country."

Now he turns to today's sermon for the faithful in downtown Dallas, just a couple of blocks from Jack Ruby's club, just down the street from where Lee Harvey Oswald has recently gone to work at the Texas School Book Depository.

The preacher is still a loyal son of the South, as loyal perhaps as General Walker. And so he decides, this Sunday, to invoke the name of another uncompromising warrior general in today's sermon. Walker is unbending, and so is First Baptist of Dallas. He is preaching about Stonewall Jackson, the Confederate general:

"A godly man, a man of deep personal piety and prayer . . . when the tide was turning against the South, Stonewall Jackson . . . led his forces in a mighty and courageous effort . . ."

Criswell adds that his church is just like the Confederate general fighting to save the South and all it stood for. It is "like a stone wall" in the "heart of this great city" standing against "the floods of infidelity and iniquity and blasphemy."[17]

Bernard Weissman still hasn't sold a single carpet in Dallas, but now he has $1,000 cash in his pocket. The money is not his—it's a deposit for the *Dallas Morning News* to reserve the full-page advertisement for November 22. The money has been raised by friends and members of the Birch Society, including H. L. Hunt's son.

The full cost of the advertisement, if it is approved, will be $1,462. The copy, written by Larrie Schmidt, is aggressive. The ad also contains eleven questions, most of which have come from a John Birch Society memo given to Schmidt by the Dallas oilman who helped raise the funds for the ad. The oilman suggested that it would be easier to secure the funding if the John Birch questions appeared in the advertisement. Schmidt has complied.

Weissman can't help but be a little nervous as he meets with the advertising officers at the *Morning News*. Weissman is still coming to grips with how he suddenly became the point person for this effort.

The oilman, Joseph Grinnan, said his name couldn't be used since he is so closely associated with the John Birch Society—which doesn't want to be publicly identified as the source of the advertisement. If Larrie Schmidt's name is on the ad, the paper will almost certainly refuse to run it. The only choice is Weissman. Schmidt points out that having an obviously Jewish name associated with such a hard-edged anti-Kennedy indictment will confuse and demoralize the leftists. He solemnly notes that using Weissman's name will inoculate conservatives from the usual charges that they are anti-Semitic.

Schmidt finally adds that he personally sold a hell of a lot more life insurance after he became publicly associated with the Adlai Stevenson incident. In Dallas, being an outspoken conservative is apparently good for business.

Weissman finally agrees to put his name on the full-page ad.

He and Schmidt realize that they need to have some sort of organization associated with the ad. So they invent one: the American Fact-Finding Committee, with Bernard Weissman as chairman.

As Weissman talks with the ad people at the *Morning News*, he strikes them as a little nervous and jumpy. An advertising man is asking him for the name of the organization Weissman represents.

Weissman pauses.

He can't recall the name. Shrugging apologetically, he begins digging through his pockets. Finally, he finds the scrap of paper he'd written the name on. He pulls it out, reads it quickly, and announces: "The American Fact-Finding Committee."

The ad people finish collecting the necessary information and give Weissman a receipt for his $1,000 deposit. Weissman listens as the man tells him that all political advertisements must be reviewed by the paper's executives. If the ad is approved, he can return in two days to pay the remainder of the balance.

A provocative political ad like this will most likely go all the way to the top floor, to Dealey's office.

General Walker is among the two hundred or so people assembled in the ballroom of the Baker Hotel on November 18 for a talk by Alabama Governor George Wallace.

He is listening attentively to one of his favorite politicians in America—but Walker is also aware that he will have to leave Dallas, and soon, well before Kennedy arrives. Tomorrow, he is scheduled to fly to Mississippi and meet with white supremacists and KKK members in Hattiesburg. That city has been on the front lines of the civil rights movement in recent months: Only twelve of the seventy-five hundred eligible African Americans in the county have been allowed to register to vote, while white registration is close to 100 percent.

Wallace would approve of Walker's mission in Mississippi. A year earlier, Wallace won his race for governor, and at his inauguration he proclaimed: "I say segregation now, segregation tomorrow, segregation forever." In June, Wallace stood in a doorway to prevent black students from enrolling at the University of Alabama. He stepped aside only after Kennedy federalized the Alabama National Guard—and not before Wallace read a fiery statement on states' rights to assembled television cameras.

Wallace is the rising star on America's far right, and he's chosen Dallas as the perfect place to make a special announcement: He is going to run for president against John Kennedy.

He has picked Dallas to launch his campaign for a very simple reason: Dallas is the financial and public relations headquarters for America's ultra-conservatives.

"People all over the nation are aroused by the implications of the Kennedy civil rights legislation," Wallace tells Walker and the others in the Dallas audience. "People all over the country are just as disturbed as we are and they are going to do something about it... The American people are going to save this country next year."[18]

As Wallace warms up, he begins denouncing Robert Kennedy's Justice Department: "It is vitally necessary that the people know exactly to what extent the Justice Department civil rights attorneys have consorted with, aided and abetted the flood of beatniks, sex perverts, narcotics addicts and common criminals who have invaded Alabama as so-called civil rights workers."[19]

Suddenly, a loud crashing sound is heard in the ballroom.

Wallace ducks instinctively.

There is momentary confusion. It takes everyone a few seconds to register what has just happened.

A TV newsman was filming General Walker as he listened to Wallace.

Walker suddenly jerked to his feet and knocked the camera out of the newsman's hands. Then he shoved the astonished reporter, who fell back onto a group of guests seated at another table, sending glasses, silverware, and dishes crashing to the floor.

The ballroom is stone silent as everyone takes in the scene.

Walker, all eyes on him, nods curtly at Wallace.

"I beg your pardon," the general says, taking his seat.

On November 19, Dealey's *Dallas Morning News* announces the Kennedy motorcade route on the front page. The President and First Lady will travel along Main Street and then exit downtown beneath the triple underpass. The map makes it clear that Kennedy will pass by Dealey Plaza and the Texas School Book Depository.

There is other news: a new city ordinance designed to crack down on the sorts of protests that greeted Adlai Stevenson. The clear intent is to protect the president during his upcoming visit. The ordinance prohibits demonstrators from "interfering with a public or private assembly by the use of insulting, threatening or obscene language or intimidation." The city attorney tells reporters: "This also gives the police the right to disperse a group and break up a demonstration."[20]

On the top floors of the newspaper building, Ted Dealey has spent the last few months preparing to step aside from his post at the paper. He has named his son Joe as president of the company. And with that title, Joe would typically review political advertisements in advance of publication. But today, Joe is at a conference in Miami, and many of the other top executives are also out of town. The old man, Ted Dealey, is on call when it comes time to review the WELCOME MR. KENNEDY advertisement from Bernard Weissman's American Fact-Finding Committee.

Dealey reads the copy, and he approves—very much.

The advertisement, as far as he can see, matches exactly what his paper has been saying about the president for years.

Bernard Weissman meets again with the advertising men at the *Dallas Morning News*. Weissman learns that his ad has been approved, and he pays the remaining balance—$462—in cash. Weissman also has a late item to insert into the advertisement. Joe Grinnan, the oilman who raised the money for the ad, brought him a scrap of paper earlier and said: "This has to go in. Go back and have them change the ad."

A twelfth question has been added to the list. This one refers to the recent executions of Diem and Nhu in Vietnam.

The newspaper adman promises to add the new material. He also has a mock-up of the advertisement. As the men view the ad, Weissman is underwhelmed. There's nothing really eye-catching about the rows of plain text. There's nothing to stop people from simply turning the page. He and the man begin discussing design changes. They agree to set WELCOME MR. KENNEDY in bigger, bolder letters across the top.

But the ad still needs something else.

Finally, Weissman figures out what it is. He suggests adding a black border to the ad. The adman tries out a one-eighth-inch border. Weissman asks him to make it even more grand. Then the adman creates a quarter-inch border. Weissman is pleased.

It doesn't occur to him until later that the black border mimics the black borders used for death notices.[21]

General Walker is in New Orleans on November 20, where he plans to spend the next two days. He has no public events scheduled. Instead, he arrives at the National American Bank building downtown for a meeting with Judge Leander Perez, a cigar-twirling local political boss who is one of America's most notorious racists. Perez has described the civil rights movement as the work of "all those Jews who were supposed to have been cremated at Buchenwald and Dachau but weren't." He describes Negroes as animals "right out of the jungle." Perez has not only incited riots against African Americans, but also organized reprisals against white parents who have allowed their children to attend integrated schools.[22]

This is not Walker's first meeting with a notorious racist. In late October, after the Adlai Stevenson riot in Dallas, he traveled to Brandon, Mississippi. He visited with Byron De La Beckwith, the man who has been arrested for murdering civil rights leader Medgar Evers. Walker later told the press that he extended his "best wishes" to Beckwith, describing the prisoner as "in good spirits and very courageous."[23]

In New Orleans, Walker spends several hours visiting with Judge Perez before he adjourns to the massive Jung Hotel on Canal Street. There he meets privately with another thirty-five ultra-conservative political leaders. The gathering continues until well past midnight. Walker plans another series of meetings for the following day.

A light rain is falling outside the White House on November 21 as John F. Kennedy carefully adjusts his back brace in his bedroom. A very long day is ahead of him, and he knows that his back will be aching by the end of it. In a couple of hours he will leave for Texas, taking along his wife, his staff, a contingent of thirteen Texas congressmen, and a planeload of reporters. His press secretary, Pierre Salinger, won't be able to accompany him on this trip because he is scheduled to fly to Tokyo. Normally Andrew Hatcher, Salinger's second in command, would replace him. But Hatcher is African American, and the Kennedy team knows that a black spokesman won't help their political efforts in Texas. Instead, a press aide named Malcolm Kilduff is assigned to make the trip with the president.

Kennedy knots his dark blue tie, fastening his PT boat clip into place. Once he finishes lacing his shoes, he inspects his appearance in the mirror. His face still has a boyish quality, but the presidency is quickly aging him. His reddish brown hair is increasingly showing strands of gray, and the wrinkles in his face are growing more pronounced. His eyes, always alert with curiosity and intelligence, also bear a hint of sadness.

Walking to the door, he calls out for his children, Caroline and John, who come running to see him. Caroline is outfitted in a blue leotard and a dark blue velvet dress. John is wearing plaid shorts. Early mornings are usually their special time with their father. Today, Jackie is busy having her hair done, and so Kennedy and the children have breakfast together. He half listens to their chatter—both children are excited about their upcoming birthdays—as he scans the morning papers, occasionally pausing to gently tease them.

At nine fifteen, the children's British nanny, Maud Shaw, arrives. It is time for Caroline to go off to school. She runs over to hug her father good-bye. "I love you, Daddy," she says. John goes off reluctantly with his nanny, but his father promises that he will get to ride in the helicopter later in the morning.

Kennedy then makes his way to the Oval Office, where he meets with two U.S. ambassadors and conducts other business. He learns that the updated weather forecasts in Texas are calling for unseasonably warm temperatures. Mrs. Kennedy has already painstakingly selected and packed an assortment of woolen winter outfits. The president is annoyed. It is too late to change now, so they'll just have to make the best of it. He really wants this first campaign trip with Jackie to be a success. His political instincts tell him that she will be a great asset on the campaign trail.

Before leaving the Oval Office, Kennedy reviews his speech for Dallas. He calls in his adviser, Ted Sorensen, for a final consultation. The two men have been working on it together for the past week, trading drafts back and forth. Sorensen brings in the latest draft and waits as the president reads it. Kennedy is pleased. The address will be a ringing defense of his record. It will also directly challenge the reactionary forces in Dallas:

> Ignorance and misinformation can handicap the progress of a city or a company, but they can, if allowed to prevail in foreign policy, handicap this country's security. In a world of complex and continuing problems, in a world full of frustrations and irritations, America's leadership must be guided by the lights of learning and reason—or else those who confuse rhetoric with reality and the plausible with the possible will gain the popular ascendancy with their seemingly swift and simple solutions to every world problem.
>
> There will always be dissident voices heard in the land, expressing opposition without alternatives, finding fault but never favor, perceiving gloom on every side and seeking influence without responsibility. Those voices are inevitable...
>
> We cannot expect that everyone, to use the phrase of a decade ago, will "talk sense to the American people." But we can hope that fewer people will listen to nonsense. And the notion that this Nation is headed for defeat through deficit, or that strength is but a matter of slogans, is nothing but just plain nonsense.

Kennedy nods approvingly as he finishes reading.

"It's good," he tells Sorensen.

But then he begins to worry that perhaps the speech is *too* serious. He suggests adding a joke or two to break the tension. Sorensen takes the papers back and promises to find some jokes.[24]

It is now 10:45 a.m. and three helicopters are waiting at the

White House helipad to carry Kennedy and his entourage to Andrews Air Force Base. The president and his son climb into Helicopter One along with JFK's secretary, Evelyn Lincoln, three Secret Service agents, and General Ted Clifton, a military aide. White House staff and pool reporters pile into Helicopters Two and Three.

Everyone is ready to leave, but one person is missing. The president sits anxiously in the helicopter, nervously tapping his fingers on his right knee. His days are scheduled in minutes, not hours. Still no Jackie. Finally, he speaks to General Clifton and Secret Service Agent Clint Hill: "See if she's waiting over there."

The two men dash back to the White House, find Jackie, and bring her out to the helicopter.[25]

Soon, at Andrews Air Force Base, the parents hug John Jr. good-bye.

"I want to come," the boy tells his father, beginning to cry.

"You can't," Kennedy says softly.

The president kisses his son again and pats him gently. Then he speaks to Agent Bob Foster, who will be helping watch over John while his parents are away.

"You take care of John, Mr. Foster," Kennedy says.

Final security preparations are being made for the presidential luncheon at the Trade Mart. Secret Service agents have asked for and received a list of key personnel working the event—the caterers, the cooks, the food handlers, the waiters, maids, porters. Even the organist at tomorrow's luncheon will receive a background check.

Some five thousand yellow roses are being brought to the Trade Mart as table decorations. Every single rose will be checked to ensure that it does not contain any explosives. The menu for the Friday meal includes steak. President Kennedy and all other Catholics attending the luncheon have received a special dispensation from the church allowing them to eat beef on that day. The president's steak will be selected at random from the thousands of meals being cooked.

Elsewhere in Dallas, cheaply printed handbills are appearing on car windshields downtown and at local universities.

The flyers are designed to look like WANTED posters, only the face they show is that of the president of the United States. Kennedy is depicted in a front view and a profile view, just like a police mug shot. Underneath the photos, in large type, the flyers read WANTED FOR TREASON, beneath which two columns of text explain the charges:

THIS MAN is wanted for treasonous activities against the United States:

1. Betraying the Constitution (which he swore to uphold): He is turning the sovereignty of the U.S. over to the communist controlled United Nations.

He is betraying our friends (Cuba, Katanga, Portugal) and befriending our enemies (Russia, Yugoslavia, Poland).

2. He has been WRONG on innumerable issues affecting the security of the U.S. (United Nations—Berlin wall—Missile removal—Cuba—Wheat deals—Test Ban Treaty, etc.)

3. He has been lax in enforcing Communist Registration laws.

4. He has given support and encouragement to the Communist inspired racial riots.

5. He has illegally invaded a sovereign State with federal troops.

6. He has consistently appointed Anti-Christians to Federal office; Upholds the Supreme Court in its Anti-Christian rulings. Aliens and known Communists abound in Federal offices.

7. He has been caught in fantastic LIES to the American people (including personal ones like his previous marriage and divorce).

The day before Kennedy is scheduled to land in Dallas, Juanita Craft announces she is planning a new kind of civil rights protest: She will hold a "Bombingham Tea" two days after Kennedy leaves Dallas.

It is a play on words, a nod to the nightmare that unfolded in September in Birmingham, Alabama, when four young girls were killed after a bomb exploded one Sunday at the 16th Street Baptist Church. The event led Craft into immediate action—she held prayer rallies, vigils, in honor of the young women. They could have been her kids, her young people, the ones she essentially adopted in Dallas. It could have happened in Dallas.

She knows there was a bomb scare when Dr. King came to Dallas several months ago. She lived in the South Dallas areas in the early 1950s when white neighborhoods were being integrated, when Dallas made national news for its string of bombings against blacks. She could have gone to be a teacher in some small, all-black town in Texas. It might have been safer. But she stayed in Dallas.

Now, with the president coming to the city, she feels like she has to do something to make a statement—and she has always held teas, socials, dances, bake sales, and get-togethers to raise money for the Dallas Youth Council of the NAACP to take trips to the national NAACP conventions. She contacted the ministers at Warren Methodist Church and asked if they were willing to allow several of her high school students to stage the "Bombingham Tea": There will be music, freedom songs, voter registration literature, displays devoted to a Stay In School project, and fund-raising for next spring's bus trip to the NAACP national convention in Washington, DC.

Craft never really tells people that her mother was a mulatto, a mixture of English, Indian, and Negro. But the older she gets, the more she has been thinking about the blood coursing through her veins. She is, of course, of African descent. But she is more than black. By now she realizes that she owes just as much allegiance to the English and the Indians as the Africans. She is fully integrated, from within. She is everything the racists fear.[26]

Her "Bombingham Tea" might show the world that here, in Dallas, there is nothing as evil, nothing as mad, as what happens in other places.

Air Force One touches down in San Antonio at 1:30 p.m. local time, on the twenty-first. Waiting for the president and First Lady are Vice President Lyndon Johnson and his wife, Lady Bird, along with other dignitaries. Texas Governor John Connally has hustled into the receiving line, having only just arrived himself. People were beginning to wonder if Connally would even show. The Texas governor is a Democrat, but a very conservative one, and he's made no secret of his disagreement with the Kennedy administration's views on civil rights.

Connally is not happy about Kennedy's visit to his state. The conservative governor is far more popular in Texas than the president, and he doesn't want to be dragged down by an association with Kennedy. Many of his allies are sympathetic. Earlier in the week, when he'd finished a speech before a lobbying group in Austin, the emcee had excused Connally from the rest of the program. Referring to Kennedy's upcoming visit, the man said, "You may get back to your preparation for the Irish wake to be held here next Friday."[27]

Now, Connally has no choice but to be hospitable to the president. As he explained it to the Dallas Citizens Council, the governor is like a captain of a ship, and the admiral is asking for permission to come aboard. You can't tell the president not to come.

In San Antonio, Jackie steps out of Air Force One ahead of her husband. She is greeted by hot, humid weather along with boisterous cheers. She is dressed in a white wool bouclé suit and a knitted black beret. She waves to the assembled crowd as she accepts a dozen yellow roses.

A motorcade leads Jack and Jackie from the airport to Brooks Air Force Base, where the president will dedicate an aerospace medical center. This is the first presidential visit to San Antonio in fifteen years, and over 125,000 people jam the streets to cheer the First Couple. San Antonio schools have declared a holiday to allow children and their families the chance to see the president. In Dallas, no such arrangements have been made. Schools will remain in session.

The crowds are exuberant. San Antonio, bolstered by Mexican American voters, favored JFK over Nixon in 1960. Now people are turning out to claim their reward. Cries of "Viva Jackie!" can be heard along the parade route as the presidential limousine glides by.

In Dallas, final security arrangements are being discussed at police headquarters. Secret Service Agents Winston Lawson and Forrest Sorrels are meeting with Police Chief Jesse Curry and his top command.

Everything seems to be in order. Three hundred fifty uniformed officers from the Dallas Police Department—a third of the entire force—will be on hand at Love Field, the Trade Mart, and the motorcade. They will be supplemented by dozens more officers from the Sheriff's Department and the Department of Public Safety. Each officer has been fully briefed about presidential security. Dallas police have also tested all radios and walkie-talkies, making sure to install fresh batteries in each unit.

A debate arises about the proper level of motorcycle protection around the president. The police envision surrounding the limousine with eight motorcycles. Agent Lawson interjects that JFK does not like motorcycles directly alongside his car because of the loud noise they make. They also interfere with the crowd's view of him. After some discussion, everyone agrees to have four motorcycles accompany the president. Two will be on each side of the limousine, just behind the rear fender.

The meeting is interrupted by an important call for Chief Curry. It has to do with a flyer circulating around Dallas. A copy of the flyer is quickly located and brought to the meeting.

The officials examining the handbill are gravely concerned. Curry has been boasting to the Secret Service that his men have infiltrated Dallas's extremist groups, but the cops are forced to admit that they have no idea who is responsible for the handbill. Curry promises an immediate investigation. As the meeting breaks up, everyone understands that while the security team has planned as well as it can, there are still threats to the president, and no one is quite certain what direction they will come from, or when or how they will strike.

*   *   *

As if by political and poetic fate, Kennedy's presidential opponent Richard Nixon is in Dallas to attend the annual convention of the American Bottlers of Carbonated Beverages. The former vice president is appearing on behalf of Pepsi-Cola, one of the corporate clients his law firm represents. Pepsi has also brought in actress Joan Crawford—she and Nixon arrived on the same company jet.

Seventy-five hundred conventioneers are gathered at Market Hall, the complex that houses the Trade Mart where President Kennedy's luncheon is to be held tomorrow. Nixon's role is to be seen and be sociable. He attends the Pepsi-Cola reception and shakes hands with many of the company's 810 delegates. He also finds time to chat with newsmen in his suite at the Baker Hotel. Nixon appears uncharacteristically relaxed. When asked about Kennedy's upcoming visit, Nixon jabs at the president, pointing out that the trip is completely political, no matter what the administration claims. Nixon also swings at LBJ, predicting that he will be dropped from the Kennedy ticket: "Lyndon was chosen in 1960 because he could help the ticket in the South. Now he is becoming a political liability in the South, just as he is in the North."

Nixon ends his talk with a statesman-like appeal:

"I hope President Kennedy will receive a courteous reception in Dallas. Just because you may disagree with his views is no excuse for discourtesy towards the President of the United States."[28]

After just two hours in San Antonio the presidential party flies to Houston, where another motorcade winds its way through the city.

Jackie has changed into a black cut-velvet suit, a double strand of pearls, and diamond earrings. In the Grand Ballroom of the Rice Hotel, she makes a short speech to the League of United Latin American Citizens, and she delivers it in nearly flawless Spanish—something she has been practicing for days back in Washington.

"I am very happy to be in the great state of Texas," she says, "and I am especially pleased to be with you who are part of the noble Spanish tradition which has contributed so much to Texas." Her husband beams proudly at the sustained applause for his wife.

Late in the evening, the presidential party flies out of Houston, arriving in Fort Worth after 11 p.m. A light rain is falling. The forecast calls for clouds and rain in Dallas all day tomorrow. The weather is appropriate, many people think, considering the reception some people fear the president is going to receive there.

The idea of John F. Kennedy visiting the city that reviles him is leading to nervous jokes. Even Vice President Johnson, who is scheduled to introduce Kennedy at a dinner in Austin—the stop after Dallas—has gotten in on the act.

Johnson plans to end his Austin speech with:

"And thank God, Mr. President, that you came out of Dallas alive."[29]

In Washington, Senator Hubert Humphrey is also thinking about Dallas as he gives a speech to the National Association for Mental Health.

Humphrey, a devout liberal, tells his audience that whole communities "can be afflicted with emotional instability, frustrations, and irrational behavior...that emotional instability that afflicts a significant but small minority in our midst that some call the extreme right, some the Birchers...They still see the world in total black or white...They are still substituting dogma for creative thought. They are still angry, fearful, deeply and fundamentally disturbed by the world around them."

Humphrey proceeds to warn the audience:

"The act of an emotionally unstable person or irresponsible citizen can strike down a great leader."[30]

There are twenty-five hundred people clutching invitations to have lunch at noon today with President John F. Kennedy and First Lady Jacqueline Kennedy. The invitation list—coordinated by the White House, by Governor John Connally, and by the Dallas Citizens Committee—sets aside one hundred seats for black residents, and most of those are handed to Rhett James for distribution as he sees fit.[1]

Juanita Craft is one of the people getting a treasured ticket to see the president and First Lady. Back in February, she and James saw President Kennedy and the First Lady in the White House. Now they will help host them in Dallas.

The black leadership in the city often remains splintered—there are people who fear Martin Luther King, those who idolize him, and many who remain suspicious of LBJ and John Connally. But there is almost a uniform feeling that Kennedy really does hold the promise of something better. Craft is hearing it from her close white friends in Dallas, too. The affection for Kennedy is almost tangible at times—except when it seems to be sucked inside the drowning pool created by a handful of misguided souls in the city.

It is also what Stanley Marcus knows, and what Rhett James knows. That a handful of men in Dallas have stolen the microphone, they have screamed louder, spent more money to be heard—they have bullied from the altar, the airwaves, the editorial pages of the newspaper. And they have done the very thing that they always swore they would never do: They have warped the very image of the city. And they have, without really understanding it, turned their city into an object of suspicion and derision.

Maybe the president's mere presence in Dallas will be the final balm, the ultimate palliative, something to cleanse away all the acidity: the awful way that some people associated Edwin Walker's segregationist armada with everyone in Dallas...the way people outside Texas remembered Reverend Criswell's racist rants and his endless, anti-Catholic diatribes, the way people thought the hedonistic rich men idled away their time spewing racism, the way the lunatic rich men like Hunt saw communists in every corner of the nation, the way Dealey had mocked the president as a weakling, a little girl bowing and scraping to Russia.

Craft knows one thing: She is going to have lunch with the president in a city where just two years ago she couldn't always sit alongside white men and white women and be served a meal.

Dawn arrives in Dallas with heavy clouds and a steady drizzle. An updated forecast judges that a cool front sweeping in from the west may clear the skies later in the day. In homes across the city, people are stepping outside into the wet dim light to claim newspapers from their lawns. All of the state's papers are reporting on the Democrats' public feuding. The *Morning News* has pounced on the story with glee. Its banner headline reads: STORM OF POLITICAL CONTROVERSY SWIRLS AROUND KENNEDY ON VISIT. Inside the paper is more bad news for the Democrats: NIXON PREDICTS JFK MAY DROP JOHNSON.

On its editorial page, however, the *News* has opted for a conciliatory message to Kennedy: "Dallas sheds its sharp cleavages of partisanship at noon today in extending the hand of fellowship to the President of the United States and his attractive wife...Dallas hopes, Mr. President, that your brief interlude here will be pleasant."

On page 14 is Bernard Weissman's full-page, black-bordered advertisement proclaiming: WELCOME MR. KENNEDY TO DALLAS:

MR. KENNEDY, despite contentions on the part of your administration, the State Department, the Mayor of Dallas, the Dallas City Council, and members of your party, we free-thinking and America-thinking citizens of Dallas still have, through a Constitution largely ignored by you, the right to address our grievances, to question you, to disagree with you, and to criticize you.

In asserting this constitutional right, we wish to ask you publicly the following questions—indeed, questions of paramount importance and interest to all free peoples everywhere—which we trust you will answer...in public, without sophistry.

These questions are:

WHY is Latin America turning either anti-American or Communistic, or both, despite increased U.S. foreign aid, State Department policy, and your own Ivy-Tower pronouncements?

WHY do you say we have built a "wall of freedom" around Cuba when there is no freedom in Cuba today? Because of your policy, thousands of Cubans have been imprisoned, are starving and being persecuted—with thousands already murdered and thousands more awaiting execution and, in addition, the entire population of almost 7,000,000 Cubans are living in slavery.

WHY have you approved the sale of wheat and corn to our enemies when you know the Communist soldiers "travel on their stomachs" just as ours do? Communist soldiers are daily wounding and/or killing American soldiers in South Viet Nam.

WHY did you host, salute and entertain Tito—Moscow's Trojan Horse—just a short time after our sworn enemy, Khrushchev, embraced the Yugoslav dictator as a great hero and leader of Communism?

WHY have you urged greater aid, comfort, recognition, and understanding for Yugoslavia, Poland, Hungary, and other Communist countries, while turning your back on the pleas of Hungarian, East German, Cuban and other anti-Communist freedom fighters?

WHY did Cambodia kick the U.S. out of its country after we poured nearly 400 Million Dollars of aid into its ultra-leftist government?

WHY has Gus Hall, head of the U.S. Communist Party praised almost every one of your policies and announced that the party will endorse and support your re-election in 1964?

WHY have you banned the showing at U.S. military bases of the film "Operation Abolition"—the movie by the House Committee on Un-American Activities exposing Communism in America?

WHY have you ordered or permitted your brother Bobby, the Attorney General, to go soft on Communists, fellow-travelers, and ultra-leftists in America, while permitting him to persecute loyal Americans who criticize you, your administration, and your leadership?

WHY are you in favor of the U.S. continuing to give economic aid to Argentina, in spite of that fact that Argentina has just seized almost 400 Million Dollars of American private property?

WHY has the Foreign Policy of the United States degenerated to the point that the C.I.A. is arranging coups and having staunch Anti-Communist Allies of the U.S. bloodily exterminated?

WHY have you scrapped the Monroe Doctrine in favor of the "Spirit of Moscow"?

MR. KENNEDY, as citizens of these United States of America, we DEMAND answers to these questions, and we want them NOW.

The organization identified as responsible for the advertisement is "The American Fact-Finding Committee, an unaffiliated and non-partisan group of citizens who wish truth."

Police Chief Jesse Curry appears on television to make a special plea to all Dallas citizens: "Because of the unfortunate incident which happened with Mr. Stevenson, people everywhere will be hyper-critical of our behavior. Nothing must occur that is disrespectful or degrading to the president of the United States. He is entitled to the highest respect, and the law enforcement agencies of this area are going to do everything possible to insure that no untoward accidents or incident occurs. We will take immediate action if any suspicious conduct is observed."

Curry has decided to deputize the entire city: "We also urge all good citizens to be alert for such conduct. Citizens themselves may take preventative action if it becomes obvious that someone is planning to commit an act harmful or degrading to the president."[2]

Walker's army has been busy overnight.

Hundreds more WANTED FOR TREASON flyers have been distributed along the motorcade route. Copies of the flyer have also been placed inside newspaper vending machines, interleaved with copies of the *Dallas Morning News*.

In a fashionable section of North Dallas, a family is gathered around their kitchen table. The father is skimming the *Morning News* and the grade-school-aged daughter is finishing her breakfast. The mother and father have been discussing Kennedy's impending visit. As the husband and daughter prepare to leave, the mother, a member of the local PTA, kisses them good-bye. As they walk out the door, the mother calls after them: "I'm going to take a gun and go to that parade and shoot him—bingo—right in the head."[3]

A small crowd is already beginning to gather at Love Field to see the Kennedys even though Air Force One is not scheduled to arrive for another four hours. Security is exceptionally tight. Dallas police are everywhere. Several are posted on rooftops overlooking the area. Others are controlling access to the airport. The cops scrutinize the onlookers and direct them to a spot behind a chain-link fence. Mixing in with the crowd are several plainclothes detectives. In all there are over two hundred law enforcement personnel on duty.

Ted Dealey's forty-four-year-old son, Joe, is glancing through the morning paper. He has been out of town in Miami for most of the week, and he only arrived back in Dallas late last night.

He is scheduled to go to the Trade Mart later as one of the guests for the Kennedy luncheon. Dealey, like his father, is no fan of John F. Kennedy, but he is more diplomatic. He has been working diligently with other Dallas business leaders to try to repair the city's tarnished image in the wake of the Stevenson incident.

He turns the page of the paper and comes face-to-face with the advertisement from the American Fact-Finding Committee. A sickening feeling washes over him. He can think of only one person who would approve an ad like this on the very day of the president's visit.

He picks up the phone and calls his father.

"It's like inviting someone to dinner and then throwing tapioca in his face," he tells his father, the man who derided Kennedy to his face.

Ted Dealey is unmoved. The old man reminds his son that the advertisement merely endorses what the *News* has been saying editorially for years.

"That's not the point," his son says. "The timing is bad."[4]

Heavy rains have been falling, but that doesn't dampen the spirits of the large crowd gathered outside the Hotel Texas, a stolid, brown brick building that rises fifteen stories above Fort Worth, just thirty miles west of Dallas, within earshot of the railroad switchyard and within sniffing distance of the famed Fort Worth stockyards. People have been gathering here since 5 a.m., hoping to catch a glimpse of the First Couple. These are the people who haven't been invited to the private chamber of commerce breakfast Kennedy will be speaking to later in the morning. These are Fort Worth's working folks—mechanics, railroad brakemen, factory workers, clerks, waiters, union people. Despite the rain, people in the crowd are laughing and talking. They've been told that the president will come out to speak to them.

On the eighth floor, inside his three-room suite, Kennedy has already showered and dressed. The Kennedys arrived after midnight, very tired, to find the air conditioner blowing full-blast. The president ordered it shut off, but the controls seemed to be stuck, and it took a while to locate someone on staff who could finally turn it off. A portable television on casters is stationed near the door of the tiny bathroom. The president is amused to see a sign on top of the TV: HOTEL TEXAS. CHECK OUT TIME IS 12:30 P.M.

IF YOU PLAN TO STAY AFTER THIS TIME PLEASE CONTACT ASSISTANT MANAGER.[5]

Jackie is still asleep in the south-facing room, in a small bed with a brass headboard made to look like harp strings. JFK can hear the loud crowd outside, and he is pleased. This trip to Texas has been going very well. People have been far friendlier than he expected. Jackie, too, has been holding up well. Although she will never be a natural campaigner, she almost seems to be enjoying herself at times.

Kennedy walks into the First Lady's room so he can look out the windows at the gathering. He gently wakes her and then checks the window. The reception is even bigger than he could have imagined. There are several thousand people down there.

"Gosh, look at that crowd!" he says, turning to his wife and smiling happily. "Just look! Isn't that terrific?"[6]

In the Will Rogers Suite on the thirteenth floor, Lady Bird Johnson is dressing. These accommodations are larger than the Kennedys'. In fact, they are the Hotel Texas's finest. The Kennedys were originally scheduled to stay here, but the Secret Service overruled the proposition because the multiple entrances make the space too difficult to guard. That's why the Kennedys have been boxed into a smaller space five floors below.

Lady Bird is normally a steady, upbeat person, but this trip has been hard on her. Her husband is under attack from both the liberal and conservative wings of the party. The president has privately chewed him out for not being able to control the competing factions. During this trip, he's been mostly ignored as the crowds focus on the charismatic Kennedys.

And there are also the ominous developments in Washington— a Senate criminal investigation is targeting LBJ's protégé Bobby Baker, and threatening to swamp Johnson as well. *Life* magazine is preparing a major story on his business affairs. Even if he avoids being indicted for corruption, his position on the Democratic ticket is hardly secure. He'd been brought aboard to keep the South in line, but now in the wake of Kennedy's actions on behalf of civil rights, the South is turning away from Kennedy—and Johnson. LBJ no longer seems to be a political asset, and rumors are swirling that the president will dump him. Her husband has been in a sour mood for a long time now.

And now they are preparing to go back to Dallas. Lady Bird is still seared by the memory of her last campaign visit to the city, three years earlier. She is positive-minded, but a dark thought keeps crossing her mind: *There might be something ugly today.*

As she adjusts her clothing, she notices that her hands are trembling.[7]

When Nixon is driven to Love Field at 8:30 a.m., he sees the large crowd gathering to welcome President Kennedy. The moment is bittersweet for Nixon. Dallas was *his* city, not Kennedy's.

Nixon has famously sworn off politics after losing the governor's race in California in 1962. "You won't have Dick Nixon to kick around anymore," he'd told the press. But his reception in Dallas has been so pleasant. He enjoyed talking to the *Morning News*, portraying himself as a statesman while spreading a little innuendo to destabilize Lyndon Johnson. Bottlers' conventions are nice, but politics is Nixon's game.

It is now boarding time for American Airlines Flight 82 to New York. Nixon quickly walks up the steps to the plane. There are no throngs to cheer him as he leaves Dallas behind.

There are 158 Dallas police officers reporting for motorcade duty. The group includes eighteen motorcycle officers who will escort the procession. The others will be stationed at various points along the route. Their job is to clear all overpasses along the route and to monitor the onlookers for any sign of trouble.

The cops are mostly worried about an ugly prank—somebody throwing rotten eggs or tomatoes at the motorcade. But the possibility of a more violent act is not out of the question, either. Most police are assigned to the downtown area, since that's where the biggest crowds are expected.

★   ★   ★

In his suite, President Kennedy greets the hotel waiter, who has brought in a cart with breakfast. Kennedy shakes the man's hand and gives him a PT-boat tie clip as a gift. Sipping coffee, the president begins skimming the morning newspapers. He's annoyed to discover the focus is on the political feuding among the Texas politicians accompanying him on this trip. The only good headlines he can find are the ones about Jackie.

He rings for his aide Kenny O'Donnell, and tells him that the bickering must end right now. O'Donnell explains how the liberal Texas Senator Ralph Yarborough refused to ride in LBJ's car yesterday. Kennedy speaks very evenly. Today, the president says, will be different. "You tell him it's ride with Lyndon—or walk."[8]

Now Kennedy puts on his best face—it's time to go speak to the huge gathering of supporters outside. It is still drizzling. Secret Service Agent Bill Greer offers Kennedy a raincoat, but the president waves him off. A huge roar erupts from the eight thousand people as the president appears. A flatbed truck has been set up with a microphone and portable amplifier system. Kennedy steps forward to speak.

"There are no faint hearts in Fort Worth," he says, smiling broadly.

People cheer in response, but several in the audience are yelling, "Where's Jackie?"

Kennedy pauses and points up at the eighth floor. "Mrs. Kennedy is organizing herself. It takes her a little longer…" The crowd begins laughing. Kennedy offers another smile. "But of course she looks better than we do when she does it." More laughter.[9]

Upstairs, Jackie Kennedy can hear her husband addressing the Texans. She rises from bed and looks out the window. It's still raining. *Good*, she thinks. She's hoping the Secret Service will affix the bubbletop to the presidential limousine today. The bubbletop may not be bulletproof, but it sure is windproof—an important consideration for Jackie. She's tired of trying to keep her coiffure in place during the steady breeze.

Morning has come too soon for her after the long day yesterday. "Oh, God," she groans. "One day's campaigning can age a person thirty years."[10]

She considers the outfit she has selected for this day. Of all the cities they will visit in Texas, her husband was most concerned about how she would look in Dallas. "There are going to be all these rich, Republican women at that lunch," he told her, "wearing mink coats and diamond bracelets. And you've got to look as marvelous as any of them. Be simple—show these Texans what good taste really is."[11]

For Dallas she has selected a strawberry-pink wool suit designed by Coco Chanel with navy trim, gold buttons, and a matching pink pillbox hat.

It is 9 a.m., and Bernard Weissman needs to leave for work in a few minutes, but for now he is still enjoying the great satisfaction of seeing his name printed at the bottom of the full-page advertisement in the *Dallas Morning News*. Everyone in Dallas will know who he is.

He gets into his car and pulls onto Reiger Avenue. His employer, Carpet Engineers, is about fifteen minutes away, and there is a sales meeting scheduled for this morning. Weissman still hasn't sold a carpet, but he has an appointment in the afternoon with a potential client. Thanks to the ad in the *News*, he feels his prospects are looking up. And it's just in time, too, since he's already gone through most of his savings.

Weissman has no intention of seeing Kennedy while the president is in town. Instead, he plans to meet with Larrie Schmidt and Joe Grinnan at the DuCharme Club at twelve thirty to have a few beers over lunch.

In the Grand Ballroom of the Hotel Texas, a well-dressed gathering of two thousand Fort Worth business leaders has finished breakfast and waits expectantly for the president and First Lady to arrive. The Kennedys were due ten minutes earlier, at 9 a.m., but the president had gone outside to speak to the crowd.

Finally, the door to the kitchen opens and several Secret Service agents come out into the ballroom, followed a few seconds later by the president of the United States. A local high school band strikes up "Hail to the Chief" as flashbulbs pop and everyone rises to applaud—and to get a better view. Kennedy is the very picture of vibrant health, standing six feet tall, smiling and deeply tanned.

Kennedy remains standing until "Hail to the Chief" finishes, then he takes his seat at the head table. The spot next to him is conspicuously empty. Jackie is listed on the program, but she is not with him. People in the audience are disappointed—many of the women in particular came to get a good look at the First Lady.

The Texas Boys Choir launches into a fervent version of "The Eyes of Texas Are Upon You." When they finish, nothing else happens. Murmured exchanges break out in the audience. On stage, Kennedy whispers briefly to the emcee. After a few more minutes of muted confusion, the Texas Boys Choir begins another song, one not listed on the program: *There was a noble ranger, They called him Mustang Gray; He left his home when but a youth, Went ranging far away . . . like a brave old Texan, a-ranging he would go . . .*

As the children sing, Kennedy edits his speech. He'd originally planned to give a twenty-minute address, but now he's striking entire passages. The boys finish singing and the emcee starts a monologue, stalling for time. Finally, after several more minutes, he shouts happily: "And now, an event I know you all have been waiting for."

The crowd stands and applauds wildly as First Lady Jacqueline Kennedy finally walks in. She is in her pink suit and white gloves. There are whistles and yells. Some men are climbing up onto their chairs to get a better view. She walks stiffly past everyone, seeming a bit embarrassed. She finally spots her husband in the crowded room and moves quickly toward him. He smiles at her warmly. If he is annoyed that she is very late for this breakfast, nothing in his face betrays it.

Now it is time for the president to speak. After seeing the reception for his wife, he decides to improvise: "Two years ago I introduced myself in Paris as the man who had accompanied Mrs. Kennedy to Paris. I'm getting somewhat that same sensation as I travel around Texas." The audience laughs appreciatively and Jackie is giggling, covering her mouth with one of her white-gloved hands. Kennedy smiles. "Nobody wonders what Lyndon and I wear."[12]

John and Jackie Kennedy return to their suite at the Hotel Texas at 10 a.m. In forty-five minutes they will leave for Dallas. Kennedy's aide Kenny O'Donnell comes into the suite with a copy of the *Dallas Morning News*. The president skimmed the headlines earlier, but didn't look through the whole paper. O'Donnell shows him the full-page advertisement denouncing him on page 14. Kennedy reads every word, grimacing. Finished, he hands the paper over to Jackie for her inspection.

He shakes his head and says to O'Donnell: "Can you imagine a paper doing a thing like that?"

Then he turns to Jackie: "Oh, you know, we're heading into nut country today."

Kennedy begins pacing around the hotel room. He stops in front of his wife: "You know, last night would have been a hell of a night to assassinate a President."

She gives him a look.

"I mean it," he continues. "There was the rain, and the night, and we were all getting jostled. Suppose a man had a pistol in a briefcase."

He points at a wall with his finger and pretends to shoot: "Then he could have dropped the gun and the briefcase and melted away in the crowd."

A few weeks earlier, he'd met in the White House with Jim Bishop, the author of *The Day Lincoln Was Shot*. Kennedy said his feelings about assassination were similar to Lincoln's:

"Any man who is willing to exchange his life for mine can do so."

And now, the ad in Dealey's paper has brought back to the surface a reality he tries to suppress—there are people in America who would like to see him dead. He walks over to a window and looks outside.

"It would not be a very difficult job to shoot the president of the United States," he muses aloud. "All you'd have to do is get up in a high building with a high-powered rifle with a telescopic sight, and there's nothing anybody could do."[13]

From Love Field, Secret Service Agent Winston Lawson is calling the Hotel Texas. He says that the weather appears to be clearing a bit. He wonders whether or not to secure the bubbletop to the presidential limousine. Kenny O'Donnell knows that the president never likes to ride under it unless it's absolutely necessary.

"If the weather is clear and it is not raining," O'Donnell says, "have that bubbletop off."[14]

In Dallas, people are tuning in to KPCN, the latest radio station to broadcast H. L. Hunt's *Life Line* program, joining other local outlets that already air the show. As families race to get ready to go see the president's motorcade, they can hear the announcer saying:

You would not be able to sing "The Star Spangled Banner" or state your Pledge of Allegiance to the American flag, because our Stars and Stripes would be replaced by the Hammer and Sickle. You would not be able to celebrate Independence Day, Memorial Day, or Labor Day. You would not be able to observe Thanksgiving as we know it today, thanking the Lord for his blessings and fruitful harvest. You would not be able to celebrate any holiday of freedom.

If communism were to come to America, never again would you be able to go off on hunting trips with friends. Private ownership and private use of firearms is strictly forbidden. No firearms are permitted the people, because they would then have weapons with which to rise up against the oppressors.[15]

Inside the Trade Mart, all of the businesses are closed. Police are stationed at all entrances, corridors, balconies, and stairways. They are also watching the meal preparations in the kitchen. Seventy plainclothes cops are also on duty, and many of these will be dispersed among the luncheon crowd.

It's not just the police who are providing security. Civilians have also been pressed into service. The local newsman who filmed the attack on Adlai Stevenson has been invited to the presidential luncheon. He has also been asked quietly, secretly, to keep an eye out for anyone he might recognize from the Stevenson incident, and to immediately report them to the FBI or Secret Service. Outside, dozens of police officers are on high alert. Cops are also posted on nearby rooftops.

Despite the heavy security, a small handful of determined protesters has arrived from the Dallas-based Indignant White Citizens Council. Each person is carrying an anti–Kennedy placard: YANKEE GO HOME; KENNEDY, KING, AND CASTRO; and HAIL CAESAR. Some of the signs have small Confederate flags attached to them. The protesters have pieces of tape over their mouths: "To show that we are being muzzled."[16]

In New York, Stanley Marcus has just sat down to lunch inside the chandeliered Le Pavillon, an exclusive French restaurant that is also a favorite of the Kennedy family. He has ordered calf's liver lyonnaise along with a bottle of French burgundy for himself and his guests: a merchant from Sweden and a young woman from Australia who has recently entered the fashion merchandising business in New York. Although Marcus is fifteen hundred miles away from Dallas, he remains extremely concerned about the president's visit. He has left instructions with his office how to reach him in case of an emergency.

The flight to Dallas will only take thirteen minutes, and during the brief up-and-down journey the president is at the rear of the plane talking to his aides—and complaining about the negative press coverage in Texas.

"It's bad," he says, holding a copy of one newspaper up for his team to see. "What's worse, it's inaccurate."

General Godfrey McHugh, Kennedy's personal military aide and the commander of Air Force One, comes to the tail-area compartment and overhears Kennedy.

"If you think that's bad, Mr. President, wait till you see *The Dallas News*," says McHugh.

"I have seen it," replies Kennedy in a thick voice.

The men watch as Kennedy paces the plane and then pauses.

"What kind of journalism do you call the *Dallas Morning News*?" he asks angrily. "You know who's responsible for that ad? Dealey. Remember him? After that exhibition he put on in the White House I did a little checking on him. He runs around calling himself a war correspondent, and everybody in Dallas believes him."

And then Kennedy mutters a curse.[17]

By eleven thirty, the early-morning clouds have blown away and the sun is shining brilliantly under bright blue skies as Air Force One completes its short flight, preparing to land at Love Field. Aboard the plane, everyone's mood has lifted with the skies. Kennedy's staff people beam at each other. They have experienced this phenomenon over and over. The president will fly into a cloudy or rainy place and suddenly the skies clear in time for his landing. They even have a name for this: They call it Kennedy Weather.

As the plane taxis to a halt, the tarmac is still wet from the early-morning rain. A crowd of thousands is gathered behind a chain-link fence. Many people have parked their cars right up at the edge of the boundary and are standing on top for a better view. This is an unusually large crowd for an airport arrival. The only question is: What kind of response will the president receive here?

Jackie emerges first from Air Force One, glancing up shyly as a huge cheer rises from the packed crowd. Her pink jacket reflects the sun, and her earrings sparkle brilliantly. In a moment she is joined by her husband, who is smiling broadly. The sunlight is dazzling, and golden rays seem to land directly on the First Couple, illuminating them with a special glow. More raucous cheering erupts. People are stamping their feet, jumping and screaming. There is mad applause for the Kennedys.

Members of the White House press corps glance at each other. This isn't the reception they expected to see in Dallas. Earlier they'd been joking about the crackpots in the city, offering each other bets on when the shooting will start.

A receiving line of local dignitaries is awaiting the Kennedys at the base of the steps on the airport tarmac. Mayor Earle Cabell's wife, Dearie, presents Jackie with a bouquet of red roses. The original plan called for yellow roses, but every yellow rose in the state has already been spoken for, including the five thousand already set up at the Trade Mart.

The crowd is screaming so loudly that it's hard for those in the receiving line to make themselves heard. As the president is greeted by Police Chief Jesse Curry, Kennedy leans in close and says:

"This doesn't look like an anti-Kennedy crowd."

Others descending from Air Force One aren't so sure. Their practiced eyes spot a few discordant notes among the welcoming signs: YANKEE GO HOME AND TAKE YOUR EQUALS WITH YOU and HELP JFK STAMP OUT DEMOCRACY. Another, referring to presumptive Republican nominee Barry Goldwater, reads LET'S BARRY KING JOHN. Most disturbing is the small, misspelled hand-lettered sign on cardboard that reads YOUR A TRAITOR. One man standing high above everyone else is waving a giant Confederate flag.

Congressman Henry B. González of San Antonio spots the oversize flag: "I sure wish somebody had invented a spit proof mask... I forgot my bulletproof vest."[18]

Some of the reporters, studying the map of the motorcade route for this visit, notice that one of the streets they'll be riding on is Turtle Creek Boulevard. They begin to speculate what might happen if the president passes by General Edwin Walker's house. It is determined that the route will actually miss Walker's residence by about ten blocks.

Secret Service agents are tailing Kennedy closely, studying the faces behind the fence. Most people are smiling and shrieking in delight at the sight of the First Couple. The agents are guiding the Kennedys toward the presidential limousine so that the motorcade can begin. The president, however, breaks out of line and walks toward the crowd, which grows frantic at his approach. Grinning broadly, he reaches over the fence and begins shaking hands with people, thanking them for their support.

The First Lady follows her husband, and Chief Curry notices

that two red buds have fallen from her bouquet. He leans over to pick them up. He plans to give them to his nine-year-old daughter as a souvenir. Curry follows the Kennedys over to the fence. A stranger who noticed his action asks if he can have one of the buds to take home for his daughter. Without hesitation the chief hands one over.

The electric charge between Kennedy and the crowd is unmistakable. Reporters observe that even some of those holding up protest signs seem charmed by the man. The huge Confederate flag, which was once being waved defiantly, has now drooped to half-mast. Much to the dismay of his Secret Service, the president continues to work the crowd for several more minutes.

"Kennedy is showing he is not afraid," writes one reporter in his notebook.[19]

Kennedy finally stops shaking hands at five minutes to noon, and the presidential motorcade prepares to depart. It is only a three-mile drive to the Trade Mart, but the procession will take a long, ten-mile route that loops through downtown in order to maximize Dallas's exposure to the president.

A car driven by a Dallas police officer will lead the motorcade. Following him are two groups of motorcycle officers who will form a flying wedge to keep curbside crowds off the street. Next is a white Ford driven by Chief Curry. Riding with Curry is Secret Service Agent Winston Lawson, who has coordinated security. In the backseat are the county sheriff and the head of the Secret Service branch in Dallas.

Five car lengths behind is the presidential limousine, a midnight-blue custom-built 1961 Lincoln Continental convertible. The car weighs nearly four tons and is over twenty feet long. It averages less than five miles per gallon. The limousine was flown in the evening before on a cargo plane and guarded overnight by police.

Texas Governor John Connally and his wife, Nellie, sit in the middle jump seat. The president and First Lady climb into the backseat. The rear seat is raised by a hydraulic lift so that it rides several inches higher than the jump seat in order to give the people of Dallas a better view of the president.

At the rear corners of the limousine are four motorcycle

officers. Their main job is to keep the crowds from surging forward toward the president. Traveling directly behind the limo is the Secret Service car: a nine-passenger 1955 Cadillac convertible with running boards for the agents to stand on. Behind the Secret Service car is the vehicle carrying Lyndon and Lady Bird Johnson. Finally, there are other cars bringing up the rear of the motorcade and carrying congressmen, Mayor Earle Cabell, and other officials. Two press buses are at the very back. As the procession gets under way, the motorcade spreads out over ten blocks.

Leaving the airport, the cars turn onto Lemmon Avenue, the main route toward downtown. Few people are out on the streets this far from the city center. The motorcade speeds along at thirty-five miles per hour. The plan is to slow down to twenty miles per hour in the crowded areas.

During this relatively deserted stretch, Jackie amuses herself by waving gaily to the line of billboards that greets their entrance into the city, advertising everything from hamburgers to whiskey. Now that the sun is out, the temperature has become very warm. Mrs. Kennedy reaches into her purse and puts on her sunglasses. Her husband reminds her to take them off—they need to be able to make eye contact with people, he explains.

About two miles into the trip, Kennedy spots a group of schoolchildren holding a long banner that reads: PLEASE STOP AND SHAKE OUR HANDS.

Kennedy calls ahead to the driver.

"Let's stop here, Bill."

The excited children rush forward and swarm the car. A woman with the children keeps shouting: "It worked! Our sign worked!"[20]

The streets are gradually becoming more packed in anticipation of the presidential parade. Many people have parked their cars along the right-of-way and are standing alongside them, waving wildly as the motorcade passes by. After several more blocks the president spots a group of nuns lined up to see him. He can't resist the nuns. He orders the motorcade halted again so that he can shake hands with them.

Now the motorcade is approaching Turtle Creek Boulevard. At this intersection is Robert E. Lee Park, with the bronze statue of the Confederate general. A half mile to the left is General Walker's home with its looming American flags. The procession turns right and passes under a twenty-two-story luxury apartment high-rise, a modernist monolith billed as the "tallest, largest, and most luxurious apartment ever erected west of the Mississippi."

Inside the building, on the nineteenth floor, Ted Dealey is making himself a drink. He has just returned from a checkup with his doctor and he's changed out of his business clothing. He's now in a sport shirt and he plans to relax. He has no intention of attending the Trade Mart luncheon on the president's behalf. He's all too happy to leave that duty to his son.

Dealey is looking out a corner window at the motorcade. It's hard to make out much detail from so high up, but he sees a flash of pink down below. That, he figures, must be Jackie Kennedy. He walks back into his den and snaps on the television, where the motorcade is being broadcast live to the entire city.

Though downtown is still three miles away, the sidewalks are filling up with spectators. In some places people are standing three- and four-deep, cheering wildly as Jack and Jackie pass by. No organized demonstrations are seen, but there are a few individual protesters. One man holds a sign announcing: I HOLD YOU JFK AND YOUR BLIND SOCIALISM IN COMPLETE CONTEMPT. Others along the way proudly brandish homemade BARRY GOLDWATER FOR PRESIDENT signs.

Main Street is only a mile away, and the crowds are growing even thicker. People are now standing five- and six-deep. The smiles on the president and First Lady grow even bigger. It is clear by now that they are experiencing the largest, friendliest crowd of the entire Texas trip. The reporters riding with the motorcade are surprised by this massive outpouring of public goodwill. This is not what they expected in Dallas. Kennedy's aides are not just relieved, they are nearly giddy with delight.

Juanita Craft wants to be on time, to get her seat, to be ready. As she puts on her best clothes, she keeps one eye on the television, watching the arrival of the president and his wife. They look so glamorous to her, and each step they take toward Dallas seems to suggest some bigger meaning.

She makes it through security at the Trade Mart and is shown to her table. The place is quickly filling up. There is a buzz in the air, the room pungent with the smell of roses, cologne, and perfume. Decorators have placed birdcages filled with canaries around the courtyard. There are dozens of uniformed waiters and hosts running alongside the tables.

And Craft waits and waits. The most powerful people in Dallas are assembling, including many of the members of the Dallas Citizens Council. She sees some familiar faces, some black preachers, including Rhett James. She has often been afraid that people like James are pushing too fast. But today, there is something for both of them to look forward to.

At the intersection with Main Street, the crowd is so large that people have flowed out onto the roadway. The police working the corner try to push everyone back as the limousine slows to turn onto Main.

The President and First Lady are now in the heart of Dallas. This is the final leg of the motorcade. The procession will travel twelve blocks through downtown until they reach Dealey Plaza and make a dogleg turn onto Elm Street. Then they will pass in front of the Texas School Book Depository before driving beneath the triple underpass and turning onto the freeway for the quick five-minute drive to the Trade Mart.

Nearly a quarter million people are jamming into downtown to get a firsthand look at the president and First Lady. The city has never witnessed a boisterously exuberant spectacle like this one: A breeze is making the red, white, and blue banners bob over the motorcade route, and showers of confetti are raining from the sky. People are stacked eight, ten, even twelve persons deep along the route, and in more places the crowds are spilling out into the streets. In the buildings overlooking Main Street, fidgeting, joyous observers are leaning out windows, waving and cheering wildly, and waiting to catch a glimpse.

When the motorcade crawls into view, when people spot Kennedy, they clap, whistle, and begin to shout: "We love you!"

The swarms are now so thick that the motorcade is forced to slow down. The speed drops from twenty to fifteen miles per hour. Then it's down to ten. Then seven.

Thousands more people are jumping, screaming, waving. For more than a few, it feels cathartic, as if Dallas is letting something go. As the happy crowds push toward Jack and Jackie, the motorcade slows even more. Secret Service agents jump off the follow-up car and surround the presidential limousine to make sure the president and First Lady are protected.

The procession is now slowly passing Neiman Marcus. Lady Bird spots a friend of hers who works at the store, and the two women wave gaily at each other. Looming above Neiman Marcus, on the opposite side of the street, is the Mercantile Building. Up on the seventh floor, in the offices of Hunt Oil, the seventy-four-year-old billionaire is somberly watching the procession from his window. He is flanked by two young secretaries. No one has to say a word. The huge roars from Dallas say it all.

Down on the street, a reporter from the *Dallas Morning News* nudges one of his colleagues and shouts:

"They've got this town wrapped around their little fingers."[21]

The president's car is finally leaving the huge throngs behind, passing out of the shadows of Dallas's skyscrapers. Directly ahead is open sky and the small green swath of Dealey Plaza. This will be the final leg of the motorcade, nearly an afterthought, this transition zone between downtown and the freeway. The live television and radio coverage of the motorcade route ended a few blocks earlier.

Here, at the hem of the Texas School Book Depository and Dealey Plaza, only a few dozen people are on hand to see the president.

Among them is Steve Witt, who works at a nearby insurance company. He has strolled over on his lunch break to see the motorcade, and even though the rain has passed, he is holding a black umbrella. Witt considers Kennedy to be an appeaser, just like

Neville Chamberlain, the British prime minister who once accommodated Hitler—and who was famous for carrying an umbrella. Kennedy has been heckled with umbrellas before, and Witt plans to open his umbrella and taunt the president when the limousine passes by.

Another spectator at Dealey Plaza is Arnold Rowland, a young man who has come with his wife, Barbara. A few minutes earlier, Rowland was looking across the street toward the Texas School Book Depository when he noticed a man standing in an upper floor window holding a rifle.

"Hey," Rowland said to his wife, "you want to see a Secret Service man?"

By the time his wife looked, however, the man had disappeared.[22]

At the entrance to Dealey Plaza, the presidential limousine turns right onto Houston Street. A man named Abraham Zapruder, standing in the shade, turns on his camera as the limousine comes into view. Though the crowds are thinner here, the enthusiasm for the president is hardly dampened. In the president's car, the passengers are still overwhelmed by the effusive reception they have just received.

Governor Connally, who'd been so worried about being tied to Kennedy, is immensely relieved.

The giant clock on the Hertz sign perched on top of the Texas School Book Depository changes to twelve thirty as Greer cuts the wheel to make the sharp left onto Elm Street.

The president and Jackie are still waving to the people cheering for them. Now that the cacophony of roaring crowds is beginning at last to abate, Nellie Connally turns around in the jump seat and speaks to John Kennedy.

"Well, Mr. President," she says buoyantly, "you can't say that Dallas doesn't love you."

Within seconds, the first shot explodes the air.

EPILOGUE

The television in Ted Dealey's living room is tuned to the local station owned by his newspaper. Coverage of the presidential motorcade ended a few moments earlier, and now a lunch-hour variety show is airing. A stylish-looking Dallas woman is modeling the latest in winter fashions when suddenly the transmission is cut. A visibly flustered local news announcer, Jay Watson, is clutching a sheaf of papers and staring intently into the camera.

"Good afternoon, ladies and gentlemen," he says, "you'll excuse the fact I'm out of breath, but..."

He tries to collect himself.

"About ten or fifteen minutes ago a tragic thing, from all indications at this point, has happened in the city of Dallas."

Across the country, millions of other viewers are also having their regular programming interrupted. Many are tuned in to CBS's hit soap opera *As the World Turns* when the screen goes black. A still image appears: CBS NEWS BULLETIN. Then Walter Cronkite's voice comes on, quaking with emotion as he breaks the news to the nation:

"In Dallas, Texas, three shots were fired at President Kennedy's motorcade in downtown Dallas. The first reports say that President Kennedy has been seriously wounded by this shooting."

Cronkite pauses.

"More details just arrived."

Another brief pause.

"These details about the same as previously. President Kennedy shot today just as his motorcade left downtown Dallas. Mrs. Kennedy jumped up and grabbed Mr. Kennedy. She called 'Oh, no.' The motorcade sped on. United Press says that the wounds for President Kennedy perhaps could be fatal."

Dealey glumly studies the frantic, breaking news reports on the television. Downtown at the *Dallas Morning News*, his reporters are already racing out the door and sprinting the three short blocks to where Kennedy was shot—just by the plaza and looming statue honoring Ted Dealey's crusading father.

And already, his newspaper's phone operators are being deluged with blistering calls blaming Dealey and his paper for the tragedy:

"I hope you're happy now," one angry caller screams into the receiver before slamming it down.[1]

A few blocks away, the phones are incessantly jangling at the Hunt Oil Company headquarters. The billionaire's wife, Ruth, finally gets through after dialing in from Southern Methodist University, where she had stopped to visit one of their children. Hunt tells her not to move. The FBI is also calling, and agents are bluntly telling Hunt to not go home. They advise him to take his family and hide somewhere out of town. Plenty of people know he hates Kennedy, that he has spent millions of his fortune on virulently anti-Kennedy *Life Line* broadcasts, that he sponsored people in Dallas churning out anti-Kennedy attacks.

Hunt only grunts at the advice, then says he will not flee Dallas. But his security chief, the former FBI Agent Paul Rothermel, keeps insisting. Hunt has his wife and his children to think about. What if harm comes to them? Finally, Hunt relents. He hurriedly packs some bags. Aides procure immediate airplane tickets, under false names, for Hunt and his wife.

The Hunts will hide out, for as long as necessary, in a suite at the Mayflower Hotel in Washington, DC.

As the news spreads, more and more frantic messages are flooding the switchboard at Dallas police headquarters. Distraught women from all over Dallas are on the phone lines. Each one is sobbing, confessing to police that she is certain that it must have been *her* husband who shot the president.

Meanwhile, in the jammed hallways of the police station, a horde of reporters has completely encircled Police Chief Jesse Curry. They are shouting questions: *What kind of weapon was used? How many shots were fired? Have the police run a trace on the rifle?*

Suddenly one reporter in the pack shouts out:

"Do you have any connection yet between this and the firing of Major General Walker?"

The beleaguered police chief seems to pause for a fraction of a second and then replies in a slow, deliberate voice:

"I do not know."

Bernard Weissman had begun the day feeling proud about the full-page ad in the *Dallas Morning News* signed in his name. Now he is in his car, along with his friend Bill Burley. They are driving across town to meet Larrie Schmidt for beers at the DuCharme Club. As the first reports of the shooting come over the car radio, Weissman is stunned.

"I hope he is not a member of Walker's group," he says. "I hope he's not one of Walker's boys."

In Louisiana, General Walker is aboard a commercial flight from New Orleans to Shreveport when the pilot announces the news of the Kennedy assassination over the intercom. Walker immediately begins gathering the names and addresses of the other passengers: He knows he will need to use them as witnesses, to prove that he was not in Dallas on November 22.

When the plane lands, a delegation from the local White Citizens Council is on hand to greet him. Walker is asked whether or not he should cancel this evening's speech, in light of the day's events.

"Hell, no!" he barks.

Across the nation, the first few moments of shock are giving way to outrage.

In Washington, John Kennedy's senior aide Timothy J. Reardon shouts out: "I'd like to take a fucking bomb and blow the fucking state of Texas off the fucking map!"[2]

Telegrams are being wired straight to the Dallas office of Mayor Earle Cabell:

> *Three years ago you assaulted Senator Johnson. Last month, you spit on and broke a sign over the head of Governor Stevenson. And today, you've killed our president . . . What kind of people are you? . . . You can take your stinking city and your stinking state and secede from the union . . .*

> *As with your ridiculous and nauseating auto slogan stickers we see—"Made in Texas by Texans"—I suppose a similar one can be adopted pertaining to the assassination . . .*

> *Dallas, the city that spawns the lunatic fringe of the far right. Dallas, the City of Hate.*[3]

Marina Oswald is at the house of her friend Ruth Paine, watching TV news updates about the shooting. She can understand only a little of what she's hearing, but Paine is translating for her. When the announcer says that the shots were fired from the Texas School Book Depository, the thought immediately enters Marina's mind: *Could my husband have done such a thing?* Yes, she decides, he could have.

She rushes out to the Paines' garage, where Oswald kept his rifle wrapped inside a blanket. A quick glance tells her that the blanket appears to still hold the weapon. She breathes a sigh of relief and returns to the house. Only later will she realize that the rifle was, in fact, gone.

Aboard Air Force One, still parked on the tarmac at Love Field while awaiting the delivery of Kennedy's body, Lyndon B. Johnson is being sworn in as the nation's thirty-sixth president. As Johnson recites the presidential oath, the newly widowed Jacqueline Kennedy is standing at his side, her husband's blood and brains sprayed across her pink Chanel suit. She has made no attempt to clean up.

Speaking quietly, she says, "I want them to see what they have done to Jack."[4]

Lee Harvey Oswald, after fleeing the School Book Depository, has shot and killed a Dallas policeman. Now he's run inside a movie theater, trying to hide. Dallas cops quickly swarm the place. As an officer moves to arrest him, Oswald stands up and begins to raise his hands. "Well, it's all over now," he says dejectedly. Suddenly he punches the cop in the face and they tumble to the floor. It takes four cops to finally subdue Oswald, who is desperately trying to reach for the pistol tucked into his waistband.[5]

Jack Ruby doesn't strike people who know him as a particularly politically minded person, but he's always expressed an admiration for President Kennedy. He mentioned JFK on stage at the Carousel Club, and he long made it a policy to ban his comedians from making any jokes about Negroes, Jews, or the Kennedys.

A couple of weeks earlier, he'd stopped by a business convention in Dallas where copies of anti-Kennedy *Life Line* scripts were being given away. Ruby picked some up and was instantly incensed. "I'm going to send this stuff to Kennedy," he threatened.[6] He stuffed the scripts into his suit jacket pocket.

As Kennedy arrived in Dallas, Ruby was among the thousands of local readers angered by Bernard Weissman's full-page ad in the *Dallas Morning News*. Ruby, sensitive to his own ethnicity in Dallas, wondered how another Jew could do such a thing.

"If this Weissman is a Jew," he told his sister, "they ought to whack the hell out of him."[7]

By lunchtime, he is at the offices of the *Dallas Morning News*, placing a new ad for his strip club and complaining to employees about their paper's anti-Kennedy screed. Then the reports come in about the shooting at Dealey Plaza. As people rush by him, some screaming, some crying, Ruby suddenly turns uncharacteristically silent. Finally, he speaks to the adman.

"I am not opening up tonight," he says.[8]

Ruby cancels his advertisement, aims for his club on Commerce

Street, and tells the employees he is closing the doors for a few days. He begins calling one person after another, sobbing about Kennedy. On the line to a sister in Chicago, he keeps repeating: "Oh, my God. What a black mark for Dallas."[9]

By nighttime, he is headed to the special services at Temple Shearith Israel in Dallas. The presiding rabbi, Hillel Silverman, has known Ruby for a decade, not as a regular attendee, but as someone who occasionally comes to worship. As Ruby enters the temple and Silverman greets him, Ruby is crying and shaking, seemingly on the verge of emotional collapse. After Ruby leaves the synagogue, he slides his .38 Colt Cobra into the front pocket of his pants.

He drives around town, checking on his competition and angrily noting that places like Club Bali Hai are staying open. *How can they disrespect the dead president?* He scans the radio for the latest news. Announcers are saying that Lee Harvey Oswald from Dallas, from the same neighborhood as Ruby, will be charged with being part of an international communist conspiracy to murder the president.

Ruby thinks about the hardworking Dallas police—many of whom he considers friends. On an impulse, he decides to order ten sandwiches from Phil's Deli to take to the cops. Even though the cops tell him they don't need the sandwiches, by 11 p.m. he is inside Dallas police headquarters. Throngs of reporters are gathered in a corridor while Oswald is interrogated behind a closed door. Newsmen and photographers are frantic to see the suspect, the communist who killed the president. Ruby quickly makes himself at home, handing out free passes to the Carousel Club and helpfully telling out-of-town reporters how to spell the names of various police officers.

One of the cops notices Ruby and calls out, asking what he's doing.

"I am helping all these fellows," Ruby says, gesturing grandly toward the reporters.[10]

After midnight, Oswald finally appears. He has been grilled by detectives for hours. Now reporters are shouting questions at him as he is escorted down the hallway. Oswald passes within two or three feet of Ruby, who still has his pistol in his front pocket. Ruby feels right at home in the Dallas police station. He is, he thinks to himself, "being carried away by the excitement of history."[11]

Saturday, November 23

Rumors are circulating that in some Dallas schools, the children broke into cheers and applause when they first heard the news of Kennedy's shooting.

In Dealey's *Dallas Morning News*, the editorial writers express sorrow for the president's death, and then add: "It cannot be charged with fairness that an entire city is in national disgrace..."[12]

The competing newspaper, the *Times Herald*, is flatly apologetic: "First there had to be the seeds of hate—and we must pray that Dallas can never supply the atmosphere for tragedy to grow again."[13]

And at the morning services, at 9 a.m. at Temple Shearith Israel, there is Ruby again. Still despondent, still emotional. Rabbi Silverman is surprised to see Ruby come back. It is out of character. Silverman thinks that Ruby is not very deep, and certainly not an intellectual or political. That he wouldn't know the difference between a communist and a totalitarian.[14]

Ruby listens to Silverman's eulogy. He hears Silverman talk about Kennedy being ambushed in Dallas, shot in the back by an enemy: "Here is a man that fought in all battles, but he didn't have a chance to fight here, he was shot from the rear."

Ruby leaves the temple thinking about what he has heard from the rabbi, about the city of Dallas, about the mad jumble of events: "I have been around people that are so smug and hard."[15]

Everyone Ruby talks to that day has the same impression: He seems extraordinarily emotional. He gets choked up when he mentions Jackie Kennedy and thinks of the children growing up without a father. As evening descends, Ruby drives over to Dealey Plaza, where he views the clusters of memorial wreaths left overnight. He also decides to take a picture of a billboard downtown that reads IMPEACH EARL WARREN—it reminds him of the anti-Kennedy ad he saw in the *Dallas Morning News*.

Rhett James was at the Trade Mart when word began spreading that Kennedy had been shot. To him it was like a mental pandemonium—not a physical one, but a mental one. As if the room and everyone in it had surrendered to something. He knew he would have to prepare sermons, eulogies, emergency services at New Hope. And he would talk about the basic things, the elemental things—about hope, about clinging to faith.

James and Lyndon Johnson had been trading letters for the last few months. Johnson and his aides seemed to rely on James's field reports about the increasingly important black voters in Texas, on how they were feeling about Texas Governor John Connally and his stances on civil rights. And LBJ and his team wondered, internally, where James was headed—what exactly he had in mind as he tried to form a new, black-based political organization in Texas.

Now LBJ is president—and James decides to send him a letter trying to provide some balm:

> *Dear Mr. President:*
> *...As we have talked in your office many times, I have been working and giving my service to your cause and the cause of our nation... Dallas is hanging its head in sorrow, more so because this shame to our nation happened in our city... As you have stated, this act was caused by conditions which could have occurred in any city. Yet, Dallas is the city it occurred... Today, things have changed, and I and thousands of Texans still feel that we are fortunate that you were the man to take over the position of President...*
>
> *Mr. President, I will continue to pray for you and work for your cause and I want you to know that I am convinced that you represent the Joshua of the hour...*[16]

In the hours after the assassination, reporters began calling Congressman Bruce Alger, demanding some reaction. Alger, uncharacteristically, refused comment.

Political observers felt Alger was someone Dallas *needed* to distance itself from. Some brooding, hidden wings of the Dallas Citizens Council probably remained deeply wary of Alger anyway. No doubt some thought he might be, as a public figure, a fiscal liability—annoying the Kennedy administration so much that it was denying Dallas the highly coveted, multimillion-dollar federal project that would turn a cheap real estate investment into a gusher of profit for the local millionaires. They loved Alger when he attacked Kennedy's politics, but loathed him when he couldn't figure out a way to convince Kennedy to green-light the lucrative federal project.

On the evening of the assassination, Alger decided to issue a statement:

"No words can express our deep sorrow in this tragic hour. God alone can sustain us in our loss."[17]

Now, on the morning following the president's death, Alger is sending three telegrams—to John Connally's wife, to Lyndon Johnson, and to Jacqueline Kennedy. The one to Mrs. Kennedy says: "We beseech God to give us strength to preserve our country, to which your husband was so dedicated."

In the immediate aftermath of the Kennedy shooting, thousands of people—including FBI agents—were very anxiously trying to find out where General Walker was and what he was doing. Finally, Walker decides to release a written statement. Walter Cronkite stops dramatically to read it on the air as part of CBS's continuing coverage:

"From Dallas Texas: The first comment from former Major General Edwin Walker, who is one of the more vocal right wing leaders in the United States. And he said: 'The death of Mr. Kennedy is not as surprising as it is tragic. The tragic events of yesterday demonstrate the internal threat that can never be underestimated.' "

Sunday, November 24

The major networks, magazines, and newspapers all have reporters combing Dallas, and many of them are rushing to prepare pieces to prosecute the city.

The Reverend W. A. Criswell of the mighty First Baptist Church knows the reporters are out and about. He awoke early in the morning, as is his custom. He has already spent hours laboring over the final lines for the day's sermons.

He has long planned his pre-Thanksgiving sermon to be about the Pilgrim fathers, about how they had brought hope and freedom to a savage world. With the president having been shot eight blocks away, he knows that he will have to offer something different today. He decides to title the new sermon: "The Red Terror."

Five blocks to the east of the church, embattled Dallas Police Chief Jesse Curry has a building crammed full of reporters and photographers amid tight security. Earlier, the police let the media know that Oswald would be transferred from the city jail to the county jail at 10 a.m. The suspect has been relentlessly interrogated for two days now, and this will be another opportunity for newsmen to get a good look at him. The reporters and photographers wait noisily, impatiently, as the clock ticks past ten with no sign of the suspect. Word passes that Oswald is being interrogated one last time upstairs before leaving the building.

At 10:19 a.m., Jack Ruby receives a call at his apartment from a Fort Worth dancer named Little Lynn. She is worried about lost income with the Carousel Club temporarily shutting down, and she is begging for a salary advance. Ruby listens and tells her he will take care of it, that he will go to the Western Union office in downtown Dallas and wire her enough money to tide her over.

Ruby picks out a neat suit, tie, cuff links, and pinkie ring. He sobs quietly as he thinks about the "Letter to Caroline" in that morning's *Dallas Times Herald*. In it, a young girl offers to share her own daddy with Kennedy's now fatherless daughter. Ruby has been telling people that he can't bear the thought that Jacqueline Kennedy would ever have to return to Dallas to confront in court the man who shot her husband.

Ruby smooths down his oiled hair and grabs his fedora. He brings his small dog, Sheba, and places her in the car. He drives downtown, passing through Dealey Plaza, where fresh wreaths have been laid overnight. He parks across from Western Union. It is 11:05. He leaves Sheba in the car.

The police headquarters is just a block away, and he can see that a crowd is still gathered, even though Oswald should have been transferred an hour ago. Inside Western Union, a line has formed. Ruby waits patiently. Finally, it is his turn, and he signs the paperwork to send the money to Little Lynn. His receipt is stamped with the exact time: 11:17.

Those few blocks to the west, the Reverend W. A. Criswell is in the pulpit, railing against communism, against Lenin, against the revolutionaries who have brought death to Dallas.

The hundreds of congregants huddle and stare at him, listening carefully to their pastor's first sermon in the wake of the murder of President John F. Kennedy, the man who Criswell once said was surely under the sway of the papal empire:

"The assassination that so darkly and tragically was enacted upon the streets of our queenly city of Dallas was perpetrated by a man who was schooled in Communist ideology . . . we have seen on the streets of our city, a typical product of Communist ideology: vengeance, blood, terror."

Finishing up at Western Union, Ruby walks down Main Street and to the Dallas police building. His dog is still in his car. Ruby has visited this building many times. He nimbly avoids the large crowd gathered out front and walks down a ramp into the basement. The policeman guarding the area doesn't even notice him. It is 11:21.

Upstairs, Oswald is finally entering the elevator for the prisoner transfer to the basement. He delayed things even more by asking for a different sweater before being taken downstairs.

As the elevator descends, Oswald is closely handcuffed to Detective Jim Leavelle. Looking over at the prisoner, Leavelle jokes, "Lee, if anybody shoots at you, I hope they're as good a shot as you are."

Finally, Oswald appears in front of the jockeying reporters and photographers. Flashbulbs are popping and reporters shout questions at him. He appears to be smirking. With everyone turning toward Oswald, Ruby finishes his short walk by joining the throng of newsmen. He has phenmetrazine, a stimulant, in his bloodstream. He's long practiced the art of getting to the front of a crowd.

Just as Criswell is finishing his First Baptist sermon about the Red Terror creeping into Dallas, the slightly balding Ruby is reaching inside his pocket for his black .38 Colt Cobra revolver.

Suddenly there is a flash of movement as Ruby darts forward and cries out: "You son of a bitch!" The explosion of the gunshot rings off the basement walls. Millions of Americans are witnessing the first-ever live murder broadcast on television.

Ruby is quickly gang-tackled and brought under control. Amid all the shouting and pushing, he looks around, seemingly confused.

"You all know me," he says. "I'm Jack Ruby!"

Later, in custody on the fifth floor, Ruby stares at the somber officers and agents looming over him. He has been stripped, searched, and relieved of H. L. Hunt's anti-Kennedy *Life Line* scripts found in his jacket. Left in his undershorts, Ruby is befuddled. He expected to be greeted as a great hero for killing the communist assassin.

Thirty minutes after his arrest, FBI Agent Forrest Sorrels sits down with him. Ruby tells the agent that his name was formerly Rubenstein, and that he changed it after coming to Dallas. Sorrels wants to know why Ruby gunned down Oswald.

He stares at Ruby and asks: "Jack—why?"

Ruby looks up at him and rambles about how he closed his club as soon as he heard the news, how he went to the synagogue and heard a eulogy for Kennedy, how his sister had recently had an operation—and how she had been hysterical. And how, when he saw that Mrs. Kennedy was going to have to appear for the trial, he thought that there probably wasn't anyone in Dallas who could do what needed to be done.

"Somebody had to do it. You all couldn't."[18]

As the days and weeks pass after the president's death, Bruce Alger perhaps begins to fathom that any backlash against Dallas will crack directly down on him. That he will be consumed by, or thrown into, the drowning pool of repulsion toward Dallas. He issues another statement, saying that he is still going to fight Kennedy's legacy, his programs, if Johnson insists on carrying them forward. Loyal opposition is a hallmark of America, argues Alger. That opposition to the president "is not based on hate, nor does the mere fact that a legislator opposes certain legislation make him a breeder of hate or an accessory to murder."

He is, of course, talking about himself: He is not a murderous accomplice—not an accessory to the murder of the president of the United States. In the city, there are already discussions that, within the year, Alger is to be dethroned and replaced by the trusty old-guard Mayor Earle Cabell, whose father had been mayor of Dallas, whose grandfather had been mayor of Dallas. And Alger decides he will remain inflexible, that he will spend the year embracing what he said in the past. Extremists really did kill Kennedy—left-wing extremists. And their goal hasn't changed. It is rather simple:

"The destruction of America."[19]

Word is spreading that when Jack Ruby was searched, there were those copies of scripts from Hunt's *Life Line* program in his pocket.

Someone drives by Mount Vernon, the Hunt estate in Dallas, and begins blasting gunshots at it. Hunt is still listed in the Dallas phone book, and now there are also ominous phone calls coming to his home in the dead of night. Threatening letters begin arriving in the mail.[20]

From the safety of the Mayflower Hotel in Washington, Hunt decides to go on the offensive. To write his own explanation for what had happened in Dallas, for what happened to the president he loathed. Two days after Ruby killed Oswald, Hunt pens an open letter to newspapers: "Grave warnings that patriots are more dangerous and do more harm than communists are outmoded."

And then he tells the FBI that he is sick of Washington, sick of being away from home. He damned well will be celebrating Christmas back in Dallas. He will never erect a real security fence around his house, hire extra bodyguards and watchmen, or remove his addresses and phone numbers from public listings. He will be, he says, as safe and welcome in Dallas as ever.

General Walker returns to Dallas and, like Hunt, refuses to abandon his house, despite the hate mail and death threats.

He also decides to make a broader statement about the assassination, one that he will personally take to the airwaves. He wants to lay the blame where it belongs. And he wants people to know that Dallas itself has been victimized—that the city was a patsy, that it has been turned into a pawn in a deadly game. He wants to thank the *Dallas Morning News* for its long-standing history of defending the right, of being unafraid to speak truth to power in Washington. A week after the assassination, Walker goes on the air:

"*Pravda*, Castro, and *The Worker* started malicious and deceptive attacks on the conservative right. That continues to spread, holding Dallas responsible."

Walker has one final, simple thing to add. He knows exactly what happened in Dallas. The assassination was a plot against the super-patriots, a way to besmirch, exile, and blame them. The assassination, in a way, might finally validate him—and prove the truth to those people claiming that he is a mad paranoiac.

"Dallas," Walker insists, "has been set up."[21]

Juanita Craft remains in a daze for two, maybe three days. She tries to follow the news, the way the stranger named Oswald was gunned down by the Jewish man who runs the girlie clubs downtown. Her friends from around the country reach out to her, asking her if she is doing well. And then it dawns on her that she still has the "Bombingham Tea" scheduled at the Methodist church. Now, of course, it almost seems absurd. It was always meant to be a slightly mocking thing—a way to show the evil bombers, the racists who had killed children, that Dallas was resilient and that it could show grace and mercy. It was meant to show that life could go on—and that, at least in a place like Dallas, people were unafraid. Now what could she say to her children in Dallas? The hundreds of idealistic young people she had conscripted in Dallas over the years?

They could read, they could see it all spelled out over and over again in the national stories: *Dallas is a city of hate. Dallas is the city that killed our president.*

She decides that the tea will go on. But the theme will change. She gathers her children in the education building at her church in South Dallas. It is a beautiful day, soothingly cool and clear, and with just the slightest breeze. She has arranged for a life-size portrait of John Fitzgerald Kennedy to be placed near the front door. She supervises as some of her children carefully, gently drape it in black. Others quietly move around the room and place large black cloths over each table. She has asked that every member of her precious NAACP Youth Council find black ribbons and black armbands to wear on their finest Sunday suits and dresses.

When the mourners begin to arrive, they stop for a second to stare at the image of the dead president—his face is creased into that easy smile, the same one that had once graced all those holiday cards distributed in Dallas when he was first running for the presidency.

As the mourners settle into the burnished church room, there are speeches, prayers, and songs. And Craft listens as her children in Dallas vow to stay the course, because that is the only way to find peace:

To remain dedicated to the principles for which this great man lived and died . . . freedom for all mankind, and dignity for all.[22]

For many in America, Ruby's public gunning down of Oswald inside police headquarters confirms their worst impressions of Dallas—a lawless, violent city careening out of control. Mayor Cabell insists that Dallas is innocent, still a hospitable place that remains open for business. He notes with disdain that Oswald wasn't a permanent resident of the city. Of the tragic sequence of murders, Cabell says stiffly: "It could have happened in Podunk as well as Dallas."[23]

After the assassination, a group of Dallas businessmen begins
fretting that out-of-state sales will be drying up for the city. They
decide on an ambitious plan—they will contact Kennedy's widow,
Jacqueline, to ask if she will sign a testimonial to Dallas hospitality.

She never responds.

Stanley Marcus, like so many others, retreats to his home to try to
make sense of the assassination. He cloisters himself in the book-
lined study of his sprawling nine-thousand-square-foot estate. He
will travel to Washington to attend the funeral. He is already hearing and feeling firsthand how Dallas is being blamed, how everyone from the city is being assailed as somehow complicit in the
president's death.

In a way, Marcus felt he really did see it coming, that his own
fears about what was waiting for Kennedy in Dallas have come
true. Some people in the city were twisted, coiled, in hysteria,
in abject fear. They saw communists and socialists creeping into
power, seizing the reins. And if you weren't a red-blooded patriot,
then surely you were a communist sympathizer. The city was in
the grip of a handful of "absolutists"—men, including those who
ran the newspaper, who refused to allow for opposite opinions
about patriotism.

Marcus decides to write an open letter. He'll pay for it to be
published in Dallas newspapers and around the nation. It will have
to be more than delicate—partly an apology, partly a path forward.

The irony of using newspapers for his message isn't lost on him—
after all, it is a lone newspaper, the *Dallas Morning News*, that he
blames especially for the vitriol, the toxicity in the city. And it is Ted
Dealey whom Marcus blames most of all: "Ted was a difficult person to voice your differences to, because he was part of the bigoted
crowd himself...Had (his father) G. B. Dealey been at the helm, he
would have said: 'We cannot permit a racist or a bigot of any type to
stand up and twist the community into a false position.' "[24]

The truth of the matter is that no one can get to know a
city in a day, a week, or a month. Those of us who have

lived here for a lifetime are so close to the picture that we too sometimes fail to see either some of the pertinent details or the entire composition....

We think that our citizens are friendly and kind-hearted human beings who extend genuinely warm welcomes to newcomers to our city.

All of this doesn't mean that there aren't things about Dallas that couldn't be improved...a city, like individuals or business institutions, must take an honest look at its inventory and be willing to consider its faults as well as its assets....

The rejection of this spirit of "absolutism" and the acceptance and insistence by all citizens on toleration of differing points of view seem to us to be essential for the future health of our community...

When he is finished, Marcus wonders what else he can do. It occurs to him that there is at least one more thing, something he will pursue in a more private fashion: He will find a way to honor the words and spirit of President Kennedy. Marcus will commission five hundred copies of an exquisitely hand-typeset and bound edition of the message the president had planned to offer to the city of Dallas:

We ask, therefore, that we may be worthy of our power and responsibility, that we may exercise our strength with wisdom and restraint, and that we may achieve in our time and for all time the ancient vision of "peace on earth, good will toward men."

That must always be our goal...

The first copy will be given to Jacqueline Kennedy. Perhaps it will bring her some closure.

Bruce Alger was defeated by Dallas Mayor Earle Cabell in the 1964 election. His teenage son died in a traffic accident in Washington, DC, that year. After his exile from Congress, Alger became a real estate developer and moved to Colorado, then Florida. In 1974, his ex-wife, Lynn Alger, was murdered in Dallas by a jealous lover. In 1979, Alger nearly drowned and was pulled unconscious from a hotel swimming pool in Boca Raton, Florida. In 1983 he donated his papers to the Dallas Public Library, where they are available for researchers. In 2012, the ninety-four-year-old Alger denounced Barack Obama as the worst president of his lifetime and warned against his reelection: "I consider this a crisis of our form of government. This could easily be our last gasp."

Earle Cabell became a U.S. congressman after defeating Bruce Alger in the 1964 election. He was successful in getting funding for the federal center in Dallas, which is today named the Earle Cabell Federal Building and Courthouse. He died in 1975 at age sixty-eight.

Joseph Civello spent the rest of his life linked to the Kennedy assassination by researchers, conspiracy theorists, and writers. He was highlighted in several books attempting to connect him to organized crime figures in New Orleans, to Jack Ruby, and to Lee Harvey Oswald. He suffered from heart troubles and died in 1970, after a short illness, at the age of sixty-seven.

Juanita Craft remained active in the NAACP and many other local organizations. In 1974 she became the first African American woman elected to the Dallas City Council, serving two terms. She received many honors, including the Linz Award, the oldest civic award in Texas, in 1969—other winners include Stanley Marcus and the *Dallas Morning News*'s Joe Dealey. Craft was invited back to the White House on several more occasions, and President Jimmy Carter referred to her as a "national treasure." She died in 1985, at the age of eighty-three, and her home in Dallas is now known as the Juanita J. Craft Civil Rights House.

W. A. Criswell was elected president of the Southern Baptist Convention in 1968 and formally renounced his earlier segregationist stance. He continued to be active in conservative politics and is regarded by many observers as a pioneer of the "Religious Right." Although Criswell had called for a separation between church and state when John Kennedy ran for president in 1960, he changed his mind with the prospect of Ronald Reagan's election, telling those assembled at the 1980 Republican Convention: "I believe this notion of the separation of church and state was the figment of some infidel's imagination." Criswell's First Baptist Church continued its dynamic expansion, and he remained active in its affairs until his death at age ninety-two in 2002.

Ted Dealey resigned as chairman of the board of the *Dallas Morning News* in 1964 but retained his position as publisher until 1968. As a dedicated animal lover, Dealey helped raise funds for the Dallas Humane Society; he also led a campaign to revitalize the Dallas Zoo. He died in 1969 at age seventy-seven. Under the direction of Dealey's son Joe, the *News* evolved toward a more moderately conservative philosophy. During the 1980s, the *News* became widely regarded as the best newspaper in Texas. It has received nine Pulitzer Prizes since 1986.

H. L. Hunt remained a target of conspiracy theorists. He became increasingly interested in health issues as he aged. He began the practice of "creeping"—crawling along the floor, which he told astonished visitors helped keep him young. In 1968 he became fascinated by aloe vera—then largely unknown in America—and helped develop and market the plant to consumers. One of his sons, Lamar Hunt, founded the American Football League and coined the term *Super Bowl* to describe the meeting between AFL and NFL teams. Two other sons, Nelson Bunker and Herbert, attempted to corner the world's silver market in 1980. At age eighty-one, H. L. Hunt told an interviewer, "I intend to live to be 140, like the people in a certain tribe in the Himalayas." He died in 1974 at age eighty-five.

H. Rhett James served as the leader of New Hope Baptist until 1986, and he oversaw the creation of a new million-dollar church building. He remained engaged in city, state, and national politics, serving with the Dallas War on Poverty and the Dallas Urban League. After helping open Bishop College in Dallas, a school with a predominantly African American student body, he served as an associate professor of social science there for twenty years. He earned his doctorate in urban administration from the University of Texas at Arlington, and graduated from the Institute for Management at Harvard. He taught at Austin College and the University of Texas at Dallas, and also worked as an assistant principal and administrator in the Dallas Independent School District. He traveled the world recruiting black teachers for the same Dallas public schools he helped integrate. He died in 2004. He was seventy-five. When he died, a scholarship in his name was created by the NAACP.

Lady Bird Johnson became one of America's most notable First Ladies, leading a public campaign to restore America's landscape. "Where flowers bloom, so does hope," she said as she lobbied for passage of the Highway Beautification Act, nicknamed Lady Bird's Bill. In 1977 President Gerald Ford awarded her the Presidential Medal of Freedom. In her home state, she co-founded the National Wildflower Research Center. In 2007, the city of Austin renamed its Town Lake "Lady Bird Lake." She died in 2007 at age ninety-four.

Lyndon Johnson became the thirty-sixth president following Kennedy's death in Dallas. Using his mastery of the legislative process, Johnson was able to pass much of Kennedy's stalled legislation, including the Civil Rights Act. Johnson won a landslide victory over conservative Barry Goldwater in 1964—even claiming a majority of the vote in Dallas. As president, Johnson proved to be far more liberal than Kennedy, passing "Great Society" legislation designed to expand opportunities for poor and minority populations. He appointed NAACP counselor Thurgood Marshall to the Supreme Court, making him the first African American justice. Johnson also deepened the nation's involvement in Vietnam, which proved to be his undoing. By the end of his term, crowds outside the White House were chanting, "Hey, hey, LBJ, how many kids did you kill today?" Johnson declined to run for reelection in 1968. He died in 1973 at age sixty-four of a heart attack.

Jacqueline Kennedy gave an exclusive interview to sympathetic journalist Theodore H. White a week after her husband's death. She compared JFK's time in office to the Broadway musical *Camelot*, which became an enduring image of the Kennedy presidency. In 1968 she married Greek shipping magnate Aristotle Onassis, one of the world's wealthiest men. Following her second husband's death in 1975, she became a successful book editor at Doubleday. She died of cancer in 1994 at age sixty-four.

Stanley Marcus became more outspoken in Dallas on selected matters of free speech and civil rights. In 1966, a plot to assassinate Marcus by ultra-right extremists in Dallas was exposed by an informant. In 1974 Marcus published a memoir, *Minding the Store*, on the eve of his retirement from Neiman Marcus. He went on to publish several more books. In the 1980s the *Dallas Morning News* hired him to write a weekly opinion column, which continued for fifteen years. He contributed to many civic causes and remained an active arts patron, bringing numerous artists to Dallas and serving as an early board member for the Georgia O'Keeffe Museum. He died in 2002 at age ninety-six.

Frank McGehee was arrested for driving under the influence in 1964. That same year, FBI agents reported that McGehee continued

to send out fund-raising appeals on behalf of the National Indignation Convention even though the organization had been inactive
for two years. In the 1970s, McGehee began offering investment
opportunities to people in Dallas, raising hundreds of thousands
of dollars. General Edwin Walker was among McGehee's biggest
investors, contributing $44,500. Walker later became suspicious of
McGehee and hired a private investigator to track him. McGehee
was eventually convicted of theft and sentenced to the maximum
of ten years in prison. He was also ordered to pay General Walker
restitution.

Robert Morris founded the University of Plano (Texas) in 1964.
The school, open until 1977, offered "psychomotor patterning"
to young people with mental health issues—the disputed regimen
involved creeping along the floor as a way to stimulate brain power.
He ran for a seat as U.S. senator from Texas in 1970, but lost in the
primary to George H. W. Bush. He also lost a bid to represent
New Jersey in the Senate in 1984. He authored five books, most of
them attacking liberals, socialists, and communists. He also wrote
"Around the World," a newspaper column that often dwelled on
international affairs. He died in 1996, in New Jersey, at the age of
eighty-two.

Larrie Schmidt was interviewed by the FBI regarding his role in
the WELCOME MR. KENNEDY advertisement, but he was not called to
testify before the Warren Commission. In 1964 Schmidt gave an
interview to *Look* magazine claiming that other conservatives in
Dallas "just didn't want to go as fast as I did. I was too advanced."
Schmidt later moved to Las Vegas, Nevada, where he worked in
advertising, managed an apartment complex, and founded a chapter of the American Historical Society of Germans from Russia.
In 2009 he returned to his native state, Nebraska, where he lives
today.

Robert Surrey was eventually identified by federal investigators as the source of the WANTED FOR TREASON pamphlet. He was

called to testify before the Warren Commission, but he refused to answer questions about the pamphlet, citing his rights under the Fifth Amendment. Surrey and his wife, Mary, broke with General Walker after Walker refused to join the American Nazi Party. Surrey helped raise funds for the ANP and headed a Nazi front group, the Board of United White Christians Majority. He separated from the ANP after the 1967 assassination of its founder, George Lincoln Rockwell. The Surreys moved to Florida and settled in Pompano Beach. Surrey died in 1987 at age sixty-two.

Edwin A. Walker was among the first to suspect that Lee Harvey Oswald had been the mystery man who'd attempted to kill him, a fact confirmed by Marina Oswald and the evidence found among Oswald's belongings. Walker testified to the Warren Commission about the attempt on his own life, but was not asked any questions about his hostile relationship with John F. Kennedy. Walker remained a committed conservative political activist but gradually faded from public view. He was arrested twice in the 1970s after fondling undercover police officers in public restrooms near his home. His personal papers were donated to the Briscoe Center for American History at the University of Texas at Austin, where they are available for researchers. Walker died of lung cancer at age eighty-two in 1993.

Bernard Weissman, who was publicly associated with the WELCOME MR. KENNEDY advertisement in the *Dallas Morning News*, no longer felt safe in the city after Kennedy's death. He left Dallas the following week and never returned. He was called before the Warren Commission and testified extensively about his relationship with Larrie Schmidt and the creation of the advertisement. Weissman also turned over to the commission his correspondence from Schmidt, which is included in the final report. Weissman lives in his native New York.

ACKNOWLEDGMENTS

Many wonderful people provided important assistance at all stages of this book's creation. We are indebted to countless good-hearted men and women who repeatedly gave their time and intelligence. Forgive us for those we inadvertently fail to mention.

Tad Hershorn and his family are to be thanked for their extraordinary generosity and insights. W. Michael Smith provided superlative fact checking and insights. Nick Swartsell, Carlos Morales, Gabino Iglesias, Emily Mathis, Wendy Grossman, and Jeff Davis offered expert, painstaking research.

We extend special thanks to Krishna Shenoy, Mark Davies, and Megan Bryant at the Sixth Floor Museum in Dallas; Pamalla Anderson, Russell Martin, and Ada Negraru at the DeGolyer Library at Southern Methodist University; Brian Collins and Adrianne Pierce in the Texas/Dallas History and Archives Division at the Dallas Public Library; Aryn Glazier, Don Carleton, Margaret Schlankey, and Brenda Gunn at the Dolph Briscoe Center for American History at the University of Texas at Austin; Maryrose Grossman and Lynsey Sczechowicz at the John F. Kennedy Presidential Library; Gerry Cristol at Temple Emanu-El in Dallas; former mayor of Dallas Wes Wise; author and educator Darwin Payne at Southern Methodist University; Sarah Cunningham and Barbara Cline at the Lyndon B. Johnson Presidential Library; Adriane Hanson at the Seeley G. Mudd Manuscript Library at Princeton University; Dorissa Martinez at the Richard M. Nixon Presidential Library; Nicci Hester and Tai Kreidler at the Southwest Collection at Texas Tech University; Jennifer Hadley at the Olin Memorial Library at Wesleyan University; Michelle Kopfer at the Dwight D. Eisenhower Presidential Library; Matthew Lutts with Associated Press Images; Jerome Sims and Ed Timms at the *Dallas Morning News*; Amy Delong at the National Archives and Records

Administration; David P. Sobonya at the FBI Records Management Division.

We are extraordinarily fortunate to have worked with the brilliant editors Cary Goldstein, Sean Desmond, and Deb Futter. Their incredible wisdom and good cheer are unparalleled—all writers would be lucky to work with folks as smart and supportive.

We are also indebted to the many other great people at Twelve and Hachette: the creative and energetic Brian McLendon and the smart and talented Libby Burton, and the exemplary copyediting team of Laura Jorstad and Carolyn J. Kurek. Too, special appreciation and respect must be extended to the excellent editor Roland Philipps with John Murray/Hachette UK. Roland provided wonderful insights and unflagging encouragement. At John Murray, thanks as well to Lyndsey Ng and Becky Walsh.

Our literary agent, David Hale Smith with Inkwell Management, deserves recognition. We are grateful to many others from Inkwell, including Lyndsey Blessing, Kristan Palmer, Lizz Blaise.

Love to Louie Canelakes, a righteous soul, and his beautiful family. Donald Payton, Chuck Nevitt, and Randy Eli Grothe in Dallas opened up several avenues of research. The wonderful author Stephen Harrigan provided great advice and support, as did Chad Hammett, Gary Cartwright, John Slate, Robert Flynn, Eddie Wilson, Connie Todd, Mary Margaret Farabee, Ben Guttery, Bill Wittliff, and Sam Pfiester. John Branch had good counsel from his vantage points in San Antonio and Houston. Glenn Frankel, Dennis Darling, Tracy Dahlby, and Rod Hart at the University of Texas at Austin were exceedingly supportive, as were colleagues at Texas State University–San Marcos: David Coleman, Joan Heath, Michele Miller, Carla Ellard, Katie Salzmann, Maggie DeBrecht, Lauren Goodley, Lyda Guz, and Mark Busby. Thanks to David Maraniss, Sir Harold Evans, Michele Stanush, Michael Nahrstedt, Ellen Kampinsky, Melissa Houtte, John Wilburn, Bob Compton, Joe Nick Patoski, Anne Lang, Shermakaye Bass, Mary Comparetto, Ben Shrake, Nina Howland, Becky Howland, Albert Mendiola, Twister Marquiss, Ernie Lazar, Paul Trejo, John McAdams, Ryan Sachetta, Jacob Payne, Loren Reimer, Laura Tolley, Joe Holley,

Shaun Castillo Fisher, Dave Mann, Brad Tyer, Susan Smith Richardson, Forrest Wilder, and Melissa del Bosque. A bow to the entire staff of the *Texas Observer*.

Bill Minutaglio offers his love to Holly, Rose Angelina, Nicholas Xavier, Linda Smeltzer, Robert, Frank, and John. Tessie, Francesco Xavier, and Tom guided things from above.

Steven L. Davis extends his gratitude to his loving family, which makes each day a special joy: Georgia, Natalie, and Lucia.

SOURCES

Archives

National Archives and Records Administration

Bruce Alger Papers, Texas/Dallas History and Archives Division, Dallas Public Library

Earle Cabell Papers, DeGolyer Library, Southern Methodist University

Juanita Craft Papers, Texas/Dallas History and Archives Division, Dallas Public Library

E. M. "Ted" Dealey Collection, Belo Records, DeGolyer Library, Southern Methodist University

Dwight D. Eisenhower Presidential Library and Museum

A. C. Greene Papers, Special Collections Division, the University of Texas at Arlington Libraries

Shel Hershorn Photographic Collection, Dolph Briscoe Center for American History, University of Texas at Austin

H. Rhett James Papers, Anacostia Community Museum

Lyndon Baines Johnson Presidential Library and Museum

John F. Kennedy Presidential Library and Museum

William Manchester Papers, Special Collections and Archives, Olin Memorial Library, Wesleyan University

Stanley Marcus Papers, DeGolyer Library, Southern Methodist University

Melvin Munn Papers, Southwest Collection, Texas Tech University

Richard M. Nixon Presidential Library and Museum

Rabbi Levi A. Olan Papers, Bridwell Library, Perkins School of Theology, Southern Methodist University

Adlai E. Stevenson Papers, Seeley G. Mudd Manuscript Library, Princeton University

Edwin A. Walker Papers, Dolph Briscoe Center for American History, University of Texas at Austin

Edwin A. Walker Papers, Department of Justice, Federal Bureau of Investigation

Books

Adams, Marion. *Alvin M. Owsley of Texas: Apostle of Americanism* (Texian Press, 1971).

Anthony, Carl Sferrazza. *The Kennedy White House: Family Life and Pictures, 1961–1963* (Touchstone, 2001).

Aynesworth, Hugh with Stephen G. Michaud. *JFK: Breaking the News* (International Focus Press, 2003).

Bainbridge, John. *The Super-Americans* (Doubleday, 1961).

Behnken, Brian D. *Fighting Their Own Battles: Mexican Americans, African Americans, and the Struggle for Civil Rights in Texas* (University of North Carolina Press, 2011).

Bugliosi, Vincent. *Reclaiming History: The Assassination of President John F. Kennedy* (W. W. Norton, 2007).

Burrough, Bryan. *The Big Rich: The Rise and Fall of the Greatest Texas Oil Fortunes* (Penguin, 2009).

Carleton, Don E. *Red Scare! Right-Wing Hysteria, Fifties Fanaticism, and Their Legacy in Texas* (Texas Monthly Press, 1985).

Caro, Robert. *The Years of Lyndon Johnson: The Passage of Power* (Knopf, 2012).

Carraro, Francine. *Jerry Bywaters: A Life in Art* (University of Texas Press, 1994).

Cartwright, Gary. *Confessions of a Washed-Up Sportswriter: Including Various Digressions About Sex, Crime, and Other Hobbies* (Texas Monthly Press, 1982).

Courtney, Kent, and Phoebe Courtney. *The Case of General Edwin A. Walker* (CSA, Conservative Society of America, 1961).

Cox, Patrick. *The First Texas News Barons* (University of Texas Press, 2005).

Cristol, Gerry. *A Light in the Prairie: Temple Emanu-El of Dallas 1872–1997* (Texas Christian University Press, 1998).

Criswell, W. A. *Standing on the Promises: The Autobiography of W. A. Criswell* (Word Publishing, 1990).

———. *These Issues We Must Face* (Zondervan, 1954).

Criswell, W. A., and Duke McCall. *Passport to the World* (Broadman Press, 1951).

Cunningham, Sean P. *Cowboy Conservatism: Texas and the Rise of the Modern Right* (University Press of Kentucky, 2010).

Curry, Jesse. *Retired Dallas Police Chief Jesse Curry Reveals His Personal JFK Assassination File* (Curry, 1969).

Dallas Morning News. *November 22: The Day Remembered as Reported by the Dallas Morning News* (Taylor, 1990).

———. *The Day JFK Died: Thirty Years Later: The Event That Changed a Generation* (Andrews and McMeel, 1993).

Dallek, Robert. *An Unfinished Life: John F. Kennedy, 1917–1963* (Little, Brown, 2003).

Davis, Steven L. *Texas Literary Outlaws: Six Writers in the Sixties and Beyond* (Texas Christian University Press, 2004).

Davison, Jean. *Oswald's Game* (W. W. Norton, 1983).

Dealey, Ted. *Diaper Days of Dallas* (Abingdon, 1966).

Diamond, Sara. *Roads to Dominion: Right-Wing Movements and Political Power in the United States* (Guilford Press, 1995).

Dudman, Richard. *Men of the Far Right* (Pyramid Books, 1962).

Dulaney, W. Marvin, and Kathleen Underwood, eds. *Essays on the American Civil Rights Movement* (Texas A&M University Press, 1993).

Eagles, Charles W. *The Price of Defiance: James Meredith and the Integration of Ole Miss* (University of North Carolina Press, 2009).

Fairbanks, Robert B. *For the City as a Whole: Planning, Politics, and the Public Interest in Dallas, Texas 1900–1965* (Ohio State University Press, 1998).

Giglio, James N. *The Presidency of John F. Kennedy* (University Press of Kansas, 2006).

Graff, Harvey J. *The Dallas Myth: The Making and Unmaking of an American City* (University of Minnesota Press, 2008).

Gray, Ed. *Henry Wade's Tough Justice: How Dallas County Prosecutors Led the Nation in Convicting the Innocent* (Dog Ear Publishing, 2010).

Green, George N. *The Establishment in Texas Politics: The Primitive Years, 1938–57* (University of Oklahoma Press, 1984).

Hanson, Royce. *Civic Culture and Urban Change: Governing Dallas* (Wayne State University Press, 2003).

Hazel, Michael V., ed. *Dallas Reconsidered: Essays in Local History* (Three Forks Press, 1996).

Hill, Patricia Evridge. *Dallas: The Making of a Modern City* (University of Texas Press, 1996).

Huffaker, Bob, et al. *When the News Went Live: Dallas 1963* (Taylor Trade, 2007).

Hunt, H. L. *Alpaca* (HLH Press, 1960).

Hurt, Harry III. *Texas Rich: The Hunt Dynasty from the Early Oil Days Through the Silver Crash* (W. W. Norton, 1981).

Irons, Peter. *Jim Crow's Children: The Broken Promises of the Brown Decision* (Viking/Penguin, 2002).

James, H. Rhett. *The Audacity to Survive* (James, 1992).

Janson, Donald, and Bernard Eisemann. *The Far Right* (McGraw-Hill, 1963).

Jeansonne, Glen. *Leander Perez: Boss of the Delta* (University Press of Mississippi, 2006).

Jones, Howard. *Death of a Generation: How the Assassinations of Diem and JFK Prolonged the Vietnam War* (Oxford University Press, 2003).

Kaiser, David. *The Road to Dallas: The Assassination of John F. Kennedy* (Belknap/ Harvard University Press, 2008).

Kennedy, Jacqueline, and Caroline Kennedy (with Michael Beschloss). *Jacqueline Kennedy: Historic Conversations on Life with John F. Kennedy, Interviews with Arthur M. Schlesinger, Jr., 1964* (Hyperion, 2011).

Leslie, Warren. *Dallas: Public and Private: Aspects of an American City* (Grossman Publishers, 1964).

Manchester, William. *The Death of a President* (Harper & Row, 1967).

Marcus, Stanley. *Minding the Store: A Memoir* (Little, Brown, 1974).

McNamara, Robert S. *In Retrospect: The Tragedy and Lessons of Vietnam* (Crown, 1995).

Mecklin, John. *Mission in Torment: An Intimate Account of the U.S. Role in Vietnam* (Doubleday, 1965).

Miller, Merle. *Lyndon: An Oral Biography* (Ballantine Books, 1981).

Minutaglio, Bill. *In Search of the Blues: A Journey to the Soul of Black Texas* (University of Texas Press, 2010).

Minutaglio, Bill, and Holly Williams. *The Hidden City: Oak Cliff, Texas* (Elmwood Press, 1990).

O'Brien, Michael. *John F. Kennedy: A Biography* (Thomas Dunne, 2005).

Payne, Darwin. *Big D: Triumphs and Troubles of an American Supercity in the 20th Century* (Three Forks Press, 1994).

————. *Indomitable Sarah: The Life of Judge Sarah T. Hughes* (Southern Methodist University Press, 2004).

————. *Quest for Justice: Louis A. Bedford Jr. and the Struggle for Equal Rights in Texas* (Southern Methodist University Press, 2009).

Perlstein, Rick. *Before the Storm: Barry Goldwater and the Unmaking of the American Consensus* (Hill and Wang, 2001).

Phillips, Michael. *White Metropolis: Race, Ethnicity, and Religion in Dallas, 1841–2001* (University of Texas Press, 2006).

Pietrusza, David. *1960: LBJ vs. JFK vs. Nixon: The Epic Campaign That Forged Three Presidencies* (Union Square Press, 2008).

Posner, Gerald. *Case Closed: Lee Harvey Oswald and the Assassination of JFK* (Random House, 1993).

President's Commission on the Assassination of John F. Kennedy. *The Warren Commission Report: Report of the President's Commission on the Assassination of President John F. Kennedy.*

Rosenberg, Jonathan, and Zachary Karabell. *Kennedy, Johnson, and the Quest for Justice* (W. W. Norton, 2003).

Rumbley, Rose-Mary. *A Century of Class: Public Education in Dallas* (Eakin Press, 1984).

Schlesinger, Arthur M., Jr. *Robert Kennedy and His Times* (Houghton Mifflin, 1978).

Schmaltz, William H. *Hate: George Lincoln Rockwell and the American Nazi Party* (Brassey's, 1999).

Schutze, Jim. *The Accommodation: The Politics of Race in an American City* (Citadel Press, 1987).

Sherwin, Mark. *The Extremists* (St. Martin's, 1963).

Shrake, Edwin. *Strange Peaches* (John M. Hardy Publishing, 2007).

Simonelli, Frederick J. *American Fuehrer: George Lincoln Rockwell and the American Nazi Party* (University of Illinois Press, 1999).

Smoot, Dan. *The Invisible Government* (Western Islands, 1962).

————. *People Along the Way: The Autobiography of Dan Smoot* (Tyler Press, 1996).

Talbot, David. *Brothers: The Hidden History of the Kennedy Years* (Free Press, 2008).

Tessmer, Charles. *Justice for Sale* (unpublished manuscript given to Minutaglio, December 16, 1991).

Thometz, Carol Estes. *The Decision-Makers: The Power Structure of Dallas* (Southern Methodist University Press, 1963).

Tolbert, Frank X. *Neiman Marcus, Texas* (Holt, 1953).

Tuccille, Jerome. *Kingdom: The Story of the Hunt Family of Texas* (PaperJacks, 1987).

Webb, Clive. *Rabble Rousers: The American Far Right in the Civil Rights Era* (University of Georgia Press, 2010).

Wilson, William H. *Hamilton Park: A Planned Black Community in Dallas* (Johns Hopkins University Press, 1998).

Wright, Lawrence. *In the New World: Growing Up with America, 1960–1984* (Knopf, 1988).

Youngblood, Rufus W. *20 Years in the Secret Service: My Life with Five Presidents* (Simon & Schuster, 1973).

Doctoral Dissertations and Master's Theses

Banitch, George. "The Ultraconservative Congressman from Dallas: The Rise and Fall of Bruce Alger, 1954–1964" (master's thesis, University of Texas at Arlington, 2001).

Brenner, Samuel. "Shouting at the Rain: The Growth and Development of Right-Wing Anti-Communist Organizations in the Era of Modern American Conservatism, 1950–1974" (PhD dissertation, Brown University, 2009).

Carney, Carolyn A. "The 'City of Hate': Anti-Communist and Conservative Attitudes in Dallas, Texas, 1950–1964" (master's thesis, University of Texas at Arlington, 1994).

Cravens, Chris. "Edwin A. Walker and the Right Wing in Dallas, 1960–1966" (master's thesis, Texas State University–San Marcos, 1991).

Gillette, Michael Lowery. "The NAACP in Texas, 1937–1957" (PhD dissertation, University of Texas at Austin, 1984).

Green, George Norris. "The Far Right Wing in Texas Politics, 1930's–1960's" (PhD dissertation, Florida State University, 1966).

Hill, Marilynn Wood. "A History of the Jewish Involvement in the Dallas Community" (master's thesis, Southern Methodist University, 1967).

Lorch, Alexander H., III. "Stanley Marcus: Minding Dallas and Promoting Civil Liberties and Civil Rights in the Metroplex" (master's thesis, Southern Methodist University, 1999).

Sprague, Stacey. "James Evetts Haley and the New Deal: Laying the Foundations for the Modern Republican Party in Texas" (master's thesis, University of North Texas, 2004).

Towns, James Edward. "The Rhetoric and Leadership of W. A. Criswell as President of the Southern Baptist Convention: A Descriptive Analysis Through Perspective and Public Address" (PhD dissertation, Southern Illinois University, 1970).

Wilson, Ava. "Left in an Unmarked Grave: Unearthing the Civil Rights and Black Power Movements in Dallas, Texas" (master's thesis, Temple University, 2010).

Magazines and Journals

American Mercury
Christianity and Crisis
Congressional Digest
Coronet
Cosmopolitan
D Magazine
Dallas Life Magazine
Dan Smoot Report
Fortune
Human Events
Humanities Texas Newsletter
Journal of Southern Religion
Library Journal
Life
Look
Nation
Newsweek
Overseas Weekly
Reporter
Social Science Quarterly
Texas Monthly
Texas Observer
Time
True
U.S. News and World Report

Newspapers

Chicago Tribune
Dallas Express
Dallas Morning News
Dallas Observer
Dallas Times Herald
Fort Worth Star-Telegram
Fort Worth Weekly
Houston Chronicle
Houston Post
Houston Press
Los Angeles Times
New York Times
San Antonio Express-News
Washington Post

NOTES

Prelude

1. Carlson, Peter. *K Blows Top: A Cold War Comic Interlude, Starring Nikita Khrushchev, America's Most Unlikely Tourist* (PublicAffairs, 2009), 210.

2. *New York Times*, September 20, 1959.

3. "The Strategy of Peace." John F. Kennedy Personal Papers, John F. Kennedy Presidential Library. Digital Identifier: JFKPP-036-004.

4. *New York Times*, June 2, 1963.

5. *Los Angeles Times*, April 1, 1961.

6. Walker to Welch, May 26, 1959. Edwin Walker Papers, Briscoe Center for American History, University of Texas at Austin. Accession 96-030, Box 2.

January 1960

1. *Dallas Times Herald*, February 22, 1956; *Dallas Morning News*, February 22, 1956; Freeman, Curtis W. " 'Never Had I Been So Blind': W. A. Criswell's 'Change' on Racial Segregation." *Journal of Southern Religion* X, 2007.

2. Clipping, vertical files on Criswell, Texas/Dallas History and Archives Division, Dallas Public Library.

3. Ibid.

4. *Dallas Morning News*, February 11, 1961.

5. *Dallas Morning News*, January 22, 1960.

6. *Dallas Morning News*, January 23, 1960.

7. Banitch, George. "The Ultraconservative Congressman from Dallas: The Rise and Fall of Bruce Alger, 1954–1964" (master's thesis, University of Texas at Arlington, 2001), 54.

8. *Dallas Morning News*, July 3, 1958.

9. Bruce Alger Papers, Texas/Dallas History and Archives Division, Dallas Public Library. Box 4, folder 2.

10. *Dallas Morning News*, December 30, 1959.

11. *Time*, April 7, 1961.

12. Williams, Juan. *Thurgood Marshall: American Revolutionary* (Broadway, 2000), 104.

13. *Dallas Morning News*, January 1, 1960.

14. *Overseas Weekly*, April 15, 1961.

15. *American Mercury*, January 1960.

16. *Dallas Morning News*, February 22, 1956.

17. Carraro, Francine. *Jerry Bywaters: A Life in Art* (University of Texas Press, 1994), 188–90.

18. *American Mercury*, January 1960.

19. Tolbert, Frank X. *Neiman Marcus, Texas* (Holt, 1953), 35.

February 1960

1. Clipping, H. L. Hunt vertical files, Texas/Dallas History and Archives Division, Dallas Public Library.

2. Sherrill, Robert. "H.L. Hunt: Portrait of a Super-Patriot." *Nation*, February 24, 1964.

3. Hunt, H. L. *Alpaca* (HLH Press, 1960), 183.

4. Bainbridge, John. *The Super-Americans* (Doubleday, 1961), 303.

5. Hurt, Harry III. *Texas Rich: The Hunt Dynasty from the Early Oil Days Through the Silver Crash* (W. W. Norton, 1981), 158.

6. *Life Line* transcript, program 95-62, April 5, 1962. Melvin Munn Papers, Southwest Collection, Texas Tech University.

7. *Life Line* transcripts, program 83-61, March 24, 1961, and program 93-61, April 3, 1961. Melvin Munn Papers.

8. Tuccille, Jerome. *Kingdom: The Story of the Hunt Family of Texas* (Paper-Jacks, 1987), 231.

9. Hurt, 255.

10. *New York Times*, August 13, 1990.

11. H. Rhett James Papers, Anacostia Community Museum.

12. Irons, Peter. *Jim Crow's Children: The Broken Promises of the Brown Decision* (Viking/Penguin, 2002). Texas State Historical Association, Handbook of Texas Online, "Mansfield School Desegregation Incident."

March 1960

1. Juanita Craft Papers, Texas/Dallas History and Archives Division, Dallas Public Library.

2. *Dallas Morning News*, March 8, 1960.

3. Ibid.

4. Ibid.

5. Juanita Craft Papers.

6. Gray, Ed. *Henry Wade's Tough Justice: How Dallas County Prosecutors Led the Nation in Convicting the Innocent* (Dog Ear Publishing, 2010), 109.

7. Letter from Joe Louis Atkins to Juanita Craft, Juanita Craft Papers.

8. Daniel, Carey. *God the Original Segregationist*, based on a sermon delivered by Daniel at First Baptist of West Dallas, May 23, 1954, the week following the Supreme Court's decision in *Brown v. Board of Education*.

April 1960

1. *Dallas Morning News*, April 8, 1960.

2. Caro, Robert. *The Years of Lyndon Johnson: The Passage of Power* (Knopf, 2012), 71.

3. *Dallas Morning News*, April 8, 1960.

July 1960

1. Criswell, W. A., and Duke McCall. *Passport to the World* (Broadman Press, 1951), 11–34.

2. Sermon by W. A. Criswell, July 3, 1960. This sermon is not available in the online W. A. Criswell Sermon Library. But it is reprinted in: Towns, James Edward. "The Rhetoric and Leadership of W. A. Criswell as President of the Southern Baptist Convention" (PhD dissertation, Southern Illinois University, 1970).

3. *Washington Post*, July 9, 1960.

4. "The 1960 Democratic Party Platform." *Congressional Digest*, October 1, 1960.

5. Pett, Saul. "Convention Comments." Associated Press syndicated column published July 11, 1960.

6. Memorandum on Texas Political Situation (as of July 21, 1960). John F. Kennedy Presidential Library, 1960 Campaign Files, Post Convention to Election Files. Box 987, Texas Organizational 6/21/60–9/26/60.

September 1960

1. *Dallas Morning News*, September 13, 1960.

2. *New York Times*, December 26, 1993.

3. Kennedy's speech is available on YouTube. The original draft also included the names Fuentes and Badillo, but Kennedy, looking out at his audience, realized that it wouldn't do him any good to mention Mexicanos.

4. *Dallas Morning News*, September 14, 1960; "Criswell's Adamant Stand," *Texas Observer*, October 1960; *Dallas Morning News*, October 2, 1960.

5. *Dallas Morning News*, September 14, 1960.

October 1960

1. *Dallas Morning News*, October 23, 1960.

2. Ibid.

3. *Dallas Morning News*, October 30, 1960.

November 1960

1. Pietrusza, David. *1960: LBJ vs. JFK vs. Nixon: The Epic Campaign That Forged Three Presidencies* (Union Square Press, 2008), 267.

2. Ibid., 266–67.

3. "Alger's Wife Tells About Wild Party." *Fort Worth Press*, December 21, 1960. Clipping in Bruce Alger Papers, Box 8, folder 30.

4. Ibid.

5. Payne, Darwin. *Big D: Triumphs and Troubles of an American Supercity in the 20th Century* (Three Forks Press, 1994), 306.

6. Miller, Merle. *Lyndon: An Oral Biography* (Ballantine Books, 1981), 330.

7. Descriptions of these scenes have been pieced together from many sources: Contemporary news reports, November 5, 1960; clippings found in Bruce Alger Papers in Dallas; interviews at the Lyndon B. Johnson Presidential Library with several eyewitnesses, including Lady Bird Johnson; articles by Lawrence Wright published in *D Magazine* and *Texas Monthly*; several books quoting eyewitness accounts, including those by Robert Dallek, Robert Caro, and other Johnson biographers.

8. Miller, 271.

9. *New York Times*, November 6, 1960.

10. Oval Office recording by Richard Nixon, speaking to Pat Buchanan on November 1, 1972. Richard M. Nixon Presidential Library and Museum, Tape 379, Conversation 379-10.

January 1961

1. *Dallas Morning News*, November 5, 1960.

2. Youngblood, Rufus W. *20 Years in the Secret Service: My Life with Five Presidents* (Simon & Schuster, 1973), 61.

3. "The Kennedy Assassin Who Failed." Smithsonian.com, December 6, 2012; "Man Accused of Plotting to Assassinate Kennedy." *Spartanburg (SC) Herald-Journal*, December 17, 1960.

4. Ted Dealey to Richard Nixon, January 23, 1961. Pre-Presidential Papers of Richard M. Nixon, Richard M. Nixon Presidential Library and Museum. General Correspondence, 1946–1962. Series 320, Box 206.

5. Ibid.

6. *Dallas Morning News*, November–December 1960.

7. *Dallas Morning News*, November 12, 1960.

8. *Dallas Morning News*, January 3, 1961.

9. *Dallas Morning News*, January 20, 1961.

10. *Dallas Express*, January 14, 1961.

11. James, Rhett. "Dateline Dallas." *Dallas Express*, January 28, 1961.

February 1961

1. *New York Times*, March 31, 1961.

2. Bruce Alger Papers, Box 10, folder 1.

3. John Birch Society. *The Blue Book*, 1961 edition, 59.

4. *New York Times*, March 9, 1961.

5. *New York Times*, December 10, 1961; clipping, Edwin Walker Papers, Accession 93-402, Box 5.

6. *New York Times*, April 7, 1961.

7. Bruce Alger Papers, Box 10, folder 1.

8. *Dallas Express*, February 11, 1961.

9. *Dallas Express*, February 4, 1961.

10. *Dallas Express*, February 18, 1961.

11. Stanley Marcus Papers, DeGolyer Library, Southern Methodist University. Box 275, folder 26.

March 1961

1. *Texas Observer,* November 10, 1961.
2. *Dallas Morning News,* April 18, 1961.
3. Robert Welch on NBC's *Meet the Press,* May 21, 1961.
4. *Dallas Morning News,* April 17, 1961.
5. *Dallas Morning News,* July 7, 1961.
6. *Time,* December 8, 1961.

April 1961

1. *New York Times,* April 18 and 23, 1961.
2. *Overseas Weekly,* April 16, 1961.
3. *Los Angeles Times,* April 15, 1961.
4. Lauris Norstad Papers, Dwight D. Eisenhower Presidential Library. Box 55/*Overseas Weekly.*
5. *Chicago Daily Tribune,* April 15, 1961.
6. *New York Times,* April 15, 1961.
7. Letter dated September 23, 1961. Edwin A. Walker FBI Papers. Sender's name is deleted.
8. Walker Papers, Accession 96-030, Box 4.
9. Walker Papers, Accession 96-030, Box 15.
10. *Dallas Morning News,* May 7, 1961.
11. *Dallas Morning News,* June 14, 1961.
12. *Life Line* transcript, program 298-61, October 25, 1961. Melvin Munn Papers.
13. *Chicago Tribune,* September 5, 1961.
14. *Chicago Tribune,* August 31, 1961.
15. *Dallas Morning News,* October 1, 1961.

June 1961

1. Schlesinger, Arthur M., Jr. *Robert Kennedy and His Times* (Houghton Mifflin, 1978), 450.
2. Dallek, Robert. *An Unfinished Life: John F. Kennedy, 1917–1963* (Little, Brown, 2003), 41.
3. *Washington Post,* July 19, 1961.

July 1961

1. Dallek, 346; Talbot, David. *Brothers: The Hidden History of the Kennedy Years* (Free Press, 2008), 68.
2. Talbot, 51.
3. *Dallas Morning News,* August 13, 1961.
4. *Dallas Morning News,* September 22, 1961.

September 1961

1. "All Is Quiet During Dallas Integration." *Florence (AL) Times,* September 6, 1961.

2. "Books Scorched by Haley's Critics." *Texas Observer*, September 22, 1961.

3. H. Rhett James Papers, Dallas Public Library oral history project, December 21, 2002.

October 1961

1. Knickerbocker to John Tower, September 27, 1961. Bruce Alger Papers.

2. *Dallas Morning News*, October 13, 1961.

3. *Dallas Morning News*, October 14, 1961.

4. Ibid.

5. *Texas Observer*, November 10, 1961.

6. These reports on the National Indignation Convention come from contemporaneous articles published in the *Dallas Morning News*.

7. *Dallas Morning News*, June 8, 1962.

8. Green, George Norris. "The Far Right Wing in Texas Politics, 1930's–1960's" (PhD dissertation, Florida State University, 1966), 238.

9. Dealey/Belo Papers, DeGolyer Library, Southern Methodist University. Box 3, folder 2.

10. Ibid.

11. Elkind, Peter. "The Legacy of Citizen Robert." *Texas Monthly*, July 1985.

12. *Dallas Morning News*, November 12, 1959.

13. Bishop, Jim. *The Day Kennedy Was Shot* (Funk & Wagnalls, 1968), 149.

14. *Dallas Morning News*, August 3, 1961.

15. Marcus, Stanley. *Minding the Store: A Memoir* (Little, Brown, 1974), 249.

16. "Success Story." *Time*, April 7, 1961.

17. Dealey/Belo Papers, Box 3, folder 2.

18. Ibid.

19. Ibid.

20. Ibid.

21. Ibid.

22. Ibid.

23. Ibid.

24. Ibid.; Bartlett, Charles, *Chattanooga Times*, November 6, 1961.

25. *Dallas Morning News*, October 28, 1961.

26. Dealey/Belo Papers, Box 3, folder 2; *Los Angeles Times*, November 17, 1961.

27. *Dallas Morning News*, October 29, 1961.

28. Dealey/Belo Papers, Box 3, folder 4.

29. Ibid.

November 1961

1. *Dallas Morning News*, November 3, 1961.

2. Edwin A. Walker Papers, Briscoe Center for American History, University of Texas at Austin.

3. *Dallas Morning News*, November 16, 1961.

4. Ibid.

5. Ibid.

6. *Dallas Morning News*, July 2, 1958.

7. *New York Times*, January 14, 1960.

8. Testimony of Lewis McWillie to House Select Committee on Assassinations, September 27, 1978.

9. *New York Times,* November 19, 1961.

10. *Dallas Morning News*, November 24, 1961.

11. Marcus, Stanley. Lyndon B. Johnson Presidential Library. Oral History, 21.

December 1961

1. *Dallas Morning News*, October 20, 1961.

2. *Dallas Morning News*, December 3, 1961.

3. *Dallas Morning News*, September 23, 1961.

4. "Opinion: Misfit in Mufti." *Time*, December 22, 1961.

5. *Dallas Morning News*, December 13, 1961.

6. "Walker Deplores Civilian Policies." *Texas Observer*, December 13, 1961.

7. Ibid.

January 1962

1. *Life* magazine, September 1961.

2. Ted Dealey Papers, DeGolyer Library, Southern Methodist University.

3. Drew Pearson syndicated column, November 21, 1961.

4. Talbot, 75.

5. Letter from Dealey to Bill Steven, November 17, 1961. Ted Dealey Papers.

6. Ibid.

7. *Dallas Morning News*, January 16, 1962.

8. "All Started Firing at Once." *Texas Observer*, July 7, 1962.

9. *Dallas Morning News*, January 21, 1962.

10. Ibid.

11. Cravens, Chris. "Edwin A. Walker and the Right Wing in Dallas, 1960–1966" (master's thesis, Texas State University–San Marcos, 1991), 86.

12. "Mixed Emotions on Walker Talk." *Texas Observer*, January 26, 1962.

February 1962

1. *Dallas Morning News*, February 3, 1962.

2. *Dallas Morning News*, February 10, 1962.

3. H. Rhett James Papers.

4. *Dallas Morning News*, February 16, 1962.

March 1962

1. *Texas Observer*, March 9, 1962.

2. Ibid.

3. McGehee to Kennedy, February 7, 1962. Bruce Alger Papers, Box 14, folder 25.

4. Bruce Alger Papers, Box 14, folder 25.

5. "Optimistic Footnote." *Texas Observer*, June 8, 1962.

6. Cravens, 93.

7. *Dallas Morning News*, September 19, 1961.

8. Memo to Mr. DeLoach from M. A. Jones, January 31, 1962. Edwin A. Walker FBI Papers.

9. Memo to Mr. DeLoach from M. A. Jones, December 4, 1961. Edwin A. Walker FBI Papers.

10. Walker Papers, Accession 96–030, Box 17.

11. Walker Papers, Accession 96–030, Box 15.

12. Ibid.

13. Ibid.

14. Ibid.

15. *Dallas Morning News*, October 1, 1961.

16. Walker Papers, Accession 96–030, Box 11.

17. Prayer for divine guidance: advertisement in *Dallas Morning News*, March 25, 1962; "My platform...": Bruce Alger Papers, Box 10, folder 23.

18. "Optimistic Footnote." *Texas Observer*, June 8, 1962.

April 1962

1. Janson, Donald, and Bernard Eisemann. *The Far Right* (McGraw-Hill, 1963), 141.

2. Walker Papers, Accession 96–030, Box 2.

3. Cravens, 96.

4. Walker Papers, Accession 96–030, Box 15.

5. Later, as controversy mounted over Walker's actions, he claimed that the reporter had elbowed him three times and attempted to block his exit from the room.

6. *Dallas Morning News*, April 21, 1962.

7. "Notes on Congress Races." *Texas Observer*, April 21, 1962.

8. *Dallas Morning News*, January 20, 1962.

9. "Downtown Dallas Intrigue: Syndicate Went to Work." *Texas Observer*, May 19, 1962.

10. *Dallas Morning News*, January 13, 1962.

11. *Dallas Morning News*, March 4, 1962.

12. *Dallas Morning News,* February 3, 1962.

May 1962

1. Cravens, 98.

2. *Dallas Morning News*, April 5, 1962.

3. Radio speech by John C. Williams. Edwin A. Walker FBI files.

4. *Dallas Morning News*, May 3, 1962.

July 1962

1. *Washington Post*, June 16, 1962.

2. *Dallas Morning News*, June 18, 1962.

3. *Dallas Morning News*, July 19, 1962.

4. *Life Line* transcript, program 113, September 9, 1963. Melvin Munn Papers.

5. *Dallas Morning News*, July 18, 1962.

6. Cravens, 100.

7. *Dallas Morning News*, July 10, 1962.

8. Leslie, Warren. *Dallas: Public and Private: Aspects of an American City* (Grossman Publishers, 1964), 112–13.

September 1962

1. *Dallas Morning News*, September 28, 1962.

2. *Dallas Morning News*, October 2, 1962.

3. Cravens, 108.

4. Eagles, Charles W. *The Price of Defiance: James Meredith and the Integration of Ole Miss* (University of North Carolina Press, 2009), 362.

5. Walker Papers, Accession 96-030, Box 6.

6. Cravens, 110.

7. Ibid.

8. Cravens, 109–10.

9. Cravens, 111.

10. *Dallas Morning News*, September 30, 1962.

11. Eagles, 360.

12. Radio and Television Report to the Nation on the Situation at the University of Mississippi, September 30, 1962. www.presidence.ucsb.edu/ws/?pid-8915.

13. Cravens, 112–13.

14. Walker Papers, Accession 96-030, Box 30.

15. Cravens, 113.

16. *Dallas Morning News*, October 2, 1962.

17. Eagles, 360.

18. Eagles, 361.

19. FBI memorandum, June 23, 1964. Edwin A. Walker FBI Papers.

20. Rosenberg, Jonathan, and Zachary Karabell. *Kennedy, Johnson, and the Quest for Justice* (W. W. Norton, 2003), 63–64.

21. Giglio, James N. *The Presidency of John F. Kennedy* (University Press of Kansas, 2006), 189.

22. Giglio, 190.

October 1962

1. Rosenberg, 83.

2. *New York Times*, January 2, 1997.

3. *Dallas Morning News*, October 4, 1962.

4. *Dallas Morning News*, October 3, 1962.

5. Walker Papers, Accession 96–030, Box 20.

6. *Dallas Morning News*, October 8, 1962.

7. Davison, Jean. *Oswald's Game* (W. W. Norton, 1983), 115.

8. Talbot, 163.

9. Talbot, 164.

10. Talbot, 165.

11. Talbot, 172.

November 1962

1. Davison, 113.

2. Davison, 119.

3. Davison, 127.

4. Walker Papers, Accession 96–030, Box 33.

5. *Dallas Morning News*, November 25, 1962.

December 1962

1. *Washington Post*, December 20, 1962.

2. Davison, 122.

January 1963

1. Juanita Craft Papers, oral history conducted by the Civil Rights Project, 1968, 30.

2. *Dallas Times Herald*, January 4–5, 1963.

3. *Dallas Express*, January 5, 1963.

4. Ibid.

5. *Dallas Express*, January 12, 1963.

February 1963

1. Letter from Larrie Schmidt to Bernard Weissman, June 13, 1963. Warren Commission exhibit 1040.

2. Swank, Patricia. "A Plot That Flopped." *Look*, January 26, 1965.

3. Letter from Larrie Schmidt to Larry Jones, undated. Warren Commission exhibit 1047.

4. Letter from Larrie Schmidt to Larry Jones, November 2, 1962. Warren Commission exhibit 1036.

5. Ibid.

6. Ibid.

7. *Dallas Morning News*, July 14, 1962.

8. Memorandum addressed to members of Conservatism USA, February 2, 1963. Warren Commission exhibit 1049.

9. O'Brien, Michael. *John F. Kennedy: A Biography* (Thomas Dunne, 2005), 833.

10. *Dallas Express*, February 9, 1963.

11. "Ruby Red Suit: Jacket and Skirt." John F. Kennedy Museum Collection, John F. Kennedy Presidential Library and Museum.

12. *Dallas Express*, February 9, 1963.

13. *Dallas Express*, February 23, 1963.

14. Posner, Gerald. *Case Closed: Lee Harvey Oswald and the Assassination of JFK* (Random House, 1993), 100.

15. Walker Papers, Accession 96-030, Box 7.

16. Walker Papers, Accession 93-402, Box 5.

17. Walker Papers, Accession 93-402, Box 15.

March 1963

1. *Dallas Morning News*, March 28, 1963.

2. Clipping from *Montgomery Advertiser-Journal*, Edwin A. Walker FBI Papers, March 10, 1963.

3. Clipping from *Nashville Tennessean*, Edwin A. Walker FBI Papers, March 14, 1963.

4. Clipping dated March 11, 1963, Edwin A. Walker FBI Papers.

5. Posner, 107–08.

6. Davison, 87.

7. Davison, 128.

April 1963

1. Davison, 129; Posner, 110.

2. President's Commission on the Assassination of John F. Kennedy. *The Warren Commission Report: Report of the President's Commission on the Assassination of President John F. Kennedy*, 183–87.

3. Cravens, 134.

4. This account comes from: the Dallas Police Department files on the shooting at Walker's residence; Edwin A. Walker FBI Papers; news clippings in Edwin Walker Papers.

5. Robert Surrey testimony to Warren Commission.

6. Dallas Police Department files on the shooting at Walker's residence.

7. Clippings, Edwin Walker Papers; Surrey testimony to Warren Commission.

8. Marina Oswald testimony to Warren Commission.

9. Ibid.

10. Posner, 117.

11. Marina Oswald testimony to Warren Commission.

12. Ibid.

13. Clipping, Edwin Walker Papers, Accession 96-030, Box 37; Cravens, 135.

14. Dallas Police Department report, April 16, 1963.

May 1963

1. Dallas Police Department report, April 18, 1963.

June–July 1963

1. *Dan Smoot Report*, June 3, 1963.
2. *Dallas Morning News*, June 14, 1963.
3. *Dan Smoot Report*, July 1, 1963.

August 1963

1. *Dallas Morning News*, August 5, 1963.
2. "Address to the Nation on the Nuclear Test Ban Treaty, 26 July 1963," Accession Number: TNC:384, John F. Kennedy Library.
3. *Dallas Morning News*, August 6, 1963.
4. Ibid, August 4, 1963.
5. *Life Line* transcript, program 163-62, June 12, 1962. Melvin Munn Papers.
6. *Dallas Morning News*, July 28, 1963.

September 1963

1. Letter from Larrie Schmidt to Bernard Weissman, June 2, 1963. Warren Commission exhibit 1037.
2. Letter from Larrie Schmidt to Bernard Weissman, October 1, 1963. Warren Commission exhibit 1033.
3. "Merchandising: Dallas in Wonderland," *Time*, October 28, 1957.
4. Stanley Marcus to Joe Buford, November 16, 1963. Stanley Marcus Papers.
5. Leslie, 197–98.
6. *Dallas Morning News*, April 19, 1963
7. Ibid.
8. *Dallas Morning News*, August 8, 1963.
9. *Dallas Morning News*, September 20, 1963.
10. *Texas Observer*, May 30, 1963.
11. Bruce Alger Papers, Box 23, folder 15.
12. *Life Line* transcript, program 19-62, January 19, 1962. Melvin Munn Papers.
13. *Dan Smoot Report*, April 8, 1963. Bruce Alger Papers, Box 33, folder 6.
14. *Dan Smoot Report*, October 7, 1963. Bruce Alger Papers, Box 33, folder 6.
15. *Washington Post*, September 21, 1963.
16. *Dallas Morning News*, September 25, 1963.
17. Leslie, 190.
18. *Dallas Morning News*, September 26, 1963.

October 1963

1. *Dallas Morning News*, October 3, 1963.
2. Larrie Schmidt to Bernard Weissman, October 1, 1963. Warren Commission exhibit 1033.
3. Ibid.
4. *Dallas Morning News,* October 24, 1963.

5. Mecklin, John. *Mission in Torment: An Intimate Account of the U.S. Role in Vietnam* (Doubleday, 1965), 178.

6. Jones, Howard. *Death of a Generation: How the Assassinations of Diem and JFK Prolonged the Vietnam War* (Oxford University Press, 2003), 385.

7. *Dallas Morning News*, October 24, 1963.

8. Ibid.

9. Cravens, 141.

10. Ibid.

11. *Dallas Morning News*, October 24, 1963.

12. Clipping, Bruce Alger Papers, Box 22, folder 20.

13. Huffaker, Bob, et al. *When the News Went Live: Dallas 1963* (Taylor Trade, 2007), 112.

14. *New York Times*, December 9, 1963.

15. Payne, *Big D*, 355.

16. *Texas Observer*, November 1, 1963.

17. Ibid.

18. AP and UPI wire service reports published October 25, 1963. Murray Schueth, a Dallas attorney who was shaking hands with Adlai Stevenson when the placard struck, spoke of the college student coming at Stevenson. Schueth was not quoted in the *Dallas Morning News*, but he is quoted in the wire service reports.

19. AP and UPI wire service reports published October 25, 1963.

20. Clipping on Adlai Stevenson, Bruce Alger Papers, Box 22, folder 20.

21. Payne, Darwin. *Indomitable Sarah: The Life of Judge Sarah T. Hughes*. (Southern Methodist University Press, 2004), 241.

22. AP and UPI wire service reports published October 25, 1963; Huffaker, 116. This was not reported in the *Dallas Morning News*.

23. Bernard Weissman testimony to Warren Commission.

24. *Dallas Morning News*, October 26, 1963.

25. *Washington Post*, October 27, 1963.

26. *Texas Observer*, November 1, 1963.

27. *Chicago Tribune*, October 27, 1963.

28. *Dallas Morning News*, October 26, 1963.

29. Wright, Lawrence. "Why Do They Hate Us So Much?" *Texas Monthly*, November 1983.

30. Earle Cabell Papers, DeGolyer Library, Southern Methodist University.

31. *Dallas Times Herald*, October 25, 1963.

32. Clipping, Bruce Alger Papers, Box 22, folder 20.

33. Ibid.

34. *Dallas Morning News*, October 26, 1963.

35. Ibid.

36. Stanley Marcus to Joe Dealey, October 29, 1963, Stanley Marcus Papers.

37. *Dallas Morning News*, October 27, 1963.

38. Ibid.

39. Ibid.

40. Ibid.

41. *Los Angeles Times*, November 1, 1963.

42. Larrie Schmidt to Bernard Weissman, October 29, 1963. Warren Commission exhibit 1052.

43. *Dallas Morning News*, November 3, 1963.

44. *Dallas Times Herald*, November 3, 1963.

45. Bruce Alger Papers, Box 22, folder 20.

46. Ibid.

November 1963

1. *Los Angeles Times*, November 2, 1963.

2. Leslie, 203; Manchester, William. *The Death of a President* (Harper & Row, 1967), 40.

3. McNamara, Robert S. *In Retrospect: The Tragedy and Lessons of Vietnam* (Crown, 1995), 84.

4. Manchester, 34.

5. Manchester, 39.

6. Ibid.

7. Larrie Schmidt to Bernard Weissman, October 29, 1963. Warren Commission exhibit 1052.

8. Hurt, 223.

9. Hurt, 224.

10. Dallas Police Department memo, Lieutenant Revill to Captain Gannaway, November 5, 1963.

11. Manchester, 9.

12. Testimony of James Hosty, House Committee on the Judiciary, December 12, 1975.

13. Schmaltz, William H. *Hate: George Lincoln Rockwell and the American Nazi Party* (Brassey's, 1999), 137.

14. Anthony, Carl Sferrazza. *The Kennedy White House: Family Life and Pictures, 1961–1963* (Touchstone, 2002), 261.

15. Manchester, 32.

16. Payne, *Big D*, 314; Miller, 379.

17. The Reverend W. A. Criswell, sermon, November 17, 1963.

18. *Dallas Morning News*, November 19, 1963.

19. *Los Angeles Times*, November 19, 1963.

20. *Dallas Morning News*, November 19, 1963.

21. Weissman testimony to Warren Commission.

22. Jeansonne, Glen. *Leander Perez: Boss of the Delta* (University Press of Mississippi, 2006), xxi.

23. United Press International, October 29, 1963.

24. Manchester, 55–57.

25. Manchester, 60.

26. Juanita Craft Papers, oral history conducted by the Civil Rights Project 1968, 9.

27. *Dallas Morning News*, November 19, 1963.

28. *Dallas Morning News*, November 22, 1963; Pollack, Jack Harrison. "The Man at the Dallas Airport, November 22, 1963." *True*, December 1973.

29. Marcus, 255.

30. Manchester, 90.

November 22, 1963

1. *Dallas Express*, November 23, 1963.

2. Bishop, 11.

3. White, Glen. "Dallas Revisited." *Cosmopolitan*, April 1964.

4. William Manchester Papers, Olin Memorial Library, Wesleyan University Special Collections and Archives. Box 43, folder 90.

5. Bishop, 30.

6. Bugliosi, Vincent. *Reclaiming History: The Assassination of President John F. Kennedy* (W. W. Norton, 2007), 12; Manchester, 112.

7. Bishop, 47; Manchester, 108.

8. Bugliosi, 16.

9. Bugliosi, 17; Bishop, 61.

10. Manchester, 114.

11. Manchester, 10.

12. Kennedy's speech to the Fort Worth Chamber of Commerce can be viewed on YouTube.

13. Bugliosi, 21.

14. Report of the Secret Service on the Assassination of President Kennedy, sent to Chief Justice Warren, December 18, 1963.

15. *Life Line* transcript, program 87, November 22, 1963. Melvin Munn Papers.

16. Manchester, 111.

17. Manchester, 126. Manchester does not specify Kennedy's curse.

18. Manchester, 130.

19. Manchester, 131.

20. Report of the Secret Service on the Assassination of President Kennedy.

21. Belo/*Dallas Morning News* Papers, DeGolyer Library, Southern Methodist University. Box 9, folder 21. Reporter Lewis Harris.

22. Bugliosi, 32.

Epilogue

1. Dealey/Belo Papers, Box 10, folder 17.

2. Manchester, 249.

3. Earle Cabell Papers.

4. "Selections from Lady Bird's Diary on the assassination: November 22, 1963." *Lady Bird Johnson: Portrait of a First Lady*. PBS, www.pbs.org/ladybird/epicenter/epicenter_doc_diary.html. Retrieved March 1, 2008.

5. Bugliosi, 105.

6. Bugliosi, 195.

7. Bugliosi, 172.

8. Posner, 372.

9. Posner, 375.

10. Posner, 377.

11. Bugliosi, 176.

12. *Dallas Morning News,* November 23, 1963.

13. Manchester, 287.

14. Federal Bureau of Investigation interview with Silverman. Warren Commission exhibits 1484–85.

15. Federal Bureau of Investigation interview with Jack Ruby, conducted by Agent C. Ray Hall. Warren Commission exhibit 3.

16. H. Rhett James Papers.

17. *San Antonio Light*, November 23, 1963.

18. Dallas Police Detective Barnard S. Clardy testimony to Warren Commission.

19. *Dallas Morning News*, December 22, 1963.

20. Hurt, 232–33.

21. Various YouTube videos of General Walker.

22. *Dallas Express*, December 7, 1963.

23. Manchester, 569.

24. Segura, Judith Garrett. *Belo: From Newspapers to New Media* (University of Texas Press, 2008), 114.

INDEX

ABOUT THE AUTHORS

BILL MINUTAGLIO has been published in the *New York Times*, *Esquire*, *Newsweek*, *Texas Monthly*, and the *Bulletin of the Atomic Scientists*. A professor at the University of Texas at Austin, he worked at the *Dallas Morning News*, *Houston Chronicle*, and *San Antonio Express-News*. He has written acclaimed books about George W. Bush, Molly Ivins, Alberto Gonzales, and America's greatest industrial disaster. He lives in Austin, Texas.

STEVEN L. DAVIS is the author of two highly praised books on Texas, and his work has appeared in several magazines and journals. Davis is a curator at the Wittliff Collections at Texas State University in San Marcos, which holds the literary papers of Cormac McCarthy and many other writers. He lives in New Braunfels, Texas.

From Byron, Austen and Darwin

to some of the most acclaimed and original contemporary writing, John Murray takes pride in bringing you powerful, prizewinning, absorbing and provocative books that will entertain you today and become the classics of tomorrow.

We put a lot of time and passion into what we publish and how we publish it, and we'd like to hear what you think.

Be part of John Murray – share your views with us at:

www.johnmurray.co.uk

 johnmurraybooks

 @johnmurrays

 johnmurraybooks